Explaining European Identity Formation

Stephanie Bergbauer

Explaining European Identity Formation

Citizens' Attachment from Maastricht Treaty to Crisis

Springer

Stephanie Bergbauer
European Central Bank
Frankfurt am Main, Germany

Dissertation at Johannes Gutenberg University Mainz, Germany

ISBN 978-3-319-67707-1 ISBN 978-3-319-67708-8 (eBook)
https://doi.org/10.1007/978-3-319-67708-8

Library of Congress Control Number: 2017954924

Printed on acid-free paper

This Springer imprint is published by Springer Nature
The registered company is Springer International Publishing AG
The registered company address is: Gewerbestrasse 11, 6330 Cham, Switzerland

Preface

The emergence of a common identity among Europeans has been the subject of intellectual debates ever since the beginnings of the European integration project. As the European Union is establishing ever closer political and economic ties between member states, this book takes a closer look at the affective bonds between the Union and its citizens.

The idea for this project sprang from my own experience with and through the European integration process. European unification gave me the freedom to study, work, live, and make friends throughout Europe. Whereas my experiences abroad gave me a strong sense of being European, this enthusiasm is not always shared by the general public. When I started this project, Europe was still recovering from the worst financial and economic crisis since the Great Depression of the 1930s. The ensuing drop in citizens' trust in European and national institutions and the resurgence of nationalist tones in the debate over European integration reinforced my interest in the sociocultural foundations of the European project. How strong are feelings of belonging together as Europeans among citizens in the member states today? Do Europeans share a common 'we-feeling' that can serve as a source of solidarity towards other Europeans in times of crisis? And what does it take for citizens to develop such a collective European identity? These are the questions at the core of this book. The analysis was completed before the referendum on EU membership in the United Kingdom, yet its findings already indicate that feelings of belonging to Europe are notably less developed in the British society than elsewhere on the continent. At the same time, this book provides advice to policymakers how to strengthen citizens' affective ties to Europe as a counterweight to Eurosceptic voices that can be heard also in other EU member states.

I am grateful to Edeltraud Roller for her extensive comments, constructive criticism, and support throughout this book project. Colleagues at the University of Mainz as well as friends and family in Mainz, Europe, and beyond provided helpful comments and encouragement at various stages of the book. Dieter Fuchs first helped me structure my thinking about EU attitudes long before the start of this project. All remaining errors are my own. The views expressed in this book are those of the author and do not necessarily reflect the views or policies of the European Central Bank.

Frankfurt am Main, Germany Stephanie Bergbauer

Contents

Chapter 1
The Relevance of a Common European Identity Among the Citizens of Europe

Why do some people see themselves as Europeans while others do not? Under which conditions do people feel attached to Europe? What does it take for citizens in the EU member states to consider themselves part of the wider community of Europeans? In short: What makes people identify with Europe? These are the questions at the core of the present analysis. It concentrates on the *subjective dimension of European identity*, i.e. *citizens' identification with Europe* rather than the contents or 'essential nature' of European identity. Broadly defined, identification with Europe denotes citizens' self-description as European and their attachment to Europe and other Europeans. European identification thus differs conceptually and empirically from EU support, which refers to positive or negative orientations towards the EU institutions and/or further steps in EU integration (Beaudonnet and Di Mauro 2012; Boomgaarden et al. 2011; Fuchs 2011; Kuhn 2015).

By concentrating on a common European identity among citizens in the EU member states, this book addresses both old and new questions in the history of European integration. In fact, European identity has been the subject of intellectual debates ever since the beginnings of European integration in the 1950s (Cerutti 2001; Stråth 2002). Early theorists of European integration had already pointed to the importance of mutual trust, loyalty, and a common 'we-feeling' among ordinary citizens for achieving further steps in European integration (Deutsch 1953a, b; Deutsch et al. 1957; Haas 1958). At the governmental level, the importance of a European identity was first recognised in 1973 when the heads of state and government of the European Communities adopted a declaration on European identity to strengthen cohesion among member states and affirm Europe's place in the world. It defined as fundamental elements of a European identity 'the principles of representative democracy, of the rule of law, of social justice [...] and of respect for human rights' (European Commission 1974, p. 492). This first attempt at establishing a common European identity from above was followed by intentional European identity politics led by the European Commission in the 1980s (Stråth 2002).

S. Bergbauer, *Explaining European Identity Formation*,
https://doi.org/10.1007/978-3-319-67708-8_1

Questions of identity received renewed interest after the adoption of the Treaty on European Union, also known as Maastricht Treaty, in 1992. As the European Communities developed into a fully-fledged political system at the European level, scholars started debating if and how decision-making by EU institutions can be democratically legitimated and whether European democracy requires a European demos with a strong collective identity (see e.g. Beetham and Lord 1998; Cederman 2001; Cerutti 2003; Decker 2002; Habermas 2001, 2004; Kaina 2009; Kielmansegg 2003; Offe 1998; Scharpf 2009; Zürn 2000).

In the post-Maastricht area, European integration took on a new quality: EU competences were successively extended to policy areas once at the core of national sovereignty, e.g. the control over national borders and the national currency; majority voting became the ordinary voting procedure in the EU Council, with the potential to force national governments to implement EU legislation they initially opposed; and EU policies had increasingly redistributive consequences, redirecting financial resources towards poorer regions and creating net contributors and net beneficiaries of EU funding among the member states. As a result, sources from which the EU previously derived legitimacy, notably common gains in economic welfare, securing peace in Europe, and an indirect legitimation of EU-level decision-making through the involvement of democratically elected national governments, appeared no longer sufficient. Instead, the legitimacy of the EU was now seen to depend on the development of a strong European identity among the mass public in the EU member states (Beetham and Lord 1998; Fuchs 2011; Habermas 2004; Kaina 2009).

The EU's enlargement to Central and Eastern Europe (CEE) in 2004/2007[1] and the financial and economic crisis the EU experienced from 2008 onwards[2] gave new impetus to scholarly and political debates on a common European identity. The accession of twelve new member states required institutional reforms that revived the debate over democratic deficits in the EU and the importance of a collective European identity for the legitimacy of EU decision-making. At the same time, enlargement was seen to add to the EU's cultural heterogeneity and scholars questioned whether the different historic trajectories and social and political experiences of 'old' Western European member states and new CEE members would be

[1]Eastern enlargement took place in two stages, with Cyprus, the Czech Republic, Estonia, Hungary, Latvia, Lithuania, Malta, Poland, Slovakia, and Slovenia joining the EU in 2004, and Bulgaria and Romania joining in 2007. For simplicity, both stages are summarised as Eastern enlargement 2004/2007. The member states that were part of the EU before 2004 will also be termed the EU15 or 'old' EU member states, while the terms 'CEE member states' or 'new' EU member states will refer to the group of countries that joined the EU in 2004/2007.

[2]The term 'financial and economic crisis' serves as an umbrella term for the interlocking crises—a banking crisis, a crisis of the real economy, and a sovereign debt crisis—that have affected EU member states since 2007/2008. For detailed accounts of the financial, economic, and sovereign-debt crises in the EU, see e.g. Copsey (2015, esp. Chap. 1), Illing (2013), Lane (2012), and Shambaugh (2012).

an obstacle to the emergence of a common European identity (Delhey 2007; Fuchs and Klingemann 2002; Gerhards 2005).

The financial and economic crisis brought a new urgency to the question of a collective European identity as it laid bare the interdependencies between European economies. To avoid sovereign defaults in the Eurozone and save the common currency, the Eurogroup agreed on extensive financial rescue mechanisms. Member states facing sovereign insolvency had to accept interventions by EU institutions and the International Monetary Fund (IMF) and implement fiscal austerity measures in exchange for financial aids. For the creditor states, on the other hand, the rescue funds implied considerable risks for national budgets in the case of default. While citizens in the deficit countries protested austerity programmes required by the troika of European Commission, European Central Bank, and IMF, rescue mechanisms and financial guarantees were equally contested in the creditor countries. As citizens were presented with successive and ever extended 'rescue packages' for which 'there is no alternative',[3] sentiments of distrust and opposition to further bailouts became more widespread,[4] cumulating in the question: 'Why should "*we*" pay for "*them*"?' (Offe 2013, p. 599; emphasis in the original).

The question why Europeans should stand by each other financially epitomises the relevance of a collective European identity and a common 'we-feeling' among Europeans. Fritz Scharpf estimates that the solidarity required in the crisis might have to equal the West-East transfers after German unification (Scharpf 2015). Intra-European redistributions of this amount, however, are hard to justify unless there is a sense of moral obligation via-à-vis the deficit countries and an understanding that measures to save the common currency are not a matter of 'altruistic donations' by the creditor states, but a matter of solidarity in its proper sense, meaning 'to do *not* what "is good for you" but "what is good for *all of us*"', in the words of Claus Offe (Offe 2013, p. 559; emphasis in the original). Citizens' acceptance of European measures of solidarity such as the financial guarantees given to member states facing sovereign default is seen to depend on a shared identity, a feeling of belonging together as Europeans, which serves as a source for feelings of loyalty and moral obligation towards other Europeans (Offe 2013; Scharpf 2015). That is, a collective European identity is considered necessary for

[3]Exemplary for this line of argumentation is German Chancellor Angela Merkel's speech before the Bundestag in Mai 2010: Referring to the recently agreed financial rescue measures for Greece, Merkel holds that, in order to safeguard the stability of the Euro system as a whole, there was 'no reasonable alternative' to providing financial assistance to Greece. She then goes on to argue that the Monetary Union was a 'community of fate'; at stake was no less than 'preserving and proving the European idea'. In this way, bailout measures become a 'historic task' because 'if the Euro fails, Europe fails' (Deutscher Bundestag 2010).

[4]In Germany, for example, opinion polls repeatedly found a majority of respondents opposed to further bailouts and debt cuts (Forschungsgruppe Wahlen 2010a, b, 2011a, b, c, 2012a, b). Similarly, public opinion in France and Britain opposed financial assistance to other EU member states between 2010 and 2012 (*Bloomberg News* 2011; PewResearchCenter 2012, 2013).

further steps to uphold the monetary union and further economic and political integration at the EU level in general.

The remainder of this introductory chapter gives an overview of the research strategy guiding the analysis. It introduces the research questions at the core of the present work (Sect. 1.1), outlines the theoretical model for explaining individual identification with Europe (Sect. 1.2), and presents the research design, data, and methods of the empirical analysis (Sect. 1.3). The introduction concludes with an outline of the remaining chapters of the book (Sect. 1.4).

1.1 Research Questions

At the core of the present analysis is the question why individuals identify with Europe. Empirically, identification with Europe is a fairly widespread phenomenon by now: a majority of EU citizens see themselves (also) as Europeans, feel attached to Europe, and are proud to be European (Citrin and Sides 2004a, b; Fuchs et al. 2009; Fuchs and Schneider 2011; Risse 2010). Yet the proportion of citizens identifying with Europe has hardly changed over time. In 1982, the first year the Eurobarometer asked citizens about their feelings of European citizenship, 52% of respondents indicated they sometimes or often thought of themselves as citizens of Europe (Commission of the European Communities 1982), compared to 59% of respondents who felt they were a citizen of the EU in autumn 2013 (European Commission 2013). That is, over a 30-year period of European integration that included actions with considerable symbolic power for a 'ever closer union among the peoples of Europe'—e.g. the free movement of persons on the Single European Market, the abolishment of physical borders between EU member states, and the introduction of the common currency—the share of citizens identifying as Europeans has hardly changed.

Substantial differences in citizens' identification with Europe also persist between EU member states (Bellucci et al. 2012; Citrin and Sides 2004b; Fuchs et al. 2009; Fuchs and Schneider 2011). While in autumn 2013 73% of Germans and 65% of Italians felt they were citizens of the EU only 42% of respondents in the UK shared this feeling (Commission of the European Communities 1982; European Commission 2013).

To address the overarching puzzle why some Europeans identify more readily with Europe than others and how we can explain differences between member states in this regard, this book formulates three sets of research questions. They address both the general trends in European identity over the past two decades as well as the specific effects of eastward enlargement and the crisis on citizens' identification with Europe.

A first set of questions takes stock of the *levels and development of European identification among EU citizens* from 1992 to 2013:

- How has citizens' identification with Europe developed since the adoption of the Maastricht Treaty 1992?
- How widespread are multiple national and European identifications in the EU population?
- Which changes in levels and development of European identification do we observe in response to the EU's enlargement to CEE in 2004/2007 and the onset of the financial and economic crisis in late 2008?

A second set of questions addresses the *salience of European identity in party discourse*. The aim is to assess whether national political parties provide citizens with arguments related to national and European identity:

- How salient are issues of European and national identity among political parties in the EU member states?
- How has the salience of identity issues in party discourse evolved between 1979 and 2014?
- Which changes do we see in party emphasis on European identity in response to the EU's eastward enlargement 2004/2007 and the onset of the financial and economic crisis in 2008?

A third and final set of questions turns to the *explanation of citizens' identification with Europe*. These address the determinants of European identification at individual and country level:

- Which individual- and country-level factors influence individual identification with Europe?
- How do individual attributes interact with country-level characteristics to influence European identification?
- Which changes do we observe in the determinants of European identification over time?

An additional question addresses the impact of the EU's enlargement to Central and Eastern Europe in 2004/2007 and the onset of the financial and economic crisis in late 2008:

- Do we observe changes in the determinants of European identification that can be traced back to the EU's enlargement to CEE in 2004/2007 and the onset of the financial and economic crisis in 2008?

The following section outlines how the analysis proceeds conceptually to answer these questions and describes the theoretical model for explaining individual identification with Europe.

1.2 Outline of the Theoretical Model for Explaining Individual Identification with Europe

The theoretical model for explaining individual identification with Europe developed in this book is rooted in theories of identity formation in social psychology on the one hand and theories of public opinion formation and EU public opinion research on the other.

Drawing on social psychological approaches to identity, individual identification with Europe is defined as *citizens' self-categorisation as European together with their evaluations of their membership in the European collective and their affective attachment to Europe and other Europeans.* Social identity theories also provide the starting point for conceptualising mechanisms of European identity formation at the individual level. Based on the idea that group identifications depend on individuals' exposure to 'persuasive communications' on the one hand and their 'public behaviour as group members' (Turner et al. 1987, p. 53) on the other, the theoretical model proposes two mechanisms of how citizens come to identify with Europe. First, an *information-based* way of European identification. In this logic, citizens' identification with Europe is rooted in exposure to elite messages and communications establishing the European community as a relevant category for self-representation. Second, an *experience-based* way of European identification. In this logic, citizens' identification with Europe is rooted in direct encounters between EU citizens and their personal experience of EU integration.

Proceeding from the idea that Europe-related information and Europe-related experiences are at the root of citizens' identification with Europe, the theoretical model assumes that individual identification with Europe will depend on (a) citizens' access to such information and (b) their opportunities to come into personal contact with other Europeans and the way they experience EU integration in their daily lives. The factors that determine individuals' access to EU-related information and their opportunities for European contacts and experiences should then also influence individuals' propensity to identify with Europe.

Information about Europe, the European community, and its shared norms and values may come from political elites, the mass media, or personal acquaintances. Citizens' access to such information is considered to depend on the supply of EU-related information in form of elite messages and personal communications on the one hand and citizens' attentiveness to such messages as well as their cognitive resources and competences to process these messages on the other. Europe-related experiences comprise citizens' personal interactions with other Europeans, their experience with the repercussions of EU integration in the national political context, as well as the national historical experiences and narratives of EU integration that citizens are exposed to within their home societies and learn in socialisation processes. Citizens' opportunities for Europe-related experiences are considered to depend on their personal and professional background as well as the macrosocial context in which they live. In sum, *individual attributes and predispositions* as well as *characteristics of the national context* are presumed to influence citizens' access to and opportunities for Europe-related information and experiences, and, therefore, should be included as explanatory factors in a model of individual identification with Europe.

From these general assumptions regarding the formation of European identifications among citizens in the member states, the book proceeds to develop a theoretical model for explaining individual identification with Europe. The explanatory model combines the idea of information- and experience-based mechanisms of European identification with insights from research on public opinion formation and attitudes towards EU integration. The final model combines three sets of individual-level and three sets of country-level determinants in a multilevel model of European identification. At the *individual level*, identification with Europe is expected to depend on citizens' *political awareness, attitudes towards the European and national community*, and *personal transnational experiences*. At the *country level*, identification with Europe is expected to depend on *party messages related to the European and national community, member states' economic position and degree of integration in the EU and global markets*, and the *ethnocultural composition of member state societies*.

The theoretical model of individual identification with Europe represents an integrated model that seeks to explain individual identification with Europe across all EU member states and periods of European integration without being restricted to a particular political, geographic, or historical context. Empirically, it will be applied to the analysis of citizens' identification with Europe after Maastricht and guide the explanatory analysis of citizens' identification with Europe over the period 2000 to 2012.

1.3 Research Design, Data, and Methods of Analysis

The present work places itself in the field of EU public opinion research and, more specifically, research on the emergence of European identity among citizens in the EU member states. Empirically, it explores levels and development as well as the determinants of individual identification with Europe from the adoption of the Maastricht treaty in 1992 until 2013, five years after the onset of the financial and economic crisis that has affected the EU and its member states since late 2008. By analysing citizens' identification with Europe over more than two decades, this book contributes to our understanding of long-term trends in European identification at the citizen level and helps answer questions about the consequences of major steps in the EU integration process on individual attitudes towards Europe.

The period under analysis in fact comprises a number of key events in the EU integration process. In 1992, the Treaty of Maastricht established the European Union, which marked the beginning of a fully-fledged political system at the European level. Other key developments falling into the period of analysis are the *EU's enlargement to Central and Eastern Europe in 2004/2007* and *the onset of the financial and economic crisis in 2008*. Eastward enlargement and the financial and economic crisis, followed by sovereign debt crises in a number of member states, are turning points in the integration process. They have had significant financial, political, and social consequences for the EU as a whole as well as for individual member states and initiated extensive debates over the future course of EU integration.

The present work explores the consequences of these key moments in EU integration for citizens' identification with Europe, develops hypotheses about potential changes in the determinants of European identification in response to these two events, and tests these hypotheses in empirical analysis. The inferences we can draw from this analysis reach beyond the immediate impact of enlargement and the economic crisis. Eastward enlargement and the economic crisis can be considered test cases for EU integration in that they resulted in a greater politicisation and polarisation of the EU (Hutter and Grande 2014; Rauh and Zürn 2014; Risse 2015). Concurrently, they made the costs of EU integration more visible to citizens in the member states. Future steps towards a closer political union, stronger European economic governance, or the accession of new EU member states are likely to trigger similar processes of politicisation and contestation. Drawing on the examples of enlargement and the economic crisis, we are able to theorise more generally about the development of a European we-feeling as EU integration progresses and becomes more politicised. In this regard, the present analysis enhances our understanding of the effects of major steps in EU integration on citizens' attitudes towards Europe and the EU.

The empirical analysis of citizens' identification with Europe proceeds in three steps, employing uni- and multivariate methods of analysis to provide new insights into the strength and sources of European identification among the EU mass public.

The *descriptive analysis of European identification*, first, presents levels and development of citizens' identification with Europe between 1992 and 2013 for the EU aggregate and individual member states. Particular attention is given to the consequences of the EU's eastward enlargement to Central and Eastern Europe in 2004/2007 and the onset of the financial and economic crisis starting in 2008. The descriptive analysis draws on public opinion data from 42 Eurobarometer (EB) waves conducted between March/April 1992 and November 2013.

The analysis of *party emphasis on issues of European and national community and identity,* second, draws on data from national party manifestos for European parliament (EP) elections to assess the salience of issues related to the European and national community and identity at the party level between 1979 and 2014. To this end, it tracks the share of manifesto statements dedicated to questions of European and national community and identity compared to the total number of arguments in a party manifesto over seven EP election campaigns. Data on national party manifestos for EP elections from 1979 to 2009 is provided by the Euromanifestos Project (EMP) at the Mannheim Centre for European Social Research (MZES). The analysis of the EMP data for 1979–2009 is supplemented by excerpts from party manifestos for the most recent EP election in spring 2014, for which EMP data was not yet available at time of writing.

The third part of the empirical analysis subjects the previously developed *theoretical model of individual identification with Europe to empirical testing*. It employs linear hierarchical regression models combining individual- and country-level data to study variation in identification with Europe across individuals and EU member states. By testing the model at several time points between the years 2000 and 2012, it provides insights in the stability of the determinants of European identification over different periods in the EU integration process. Depending on the period under investigation, the analysis includes either the EU15 or the EU27 member states. Individual level data come from seven EB surveys conducted between 2000 and 2012.[5] Country level data mainly come from Eurostat, supplemented by data from the EU Commission, the Euromanifestos Project (EMP) at the Mannheim Centre for European Social Research (MZES), the IMF, and the Worldbank.

1.4 Overview of the Book

The remainder of this book is divided in six chapters. *Chapter 2* defines the *concept of individual identification with Europe* as the central construct of interest for the present work. Individual identification with Europe is considered to comprise cognitive, affective, and evaluative components and allow for identification with multiple social groups, leading to a discussion of the relation between European identification and national identification as the most important 'rival' identification in the context of European integration. The chapter derives two mechanisms of individual identification with Europe: first, an *information-based way of European identification* assuming that citizens will identify with Europe to the extent that they receive information about the community of Europeans from political elites, the media and credible others; second, a *contact- and experience based way of European identification* assuming that citizens will identify with Europe to the extent that they personally interact with other Europeans and/or European institutions. Again, European and national identifications are juxtaposed to illustrate parallels and differences in the formation of both types of attachments and highlight the particularities in the development of European identification.

Chapter 3 takes these two mechanisms as a starting point for developing a theoretical model of individual identification with Europe. The model explains citizens' identification with Europe by factors shaping either citizens' access to Europe-related information or their opportunities for personal experiences with other Europeans and EU politics. It argues that access to Europe-related information and personal European experiences depend on *individual attributes*, on the one hand, and the *national context in which citizens live* on the other. Accordingly, the

[5]EB 54.1 (Nov/Dec 2000), EB 60.1. (Nov/Dec 2003), EB 62.0 (Oct/Nov 2004), EB 65.2 (March/May 2006), EB 67.2 (April/May 2007), EB 73.3 (March/April 2010), EB 77.3 (May 2012).

model includes both individual attributes and country characteristics as explanatory factors of individual identification with Europe and develops hypotheses for both sets of variables. Additional hypotheses address the consequences of the EU's enlargement to CEE in 2004/2007 and the onset of the financial and economic crisis in 2008 for the determinants of European identification.

Chapter 4 traces the *development of citizens' identification with Europe from Maastricht to the crisis*. Drawing on survey data from the Eurobarometer, it tracks individual identification with Europe in the EU aggregate and at the member state level between 1992 and 2013, allowing conclusions regarding the emergence of a collective European identity in the EU public. The empirical evidence shows that a collective European identity has developed in the EU public alongside national identities, with a majority of citizens seeing themselves (also) as European and expressing attachments to the European community. While European identity cannot match national identities in extent or intensity, multiple collective identities are a reality for EU citizens by now. As regards the consequences of the EU's enlargement and the financial and economic crisis, we observe a slight increase in citizens' identification with Europe after the 2004 accession round. In the case of the crisis, negative effects appear to accumulate over time, gradually weakening of citizens' affective ties to the European community.

Chapter 5 examines the *salience of European and national identity issues for political parties across Europe* between 1979 and 2014. It draws on data from national party manifestos for European parliament elections to explore to what extent parties provide citizens with arguments and considerations about the European community, a common European identity, and the consequences of European integration for the national community and national identity. The analysis of party manifestos shows that parties dedicate sizeable shares of their election programmes to identity-related issues. Identity issues become more salient for parties in the context of the EU's enlargement 2004. Under the impression of the financial and economic crisis, in contrast, parties' attention initially shifts away from questions of identity in the 2009 EP campaign. Yet, excerpts from the 2014 EP election manifestos provide some evidence that economic issues and identity issues become more closely linked to each other as the crisis continued.

Chapter 6 turns to *explaining European identification and the impact of enlargement and the crisis on feelings of European identity among EU citizens*. It starts by outlining the research design, specifies a set of hierarchical linear regression models predicting individuals' identification with Europe from individual- and country-level predictors, and introduces operationalisations of the dependent and independent variables at the individual and country level. The subsequent statistical analysis shows that individual identification with Europe is influenced mainly by individual-level determinants while country-level characteristics have only limited effects on European identification. The findings show stable individual-level effects on European identification over the years. At the country level, economic aspects and redistributive considerations become more relevant for European identification in the wake of enlargement and the crisis.

Chapter 7 summarises *the state of European identity after the crisis and implications for research and policymaking*. It revisits the initial question why people identify with Europe and summarises the central findings of the analysis. From there, it proceeds to discuss the implications of the present work for theorising European identity formation and the conclusions we can draw from these findings with regard to the state of European identity and its role in EU legitimacy after Maastricht. Finally, it points out strategies for policymakers interested in strengthening a common European identity among EU citizens and shows possible paths for further research on individual identification with Europe.

References

Beaudonnet, L., & Di Mauro, D. (2012). Support for Europe: Assessing the complexity of individual attitudes. *European Integration online Papers, 12*(2), 241–266.

Beetham, D., & Lord, C. (1998). *Legitimacy and the EU (Political dynamics of the EU)*. London/New York: Longman.

Bellucci, P., Sanders, D., & Serricchio, F. (2012). Explaining European identity. In D. Sanders, P. Bellucci, G. Tóka, & M. Torcal (Eds.), *The Europeanization of national polities? Citizenship and support in a post-enlargement union* (pp. 61–90). Oxford: Oxford University Press.

Bloomberg News. (2011). French People Oppose Second Greek Bailout, Ifop Poll Shows.

Boomgaarden, H. G., Schuck, A. R. T., Elenbaas, M., & de Vreese, C. H. (2011). Mapping EU attitudes: Conceptual and empirical dimensions of Euroscepticism and EU support. *European Union Politics, 12*(2), 241–266.

Cederman, L.-E. (2001). Nationalism and bounded integration: What it would take to construct a European demos. *European Journal of International Relations, 7*(2), 139–174.

Cerutti, F. (2001). Towards the political identity of the Europeans. An introduction. In F. Cerutti & E. Rudolph (Eds.), *A soul for Europe* (pp. 1–31). Leuven/Sterling: Peeters.

Cerutti, F. (2003). A political identity of the Europeans? *Thesis Eleven, 72*(1), 26–45.

Citrin, J., & Sides, J. (2004a). Can Europe exist without Europeans? Problems of identity in a multinational community. In M. G. Hermann (Ed.), *Advances in political psychology* (Vol. 1, pp. 41–70). Amsterdam: Elsevier.

Citrin, J., & Sides, J. (2004b). More than nationals: How identity choice matters in the New Europe. In R. K. Herrmann, T. Risse, & M. B. Brewer (Eds.), *Transnational identities. Becoming European in the EU* (pp. 161–185). Rowman & Littlefield: Lanham.

Commission of the European Communities. (1982). *Euro-barometre N.17 June 1982. Public Opinion in the European Community in Spring 1982. (Vol. 17)*. Brussels.

Copsey, N. (2015). *Rethinking the European Union*. London: Palgrave.

Decker, F. (2002). Governance beyond the nation-state. Reflections on the democratic deficit of the European Union. *Journal of European Public Policy, 9*(2), 256–273.

Delhey, J. (2007). Do enlargements make the European Union less cohesive? An analysis of trust between EU nationalities. *Journal of Common Market Studies, 45*(2), 253–279.

Deutsch, K. W. (1953a). *Nationalism and social communication: An inquiry into the foundations of nationality*. Cambridge, MA: MIT Press.

Deutsch, K. W. (1953b). *Political community at the international level: Problems of definition and measurement*. Princeton, NJ: Princeton University Press.

Deutsch, K. W., Burrell, S. A., & Kann, R. A. (1957). *Political community and the North Atlantic area: International organization in the light of historical experience*. Princeton, NJ: Princeton University Press.

Deutscher Bundestag. (2010). *Plenarprotokoll 17/42: Stenografischer Bericht, 42*. Sitzung. Berlin, Mittwoch, den 19. Mai 2010. Berlin.

European Commission. (1974). *Seventh general report on the activities of the European Communities 1973*. Brussels/Luxembourg.

European Commission. (2013). Standard Eurobarometer 80. Autumn 2013. *Public Opinion in the European Union. First Results*. In D.-G. f. Communication (Ed.), (Vol. 80). Brussels.

Forschungsgruppe Wahlen. (2010a). Politbarometer Dezember II 2010: Mehrheit gegen stärkere Finanzhilfen für verschuldete EU-Staaten. *Politbarometer*.

Forschungsgruppe Wahlen. (2010b). Politbarometer März II 2010: Zwei Drittel der Bürger gegen deutsche Kredite für Griechenland. *Politbarometer*.

Forschungsgruppe Wahlen. (2011a). Politbarometer Juni 2011: Mehrheit gegen weitere Finanzhilfen für Griechenland. *Politbarometer*.

Forschungsgruppe Wahlen. (2011b). Politbarometer Oktober I 2011: Mehrheit gegen Schuldenschnitt für Griechenland. *Politbarometer*.

Forschungsgruppe Wahlen. (2011c). Politbarometer September I 2011: Deutliche Mehrheit gegen Erweiterung des Euro-Rettungsschirms. *Politbarometer*.

Forschungsgruppe Wahlen. (2012a). Politbarometer August 2012: Griechenland: Zwei Drittel gegen mehr Zeit. *Politbarometer*.

Forschungsgruppe Wahlen. (2012b). Politbarometer Januar II 2012: Mehrheit gegen Aufstockung des Euro-Rettungsschirms. *Politbarometer*.

Fuchs, D. (2011). Cultural diversity, European identity and legitimacy of the EU: A theoretical framework. In D. Fuchs & H.-D. Klingemann (Eds.), *Cultural diversity, european identity and the legitimacy of the EU* (pp. 27–57). Cheltenham: Edward Elgar Publishing.

Fuchs, D., & Klingemann, H.-D. (2002). Eastward enlargement of the European Union and the identity of Europe. *West European Politics, 25*(2), 19–54.

Fuchs, D., & Schneider, C. (2011). Support of the EU and European identity: Some descriptive results. In D. Fuchs & H.-D. Klingemann (Eds.), *Cultural diversity, European identity and the legitimacy of the EU* (pp. 61–85). Cheltenham: Edward Elgar Publishing.

Fuchs, D., Guinaudeau, I., & Schubert, S. (2009). National identity, European identity, and Euroscepticism. In D. Fuchs, R. Magni-Berton, & A. Roger (Eds.), *Euroscepticism. Images of Europea among mass publics and political elites* (pp. 91–112). Opladen/Farmington Hills: Barbara Budrich Publishers.

Gerhards, J. (2005). *Kulturelle Unterschiede in der Europäischen Union: Ein Vergleich zwischen Mitgliedsländern, Beitrittskandidaten und der Türkei*. Wiesbaden: VS Verlag für Sozialwissenschaften.

Haas, E. B. (1958). *The uniting of Europe: Political, social, and economic forces 1950–57*. Stanford, CA: Stanford University Press.

Habermas, J. (2001). *Zeit der Übergänge*. Frankfurt am Main: Suhrkamp.

Habermas, J. (2004). *Der gespaltene Westen*. Suhrkamp: Frankfurt am Main.

Hutter, S., & Grande, E. (2014). Politicizing Europe in the national electoral arena: A comparative analysis of five West European countries, 1970–2010. *Journal of Common Market Studies, 52* (5), 1002–1018.

Illing, F. (2013). *Die Euro-Krise*. Wiesbaden: Springer Fachmedien.

Kaina, V. (2009). *Wir in Europa: kollektive Identität und Demokratie in der Europäischen Union*. Wiesbaden: VS Verlag für Sozialwissenschaften.

Kielmansegg, P. G. (2003). Integration und Demokratie (mit Nachwort zur 2.Auflage). In M. Jachtenfuchs & B. Kohler-Koch (Eds.), *Europäische integration* (2nd ed., pp. 49–83). Opladen: Leske+Budrich.

Kuhn, T. (2015). *Experiencing European integration: individual transnationalism and public orientations towards European integration*. Oxford: Oxford University Press.

Lane, P. R. (2012). The European sovereign debt crisis. *The Journal of Economic Perspectives, 26* (3), 49–67.

Offe, C. (1998). Demokratie und Wohlfahrtsstaat: eine europäische Regimeform unter dem Stress der europäischen Integration. *Swiss Political Science Review, 4*(4), 35–56.
Offe, C. (2013). Europe entrapped. *European Law Journal, 19*(5), 595–611.
PewResearchCenter. (2012). European Unity on the rocks. *PewResearchCenter Global Attitudes & Trends.*
PewResearchCenter. (2013). The new sick man of Europe: The European Union. *PewResearchCenter Global Attitudes & Trends.*
Rauh, C., & Zürn, M. (2014). Zur Politisierung der EU in der Krise. In M. Heidenreich (Ed.), *Krise der europäischen Vergesellschaftung? Soziologische Perspektiven* (pp. 121–145). Wiesbaden: Springer Fachmedien.
Risse, T. (2010). *A community of Europeans? Transnational identities and public spheres.* Ithaca: Cornell University Press.
Risse, T. (2015). European public spheres, the politicization of EU affairs, and its consequences. In T. Risse (Ed.), *European public spheres: Politics is back* (pp. 141–164). Cambridge: Cambridge University Press.
Scharpf, F. W. (2009). Legitimacy in the multilevel European polity. *European Political Science Review, 1*(02), 173–204.
Scharpf, F. W. (2015). Political legitimacy in a non-optimal currency area. In O. Cramme & S. B. Hobolt (Eds.), *Democratic politics in a European Union under stress* (pp. 19–47). Oxford: Oxford University Press.
Shambaugh, J. C. (2012). The Euro's three crises. *Brookings Papers on Economic Activity, Spring 2012*, 157–231.
Stråth, B. (2002). A European Identity. To the historical limits of a concept. *European Journal of Social Theory, 5*(4), 387–401.
Turner, J. C., Hogg, M. A., Oakes, P. J., Reicher, S. D., & Wetherell, M. S. (1987). *Rediscovering the social group. A self-categorization theory.* Oxford/New York: Basil Blackwell.
Zürn, M. (2000). Democratic governance beyond the nation-state: The EU and other international institutions. *European Journal of International Relations, 6*(2), 183–221.

Chapter 2
Conceptualising European Identification and Mechanisms of European Identity Formation

This chapter specifies the concept of individual identification with Europe as the central construct of interest of the present analysis and clarifies the mechanisms through which citizens come to identify with Europe (Sect. 2.1). These conceptualisations provide the starting point for the theoretical model for explaining individual identification with Europe developed in subsequent chapters of this book.

Drawing on social psychological theories of identity, *individual identification with Europe* is defined in the following as citizens' self-categorisation as European, which comprises cognitive, affective, and evaluative components (Sect. 2.1.1). It is assumed that individuals (can) identify with multiple social groups, which leads to a discussion of the relation between citizens' European identification and national identification, the most pertinent 'rival' identification in the context of European integration (Sect. 2.1.2). A further distinction is made between *identification with Europe as an individual-level characteristic* denoting citizens' self-categorisation as European and *collective European identity as the shared 'sense of community'* among European citizens, which is a characteristic of the European community at the macro level of analysis (Sect. 2.1.3). By clearly separating between the two concepts, the present work aims at more conceptual clarity in research on EU public opinion, which often uses the terms 'European identity', 'EU identity', 'collective European identity', or 'identification with Europe' interchangeably.

Building once more on insights from identity research in social psychology, the second part of the chapter clarifies the mechanisms presumed to underlie citizens' identification with Europe (Sect. 2.2). Two ways of individual identification with Europe are introduced: first, an information-based way of European identification built on the assumption that citizens will identify with Europe to the extent that they receive information about the community of Europeans from the media and credible others (Sect. 2.2.1); second, a contact- and experience-based way of European identification built on the assumption that citizens will identify with Europe to the extent that they personally interact with other Europeans and/or European institutions (Sect. 2.2.2). Again, European and national identifications are juxtaposed to

S. Bergbauer, *Explaining European Identity Formation*,
https://doi.org/10.1007/978-3-319-67708-8_2

illustrate parallels and differences in the formation of both types of attachments and highlight the particularities in the development of European identification (Sect. 2.2.3). Compared to national identification, European identification is presumed to have a stronger cognitive component and develop predominantly via an information-based way of identity building.

2.1 Conceptualising Individual Identification with Europe and Collective European Identity

The present section introduces the concept of individual identification with Europe that will guide the subsequent empirical analysis. The term 'European identification' will refer to citizens' self-categorisation as European as opposed to 'collective European identity', which is used to describe a shared sense of community among EU citizens at the group-level. European identification is understood to comprise cognitive as well as affective and evaluative components, and does not exclude identification with other social collectives, in particular the national community.

The following sections define the concept of individual identification with Europe (Sect. 2.1.1) and discuss the relation between identification with Europe and other collective identifications in the context of EU integration, notably citizens' identification with the national community (Sect. 2.1.2). A final sub-section maps out the relationship between identification as an individual attribute and collective identity as a group-level attribute (Sect. 2.1.3).

2.1.1 The Concept of Individual Identification with Europe

The starting point for defining citizens' identification with Europe are concepts of social identity developed in the framework of Social Identity Theory and its derivative Self-Categorization Theory (Tajfel 1974, 1981, 1982; Tajfel and Turner 1979; Turner 1985; Turner et al. 1987).

Social Identity Theory (SIT) and Self-Categorization Theory (SCT) understand social identity as the perception of self as part of a larger group or social collective which provides a link between the individual and the group(s) to which he or she belongs (Brewer 2001; Hogg and Abrams 1988). Accordingly, social identity is defined as 'that part of an individual's self-concept which derives from his knowledge of his membership of a social group (or groups) together with the value and emotional significance attached to that membership' (Tajfel 1981, p. 255).

Tajfel's definition of social identity has several implications. It underlines that the merely nominal allocation of individuals to a collective by outsiders, typically based on externally observable attributes such as race, gender, or nationality, does not suffice for the emergence of social identity. Rather, identification with social groups is an individual psychological attribute which results from *subjective* claims to group membership and a person's acknowledgement and acceptance of her membership in a social group as self-defining (Ashmore et al. 2004). What is more, conceptualising social identity as an individual psychological attribute also implies that identification is a continuous variable that may vary between individuals and/or within individuals over time (David and Bar-Tal 2009).

Definitions of social identity in the tradition of SIT and SCT further emphasise that identification with social groups is a phenomenon that comprises cognitive as well as evaluative and affective aspects. Social identities are thus premised, first, on *cognitive processes of in-group/out-group categorisation and self-categorisation as a member of the in-group*. Self-categorisation is the most basic process underlying social identity and a precondition for other dimensions of identification (Ashmore et al. 2004). In-group/out-group categorisations result from the perception of similarities and differences between individuals and the cognitive grouping of oneself and others as similar in contrast to other persons who do not share the common feature(s) of the in-group. Self-categorisation is assumed to follow the principle of meta-contrast; that is, individuals will categorise themselves as members of the in-group to the extent that they perceive differences between themselves and members of the in-group as less than differences between themselves and members of other groups (Turner et al. 1987).

Besides cognitive processes of in-group/out-group categorisation, social identities, second, imply *evaluation and social comparisons*. Social groups and group memberships carry positive or negative value for the self because they are associated with specific value connotations. These value connotations result from processes of social comparison between the in-group and relevant out-groups; the more favourably a social group compares to other groups, the more positively connoted the social identity associated with this group, and the higher the prestige of group membership. Vice versa, negative evaluations relative to other social groups lead to negative social identities and low prestige (Hogg et al. 1995; Tajfel and Turner 1986; Thoits and Virshup 1997). To the extent that individuals have internalised their membership in a particular group as part of their self-concept, positive group evaluations will increase their personal self-esteem; negative evaluations, on the other hand, should lead group members to either leave the group or try to enhance its prestige because individuals generally try to uphold a positive self-concept (Tajfel and Turner 1986).

Third, social identities comprise *affective components and emotional attachments*. Individual group members are considered to develop feelings of love, care, and concern for the group because group membership provides them with reasons for positive self-esteem and personal value. These affective attachments are expected to give rise to a sense of loyalty and obligation toward the group that leads its members to subordinate their individual goals to the goals of the larger group (Brewer and Silver 2000; Herrmann and Brewer 2004; Lilli 1998; Thoits and Virshup 1997). Group loyalty and the perceived 'identity of interests in terms of the needs, goals and motives associated with ingroup membership' (Turner et al. 1987,

p. 65), in turn, increase group cohesion and facilitate co-operation between group members.

Based on social psychological approaches to identity, we can thus define individual identification with Europe as follows: *Individual identification with Europe refers to citizens' self-categorisation as European together with their evaluations of their membership in the European collective and their affective attachment to Europe and other Europeans.*

Defining individual social identity as a phenomenon comprising cognitive as well as evaluative and affective aspects does not imply that all three aspects must be present or equally pronounced for all members of the in-group at all times (David and Bar-Tal 2009). Empirical research in social psychology in fact shows that the different dimensions of identification are not necessarily correlated and the relationship between them is likely to vary as a function of the particular social identity in question, the characteristics of the subject population under analysis, and the social context in which individual subjects operate (Ashmore et al. 2004; David and Bar-Tal 2009). Applying these insights to European identity, we may thus speculate that identification with Europe has stronger cognitive and weaker emotional components than, e.g. national identities; likewise, the relative strength of the different components of European identification may well vary between citizens and EU member states, with, e.g. the French feeling emotionally attached to Europe while the British identify as European primarily because they recognize their country's membership in the EU and their own legal status as EU citizens; finally, differences in member states' national political context could lead to differences in the strength of European identifications among EU citizens, for example if eurosceptical political parties are present in some countries and not in others.

Social psychological approaches to identity tend to remain on an abstract level regarding the dimension(s) along which in-group/out-group categorisation ought to take place for social identity to emerge; for example, Turner et al. (1987, p. 45) state rather generally that in-group/out-group categorisations underlying social identities are 'based on social similarities and differences between human beings that define one as a member of certain social groups and not others (e.g. 'American', 'female', 'black', 'student', 'working class')'. Yet the question which similarities individuals need to perceive in order to develop strong ties to a collective is particularly pertinent in the case of large-scale political communities such as modern nation-states and the European Union. With regard to Europe, two opposing views emerge from the discussion of the preconditions and similarities deemed necessary for the development of a common European identity.

On the one hand, proponents of *'essentialist' or 'culturalist' approaches* discuss the emergence of a common European identity against the background of national identity building. In this view, national identities always (also) build on cultural roots; the national community is seen as bound together by common historic experiences, myths, symbols, and traditions (see, e.g. Anderson 1991; Smith 1991). National identities are considered the product of long historical processes in which the national community has acquired common memories, values, and traditions. This shared heritage unites members of a nation internally and demarcates them from other communities. Compared to the long-term processes of identity building in the national realm, the outlooks for a common European identity appear bleak. In effect, 'essentialists' argue that a common European identity cannot build on such cultural bonds because unlike nation-states, the European Union is 'not a "community of communication", barely a "community of memory", and only to a very limited degree a "community of experience"' (Kielmansegg 2003, p. 58; author's translation). The few commonalities that exist among Europeans are deemed too weak for individuals to develop strong affective ties to Europe and the community of Europeans.

Other authors take a more positive stance, maintaining that a *shared political culture and shared political practices* can provide a basis for European identification (Cerutti 2003; Fuchs 2000; Habermas 2001, 2004; Meyer 2004). Furio Cerutti argues that European traditions overlap with regard to norms of solidarity and social cohesion, forming a European social model that unites Europeans and sets them apart from countries with more individualistic orientations (Cerutti 2003). Following this line of reasoning, the perception of shared social and political values together with the experience of common participation in European politics will lead citizens in the member states to identify with Europe and their fellow Europeans.

Ultimately, it remains an open empirical question, which similarities citizens in the member states perceive among Europeans and whether these similarities are substantial enough for citizens to not only acknowledge their legal status as an EU citizen, but also develop affective ties to Europe and the community of Europeans. As it is, it seems plausible to assume that most citizens in the EU member states are aware of the European Union and their country's membership therein, and, on this basis, will self-categorise as European. As regards the perception of further—more substantial—similarities among Europeans, the (scarce) empirical evidence indicates that citizens in fact base their identification with Europe on the perception of both political and cultural ties among Europeans. Pichler (2008, 2009) finds that EU citizens explain their feelings of 'being European' with shared rights and duties related to EU citizenship as well as shared membership in a common European civilisation and society[1]; Fuchs and Schneider (2011) find that Europeans predominantly see democratic values at the base of a European identity.[2] While more

[1]The exact question wording of the item analysed by Pichler and included in Eurobaromenter 57.2 (2002) reads, 'Different things or feelings are crucial to people in their sense of belonging to Europe. To what extent do you agree with the following statement: I feel European because I share with my fellow Europeans . . .?' Respondents were given fourteen options, which could be rated on a scale from 1 'strongly agree' to 4 'strongly disagree' (for details on question wording and coding, see Pichler 2008, pp. 414–415 and p. 420). Given that the item explicitly prompts respondents to think about what they *share* with their fellow Europeans, the indicator appears a valid measure for perceived similarities among Europeans.

[2]The exact question wording of the item analysed by Fuchs and Schneider and included in Eurobaromenter 71 (2009) reads, 'In your opinion, which of the following are the two most important elements that go to make up a European identity?' Respondents were given seven options from which they could select two (for details, see Fuchs and Schneider 2011). Unlike the

research is needed to clarify the substantial bases that citizens perceive as underlying European identification, these findings nevertheless indicate that citizens in the member states have developed some idea of what they have in common with their fellow Europeans. These perceived similarities should not only reinforce citizens' cognitive-based self-categorisation as European, but also support the formation of positive evaluations of and affective ties to Europe and their fellow Europeans.

2.1.2 *The Configuration of Multiple Identities in the European Context*

The question which similarities citizens perceive among Europeans and whether these similarities are substantial enough to foster a European 'we-feeling' that can fulfil functions similar to those of national identities touches on a further conceptual and empirical issue in European identity formation. What is the relation between European identifications and citizens' identification with other collectives, most importantly identification with the national community?

Collective national identities are thought to develop in long historical processes and to be deeply rooted in the collective memory and national history of a country (Anderson 1991; Fuchs 2011; Smith 1991). National identities thus become embedded in institutions and political culture and therefore prove relatively resistant to change; symbols like the national flag, the national anthem, or national holidays serve as constant reminders of the national community and its unique myths and traditions (Risse 2010; Risse and Engelmann-Martin 2002). At the individual level, national identity is typically acquired through childhood socialisation and persuasive communications (Herrmann and Brewer 2004; Turner et al. 1987), so that national attachments should constitute rather deeply rooted and stable orientations. As a result, national identifications will likely persist alongside potential European identifications, raising questions about the relationship between citizens' identification with the nation and their identification with Europe and about the conceptualisation of multiple identities more generally.

Social psychological approaches to identity explicitly allow for the existence of multiple social identities. Multiple social identifications are assumed to co-exist within a hierarchical system of self-categorisations. In this system, self-categorisations form at different levels of abstraction and each social category is included within the next-highest category (Turner et al. 1987). Which identification

indicator used by Pichler, this item does not refer to respondents' personal feeling as European nor does it incite respondents to think about shared identity elements that Europeans have in common. Therefore, the indicator should at best be considered an indirect measure of perceived similarities among Europeans (Fuchs and Schneider 2011). Nevertheless, it provides some additional information about citizens' perceptions of the foundations of European identity.

becomes salient at a given moment is expected to depend on the characteristics of both the person and the situation. It may vary across different social contexts as well as over time (Ashmore et al. 2004; David and Bar-Tal 2009; Turner et al. 1987). Social Identity Theory and Self-Categorization Theory thereby more or less implicitly assume that in any given situation only one social identity—the most salient one—will have consequences for individuals' attitudes and behaviour (cf. Turner et al. 1987, especially Chap. 6). Accordingly, SIT and SCT would expect citizens to identify with both the national community and with Europe as the superordinate and more inclusive level; because national and European identifications are expected to become salient at different times, individuals should be able to juggle both allegiances without greater difficulties.

The idea that different social identities become salient for individuals at different times and in different situations—and therefore do not pose problems of conflicting loyalties—may indeed apply to social groups and identities that are clearly demarcated from each other in terms of membership and/or function. For example, a person's belonging to and identification with a political movement has little connection or overlap with her belonging to and identification with her sports team, and, therefore, should not lead to situations in which she is forced to decide to be loyal to one group or the other. It seems questionable, however, whether the assumption of separate group memberships and allegiances also holds for large-scale social categories with overlapping memberships and potentially opposing demands for allegiance, e.g. nation, ethnicity, and social class (Brewer 2001; Cinnirella 1996).

National and European identities are a case in point: Within the European system of multi-level governance, competences and responsibilities are not always clearly allocated to either the member states or the EU; both levels claim sovereignty and decision-making authority. In this regard, national and European identity both refer to the political realm, yet involve overlapping political communities with potentially conflicting loyalties and allegiances. Consider for example the situation of a German citizen whose identification with the national community may lead her to oppose further German financial assistance to other EU member states while her identification with Europe implies loyalty to EU member states in difficulty and should lead her to support further assistance.

The example of the German European indicates that conceptualising national and European identities as separate or independent social identities is theoretically and empirically unrewarding. More appropriate appear conceptualisations of national and European identifications as interrelated or interdependent. These allow for mutual influences and overlaps between the national and European level and in principle can take two forms: on the one hand, we can think of multiple identifications as conflicting and in competition; on the other hand, we can assume concordance between different levels of identification (Westle 2003).

In a *conflict model of multiple identifications*, national and European identifications are conceived as competing and adversarial. In this view, the ideas and criteria underlying identification with the nation and the related affects and evaluations exclude feelings of belonging to the wider community of Europeans. Strong national attachments should therefore depress citizens' identification with Europe; by the same token, citizens' identification with Europe can only develop at the expense of national identification—I can either be a committed Brit or a committed European, but my identification with the latter will necessarily weaken my loyalty to the former and vice versa.

Models assuming *concordance of multiple identifications*, in contrast, conceive of national and European identifications as complementary; citizens are expected to combine and reconcile their national and European attachments without further problem. An example is the concept of 'nested identities', which considers that multiple identifications are ordered hierarchically; in this perspective, the national community and identity are subsumed ('nested') in the next-larger and more encompassing European community and identity (Diez Medrano and Gutiérrez 2001; Herrmann and Brewer 2004; Risse 2010). Accordingly, citizens who identify with the nation should also identify with Europe, although it remains unclear whether strong identifications with lower levels goes together with stronger or weaker identifications with higher-order communities (Diez Medrano and Gutiérrez 2001). Similarly, Risse's 'marble cake model of multiple identities' (Risse 2004, 2010) holds that national and European identities are compatible, but conceptualises national and European identifications as intertwined rather than hierarchically ordered. That is, multiple identities are seen to 'influence each other, mesh and blend into each other' (Risse 2004, pp. 251–252) so that citizens' identification with Europe becomes part of and inseparable from identification with the national community and vice versa. In this perspective, shared understandings of membership in the national group also contain elements of 'Europeanness' so that the common interest and experience of the national group are perceived to be connected to Europe and the community of Europeans—I cannot be a loyal German without being a loyal European.

The present analysis follows concepts that assume interdependence between multiple social identifications. Accordingly, it conceptualises national and European identifications as interrelated and mutually influencing. As the present work seeks to explain citizens' identification with Europe, the empirical analysis will concentrate on the effects of national identifications on European identifications and not further explore potential reverse effects of European on national identification.

2.1.3 The Concept of Collective European Identity

The conceptual discussion so far has focused on the individual-level processes underlying social identity in terms of individuals' self-categorisation as belonging to a particular group and the evaluative and affective consequences associated with group membership. In contrast, the functions and outcomes associated with social identities—which are often the reason for studying identification in the first place—are typically situated at the macro-societal level. These include, for example the role ascribed to collective identities in achieving and maintaining system integration, political legitimacy, regime support and regime stability as well as social mobilisation and collective action. Analyses of European identity in particular tend to adopt a functional perspective, which considers the emergence of a collective identity among Europeans a prerequisite for legitimising the European polity and solving the EU's democratic deficit (see, e.g. Cerutti 2003, 2008; and Introduction).

Given that the analytical value of the concept of European identity thus lies at the macro level, the present subsection will focus on the shift from the micro- to the macro level of analysis and discuss how individual identification is related to the collective identity of social groups and the functions of collective identity at the macro-societal level. A review of the literature on collective identities reveals two approaches to conceptualising collective identities and the relationship between collective identity as an aggregate characteristic and identification with a social group as a characteristic of individual group members. On the one hand, we find approaches to collective identity based in social psychology, which trace collective identities back to the prevalence of group identifications among the members of a society; on the other hand, we find sociological approaches to collective identity, which conceptualise collective identity as an aggregate characteristic from the outset on. These two research traditions have different implications for the empirical assessment of collective identities in the European context.

Among *social psychological approaches* to collective identity, David and Bar-Tal (2009) suggest a distinction between identification at the micro-sociopsychological level and collective identity at the macro-sociopsychological level in order to clarify the relationship between individual and group levels of identity. Identification is defined as the process by which individuals self-categorise as belonging to a group together with the cognitive, emotional, and motivational consequences associated with group membership. Collective identity, in contrast, refers to the *joint* awareness and recognition by group members that they share membership in and identification with the same group; it is defined as '*a situation in which individuals in a society identify with the collective and are aware that other members identify with this collective as well*' (David and Bar-Tal 2009, p. 361; emphasis in the original).

David and Bar-Tal's definition of collective identity has two central elements: individuals' identification with the group and their awareness of *other* group members' identification with the collective. By tracing collective identity back to the prevalence of individual group identifications among the members of a society, their definition provides a link between identification as an individual psychological attribute and collective identity as a characteristic of the group at the macrosocietal level. The second part of the definition, i.e. group members' awareness of their *shared* identification with the group, is more demanding. In David and Bar-Tal's understanding, collective identity exists only when group members identify with and attach emotional value to the group, *and*, at the same time, are conscious that *other* members of the group hold similar feelings and beliefs. This mutual awareness of group identification is considered a precondition for the cognitive, emotional, and behavioural consequences associated with collective identities at the macrosocial level. In particular, it is considered necessary for collective mobilisation and coordinated activity that serves the benefit of the group, even against individual members' interests. The idea is that the more group members are aware that not only *they* identify with the group, but that *others* share this feeling of belonging and the values and emotions associated with group membership, the greater group cohesiveness, and the greater individual members' willingness to make sacrifices for the group as a whole. Conceptually, introducing shared awareness of group membership as a second definitional element of collective identity thus helps bridge the gap between individual group identification and the functions associated with collective identity at the group level.

The second approach to conceptualising collective identity draws on *sociological* concepts of collective identity in the tradition of David Easton's 'we-feeling' or 'sense of community' (Easton 1965, p. 185). Whereas social psychological approaches start from individual identifications to construct group-level measures of identity, sociological conceptualisations in the tradition of Easton conceive of collective identity as an aggregate characteristic; from the outset on, the main focus is on the functions of collective identity at the macrosocial level. Easton restricts his analysis to the collective identity of political communities, i.e. groups of persons who are bound together by their participation in common political structures and processes. 'Sense of community' refers to the affective ties among the members of a political community; it 'consists of the feeling of belonging together as a group which, because it shares a political structure, also shares a political fate' (Easton 1965, p. 185). The 'we-feeling' of a community thus indicates the degree of political cohesion and solidarity among the members of a political community; a strong sense of community is considered to foster mutual sympathy and loyalty, which, in turn, provide resources for collective action and constitute a source of support for common political structures, the acceptance of collectively binding decisions, and participation in the decision-making process. In other words, if citizens feel they belong together as a political community, they should show solidarity with their fellow community members and be in favour of common political structures for regulating their political matters.

The definition of collective identity as, respectively, joint awareness of group membership and identification (David/Bar-Tal) or common we-feeling (Easton) also has implications for the operationalisation and empirical assessment of collective identities. Even if collective identity is considered a characteristic at the group level, it ultimately rests on individual psychological attributes and processes (Fuchs 2011). Therefore, individual members' identification with and feelings of belonging to the community ought to be the starting point for constructing an empirical measure of collective identity. Applied to the case of European identity, this means that a collective European identity can be constructed from citizens' individual identification with Europe. Based on the conceptual considerations above, we can define *collective European identity* in the following operational terms: *A collective European identity will be the stronger, the higher the number of EU citizens who identify with Europe, the stronger citizens' identification with Europe, and the more citizens are aware of other citizens' identification with Europe.*

Methodologically, the shift from individual identification at the micro level to the collective identity of a community at the macro level can be achieved via the related mechanisms of aggregation and distribution (Fuchs 2011). Thus, we can construct an empirical measure of a collective European identity by aggregating citizens' individual identifications with Europe and determine how European identifications are distributed among the EU population; the proportion of citizens identifying as European, either in the European Union as a whole or within individual member states, then serves as a measure of the strength of the macro-level phenomenon of a collective European identity. It can be compared across (different configurations of) EU member states and/or over time.

A measure of European identity based on the aggregate share of citizens' identification with Europe, however, can only be indicative of the strength of a collective European identity in terms of its extensity, i.e. the total number of citizens identifying with Europe, and its intensity, i.e. the strength of citizens' European attachments (Fuchs 2011); it does not allow conclusions about the extent to which citizens share awareness of their mutual identification with Europe. A measure of shared awareness would require that citizens not only know of their own identification, but also know whether their fellow citizens across the EU identify or not with Europe. While citizens may well be familiar with their friends' and family's attitudes toward Europe, the EU as a whole is far too large a community for citizens to personally know all other members of the community and be aware of their European identifications. Hence, a measure of joint awareness can only build on citizens' subjective perception of others' feelings and beliefs towards the European community and the assumptions they hold regarding the prevalence of European identifications in the EU population. In light of these problems, the present analysis will focus on the strength of a collective European identity in terms of the share of citizens' identifying with Europe together with the intensity of these attachments; it will not further pursue the aspect of shared awareness.

2.2 Mechanisms of Individual Identification with Europe

Having defined the concept of individual identification with Europe, the remainder of this chapter will discuss how citizens *develop* collective identifications. By specifying the conditions under which we should expect citizens to identify with Europe, it provides the basis for the theoretical model explaining European identification at the individual level presented in Chap. 3. Drawing again on identity research in social psychology, it starts by illustrating the general mechanisms presumed to underlie the formation of group identifications. In a second step, these ideas are applied to the emergence of group identifications in Europe. Citizens' identification as European is expected to develop via two mechanisms: first, an *information-based way of European identification*; second, an *experience-based way of European identification*. These are discussed in turn.

Social psychological approaches to identity assume that in case of large-scale, preformed social categories such as gender, nation, or race, i.e. categories to which people belong by birth rather than by choice, the internalisation of in-group/out-group categorisations underlying social identities follows general mechanisms of attitude change and social influence (Turner et al. 1987). Thus, Turner and his colleagues hypothesise that individuals will internalise group memberships and self-identify as a member of some preformed social category under one of two conditions, namely '(1) simply as a result of persuasive communications from credible, prestigious, or attractive others (or in the terms of the present theory, from others with whom they identify), and (2) on the basis of public behaviour as group members leading to private self-attitude change' (Turner et al. 1987, p. 53).

Implicitly, both explanations trace group identifications back to the prominence of the group in the lives and minds of group members and to factors—persuasive messages on the one hand, personal contacts and direct experiences on the other—which have the potential to make group membership (more) meaningful for the individual. These explanations thus seize on the notion of salience, the central determinant of group identification in social psychology (Hogg et al. 1995; Turner et al. 1987). While individuals are assumed to identify with multiple social categories, social-psychologists argue that whether a particular self-categorisation becomes cognitively dominant for individuals in a given situation, and, as a result, has immediate consequences for their attitudes and behaviour, depends on the salience of the respective category in that situation. The more accessible a social category, and the better the perceived fit between self and the defining characteristics of the social group, the more individuals will self-categorise as group members (Turner et al. 1987). In other words, individuals are expected to affirm their identification with a collective to the extent that the latter is present in citizens' minds as a relevant category for self-categorisation (Castano 2004).

Two basic mechanisms of group identification emerge from the discussion of collective identification formation and identity change in social psychology: on the one hand, we can trace individual group identification back to individuals' exposure to persuasive messages—'persuasive communications' in Turner's et al. terms—about the meaning and importance of the group, similarities among group members, and the group's shared identity; on the other hand, we can trace identification back to the personal experiences individuals make in their capacity as a member of a collective—i.e. when and if they 'publicly behave as group members' in Turner's et al. terms.

These general reflections on the formation of group identifications can now be applied to citizens' identification with Europe, resulting in two ways of how EU citizens may come to identify with Europe: first, *identification based on exposure to Europe-related information*; second, *identification based on personal contacts and direct experiences with the European community and other Europeans*. Citizens who receive more information about Europe and other Europeans and/or have more personal experience with the EU and citizens from other member states are expected to be more aware of the European community and the commonalities they share with other Europeans. As a result, they should also identify more readily with Europe than citizens who receive less information about Europe and/or have less personal experience with other Europeans and the consequences of EU integration.[3]

The following subsections discuss these two mechanisms of European identification and clarify which type of messages and information on the one hand and personal contacts and experience on the other are expected to affect citizens' propensity to identify with Europe. The discussion starts by specifying aspects of 'exposure to Europe-related information' and its relation to European identification (Sect. 2.2.1); a second sub-section discusses different dimensions of Europe-related experiences and opportunities for citizens to gain such experience and how these may affect European identification (Sect. 2.2.2). Tying in with the earlier discussion on multiple identifications in the European context, special attention will be given to the comparison between European identification and national identification (Sect. 2.2.3).

2.2.1 Exposure to Europe-Related Information and Individual Identification with Europe

The notion of information-based identification with Europe builds on the *idea of persuasive messages as a source of group identification*. The central assumption is that exposure to messages and information establishing the European community as an object of identification and a relevant group for citizens' self-description is at the root of European identification. Citizens are expected to identify with Europe to the extent that they receive messages and information about the community of Europeans and thus are reminded of their own status as European and the communalities they share with other Europeans. In short, more information about the

[3]It is of course possible that citizens who receive more information about and/or have more personal contacts with other Europeans not only learn more about what they have in *common* with other Europeans, but also what *sets them apart*. In this way, Europe-related information and experiences may have reverse effects, leading to less rather than more identification with Europe among EU citizens. Either way, however, the presumed underlying mechanism remains the same: more information/more experience leads to changes in identification.

The theories of social identity formation in social psychology on which the idea of information- and experience-based identification builds almost exclusively presume a positive association between group salience and group identification. In line with these approaches, I initially focus on positive effects of Europe-related information and experience on citizens' identification with Europe. However, the in-depth discussion of the two mechanisms of European identification in the following subsections as well as the empirical analysis of European identification in later chapters will take into account both positive and negative effects of more Europe-related information and experience on citizens' propensity to identify with Europe.

European community is expected to increase the salience of the European group in citizens' minds and thus affect citizens' identification with Europe.[4]

The notion that identification with Europe is fostered by better information and persuasive messages about the European community and a common European identity ties in with general theories of opinion formation and models of mass communication that see messages by political elites at the root of public opinion formation and opinion change (Kinder 1998; Mutz et al. 1996; Zaller 1992). The notion of elite effects and mass communication as a source of public opinion has also been taken up in the European context. Empirical analyses confirm the influence of political parties (de Vries and Edwards 2009; Gabel and Scheve 2007a, b; Maier et al. 2012; Ray 2003) and the mass media (Azrout et al. 2012; de Vreese and Boomgaarden 2006; Schuck and de Vreese 2011) on attitudes towards the EU and European integration. The notion of an information-based mechanism of attitude formation towards the EU is further supported by research on EU support showing that citizens who are better informed about the EU also hold more positive attitudes towards EU-level policy making (Clark and Hellwig 2012).

Citizens' exposure to information about Europe can vary along two dimensions—supply of Europe-related information and demand for such information. From these, we can derive more specific determinants of citizens' identification with Europe.

From a supply-side perspective, exposure to Europe-related information depends on the extent to which citizens *are provided* with arguments and considerations that refer to the European Union and, more specifically, the community of Europeans, its shared norms and values, and the meaning of a shared European 'we-feeling'. Sources of such information can either be political elites who disseminate Europe-related arguments and considerations via the mass media; or other citizens who transmit Europe-related arguments in personal communication.

From a demand-side perspective, exposure to Europe-related information depends on the extent to which citizens *are aware of* elite messages and personal communications regarding the European Union and the community of Europeans. Awareness of Europe-related information, in turn, is considered to depend on, first, citizens' attentiveness to such information, i.e. their interest in and motivation to receive elite messages and personal communications; and, second, on citizens'

---

[4]As regards the direction of the effect of Europe-related information on European identification, in principle, both positive and negative effects seem plausible. A priori, the present analysis postulates that more information about Europe and the European community leads to changes in citizens' propensity to identify with Europe. Based on the existing empirical record, which largely finds a *positive* association between information-related indicators such as media exposure, political interest and engagement in political discussions, or factual knowledge of EU politics on European identification (e.g. Bellucci et al. 2012; Diez Medrano and Gutiérrez 2001; Duchesne and Frognier 1995), the following discussion concentrates on positive effects of citizens' exposure to Europe-related information on European identification. Nonetheless, the theoretical model developed in Chap. 3 will include hypotheses for both negative and positive effects of information-related indicators on individual identification with Europe.

capability to receive such information, i.e. their cognitive resources and competence to process elite messages and personal communications they are exposed to.

The notion that exposure to information is a two-dimensional phenomenon leads to two sets of explanatory factors expected to affect individuals' identification with Europe: on the one hand, factors related to the *provision of information* by third parties, i.e. attributes of elite messages and/or personal communications about the community of Europeans; on the other hand, factors related to the *processing of information* by the individual, i.e. attributes of the individual receiving elite and personal messages about Europe.

As regards factors related to the provision of Europe-related information, a first determinant is the intensity or amount of elite messages and personal communications about the European community that individuals are exposed to, i.e. how salient Europe-related messages are in public or private debates. A second determinant is the content or direction of elite messages and personal communications, i.e. to what extent Europe-related messages promote a European we-feeling. The more salient Europe-related messages are and the more these messages paint a positive picture of the European community, the more citizens should identify with Europe.[5]

As regards explanatory factors related to the processing of Europe-related information, a first determinant is citizens' interest in politics and, in particular, their interest in European politics (motivation); a second determinant is citizens' cognitive resources, most often assessed in terms of their level of education (competence). Again, the more citizens are interested in (European) politics and the better their cognitive competences, the more we would expect them to identify with Europe.

2.2.2 Europe-Related Experience and Individual Identification with Europe

The second path to European identification is thought to be experience-based. It builds on the *idea of personal contacts and direct experiences as a source of group identification*. Accordingly, citizens' identification with Europe ought to be rooted in direct encounters with other EU citizens and the personal experience of being part of the European community. Citizens are expected to identify with Europe to the extent that they interact face-to-face with other Europeans and/or experience the consequences of EU policies in their daily lives. Thus, they are in a position to perceive directly what Europeans have in common in terms of shared experiences, norms, and values. As in the case of more information about the European community, more experience with other Europeans and the awareness of the

[5]Vice versa, if citizens predominantly receive negative messages about the European community, we should expect them to identify less with Europe.

consequences of EU integration are expected to increase the salience of the European group in citizens' minds, resulting in an increase in citizens' identification with Europe.[6]

The notion of a positive effect of personal contacts with other Europeans on citizens' identification with Europe ties in with theories of intergroup relations which expect increased intergroup contact to reduce intergroup bias and conflicts between social groups (Allport 1954; Amir 1969; Dovidio et al. 2003; Pettigrew 1998). Empirical work in this research tradition shows that increased contacts and personal acquaintances between members of different social groups change group members' perceptions; rather than perceiving the different groups as separate entities, they start to see a single, more inclusive group and develop a common in-group identity (Gaertner et al. 1993, 1994, 1996). In the European context, the relevance of personal contacts for a common identity is emphasised by work in the tradition of Deutsch's transactionalist approach. Deutsch considered transnational communications and cross-border networks as crucial for promoting a common identity and trust among Europeans (Deutsch 1953; Deutsch et al. 1957). Recent empirical analyses confirm that individuals with more transnational contacts are indeed more supportive of European integration and more likely to identify as European (Kuhn 2011, 2012a, b, 2015).

The notion of an experience-based way of European identification holds that citizens will identify with Europe to the extent that they come into contact with other Europeans and/or European institutions and directly perceive the consequences of EU integration and European communalities in their daily lives. Such Europe-related experiences can take different forms, depending on the immediacy of contacts and interactions between citizens and other Europeans and/or European institutions they imply. Three types of experiences are discussed in the following *individual personal contacts and direct interactions with other EU citizens*; citizens' *experience with the repercussions of EU integration in the national political context*; and member states' *national historical experiences and 'narratives' of EU integration* to which citizens are exposed within their home societies.

In a narrow sense, first, Europe-related experience signifies an individual's *personal contacts and direct interactions with other Europeans*, e.g. when working or living abroad and socialising with other Europeans for private or professional reasons. This is the most immediate form of experience related to the European community in that it implies face-to-face contacts with other EU citizens. Direct personal contacts are thought to facilitate the perception of communalities among Europeans, which, in turn, should foster a common European we-feeling. Empirically, such changes in perception due to increased contact with citizens from other

[6]As in the case of Europe-related information, it cannot be excluded that Europe-related experience actually has the reverse effect, leading to a de- rather than increase in European identification. The focus on positive effects of Europe-related experiences on citizens' identification with Europe is again based on the existing empirical record, which has repeatedly shown a positive association between citizens' experience with other Europeans and their propensity to identify with Europe (e.g. Braun and Müller 2012; Kuhn 2012b, 2015; Recchi 2008; Rother and Nebe 2009).

EU member states have been observed among Erasmus exchange students, for example, who report a better understanding of the host country and an increased sense of belonging to a European cultural space after their year abroad (King and Ruiz-Gelices 2003).

To what extent citizens engage in personal exchanges with other EU citizens is expected to depend on their personal background and professional environment. That is, the degree of personal contacts and direct interactions with other Europeans is a form of Europe-related experience that varies at the *individual level* and across EU citizens. In this regard, this first category of Europe-related experience differs from two categories of experience discussed in the following, namely the domestic consequences of EU integration and national histories and 'narratives' of EU integration. Both are forms of Europe-related experiences that are tied to the national political context in which citizens live and, therefore, vary at the *country level* and across EU member states, but are constant for citizens within the same member state.

In a broader sense, second, Europe-related experience is seen to include *citizens' experience with the repercussions of EU integration in the national political context* and the consequences of EU integration for their home country. For example, the free movement of goods, capital, services, and labour, the abolition of border controls within the Schengen area, or the introduction of the euro as a common currency let citizens experience the consequences of EU integration without necessarily coming into direct contact with other Europeans. Likewise, a country's relative economic strength within the EU, its net contribution to the EU budget or the degree of a country's integration in the European market are correlates of EU integration that citizens are confronted with in their national context. Even though they do not imply personal contacts with other Europeans, these are occasions where EU citizens gain Europe-related experience and get an idea of what it means to be part of the European community. In this sense, citizens' exposure to EU policies and the implications of their country's integration in the EU can be thought of as a form of everyday experience related to Europe that is likely to shape their perceptions of the European community and, eventually, their propensity to identify with Europe.

The assumption that experience with the consequences of EU integration in the domestic context shapes European identification needs to be qualified with regard to the nature of experiences, however. Thus, we should expect citizens to identify more with Europe, the more positively they assess the consequences of EU integration in the national context. Vice versa, negative perceptions of the consequences of EU integration are likely to depress citizens' identification with Europe. To give an example from the economic realm, we may expect citizens from net recipient countries of EU funding to identify more with Europe than citizens from net contributor countries assuming that the former will hold a more positive image of Europe and redistribution among EU member states than the latter.

Third, we can think of Europe-related experiences as the *historical experiences and 'narrative' of EU integration that citizens are exposed to within their home society* and that they learn as part of socialisation processes. This conveyed or indirectly acquired form of Europe-related experience corresponds to what Fuchs terms 'collective memory'. Collective memories provide information about a country's history, become incorporated in national symbols, writings, and monuments, and are internalised by the individual citizen during socialisation (cf. Fuchs 2011, p. 49). The relevant societal memories with regard to Europe are interpretations of a member country's historical approach to EU integration—its 'European history'. These are transmitted to citizens in socialisation processes and become manifest at the individual level in the form of particular attitudes towards Europe, the national community, and the role of one's own country in EU integration. For example, we may expect that EU integration and EU membership as well as the question of who belongs or should belong to the community of Europeans are discussed differently depending on the time and circumstances under which a country joined the EU. Thus, the topic of EU unification as a means to secure peace on the continent may be stronger in the six EU founding states whereas economic connotations may dominate in member states which joined later on; in contrast, in the Central and Eastern European member states that joined the EU in 2004/2007, EU accession will likely be interpreted first and foremost as part of (re-) integration with the West after communism. Likewise, we may expect that different historical trajectories lead to different conceptions of the relationship between the nation and Europe. Risse's (2010) analysis of national identity constructions indeed shows that the relation between national identity and Europe is discussed in very different terms in different member states. For example, European integration and EU membership were incorporated in the image of a 'modern Germany' after World War II; in contrast, the debate in the UK has traditionally sought to support the idea of a unique English or British identity that ought not be affected by British EU accession and European integration (Risse 2010). These particular national perceptions of European integration and the relation between the nation and Europe can be thought of as a society's 'collective experience' with Europe and the EU. Individual citizens are exposed to member state-specific collective experiences through the way European affairs are framed in the domestic context, e.g. in public discourse, the national education system, or the national media. In this sense, national cultures work as a filter through which citizens perceive the EU and European integration. As a result, some aspects of European integration may be equally important across all EU member countries whereas others become salient only in some member states (Diez Medrano 2003). Qualitative research on citizens' perceptions of European integration by Diez Medrano (2003) confirms that particular national understandings and representations of European integration are also reflected at the individual level. For example, Germans are found to interpret European integration as a chance for reconciliation after WWII while British citizens are more concerned with the consequences of European integration for national sovereignty and identity (Diez Medrano 2003, esp. Chap. 2).

To sum up, particular national understandings of Europe imply neither direct contacts with other EU citizens nor concrete experiences with EU policies in citizens' daily lives. Nevertheless, they can be thought of as a form of experience with the European community in that they transmit particular perceptions of Europe and the European community. These perceptions, in turn, translate into particular understandings of European integration at the individual level that are likely to affect citizens' propensity to identify as European. Again, how national perceptions of European integration and their reflections at the individual level affect citizens' European identifications will likely vary depending on the nature and focus of these perceptions. For example, we may expect that citizens who predominantly conceive of European integration as an opportunity for positive change in their home country, be it in terms of reconciliation (e.g. Germany after WWII), democratisation (e.g. Spain after Franco), or modernisation and economic progress (e.g. Eastern Europe after 1989/1990), will generally hold a more positive image of Europe and more likely identify as European. In contrast, citizens who perceive European integration first and foremost as a threat to the national community and its sovereignty should identify less with Europe.

If we assume that experiences with the European community are at the basis of citizens' European identifications, their propensity to identify as European should vary with the opportunities they have to gain such experiences. Two sources of opportunities for Europe-related experiences can be distinguished: on the one hand, opportunities for Europe-related experiences may arise from individuals' personal background and their professional position; on the other hand, such opportunities may arise from the macrosocial context in which citizens live. Individual and macrosocial context do not provide for all three forms of Europe-related experiences alike, however. Thus, personal background and professional environment will likely determine the extent to which citizens directly interact with other Europeans; likewise, particular perceptions of European integration that were internalised in socialisation processes are attributes at the individual level. The macrosocial context citizens live in, on the other hand, conditions both the extent of citizens' opportunities for personal contacts with other Europeans and the extent and nature of citizens' everyday experiences with EU policies and the domestic consequences of European integration.

2.2.3 Ways of European and National Identification Compared

To summarise the argument so far, Europeans are expected to identify with Europe to the extent that they perceive Europe as a salient category for self-identification; the salience of the European category for the individual citizen is presumed to depend on the information about Europe and the European community they are exposed to and the degree of their personal experience with other Europeans and the consequences of EU integration in the domestic context. The present section will juxtapose the mechanisms presumed to underlie European identification with the development of citizens' attachments to their national community. The aim is to show that we should expect the formation of European identification to differ fundamentally from how citizens come to identify with their national community. While individuals are socialised into the shared beliefs underlying national identity from an early age on and constantly (re-)experience institutionalised forms of national identity and solidarity, citizens' identification with Europe will rely mainly on cognitive processes and the information citizens receive and the knowledge they have of the EU and the European community.

National identities are typically thought to be 'deeply rooted', 'profound' collective identities (Fuchs 2011, p. 41). They stem from common historic experiences and strong common beliefs, and, for some, also from substantial commonalities such as shared ethnicity, religious affiliation, or cultural affinity, which translate into feelings of togetherness and solidarity among the members of a nation (Fuchs 2011; Kantner 2006). Individuals are socialised into the shared beliefs underlying national identity from an early age on and constantly (re-)experience these shared values and beliefs as the latter have become institutionalised, for example in the constitution, in national welfare state regimes, or particular national views on foreign and defence policy. Political and social institutions also provide opportunities for shared experiences and shared social norms, e.g. through participation in general elections, enrolment in the education system, or during military and community service (see Herrmann and Brewer 2004 for a discussion of how political institutions shape collective identities). National citizens also regularly experience institutionalised forms of solidarity among the members of the national community, e.g. in the form of redistributive social policies. Finally, even if national communities remain 'imagined communities' (Anderson 1991) in that members of the national community do not personally know the majority of their fellow-nationals, they still directly interact with a significant number of them on a regular basis. The expectation is that such constant direct experiences with other nationals, with the institutions representing the community's shared values, and with institutionalised forms of solidarity strengthen an individual's emotional attachment to the national community.

The situation is fundamentally different in the case of European identity. Not only does the EU lack the common historical experiences and cultural cohesion underlying national identities, there are also few occasions for citizens in the member states to experience European values through EU policies or interact directly with European institutions and other EU citizens.

In effect, there is no European constitution, which could serve as a point of reference for shared European values; likewise, most EU policies remain regulative in nature. Thus, they do not involve the same type of moral issues or value-laden questions as some of the policy areas under national jurisdiction and, as a result, provide fewer opportunities for emotional attachment (see Kantner 2006 for a discussion of the problems of integrating highly value-laden policy areas at the EU level). An example would be national welfare regimes or security politics. Research on national identities shows that citizens see their country's social security system as a reason for national pride and identification with the national level; likewise, the military is cited as a source of national pride (Evans and Kelley

2002; Hjerm 1998). The EU, in contrast, has little competences in these highly sensitive policy areas and thus cannot rely on them as a reference point for a common European identity.

What is more, although the EU has far-reaching competences in numerous (other) policy fields, EU legislation and policy programmes are implemented in the member states not by EU institutions, but by their national counterparts, and EU representatives are rarely present in the member states. This division of labour between the European and the national level leaves few occasions for citizens to interact directly with European actors.

Apart from elections to the European Parliament, there are also few institutionalised opportunities for experiences that are shared by citizens across EU member states. Similarly, tangible forms of pan-European solidarity are typically restricted to small parts of the EU population, such as subsidies for farmers or the Structural and Cohesion funds for poorer regions within EU member states. At the citizen level, personal contacts between citizens from different EU member states are restricted to small parts of the EU population and primarily occur among the young, the highly educated, and those in higher-status occupations (see descriptive results in Fligstein 2008; Kuhn 2011, 2012b, 2015).

The expectation is that in the absence of direct personal experiences with EU representatives and citizens from other member states, the greater part of EU citizens will develop European identifications based on information about the European community they receive from third parties and the way they experience the consequences of European integration in the domestic context. For the same reason, we may expect that European identification has a stronger cognitive than affective component; citizens will probably be aware of their home country's membership in the EU and geographical location on the European continent and, therefore, self-categorise as European, yet without necessarily showing strong emotional attachments to Europe and their fellow Europeans.

The characteristics that are assumed to distinguish the formation of European identification in the mass public from identification with the national community—low salience of European issues and few personal interactions with other Europeans in citizens' everyday lives, reliance on third-party information, and a stronger cognitive component—also have implications for the explanation of citizens' identification with Europe. An explanatory model of European identification must take into account that, for a large part of EU citizens, Europe as the object of identification has little relevance and few are familiar with European affairs and/or other Europeans. What is more, we need to account for the fact that, for most citizens, experience with Europe takes place in the national political context; that is, citizens gain experience with Europe not by interacting directly with EU institutions or other Europeans, but by experiencing the consequences of European integration in their home country. In this manner, characteristics of the national political context are likely to shape how citizens perceive and evaluate the EU integration process and ought to be taken into account in the explanation of European identification.

References

Allport, G. W. (1954). *The nature of prejudice*. Cambridge, MA: Addison-Wesley.
Amir, Y. (1969). Contact hypothesis in ethnic relations. *Psychological Bulletin, 71*(5), 319–342.
Anderson, B. (1991). *Imagined communities: Reflections on the origins and spread of nationalism*. London/New York: Verso.
Ashmore, R. D., Deaux, K., & McLaughlin-Volpe, T. (2004). An organizing framework for collective identity: Articulation and significance of multidimensionality. *Psychological Bulletin, 130*(1), 80–114.
Azrout, R., van Spanje, J., & de Vreese, C. (2012). When news matters: Media effects on public support for European Union enlargement in 21 countries. *Journal of Common Market Studies, 50*(5), 691–708.
Bellucci, P., Sanders, D., & Serricchio, F. (2012). Explaining European identity. In D. Sanders, P. Bellucci, G. Tóka, & M. Torcal (Eds.), *The Europeanization of national polities? Citizenship and support in a post-enlargement union* (pp. 61–90). Oxford: Oxford University Press.
Braun, M., & Müller, W. (2012). National and transnational identities of intra-European migrants. In F. Höllinger & M. Hadler (Eds.), *Crossing borders, shifting boundaries: National and transnational identities in Europe and beyond. Festschrift für Max Haller* (pp. 263–287). Campus Verlag: Frankfurt/New York.
Brewer, M. B. (2001). The many faces of social identity: Implications for political psychology. *Political Psychology, 22*(1), 115–125.
Brewer, M. B., & Silver, M. D. (2000). Group distincitiveness, social identification, and collective mobilization. In S. Stryker, T. J. Owens, & R. W. White (Eds.), *Self, identity and social movements* (pp. 153–171, Social movements, protest, and contetion, Vol. 13). Minneapolis: University of Minnesota Press.
Castano, E. (2004). European identity: A social-psychological perspective. In R. K. Herrmann, T. Risse, & M. B. Brewer (Eds.), *Transnational identities. Becoming European in the EU* (pp. 40–58). Rowman & Littlefield: Lanham.
Cerutti, F. (2003). A political identity of the Europeans? *Thesis Eleven, 72*(1), 26–45.
Cerutti, F. (2008). Why political identity and legitimacy matter in the European Union. In F. Cerutti, & S. Lucarelli (Eds.), *The search for a European idenity. Values, policies and legitimacy of the European Union* (pp. 3–22, Routledge/GARNET series: Europe in the World). Abingdon/New York: Routledge.
Cinnirella, M. (1996). A social identity perspective on European integration. In G. M. Breakwell & E. Lyons (Eds.), *Changing European identities: Social psychological analyses of social change* (pp. 253–274). Oxford: Butterworth-Heinemann.
Clark, N., & Hellwig, T. (2012). Information effects and mass support for EU policy control. *European Union Politics, 13*(4), 535–557.
David, O., & Bar-Tal, D. (2009). A sociopsychological conception of collective identity: The case of national identity as an example. *Personality and Social Psychology Review, 13*(4), 354–379.
de Vreese, C. H., & Boomgaarden, H. G. (2006). Media effects on public opinion about the enlargement of the European Union. *JCMS: Journal of Common Market Studies, 44*(2), 419–436.
de Vries, C. E., & Edwards, E. E. (2009). Taking Europe to its extremes: Extremist parties and public euroscepticism. *Party Politics, 15*(1), 5–28.
Deutsch, K. W. (1953). *Nationalism and social communication: An inquiry into the foundations of nationality*. Cambridge, MA: MIT Press.
Deutsch, K. W., Burrell, S. A., & Kann, R. A. (1957). *Political community and the North Atlantic area: International organization in the light of historical experience*. Princeton, NJ: Princeton University Press.
Diez Medrano, J. (2003). *Framing Europe: Attitudes to European Integration in Germany, Spain, and the United Kingdom*. Princeton, NJ: Princeton University Press.

Diez Medrano, J., & Gutiérrez, P. (2001). Nested identities: National and European identity in Spain. *Ethnic and Racial Studies, 24*(5), 753–778.

Dovidio, J. F., Gaertner, S. L., & Kawakami, K. (2003). Intergroup contact: The past, present, and the future. *Group Processes and Intergroup Relations, 6*(1), 5–21.

Duchesne, S., & Frognier, A.-P. (1995). Is there a European identity? In O. Niedermayer & R. Sinnott (Eds.), *Public opinion and internationalized government. Vol. 2 of Beliefs in government* (pp. 193–226). Oxford: Oxford University Press.

Easton, D. (1965). *A systems analysis of political life*. New York: Wiley.

Evans, M. D. R., & Kelley, J. (2002). National pride in the developed world: Survey data from 24 nations. *International Journal of Public Opinion Research, 14*(3), 303–338.

Fligstein, N. (2008). *Euroclash: The EU, European identity, and the future of Europe*. Oxford: Oxford University Press.

Fuchs, D. (2000). Demos und Nation in der Europäischen Union. In H.-D. Klingemann & F. Neidhardt (Eds.), *Zur Zukunft der Demokratie. Herausforderungen im Zeitalter der Globalisierung* (pp. 215–236). Berlin: Edition Sigma.

Fuchs, D. (2011). Cultural diversity, European identity and legitimacy of the EU: A theoretical framework. In D. Fuchs & H.-D. Klingemann (Eds.), *Cultural diversity, European identity and the legitimacy of the EU* (pp. 27–57). Cheltenham: Edward Elgar Publishing.

Fuchs, D., & Schneider, C. (2011). Support of the EU and European identity: Some descriptive results. In D. Fuchs & H.-D. Klingemann (Eds.), *Cultural diversity, European identity and the legitimacy of the EU* (pp. 61–85). Cheltenham: Edward Elgar Publishing.

Gabel, M. J., & Scheve, K. (2007a). Estimating the effect of elite communications on public opinion using instrumental variables. *American Journal of Political Science, 51*(4), 1013–1028.

Gabel, M. J., & Scheve, K. (2007b). Mixed messages: Party dissent and mass opinion on European integration. *European Union Politics, 8*(1), 37–59.

Gaertner, S. L., Dovidio, J. F., Anastasio, P. A., Bachman, B. A., & Rust, M. C. (1993). The common ingroup identity model: Recategorization and the reduction of intergroup bias. *European Review of Social Psychology, 4*(1), 1–26.

Gaertner, S. L., Rust, M. C., Dovidio, J. F., Bachman, B. A., & Anastasio, P. A. (1994). The contact hypothesis: The role of a common ingroup identity on reducing intergroup bias. *Small Group Research, 25*(2), 224–249.

Gaertner, S. L., Dovidio, J. F., & Bachman, B. A. (1996). Revisiting the contact hypothesis: The induction of a common ingroup identity. *International Journal of Intercultural Relations, 20* (3–4), 271–290.

Habermas, J. (2001). *Zeit der Übergänge*. Frankfurt am Main: Suhrkamp.

Habermas, J. (2004). *Der gespaltene Westen*. Suhrkamp: Frankfurt am Main.

Herrmann, R. K., & Brewer, M. B. (2004). Identities and institutions: Becoming European in the EU. In R. K. Herrmann, T. Risse, & M. B. Brewer (Eds.), *Transnational identities. Becoming European in the EU* (pp. 1–22). Lanham: Rowman & Littlefield.

Hjerm, M. (1998). National Identities, national pride and xenophobia: A comparison of four Western countries. *Acta Sociologica, 41*(4), 335–347.

Hogg, M. A., & Abrams, D. (1988). *Social identifications: A social psychology of intergroup relations and group processes*. New York: Routledge.

Hogg, M. A., Terry, D. J., & White, K. M. (1995). A tale of two theories: A critical comparison of identity theory with social identity theory. *Social Psychology Quarterly, 58*(4), 255–269.

Kantner, C. (2006). Collective identity as shared ethical self-understanding. *European Journal of Social Theory, 9*(4), 501–523.

Kielmansegg, P. G. (2003). Integration und Demokratie (mit Nachwort zur 2.Auflage). In M. Jachtenfuchs & B. Kohler-Koch (Eds.), *Europäische integration* (2nd ed., pp. 49–83). Opladen: Leske+Budrich.

Kinder, D. R. (1998). Communication and opinion. *Annual Review of Political Science, 1*(1), 167–197.

King, R., & Ruiz-Gelices, E. (2003). International student migration and the European 'Year Abroad': Effects on European identity and subsequent migration behaviour. *International Journal of Population Geography, 9*(3), 229–252.
Kuhn, T. (2011). Individual transnationalism, globalisation and euroscepticism: An empirical test of Deutsch's transactionalist theory. *European Journal of Political Research, 50*(6), 811–837.
Kuhn, T. (2012a). Europa ante portas: Border residence, transnational interaction and Euroscepticism in Germany and France. *European Union Politics, 13*(1), 94–117.
Kuhn, T. (2012b). Why educational exchange programmes miss their mark: Cross-border mobility, education and European identity. *JCMS: Journal of Common Market Studies, 50*(6), 994–1010.
Kuhn, T. (2015). *Experiencing European integration: Individual transnationalism and public orientations towards European integration*. Oxford: Oxford University Press.
Lilli, W. (1998). Europäische Identität: Chancen und Risiken ihrer Verwirklichung aus einer sozialpsychologischen Grundlagenperspective. In T. König, E. Rieger, & H. Schmitt (Eds.), *Europa der Bürger? Voraussetzungen, Alternativen, Konsequenzen* (pp. 139–158). Frankfurt am Main/New York: Campus Verlag.
Maier, M., Adam, S., & Maier, J. (2012). The impact of identity and economic cues on citizens' EU support: An experimental study on the effects of party communication in the run-up to the 2009 European Parliament elections. *European Union Politics, 13*(4), 580–603.
Meyer, T. (2004). *Die Identität Europas. Der EU eine Seele?* Frankfurt am Main: Suhrkamp.
Mutz, D. C., Sniderman, P. N., & Brody, R. A. (Eds.). (1996). *Political persuasion and attitude change*. Ann Arbor: University of Michigan Press.
Pettigrew, T. F. (1998). Intergroup contact theory. *Annual Review of Psychology, 49*(1), 65–85.
Pichler, F. (2008). European identities from below: Meanings of identification with Europe. *Perspectives on European Politics and Society, 9*(4), 411–430.
Pichler, F. (2009). Cosmopolitan Europe. *European Societies, 11*(1), 3–25.
Ray, L. (2003). When parties matter: The conditional influence of party positions on voter opinions about European integration. *Journal of Politics, 65*(4), 978–994.
Recchi, E. (2008). Cross-state mobility in the EU. *European Societies, 10*(2), 197–225.
Risse, T. (2004). European institutions and identity change: What have we learned? In R. K. Herrmann, T. Risse, & M. B. Brewer (Eds.), *Transnational identities. Becoming European in the EU* (pp. 247–271). Rowman & Littlefield: Lanham.
Risse, T. (2010). *A community of Europeans? Transnational identities and public spheres*. Ithaca: Cornell University Press.
Risse, T., & Engelmann-Martin, D. (2002). Identity politics and European integration: The case of Germany. In A. Pagden (Ed.), *The idea of Europe. From antiquity to the European Union* (pp. 287–316). Cambridge/New York: Cambridge Unversity Press.
Rother, N., & Nebe, T. M. (2009). More mobile, more European? Free movement and EU identity. In E. Recchi & A. Favell (Eds.), *Pioneers of European Integration: Citizenship and mobility in the EU* (pp. 120–155). Cheltenham: Edward Elgar.
Schuck, A. R. T., & de Vreese, C. H. (2011). Public support for referendums: The role of the media. *West European Politics, 34*(2), 181–207.
Smith, A. D. (1991). *National identity*. Reno, NV: University of Nevada Press.
Tajfel, H. (1974). Social identity and intergroup behaviour. *Social Science Information, 13*(2), 65–93.
Tajfel, H. (1981). *Human groups and social categories. Studies in social psychology*. Cambridge: Cambridge University Press.
Tajfel, H. (Ed.). (1982). *Social identity and intergroup relations*. Cambridge: Cambridge University Press.
Tajfel, H., & Turner, J. C. (1979). An integrated theory of intergroup conflict. In W. G. Austin & S. Worchel (Eds.), *The Social psychology of intergroup relations* (pp. 33–47). Monterey: Brooks/Cole.

Tajfel, H., & Turner, J. C. (1986). The social identity theory of intergroup behaviour. In S. Worchel & W. G. Austin (Eds.), *Psychology of Intergroup Relations* (pp. 7–24). Chicago: Nelson-Hall.

Thoits, P. A., & Virshup, L. K. (1997). Me's and we's. Forms and functions of social identities. In R. D. Ashmore & J. Lee (Eds.), *Self and identity. Fundamental issues* (pp. 106–133). New York/Oxford: Oxford University Press.

Turner, J. C. (1985). Social-categorization and the self-concept: A social cognitive theory of group behaviour. In E. J. Lawler (Ed.), *Advances in group processes: Theory and reseach* (Vol. 2, pp. 77–122). Greenwich: JAI Press.

Turner, J. C., Hogg, M. A., Oakes, P. J., Reicher, S. D., & Wetherell, M. S. (1987). *Rediscovering the social group. A self-categorization theory*. Oxford/New York: Basil Blackwell.

Westle, B. (2003). Europäische Identifikation im Spannungsfeld regionaler und nationaler Identitäten. Theoretische Überlegungen und empirische Befunde. *Politische Vierteljahresschrift, 44*(4), 453–482.

Zaller, J. (1992). *The nature and origins of mass opinion*. Cambridge: Cambridge University Press.

Chapter 3
The Sources of European Identity: A Theoretical Model for Explaining Individual Identification with Europe

Chapter 2 developed the idea that Europe must be perceived as a tangible category for self-categorisation in order for citizens to identify as European. Citizens with better access to information about Europe and/or better opportunities for every day experiences with citizens from other EU member states should be more aware of the commonalities shared by Europeans and have a clearer idea of membership in the European community. As a result, they should more readily identify as European than citizens who have only little knowledge about Europe and/or experience with the EU and other Europeans.[1] Based on these considerations, two mechanisms underlying citizens' identification with Europe have been suggested: The first is information-based and assumes that exposure to elite messages and communications establishing the European community as an object of identification and a relevant category for self-representation is at the root of citizens' European identification. Citizens are expected to identify with Europe to the extent that they receive information about the community of Europeans and thus become aware of its shared norms and values as well as the meaning and importance of a shared European 'we-feeling'. The second is experience-based and considers that direct encounters with other EU citizens and the personal experience of being part of the European community are at the root of citizens' European identification. Citizens are expected to identify with Europe to the extent that they interact with other Europeans and/or European institutions and directly perceive what Europeans have in common in terms of shared experiences, norms, and values.

The present chapter takes these two mechanisms as a starting point for developing a theoretical model of individual identification with Europe among EU citizens. Building on the idea of information- and experience-based identification, the model starts out from the assumption that citizens' propensity to identify with

[1]As previously discussed, reverse effects are equally possible, with better informed citizens and those with more experience with other Europeans and EU integration identifying less with Europe. The theoretical model of European identification with Europe accounts for both positive and negative effects by developing alternative hypotheses for empirical analysis.

S. Bergbauer, *Explaining European Identity Formation*,
https://doi.org/10.1007/978-3-319-67708-8_3

Europe will depend on their access to Europe-related information on the one hand and the opportunities they have for personal contacts with other Europeans and the way they experience EU integration on the other. Accordingly, the theoretical model explains citizens' identification with Europe by factors that shape either citizens' access to Europe-related information or their opportunities for personal experiences with other Europeans and EU politics. The degree of citizens' access to information about Europe and opportunities for personal contacts among Europeans is considered to depend on, first, *citizens' individual attributes and predispositions*, and, second, the *national context in which citizens live*. Therefore, the model includes both individual attributes and predispositions and contextual attributes at the member state level as explanatory factors of individual identification with Europe.

The resulting explanatory model systematically links conceptualisations of group identity and the formation of group identifications in social psychology to explanatory factors of European identification deduced from (EU) public opinion research. It provides a comprehensive framework for analysing European identification in the mass public that aims at explaining individual identification with Europe across all EU member states and periods of European integration without being restricted to a particular political, geographical, or historical context. It will be applied to the explanation of European identification in the mass public after Maastricht with a particular view to two decisive periods in the recent history of European integration: the EU's enlargement to Central and Eastern Europe in 2004/2007 and the financial and economic crisis that has affected the EU and its member states since late 2008.

Eastward enlargement and the financial and economic crisis, followed by sovereign debt crises in a number of member states, are turning points in the integration process in that they had significant financial, political, and social consequences for the EU as a whole as well as for individual member states, and initiated extensive debates over the future course of EU integration. The present analysis theoretically and empirically explores how these key moments in the EU integration process have affected citizens' identification with the European community. The inferences we can draw from this analysis for the development of European identification in the mass public reach beyond the immediate impact of these two events. Eastward enlargement and the economic crisis can be considered test cases in the EU integration process. They made the costs of EU integration more visible to citizens in the member states and resulted in a greater politicisation and polarisation of the EU (Hutter and Grande 2014; Rauh and Zürn 2014; Risse 2015). Future steps towards a closer political union, a stronger European economic governance, or the accession of new EU member states are likely to trigger similar processes of politicisation and contestation. The examples of enlargement and the economic crisis thus allow us to theorise more generally about the development of a European we-feeling as EU integration becomes more politicised.

The remainder of the present chapter is divided in three main parts. Section 3.1 presents the conceptual foundations of the theoretical model of European identification. Section 3.2 builds on these foundations to develop a theoretical model for explaining individual European identification that links individual- and country-level determinants of citizens' identification with Europe to the information- and experience-based mechanisms of European identification deduced in Chap. 2. The final section explores the impact of EU enlargement to CEE and the financial and economic crisis on individual identification with Europe (Sect. 3.3). This last part discusses in detail how turning points in the EU integration process affect citizens' identification with Europe and which changes in the determinants of European identification we expect in response to EU enlargement 2004/2007 and the onset of the financial and economic crisis in 2008.

3.1 Theoretical Foundations for an Explanatory Model of Individual Identification with Europe

The present section presents the conceptual foundations for the explanatory model of individual identification with Europe developed in the following. These are in particular John Zaller's work on the nature and origins of mass opinion (Zaller 1992), and Dieter Fuchs' model of mass opinion towards the EU and European identity, which adapts Zaller's insights to the formation of attitudes in the context of European integration (Fuchs 2011).

John Zaller's Model of the Nature and Origins of Mass Opinion In his 1992 study on '*The Nature and Origins of Mass Opinion*', John Zaller explores how individuals form political preferences; in particular, preferences and attitudes towards objects and events which are beyond their immediate experience and full personal understanding. His central conjecture is that political attitudes are a function of, on the one hand, information carried in elite discourse and, on the other hand, the degree of individuals' attention to this information together with individuals' political values and predispositions mediating their reaction to elite information.

The starting point of Zaller's theory of public opinion formation are messages by political elites that individuals receive and convert into political opinions. Zaller distinguishes two types of messages carried in elite discourse. On the one hand, *persuasive messages* which are 'arguments or images providing reasons for taking a position or point of view' (Zaller 1992, p. 41); if accepted by the individual, these may be used as a consideration when forming an opinion about a political issue. On the other hand, *cueing messages* which 'consist of "contextual information" about the ideological or partisan implications of a persuasive message' (Zaller 1992, p. 42); this information allows individuals to evaluate the persuasive messages they receive in light of their own political predispositions and respond critically to these messages.

The extent to which individuals are exposed to and receive messages by political elites is considered to be a function of their level of political awareness (cognitive engagement); whether individuals accept or reject a particular elite message is considered to depend on their (pre-existing) political dispositions and the availability of contextual information enabling them to correctly perceive the relationship between the arguments they receive from political elites and their own values, interests, and experiences. When asked to give an opinion statement, individuals sample from the pool of elite arguments and considerations they have previously encountered and base their opinion on the most accessible considerations, i.e. those considerations which have been thought about most recently and, therefore, are still at the top of people's minds.

Zaller's conceptualisation of the processes underlying public opinion formation are the starting point for the explanatory model of individual identification with Europe developed in this book. Although Zaller is predominantly concerned with public opinion and electoral choice in U.S. legislative and presidential elections, he presents his work as a general model of the formation of political preferences. As such, it applies to a wide range of problems in research on public opinion and political behaviour (cf. Zaller 1992, p. 1), and also lends itself to the study of public opinion towards the EU and the formation of European identification among EU citizens. In fact, Zaller tailors his model to public opinion formation in situations where citizens have little first-hand experience with the matter or object in question, lack a full understanding of the event, and, therefore, rely on leadership cues and the information they receive from political elites to form an opinion (cf. Zaller 1992, p. 14). The EU appears to present a prime example of such an obscure and far removed object; in effect, the majority of the EU population has little knowledge of EU affairs (Maier and Bathelt 2013; Westle and Johann 2010), feels ill-informed about EU politics, and relies on the mass media to gather information about the EU and its policies (European Commission 2011b, 2012b). Against this background, Zaller's model of the construction of public opinion appears to be an adequate theoretical basis for the analysis of EU public opinion and the development of citizens' identification with Europe.

Dieter Fuchs' Model of the Construction of Mass Opinion Towards the EU and European Identity Fuchs (2011) takes up the notion of public opinion formation under conditions of low salience and develops a model of the construction of mass opinion towards the EU and European identity that takes Zaller's model as its theoretical basis. In Fuchs' model of EU mass opinion, the individual orientations to be explained are 'support for the EU' and 'European identity'. The central explanatory factors at the individual level are respondents' level of political awareness, considered to affect the degree of exposure to elite messages, and respondents' political predispositions, considered to regulate the acceptance or rejection of elite arguments. At the system level, the focus is on the discourse of political elites, considered the central determinant of the degree of citizens' exposure to political communications. For Fuchs, the relevant elite messages for attitudes towards Europe and the EU stem from party contestation over EU integration and the politicisation of European questions in party discourse (Fuchs 2011, p. 47).

Fuchs introduces a number of modifications to adapt Zaller's original model to the analysis of EU public opinion. First, Fuchs includes '*framing messages*' as an additional type of elite message to which citizens are exposed to. Framing messages are considered interpretative or ideational packages that convey a specific definition, causal interpretation, or evaluation of a problem (see the definitions by Entman (1993) and Polletta and Ho (2006) cited in Fuchs 2011). Furthermore, Fuchs argues that political awareness should not be considered in isolation, but is itself determined by respondents' interest in politics and their level of education. Accordingly, he adds '*motivation*' (general political interest) and '*competence*' (level of education) as predictors of individual political awareness. He further points to the relevance of *everyday experiences* for political choices and preferences as demonstrated in electoral research and hypothesised by socialisation models of identity change. Accordingly, Fuchs extends Zaller's model by including citizens' 'everyday experiences' as additional determinant of the acceptance or rejection of elite messages and thus independent source of opinion formation at the individual level.

At the system level, Fuchs extends Zaller's original model by including '*critical events*', *political institutions*, and '*collective memory*' as additional contextual influences affecting the structure and content of elite messages as well as individuals' political predispositions. All three context characteristics are expected to have a particular bearing on attitudes towards the EU.

Critical events are defined by Fuchs as events with substantial consequences for national societies that lead to significant changes in elite positions and individual political preferences (cf. Fuchs 2011, p. 48). The financial and economic crisis may present such a watershed moment for European societies in that it led to significant shifts in economic, financial, and monetary policies at both the EU and the national level, sometimes with drastic consequences for national societies, as the examples of austerity programmes in Greece and elsewhere show.

Political institutions, in turn, affect elite messages and individual predispositions by shaping the structure of national political conflict as well as citizens' expectations towards the political system. For example, types and degree of national welfare regimes, national party systems, and electoral context have all been shown to systematically influence citizens' attitudes towards the EU and EU integration (see the analyses by, e.g. de Vries and Edwards 2009; Hooghe and Marks 2005; Ray 2003; Steenbergen et al. 2007).

Collective memory, finally, is defined by Fuchs as the substance and structure of political conflict in a country together with the political predispositions of its citizens, both determined by national history (cf. Fuchs 2011, p. 49). A country's collective memory becomes manifest in its national symbols, monuments, writings, and other iconic representations, and provides a pool of references and information about a country's history. Citizens internalise these references in socialisation processes and political elites can draw on them to mobilise public opinion and provide a particular interpretation of issues of public debate. As regards elements of collective memory related to European integration, research on national identity constructions and national perceptions of European integration shows that there are indeed country-specific understandings and representations of the EU and EU integration. These can be traced back to member states' different historical trajectories and are empirically observable both among national elites (see, e.g. Risse 2010; Risse and Engelmann-Martin 2002) and ordinary citizens (see, e.g. Diez Medrano 2003) in the member states.

Fuchs' model of the construction of EU public opinion provides the starting point for the explanatory model of individual identification with Europe developed in the remainder of this chapter. The next step is to apply the general premises of Fuchs' model to the analysis of citizens' identification with Europe. This adaptation requires adjustments in two regards.

First, we need to discuss how the general constructs that Fuchs introduces as determinants of EU mass opinion can be adapted to the specific case of explaining European identification. Which are the relevant individual political predispositions and everyday experiences likely to affect citizens' identification with Europe? Likewise, which issues must be politicised in elite discourse so that we can expect elite messages to influence citizens' identification with Europe? In short, we need to replace general concepts of opinion formation with specific predictors of European identification.

Second, we need to discuss whether additional explanatory factors ought to be added to the model to account for the specific conditions of the formation of European identification. This also requires a discussion of how Fuchs' model of the construction of mass opinion towards the EU and European identity can be aligned with the idea that identification with Europe develops along two distinct paths, either through information about the EU and the community of Europeans or through personal contacts and experience with other Europeans. Section 3.2 will take up these questions and develop a theoretical model for explaining individual identification with Europe. While taking Fuchs' work as a starting point, the theoretical framework for explaining European identification modifies his model in such a way as to adapt it to the particular case of individual identification with Europe and deduct empirically falsifiable hypotheses about the sources of individual identification with Europe.

3.2 A Model for Explaining Individual Identification with Europe

The remainder of this chapter develops the theoretical model for explaining individual identification with Europe that will form the basis of the empirical analysis of European identification in the EU mass public. The presentation of the model starts with an overview of the theoretical assumptions underlying the model of European identification (Sect. 3.2.1). The subsequent sections discuss the explanatory variables and the theoretical expectations regarding the relationship between explanatory variables and citizens' identification with Europe in detail (Sects. 3.2.2, 3.2.3, and 3.2.4).

3.2.1 Citizens' Access to Europe-Related Information and Europe-Related Experience and Individual Identification with Europe

The following introduction outlines the explanatory model of European identification developed in the remainder of this chapter. It seeks to clarify how information- and experienced-based processes of European identification deduced from Social Identity Theory can be linked to specific individual- and country-level characteristics in order to build a comprehensive theoretical model of citizens' identification with Europe that can be subjected to empirical analysis.

Individual identification with Europe has previously been defined as citizens' self-categorisation as European together with their evaluation of their membership in the European collective and their affective attachment to Europe. Drawing on social identity theories in social psychology, we deduced two mechanisms of identity formation presumed to underlie individual identification with Europe. Citizens are expected to come to identify with Europe through *exposure to information about Europe and the community of Europeans* and *personal contacts with other Europeans and the experience of EU integration* in their daily lives. Consequently, individual identification with Europe should depend, on the one hand, on the opportunities and abilities citizens have to receive and process information about Europe, and, on the other hand, on citizens' opportunities to come in personal contact with other Europeans and the way they experience the consequences of EU integration in their everyday lives.

The extent of citizens' access to information about Europe and personal encounters with other Europeans as well as the way citizens experience the consequences of EU integration in their daily lives are considered to be influenced by both *citizens' individual attributes and predispositions* and *characteristics of the national context* in which citizens live. To concretise these individual- and country-level influences, I make use of the explanatory factors proposed by Zaller (1992) and Fuchs (2011) and allocate these to either of the two mechanisms of European identification, adding further determinants where appropriate.

At the *individual level*, Zaller and Fuchs suggest *political awareness, political predispositions*, and *everyday experiences* as relevant factors for influencing public opinion and attitudes towards the EU and European identity. These general concepts are adapted to the analysis of European identification in the following way:

Political awareness is extended to include *general political interest, interest in European politics,* and *knowledge of EU politics*; the aim is to capture not only citizens' general interest in political affairs, but also their attention to and knowledge of politics at the European level as the primary object of identification and reference point for feelings of European identity.

Political predispositions considered relevant for European identification are citizens' attitudes towards the European and the national community. These include citizens' conception of Europe and the European community in terms of a shared cultural heritage and/or common political fate as opposed to a means to individual benefits; the degree of national identification; and citizens' conception of national community, i.e. whether they conceive of membership in their national community as universalistic (based on the belief in common political values) or particularistic (based on a common cultural ancestry, ethnicity, language, or religion).

Finally, as regards *everyday experiences*, I assume that the relevant experiences for European identification are instances in which citizens interact with their counterparts in other EU member states. Accordingly, *personal transnational experiences* in the form of private and professional contacts and interactions with other Europeans, either across EU member state borders or within the home country, are included as a further predictor of identification with Europe at the individual level.

At the *country level*, Zaller and Fuchs both focus on the role of *political elites and elite messages* in public opinion formation. Building on this idea, I argue that the elite messages most likely to affect citizens' identification with Europe are *party messages* related to issues of European identity and the European community on the one hand and party messages related to issues of national identity and the national community on the other. Accordingly, a first set of country-level predictors included in the model of European identification are *party messages related to the European and national community*, i.e. the degree to which national political parties either emphasise communalities among Europeans and shared European values and traditions or point to the distinctiveness of the national community and invoke a strong national identity. Thus, party messages represent a measure of Europe-related information and, more particularly, information about the European and national community that citizens receive within the national political context.

Expanding on Zaller and Fuchs, I include two additional sets of country-level predictors in the model of European identification. The first are member states' *economic position and degree of integration in the EU and global markets*, which refers to member states' *membership in the Eurozone, net contribution to the EU budget*, and *share in international trade*. These measures represent proxies for how citizens experience the economic dimension of European integration and its consequences for the national economy.

Second, I include measures of member state societies' *ethnocultural composition* as additional country-level predictors. *Ethnocultural composition* thereby refers to the *overall share of foreigners* and the *share of EU nationals* living in a country as a measure of member states' cultural heterogeneity and diversity of the national population. These are considered proxies for the likelihood of personal contacts between foreign (EU) nationals and the native population.

Figure 3.1 provides an overview of the individual- and country-level predictors included in the model of individual identification with Europe. Country-level predictors are displayed in the upper half of the figure; individual-level predictors are displayed in the bottom half. Shaded boxes indicate predictors allocated to an experienced-based mechanism of European identification.

Having introduced the individual- and country-level determinants of European identification included in the explanatory model, the next step is to clarify whether and how these relate to the idea of information- and experience-based ways of

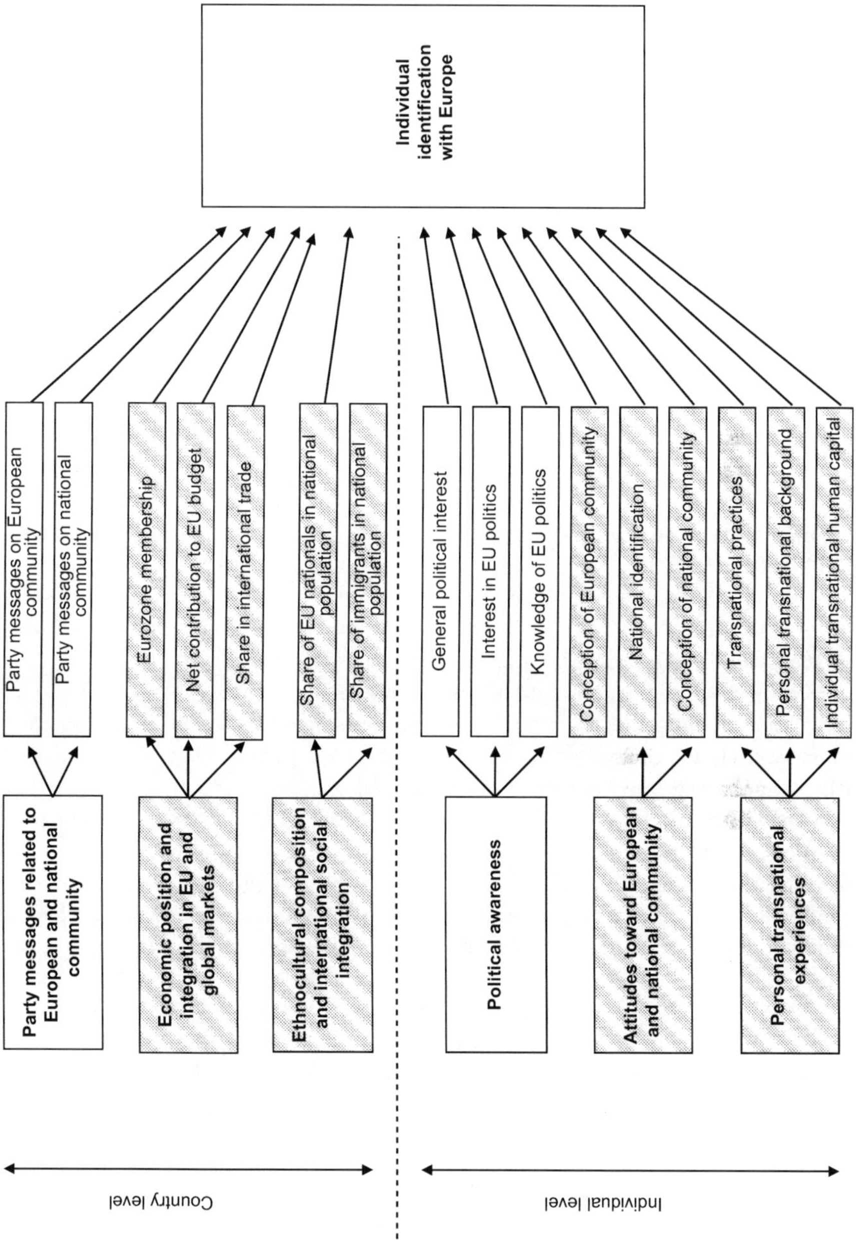

Fig. 3.1 Explanatory model of individual identification with Europe (without interaction effects)

identification with Europe. The aim is to show how approaches to European identification that draw on social psychology on the one hand and research in the field of public opinion formation on the other can be linked in order to develop a comprehensive theoretical framework for explaining individual identification with Europe.

Starting with *individual-level determinants* of European identification, *political awareness*, in the form of citizens' knowledge of and their attention to (European) politics, clearly points to an information-based way of identification. The assumption is that political awareness influences how likely citizens are to receive information about Europe and the European community on which European identification may build.

Citizens' *attitudes towards the European and the national community* as well as *personal transnational experience*, in contrast, are associated with an experience-based way of identification.

Starting with the latter, *personal transnational experiences* provide a direct measure of Europe-related experience: private and professional contacts and interactions with citizens from other member state, either across member state borders or within the home country, represent a very direct form of experience with the European community. This experience is thought to facilitate the perception of communalities among Europeans, which, in turn, should affect citizens' likelihood to identify with Europe.

Attitudes towards the European and the national community, on the other hand, represent measures of indirect experiences with the European community or experiences with the European community once removed. Over the course of their lives, citizens are exposed to particular national perceptions of European integration—the 'collective memory' of a country's European history—passed on in socialisation processes, via the education system, and in the mass media. They also experience EU policies and the consequences of EU integration at the national level and in their everyday lives, e.g. in the form of open borders, the common currency, or EU-funded infrastructural projects. Likewise, citizens acquire conceptions of national identity and national community in socialisation processes; over the course of life, these conceptions are reinforced through experiences with other members of the national community and social and political institutions embodying the community's shared values and beliefs (cf. Chap. 2). While these experiences do not necessarily imply personal contacts with other Europeans, they still constitute a form of experience with Europe expected to shape citizens' outlook on the European and the national community and their perception of the relation between the national and the European level. These attitudes, in turn, are expected to influence citizens' feelings of belonging to Europe.

As regards the allocation of *country-level determinants* to different paths of European identification, *party messages related to the European and national community* are assumed to affect European identification via an information-based process. In effect, party messages about the European community, a common European identity, and its relation to the national level provide a direct measure of the extent and type of Europe-related information that citizens are exposed to. This is also the case for party messages about the national community: by emphasising the nation, its unique values and traditions, and a national way of life, parties implicitly or explicitly invoke the distinctiveness of the national community, thus underlining differences rather than communalities among Europeans. In this regard, party messages about the national community, too, represent a form of Europe-related information. Overall, party messages thus represent the supply side of an information-based path of European identification: they provide citizens with arguments and considerations about Europe, the European community, and the relation between the national and the European level, which, in turn, should influence citizens' propensity to identify with Europe.

Member states' *economic position and degree of integration in the EU and global markets* as well as member state societies' *ethnocultural composition*, on the other hand, are considered to affect European identification via an experience-based process of identification.

As regards member states' *economic position and degree of economic integration*, the idea is that indicators of a country's economic strength and degree of integration in the European market such as its net contribution to the EU budget, membership in the Eurozone, or share in trade represent corollaries of EU integration that citizens experience in the domestic context; either directly because they use the euro as the common currency or are employed in trade-dependent industries, or indirectly, in that contributions to the EU budget and trade dependency represent aspects that are relatively frequently communicated and discussed in the national political debate and mass media, not only in relation to EU integration, but also in the wider debate on the state of the national economy. Moreover, economies that are more open and more export-oriented industries also provide more opportunities for citizens to meet personally with citizens from other EU member states for professional reasons, thus increasing the chance for everyday experiences with other Europeans.

A similar argument applies to the relation between member states' *ethnocultural composition* and citizens' propensity to identify with Europe. The idea is that indicators of sociocultural diversity such as the share of EU nationals living in a country and the overall share of immigrants in a country's population provide proxies for citizens' opportunities to interact with non-nationals and make the kind of everyday experiences and personal encounters expected to influence identification with Europe. Based on these considerations, measures of member states' ethnocultural diversity are associated with an experience-based process of European identification.

The following subsections discuss the different sets of explanatory variables of European identification in detail and derive hypotheses for empirical analysis. I will develop, first, an *individual-level model of identification with Europe* (Sect. 3.2.2); in a second step, I will add *explanatory factors at the country level* to the individual-level model to build a multilevel model of European identity (Sect. 3.2.3). Third, I will discuss how individual predispositions such as political interest and identification with the nation mediate the effect of country characteristics on citizens' propensity to identify with Europe and specify potential *interaction effects between individual- and country-level determinants* (Sect. 3.2.4). The final part of this chapter discusses *the impact of EU enlargement to CEE and the financial and economic crisis on individual identification with Europe* (Sect. 3.3). To explore whether and how the bases of citizens' identification with Europe change at key moments in the integration process, the EU's eastward enlargement 2004/2007 and the onset of the financial and economic crisis in 2008 are taken as test cases for the general model. Thus, a final set of hypotheses addresses potential changes in the determinants of European identification under the impact of enlargement and economic turmoil in the EU member states. The aim is to explore theoretically and empirically how turning points in the integration process affect citizens' identification with Europe and contribute to our understanding of the development of EU public opinion in light of substantial changes in the composition of EU member countries and changing economic relations between EU member states.

3.2.2 *Individual-Level Determinants of Individual Identification with Europe*

The explanatory model of individual identification with Europe developed in the following includes three categories of individual-level variables expected to affect the formation of European identification among EU citizens: political awareness, attitudes toward the European and national community, and personal transnational experiences.

3.2.2.1 Political Awareness

Political awareness, understood as individuals' cognitive engagement with politics (cf. Zaller 1992, p. 43), is associated with an information-based process of European identification in that it influences the likelihood of citizens' exposure to information about Europe and the European community. The concept of political awareness comprises two components, *political interest* on the one hand and *political knowledge* on the other, which are adjusted to the European context. Given that individual identification with Europe refers to an object of identification that is located outside the national political context, we may expect that what affects identification with Europe is not so much or not only individuals' interest in and knowledge of national politics or politics in general, but their interest in and knowledge of *European politics*. Assuming that citizens who are generally more interested in politics will also be more likely to pick up news and information on the EU, even if they do not take a specific interest in European affairs in the first place, both *general political interest* and *interest in European politics* are included as predictors of individual identification with Europe. Furthermore, the individual-level model includes *knowledge of European politics* as a predictor of European identification.

As regards the direction of the expected effect, both positive and negative effects on European identification seem plausible. On the one hand, we may expect that the more interested people are in politics and issues of European integration and the more knowledgeable about the EU, the more likely they are to identify with Europe. If people are familiar with and interested in European politics, they should have a better understanding of the workings of the EU system, and, therefore, be less likely to perceive European integration as a threat; they should also be more aware of the potential benefits of European integration, be it for them personally, their country, or Europe as a whole, and have a better grasp of the relevance of European integration for their everyday lives. Empirically, this line of reasoning is supported by analyses of European identification that find positive effects of consumption of international news (Diez Medrano and Gutiérrez 2001), general political interest, and knowledge of EU politics on identification with Europe (Bellucci et al. 2012; Duchesne and Frognier 1995; Scharkow and Vogelgesang 2010). Furthermore, there is evidence from research on EU support that citizens who are better informed about the EU indeed hold more positive views of policy making at the EU-level (Clark and Hellwig 2012). The above considerations and the existing empirical evidence lead to three hypotheses predicting positive effects of political interest and political knowledge on European identification:

H_{1a}: The more interested individuals are in politics, the more they identify with Europe.

H_{2a}: The more interested individuals are in EU politics, the more they identify with Europe.

H_{3a}: The more knowledgeable individuals are of the EU and EU integration, the more they identify with Europe.

The alternative hypothesis expects that *those who are more familiar with European politics are less likely to identify with Europe*. Negative information effects are likely if greater knowledge of and interest in European affairs also makes citizens more aware of the potential risks and downsides of European integration; as a result, the community of Europeans may no longer be perceived as an object of positive identification and citizens will become less likely to identify with Europe. Again, three empirically testable hypotheses are formulated:

H_{1b}: The more interested individuals are in politics, the less they identify with Europe.

H_{2b}: The more interested individuals are in EU politics, the less they identify with Europe.

H_{3b}: The more knowledgeable individuals are of the EU and EU integration, the less they identify with Europe.

Negative effects of knowledge and political interest on European identification appear particularly plausible at times when EU topics gain in attention and become more politicised in domestic debates. The economic and financial crisis affecting the EU over the past years represents such a period of politicisation and polarisation of EU integration (Hutter and Grande 2014; Hutter and Kerscher 2014; Risse 2015). The financial and economic turmoil of the past years has made apparent the strong financial and economic interdependencies among EU member states. It showed that EU integration can have redistributive consequences creating winners and losers of integration. In such periods of crisis, greater knowledge of and interest in EU affairs also implies greater awareness of the risks and potential negative consequences of EU integration. As a result, we may expect negative effects on European identification. Likewise, we may expect that negative effects of knowledge and political interest on European identity are stronger among citizens in member states hit hardest by the crisis, in particular in countries where national governments imposed austerity measures in order to comply with conditions for EU financial aids, e.g. Greece or Portugal. To account for such variation in the effects of political awareness, subsequent sections will discuss interaction effects between individual political interest and characteristics of the national context.

3.2.2.2 Attitudes Towards European and National Community

Attitudes towards the European and the national community represent a second set of individual-level determinants of citizens' identification with Europe. Resulting from socialisation processes and citizens' experiences with European integration on the one hand and the national community and national institutions on the other, they are associated with an experience-based process of European identification.

Two sets of predispositions appear particularly relevant in the context of European identification: *attitudes towards the European community* as reflected in citizens' *conception of Europe and the European community*, and *attitudes towards the national community*, understood here as comprising citizens' *identification with the nation* and their *conception of national community*.

Conceptions of Europe and European Community Regarding, first, *conceptions of Europe and the European community* as predictor of European identification, we may assume that citizens' identification with Europe also depends on their notion of the substantive contents of a common European identity and the meaning they ascribe to Europe.

Conceptual analyses of European identity and European community often distinguish between *civic (or political) conceptions* of community on the one hand and *cultural conceptions* of community on the other (see e.g. Bruter 2004, 2005; Cerutti 2003; Delanty 2002; Schlenker 2013). *Civic conceptions* of European community emphasise the universalistic values of democracy, human rights, and civil liberties underlying European unification and uniting Europeans in a *common political project*. *Cultural conceptions* of European community, in contrast, emphasise a *common European cultural heritage* defined by, inter alia, a Greco-Roman legacy, Humanism, the experience of Reformation and Enlightenment, and religious roots in Christianity.

The distinction made here with regard to citizens' conceptions of Europe and the European community differs from the above distinction between civic and cultural conceptions of community. The focus is not on whether citizens see political or cultural communalities as the foundation of the community of Europeans; rather, different conceptions of European community are distinguished based on whether citizens conceive of Europe and European integration as a *common endeavour*—based on either a common culture or a common political fate—or as a *means for individual material benefits*.

Citizens who feel that a common culture and common history is at the basis of European integration evidently see Europe as a cultural sphere and perceive sociocultural communalities among Europeans across EU member states. Given the crucial role that the perception of such commonalities plays for collective identity formation, these citizens should be more likely to identify with Europe. A similar argument applies to citizens for whom European integration primarily signifies peace and democracy. These ideals invoke a shared political fate that provides a basis for the development of a common we-feeling and collective identity. Therefore, we should expect citizens who associate Europe with the ideals of peace and democracy to be more likely to identify with Europe.

In contrast, citizens who think of Europe primarily in terms of entrepreneurship or the freedom to travel, study, and work across the EU appear to associate Europe mainly with individual benefits. Perceptions of individual benefits of integration, however, do not imply strong sociocultural ties, a community of fate, or a common political project among Europeans on which a common European identity may build. Therefore, we should expect citizens for whom Europe signifies primarily individual benefits to be less likely to identify with Europe.

The following two hypotheses summarise these expectations:

H_{4a}: The more individuals associate Europe with a common cultural heritage and/or a common political fate, the more they identify with Europe.

H_{4b}: The more individuals associate Europe with individual benefits, the less they identify with Europe.

National Identification and Conceptions of National Community A second set of individual predispositions expected to affect European identification are attitudes towards the national community. These include, on the one hand, the *strength of national identification*, and, on the other hand, citizens' *conception of national identity and the criteria for inclusion in the national community*.

As regards the relation between *national identification* and identification with Europe, the theoretical discussion and empirical evidence so far remain inconclusive. Conceptually, we can think of national and European identifications as either conflicting or complementary, leading us to expect national attachments to be either negatively or positively related to attachments to Europe (cf. Chap. 2; see also discussion in, e.g. Fuchs et al. 2009; Herrmann and Brewer 2004; Risse 2010; Westle 2003, 2012). Empirically, the majority of analyses find positive effects of national identification on identification with Europe although the strength and direction of these effects vary between EU member states (see results in, e.g. Citrin and Sides 2004; Duchesne and Frognier 1995, 2008; Fuchs et al. 2009; Westle 2003, 2012). In light of the on-going conceptual discussion and conflicting empirical evidence, alternative hypotheses will assess the influence of national attachments on citizens' identification with Europe.

On the one hand, we may expect that the more citizens identify with the nation, the *more* they will identify with Europe. Drawing on research in social psychology, the assumption here is that individuals hold multiple identities which correspond to different levels of abstraction and become salient in different situations (Brewer 2001; Turner 1987). Accordingly, national and European attachments either should be uncorrelated or even reinforce each other. This may be the case if citizens believe that their country plays an important role in or has a lot to gain from European integration, or if they feel that being European is an integral part of the national identity (cf. the discussion on the Europeanisation of national identities in Risse 2001, 2010).

On the other hand, we can hypothesise that the more citizens identify with the nation, the *less* they will identify with Europe. The underlying assumption is that citizens who feel strongly attached to the nation are also more concerned with national sovereignty and integrity and thus more likely to perceive Europe and European integration as a threat to the nation state, national culture, and national traditions (McLaren 2002). As a result, we should expect these citizens to see European identity as conflicting with their national identity and, hence, identify less or not at all with Europe.

H_{5a}: The more individuals identify with the nation, the more they identify with Europe.
H_{5b}: The more individuals identify with the nation, the less they identify with Europe.

Whether citizens perceive their national identity as compatible or conflicting with European identity will likely depend on how these issues are debated in the domestic context. For example, we may expect that in Germany—where European integration and EU membership were incorporated in the image of a 'modern Germany' after the Second World War (Risse 2010)—citizens tend to perceive national and European identifications as compatible. In Britain, in contrast, the idea of a unique English or British identity has traditionally been stronger (Risse 2010). As a result, citizens are more likely to perceive national and European identifications as conflicting.

Likewise, we may expect that the relationship between national and European identifications changes in response to the widening and deepening of European integration over time. Thus, concerns for the cultural integrity of the national community and the threat posed by European integration may have been less eminent in the EU12 or EU15, uniting culturally relatively homogeneous Western European countries. This homogeneity has shown cracks since the accession of the new CEE member states; it appears to erode even further with the potential enlargement of the EU to Southeast Europe and the Balkans. Similarly, as long as European integration mainly aimed for the completion of the common market, transfers of national sovereignty to the EU appeared controllable. As the EU has started to pursue greater political unity and, in the context of the economic crisis, has pushed for economic oversight by Brussels and financial redistribution between member states, concerns for national sovereignty have resurged. These renewed concerns for national community and sovereignty may also influence the relationship between national and European identification. Section 3.3 will discuss such variation in the effects of national identification on citizens' identification with Europe in more detail, focussing on the consequences of eastward enlargement and the economic crisis for the relation between attachment to the nation and attachment to Europe.

Other than the strength of national attachments, citizens' *conception of national community* is expected to influence their propensity to identify with Europe. Research on nationalism, national identity, and conceptions of community distinguishes between two main types of nation and national community (Anderson 1991; Brubaker 1992). On the one hand, a particularistic or cultural type (*Kulturnation*), which defines membership in the national community based on criteria such as common ancestry, ethnicity, language, and religion; i.e. criteria which imply a sharp demarcation from outsiders and make membership in the national community highly exclusive. On the other hand, a universalistic or voluntary type (*Staatsnation*), which defines membership in the national community based on criteria such as the common belief in democratic values, individual rights, and civil liberties; i.e. criteria which, in principle, open up membership in the national community to anyone adhering to these values and, therefore, make membership in the national community highly inclusive (for more extensive discussions, see Guinaudeau 2011; Schlenker-Fischer 2009, 2011).

Different conceptions of national community appear more or less compatible with European identification. While particularistic definitions of national community based on shared cultural traits seem to exclude identification with other political communities, value-based universalistic conceptions of community are seen to allow for identification with higher-level communities such as the European community (Guinaudeau 2011; Schlenker-Fischer 2011). Empirically, these expectations have been confirmed by Fuchs et al. (2009) who find that exclusive definitions of national community indeed depress citizens' attachment to Europe.

Based on these considerations and prior empirical findings, we can hypothesise that citizens for whom membership in the national community primarily depends on cultural affinity and a common ethnic and religious heritage are less likely to identify with Europe than citizens for whom membership in the national community primarily depends on shared political values.

H_{6a}: The more individuals associate membership in the national community with common political values, the more they identify with Europe.

H_{6b}: The more individuals identify associate membership in the national community with a common ethnic and religious heritage, the less they identify with Europe.

3.2.2.3 Personal Transnational Experiences

Personal transnational experiences are a third set of individual-level determinants of European identification. These experiences comprise citizens' encounters with other Europeans in the form of private and professional contacts and interactions, either across EU member state borders or within the home country. Personal transnational experiences thus correspond to Fuchs' concept of 'everyday experiences' as a determinant of EU public opinion (Fuchs 2011), and are associated with an experience-based process of European identification.

Transactionalist theories of European identity formation have pointed to the role of personal contacts and interactions for community building from early on in the European integration process (Deutsch 1953a, b; Deutsch et al. 1957). I draw on these theories as well as recent approaches to European identity formation in this tradition (cf. Büttner and Mau 2010; Fligstein 2008; Kuhn 2011, 2012, 2015; Recchi 2012; Sigalas 2010) to develop hypotheses regarding the influence of personal experiences with other Europeans for citizens' propensity to identify with Europe.

Frequent personal contacts with citizens from other EU countries are expected to have a positive impact on European identification because the more citizens interact cross-nationally, the more they should become aware of the values, interests, and experiences they share with other EU citizens. Eventually, this process should lead citizens to see themselves (also) as Europeans and develop feelings of belonging to Europe (Büttner and Mau 2010; Fligstein 2008; Kuhn 2011, 2012, 2015; Recchi 2012; Sigalas 2010). Besides citizens' active involvement with other Europeans, holding dual citizenship as well as possessing the necessary skills and competences to live and work abroad, e.g. foreign language skills, are considered to foster European identification (Kuhn 2011).

Previous empirical analyses largely confirm the expected positive effect of transnational interactions and experience on European identifications. Thus, frequent cross-border trips and contacts with other Europeans haven been shown to increase the probability of identification with Europe (Kuhn 2015; Mau et al. 2008); intra-European migrants and those holding foreign citizenship are significantly more likely to identify with Europe than citizens who stayed in their country of origin (Braun and Müller 2012; Kuhn 2012; Recchi 2008; Rother and Nebe 2009); and individuals with more transnational human capital have been found to more readily identify with Europe (Diez Medrano 2014; Fligstein 2008; Green 2007; Kuhn 2015).

Accordingly, I expect positive effects of transnational practices, transnational background, and transnational human capital on citizens' propensity to identify with Europe as the following hypotheses suggest:

H_7: The more individuals engage in transnational practices involving other Europeans in their daily lives, the more they identify with Europe.

H_8: Individuals with a personal transnational background identify more with Europe than individuals without a transnational background.

H_9: The more transnational human capital individuals possess, the more they identify with Europe.

By tracing systematically how citizens' attitudes and experiences come to influence their propensity to identify with Europe, the explanatory model developed so far contributes to our understanding of the individual-level processes underlying European identification. The next step is to go beyond individual-level influences on European identification and explore how member state characteristics affect citizens' identification with Europe. The following section will extend the individual-level model to the country level and develop a multi-level framework of individual identification with Europe.

3.2.3 Country-Level Determinants of Individual Identification with Europe

On several occasions, the discussion of individual-level determinants of European identification pointed out that the influence of individual characteristics will also depend on the context in which citizens are socialised, absorb information about Europe, and experience the consequences of EU integration in their daily lives. In effect, the empirically observed country-differences in aggregate levels of European identification (see, e.g. results in Fuchs and Schneider 2011; Kaina 2009) appear too great to be explained by differences in individual characteristics alone, underlining the need to add characteristics of the national context in which citizens live to the explanatory framework of European identification. Against this background, the present section explores the impact of country characteristics on citizens' identification with Europe. The aim is to illustrate how political, economic, and social conditions within EU member states influence citizens' propensity to identify with Europe in addition to individual attitudes and experiences. Three sets of country-level characteristics are added to the explanatory model of European identification to capture the political, economic, and social conditions in which citizens form orientations towards Europe. These are, first, *party messages related to the European and national community*, i.e. the degree to which national political parties either emphasise communalities among Europeans and shared European values and traditions, or point to the distinctiveness of the national community and invoke a strong national identity. Second, member states' *economic position and degree of integration in the EU and global markets,* as reflected in *member states' membership in the Eurozone, net contributions to the EU budget,* and *share in international trade*. Third, member state societies' *ethnocultural composition* serves as a proxy for the density of transnational relations and personal contacts between foreign nationals and the native population.

The choice of the three sets of country characteristics as additional determinants of individual identification with Europe is motivated as follows: Messages by national political parties, countries' macroeconomic strength, and societies' ethnocultural characteristics are country-level attributes to which citizens are exposed in their daily lives, without much effort or initiative by citizens. At the same time, these country characteristics provide citizens with information and experiences likely to affect their attitudes towards Europe and European identification: because they convey a certain picture of Europe, make the European community more or less salient in the national political debate, or offer opportunities for citizens to interact with other Europeans. In other words, these characteristics regulate the nature and amount of Europe-related information citizens receive and shape the way citizens experience EU integration in their everyday lives.

3.2.3.1 Party Messages Related to the European and National Community

The first country-level characteristic expected to influence European identification are *party messages related to the European and national community*. Party messages are associated with an information-based process of European identification as these messages provide citizens with arguments about Europe and the European community and/or the implications of European integration for the national community.

Analyses of party systems in the member states find national party competition over European integration to be structured along two dimensions: first, an *economic* dimension arising from the opposition between market liberalism and market regulation; second, a *political-cultural* dimension arising from the opposition between national sovereignty and supranational governance on the one hand and between libertarian-universalistic and traditionalist-communitarian values on the other (Bornschier 2011; Hix 1999; Hooghe and Marks 2009; Hooghe et al. 2002, 2004; Kriesi 2007, 2010; Kriesi et al. 2006). At its core, this second dimension revolves around conflicts over the role of community in an increasingly integrated European Union, which has established a new supranational political community with extensive decision-making competences while reducing the autonomy of the national community (Bornschier 2011).

Research on party competition over European integration has explored both parties' *position* on European integration (e.g. Arnold et al. 2012; Helbling and Tresch 2011; Marks et al. 2002, 2006, 2007; Marks and Wilson 2000; Ray 1999, 2007; Rohrschneider and Whitefield 2010; Whitefield et al. 2007) and the *salience* parties attach to EU integration (e.g. Netjes and Binnema 2007; Pennings 2006; Spoon 2012; Steenbergen and Scott 2004). Furthermore, there is evidence that party positions on EU integration and the salience of EU integration in national party systems affect public opinion towards European integration (e.g. Carrubba 2001; de Vries and Arnold 2011; de Vries and Edwards 2009; Franklin et al. 1994; Gabel and Scheve 2007b; Hellström 2008; Hooghe and Marks 2004, 2005; Netjes and Edwards 2005; Ray 2003; Steenbergen et al. 2007); likewise, previous analyses indicate that party positions mediate the relation between national identity and EU support (e.g. de Vries and Edwards 2009; Gabel and Scheve 2007a, b; Hooghe and Marks 2005; Maier et al. 2012; Ray 2003; Steenbergen et al. 2007).

I build on these analyses by including party messages as a country-level determinant in the explanatory model of European identification. In contrast to previous analyses, however, I do not focus on the effects of parties' overall position on EU integration or the overall salience of EU integration in national political conflict, but the *specific salience of issues related to the European and national community* in the national party discourse. The assumption is that in order to affect identification with Europe, it is not enough for parties to emphasise European integration in general or economic terms, e.g. by voicing their support for or opposition to further political integration or a European economic government, because these general or economic questions are relatively far removed from questions of identity and community. Rather, parties need to address the role of community and identity in an increasingly integrated Europe in a direct way, allowing the public to connect party messages to their own feelings of belonging. Therefore, the present analysis will employ more fine-grained measures of party emphasis on European and national community. These include, on the one hand, references to the *European community*, its members, and the values, interests, and experiences which are shared by Europeans and may thus form the basis for collective identity building at the European level; on the other hand, references to the *national community* which, for most citizens, remains the primary level of identification, and, at the same time, represents the political community most directly affected by the widening and deepening of European integration.

I expect a positive effect on European identification if national political parties invoke the wider community of Europeans and emphasise common European values, interests, and experiences as well as a distinct European way of life. In this way, parties contribute to citizens' awareness of what they have in common with other Europeans, even in the absence of personal experiences with citizens from other member states. Vice versa, I expect negative effects of party messages on European identification if national political elites predominantly invoke the national community and national identity and emphasise the distinctiveness of the national community based on unique national values, interests, traditions, and experiences. As more emphasis is put on the national community, citizens will likely become more aware of the potential threats the EU poses to the integrity of the national community and the national way of life, making them more likely to perceive European identity as conflicting with their national identity. These considerations lead to two hypotheses regarding the effect of party messages on European and national community and identity on individuals' propensity to identify with Europe:

H_{10}: The more political parties in a country address issues of European community and identity in the national political debate, the more individuals from this country identify with Europe.

H_{11}: The more political parties in a country address issues of national community and identity in the national political debate, the less individuals from this country identify with Europe.

While differences in the national party discourse are expected to explain some of the variation in individual European identification across EU member states, party messages are unlikely to affect all citizens within a member state in the same way. For example, citizens who are politically more interested and pay greater attention to (European) politics have greater chances to receive party messages that invoke issues of community and collective identity. That is, individuals' degree of political awareness mediates the effect of party messages on European identification. Likewise, we may expect that individuals' predispositions with regard to the national community mediate the effect of party messages. Individuals who feel strongly attached to the nation may respond differently to party messages invoking the national community than individuals with a weaker sense of national identity. Section 3.2.4 discusses such interaction effects between party messages and individual attributes and predispositions in detail.

3.2.3.2 Economic Position and Degree of Integration in the EU and Global Markets

The second set of country-level determinants included in the model of European identification refers to member countries' *economic position and degree of integration in the European and global markets*, as measured by member states' *membership in the Eurozone, net contributions to the EU budget,* and *share in international trade*. These measures represent proxies for how citizens experience the economic dimension of European integration and its consequences for the national economy in their everyday lives and, therefore, are associated with an experience-based process of identification with Europe.

In effect, European integration has long been a predominantly economic project, focused on completing the Single European Market, based on the free movement of goods, capital, services, and labour, a Europe-wide competition policy, and the euro as the common currency. Accordingly, public debates over European integration in the member countries—as assessed by media coverage of EU integration and the salience of European issues in national political competition—have largely centred on economic aspects of EU integration (de Vreese 2003; Diez Medrano 2003; Diez Medrano and Gray 2010; Koopmans and Erbe 2004; Koopmans et al. 2010; Koopmans and Pfetsch 2006; Peter et al. 2003). Qualitative analyses of how citizens conceive of European integration indicate that the dominance of economic aspects in the political debate is mirrored at the individual level. While people offer a variety of arguments to clarify their attitudes towards the EU and European integration, they tend to converge on themes related to the common market and economic integration (Diez Medrano 2003).

Given the dominance of economic aspects in both public debate and representations of European integration among EU citizens, it seems plausible to assume that individuals' identification with Europe will be influenced by how they experience the economic dimension of EU integration.

Membership in the Eurozone is expected to have a positive effect on citizens' identification with Europe. Using the euro as the common currency is a daily reminder for citizens that they are members of the European community; the euro also lets citizens directly experience tangible benefits of economic integration at the EU level, for example by reducing the need to exchange money abroad and facilitating cross-border shopping.

Regarding the impact of EU budget contributions, I hypothesise that citizens from net recipient countries of EU funding will identify more with Europe than citizens from net contributor countries to the EU budget. Citizens from net recipient countries are expected to have a more positive image of Europe because they are more likely to experience the benefits of EU funding for their home country, e.g. in form of EU-funded infrastructural projects. This should result in a higher propensity to identify as European. Vice versa, citizens from net contributor countries should have a more negative image of Europe because of the financial cost their country incurs by contributing more to the EU budget than what it gets back in EU funding. As a result, we should expect citizens from net contributing member states to identify less with Europe.

Likewise, citizens from countries with a more open economy (in terms of shares of exports and imports in GDP) are expected to identify more with Europe than citizens from economically less integrated countries because their country benefits disproportionally from the common market. The perception of benefits should lead to positive outlooks on EU integration, and, in turn, to a higher propensity to identify with Europe. What is more, greater trade openness also provides more opportunities for citizens to interact personally with other Europeans and non-nationals, e.g. because a higher share of the population is employed in the exporting industry and has professional contacts abroad, which are expected to foster identification with Europe.

Empirically, analyses in the field of 'horizontal Europeanisation' confirm a positive effect of a country's degree of economic integration on the prevalence of transnationalist activities in its population (Kuhn 2015; Mau and Mewes 2012). In contrast, few analyses so far have directly assessed the effect of economic factors on European identification among EU citizens. Among these, Isernia's et al. study of aggregate levels of European identification finds higher levels of identification in net recipient countries of EU funding than in net contributor countries. Likewise, levels of identification with Europe are shown to be higher in member states with higher shares of intra-EU trade (Isernia et al. 2012; Kuhn 2015). Based on the above considerations and the empirical record so far, the following hypotheses summarise the expected effects of different economic indicators on individuals' identification with Europe:

H_{12}: Individuals from Eurozone member states identify more with Europe than individuals from member states outside the Eurozone.

H_{13}: Individuals from net contributor countries of EU funds identify less with Europe than individuals from net recipient countries of EU funds.

H_{14}: The more economically integrated a country in the European and global markets, the more individuals from this country identify with Europe.

As in the case of party messages, we should expect the effect of economic indicators on European identification to vary by individual dispositions. Section 3.2.4 will discuss such interaction effects between measures of economic integration and individual political interest on the one hand and between economic measures and national identification on the other.

3.2.3.3 Ethnocultural Composition of Member State Societies

The *ethnocultural composition of member state societies* represents a third set of country-level determinants in the model of individual identification with Europe. Member states' *ethnocultural composition* refers to member states' cultural heterogeneity and diversity of the national population in terms of the *share of EU nationals* and the *total share of foreigners* living in a country. Both measures represent proxies for citizens' opportunities to interact with non-nationals and thus make the kind of experiences that influence identification with Europe; accordingly, they are associated with an experience-based process of identification with Europe.

As regards the *share of EU citizens in the national population*, I assume that with more citizens from other EU member states living in a country, national citizens have more chances to interact personally with other Europeans. These personal contacts and interactions are expected to make citizens more aware of the commonalities they share with citizens from other EU member states and create a sense of togetherness as Europeans which, ultimately, should result in a higher propensity to identify with Europe (Mau and Mewes 2013). Accordingly, the corresponding hypothesis expects a positive correlation between the share of EU nationals in a country and citizens' propensity to identify with Europe.

H_{15}: The higher the share of EU nationals in a country, the more individuals from this country identify with Europe.

Regarding the impact of the *overall share of immigrants in a country* on citizens' propensity to identify with Europe, alternative expectations seem plausible. In line with the above argumentation, we may expect that higher overall numbers of non-nationals living in a country, regardless of their country of origin, give citizens more opportunities to interact with non-nationals and perceive commonalities between themselves and foreigners. These experiences should make citizens generally more cosmopolitan in their outlooks and thus more inclined to identify with supranational communities.

On the other hand, we may expect negative effects of higher shares of immigrants on citizens' identification with Europe. In this view, higher numbers of immigrants in a country increase the chances that national citizens perceive negative effects of more open borders. Higher shares of immigrants may thus lead to greater fears of a loss of national traditions and identity as well as fears of economic disadvantages and increased competition on the national labour market. Given the important role of European integration for the opening of national borders and markets, citizens are likely to project such fears on the European Union and, as a result, identify less with Europe.

Two alternative hypotheses capture the diverging theoretical considerations regarding the effect of overall immigrant shares on European identifications among citizen in the member states:

H_{16a}: The higher the overall share of immigrants in a country, the more individuals from this country identify with Europe.
H_{16b}: The higher the overall share of immigrants in a country, the less individuals from this country identify with Europe.

As in the case of other country-level predictors, the effect of sociocultural indicators on individual identification with Europe is likely to vary across individuals; in particular, we should expect a mediating effect of citizens' attachment to the nation on the relation between immigrant shares and individual identification with Europe. Section 3.2.4 will discuss such interaction effects between individual attributes and predispositions and share of (EU) immigrants in the national population on citizens' identification with Europe.

3.2.4 *Interaction Effects Between Individual- and Country-Level Determinants of Individual Identification with Europe*

The presentation of the explanatory model of individual identification with Europe thus far has concentrated on direct effects of individual- and country-level characteristics on European identification. Yet there is reason to assume that country characteristics do not affect all citizens within a member state in the same way. Individual predispositions and characteristics are likely to mediate the effect of country-level determinants on individual identification with Europe.[2] Therefore,

[2]A second source of heterogeneity in the formation of European identification may spring from developments at the European level. That is, while singular events and changes in the process of European integration over time a priori affect all EU member states, citizens within member states may still perceive and experience these changes and events in different ways, depending on differences in member states' political, economic, or social characteristics. Section 3.3 will discuss this second source of variation in European identification by exploring variation in the determinants of European identification by member state, first, in response to the EU's eastward enlargement 2004/2007, and, second, the wake of the economic and financial crisis starting in 2008.

the following section discusses *interaction effects between individual- and country-level determinants of European identification* among EU citizens. The focus lies on mediating effects of, first, *political interest* and, second, *national identification* on the effects of country-level determinants on European identification. In technical terms, I include interaction terms between country-level predictors and political interest and between country-level predictors and national identification in the explanatory model of individual identification with Europe.

Political interest is included as a mediator variable of the effect of country characteristics on individual European identification to account for differences in the attention people pay to party messages and the national economic environment. In this regard, the model of European identification follows longstanding research traditions in public opinion studies that point to political awareness and sophistication as the main causes of differences in opinion formation and attitude structures among individuals (Bartle 2000; Converse 1964; Delli Carpini and Keeter 1996; Kinder 2006; Luskin 1987, 1990; Sniderman et al. 1991; Zaller 1990, 1992). Political interest not only influences individuals' knowledge and awareness of political affairs (Delli Carpini and Keeter 1996; Kriesi 2005; Luskin 1990), but also mediates the impact of elite messages (Zaller 1992), party campaigns (Kriesi 2005, 2012), and the media (Chong and Druckman 2007; Krosnick and Brannon 1993; McGuire 1985; Valentino and Nardis 2013) on individual attitudes and vote choice. These findings also hold for the EU context: interest in politics affects individuals' knowledge of European affairs (Maier and Bathelt 2013; Westle and Johann 2010), and mediates the effect of party messages (Gabel and Scheve 2007b; Slothuus and de Vreese 2010) and the mass media (de Vreese 2007; de Vreese and Boomgaarden 2006b, c; Scharkow and Vogelgesang 2010) on attitudes towards the EU and European integration.

Besides political interest, the explanatory model of European identification includes *national identification* as a second variable mediating the effect of country characteristics on individual European identification. Individual national identification is interacted with member state characteristics in order to account for differences in peoples' perception and evaluation of party messages, their country's contribution to the EU budget as well as the share of immigrants living in their country that are due to differences in how strongly they identify with the national community. As in the case of political interest, the choice of national identification as a moderator variable is motivated by the theoretical and empirical insights of the (EU) public opinion literature.

Research on belief systems and processes of opinion formation points to the role of affect for political reasoning, arguing that people often rely on their likes and dislikes of social groups when forming political opinions (Converse 1964; Kinder 2003, 2006; Sniderman et al. 1991). For Donald Kinder, public opinion is thus shaped 'in powerful ways by the feelings citizens harbor toward the social groups they see as the principle beneficiaries (or victims) of the policy' (Kinder 2003, p.18). Empirically, this research shows that group-centrism and ethno-centrist orientations shape attitudes towards, e.g. foreign and security policy (Kam and

Kinder 2007; Kinder 2003), the welfare state (Kinder and Kam 2010), and immigration (Citrin et al. 1990; Kinder 2003).

The literature on EU public opinion has incorporated these ideas, pointing to the role of national identity as a short cut or 'cue' for citizens when forming attitudes towards the EU and European integration. Hooghe and Marks expect citizens to rely on feelings of identity in situations where they lack the knowledge and resources to determine their (economic) interests in relation to EU issues, but have a clear idea of the implications for the national community (cf. Hooghe and Marks 2009, pp. 10, 13). Analyses of EU support have tested these propositions using the concept of 'exclusive national identity', which differentiates between citizens who identify exclusively with the nation and citizens who hold multiple identities. Exclusive national identifications have been shown to mediate the effect of elite division over EU integration (Hooghe and Marks 2005); the influence of party messages, in particular, the effects of campaigns by extreme right-wing parties (de Vries and Edwards 2009); and the impact of net transfer payments from the EU (Garry and Tilley 2009).The following sections discuss in detail how political interest and national identification interact with country-level characteristics to influence European identification among EU citizens.

3.2.4.1 Cross-Level Interactions with Political Interest

Country-level characteristics such as the discourse of political elites or the dependence of the national economy on European and global markets can only affect citizens' identification with Europe to the extent that the latter actually pay attention to party messages and have some understanding of the information they are exposed to. Given the well-known differences in citizens' attention to politics (van Deth 1991; van Deth and Elff 2004), we should expect the effect of macrosocial characteristics to vary across individuals depending on their level of political interest. To account for this individual-level variation in political interest and exposure to Europe-related messages and information, the explanatory model of European identification includes interaction terms between individuals' interest in politics and country-level determinants.

To recall, Sect. 3.2.3 discussed three sets of country-level characteristics likely to affect citizens' identification with Europe, namely party messages on issues of national and European community, member states' economic position and degree of integration in European and world markets, and the ethnocultural make-up of member state societies. I assume that individual political interest will first and foremost mediate the effect of party messages, of member states' status as net contributors to the EU budget, and of the degree of integration in European and global markets. Party messages and macroeconomic indicators like trade openness will only be effective in shaping citizens' orientations toward Europe if citizens actually perceive these messages and are aware of the economic dimension of European integration and its effects for the national economy. This requires a certain level of attention to current affairs on the part of the citizens, as they are unlikely to be personally approached by political elites or consult data on the situation of the national economy independently.

In the case of the euro as the common currency as well as immigration rates, in contrast, the causal mechanism is expected to work via personal experiences and direct contacts. Citizens use the euro on a daily basis; if more EU immigrants live in a country, citizens have greater chances to interact with non-nationals and make the kind of experience expected to shape attitudes towards Europe and European identification. To the extent that these experiences are considered part of citizens' everyday lives, they occur independently of citizens' engagement with politics and should not be mediated by individuals' level of political interest.

Based on these considerations, we can hypothesise that the more politically interested individuals are, the more party messages on national and European community and identity they will receive, and the more these messages will affect their identification with Europe. In technical terms, there should be a positive interaction effect of political interest and party messages on European identification as proposed by the following hypothesis:

H_{17}: The more interested individuals are in politics, the stronger the relationship between party messages and individual identification with Europe.

A priori, the mediating effect of political interest should occur independently of the contents of party messages. We can further specify the direction of the effect by taking into account whether national political elites emphasise the European community and issues related to a common European identity or the national community and issues related to national identity. On the one hand, we can assume that political interest reinforces the previously expected positive influence of party messages emphasising the European community and a common European way of life on identification with Europe (cf. H_{10}). Hence, we should observe a positive interaction effect of political interest and party messages on European community and identity. Vice versa, the previously expected negative effect of party messages emphasising national identity on European identification (cf. H_{11}) should be reinforced among politically more interested individuals. That is, we should observe a negative interaction effect of political interest and party messages on national community and identity. The following two hypotheses summarise these expectations:

H_{17a}: The more interested individuals are in politics, the stronger the positive relationship between party messages on issues of European community and individual identification with Europe.

H_{17b}: The more interested individuals are in politics, the stronger the negative relationship between party messages on issues of national community and identity and individual identification with Europe.

In a similar vein, we can expect interaction effects between political interest and *measures of economic integration* on individual identification with Europe. The politically more interested should also have a better understanding of the economic dimension of European integration and its effects for the national economy than their less interested peers. Therefore, they should be more likely to take into account economic considerations when forming an opinion about Europe and European identification. As a result, a country's net contributions to the EU budget and its degree of integration in European and global markets should have a greater influence on identification with Europe among citizens with greater interest in political affairs.

H_{18}: The more interested individuals are in politics, the stronger the effect of member states' status as a net contributor country of EU funds on individual identification with Europe.

H_{19}: The more interested individuals are in politics, the stronger the effect of member states' degree of integration in the European and global markets on individual identification with Europe.

3.2.4.2 Cross-Level Interactions with National Identification

The second variable expected to mediate the effect of country-level characteristics on individual European identification is citizens' *identification with the national community*. National attachments are interacted with party messages related to the European and national community, member states' contribution to the EU budget, and the share of immigrants in the national population. In this way, the model accounts for differences in how citizens perceive and evaluate these country characteristics depending on the strength of their national attachments. As in the case of political interest, the choice of national identification as an intervening variable builds on insights from research on public opinion formation as well as the EU public opinion literature.

The expectation is that citizens' attachments to the national group will colour their assessment of the political, social, and economic consequences of European integration for the national community. Citizens who identify strongly with the nation are likely to be more concerned with the integrity and the traditions of the national community, and, therefore, react differently to the consequences of European integration for their country than citizens who feel only weakly attached to the national level. For example, people who feel strongly attached to the nation have been shown to hold more negative views on immigration (Curtis 2014) and thus will likely react more negatively to higher shares of immigrants in the national population than their less attached peers.

I expect that national attachments mediate in particular the effect of member state characteristics that have direct social and financial implications for the national community. As is argued in the following, this is foremost the case for party messages emphasising the national and European community and identity, national contributions to the EU budget, and increased ethnocultural diversity in the national society.

Party messages related to questions of national and European community and identity directly invoke questions of community and belonging at the national and

European level. I expect that citizens with strong national identifications respond more strongly to these messages because they are more sensitive to threats to the national community and its values and traditions than citizens who identify only weakly with the nation. As a result, we should see national identification mediate the effect of identity-related party messages on individual identification with Europe. In technical terms, there should be a positive interaction effect of national identification and party messages, as the following hypothesis states:

H_{20}: The more individuals identify with the nation, the stronger the relationship between party messages and individual identification with Europe.

More specifically, we may expect that people who feel strongly attached to the nation are particularly perceptible to party messages emphasising the national community. In this case, the previously expected negative effect of party messages focussing on national community and identity (cf. H_{11}) should be reinforced among citizens with strong national identifications. Hence, we should find a negative interaction effect of national identification and party messages on national community and identity. The following hypothesis reflects this expectation:

H_{20a}: The more individuals identify with the nation, the stronger the negative relationship between party messages on issues of national community and individual identification with Europe.

Similar effects seem plausible for the *interplay between national identification and national contributions to the EU budget*. The assumption is that individuals who identify strongly with the nation evaluate their country's status as a net recipient or net contributor of EU funding differently than individuals who identify less with the national level. Member states' contributions to the EU budget are a clear indicator of the economic consequences of EU integration and, in particular, the potential costs of EU integration for the nation state. Therefore, we should expect strong national attachments to reinforce the expected negative effects of member states' status as net contributors to the EU budget on citizens' identification with Europe. Thus, there should be a negative interaction effect of national identification and member states' status as a net contributor to the EU budget as the following hypothesis proposes:

H_{21}: The more individuals identify with the nation, the stronger the negative relationship between member states' status as a net contributor country to EU funding and individual identification with Europe.

Finally, the model includes *interaction effects between national identification and member states' ethnocultural composition*. The expectation is that people who identify strongly with the nation are more likely to perceive the ethnocultural diversity that comes with open borders as a threat to the national community and, as a result, evaluate European integration more critically and identify less with Europe. Hence, I expect individual national identification to intensify potential negative effects of international social integration and immigration on European identification as the following hypothesis states:

H_{22}: The more individuals identify with the nation, the greater the negative effect of member states' overall share of immigrants on their propensity to identify with Europe.

The costs and benefits to the national community are les apparent in case of the other country-level determinants included in the model of European identification. For example, the immediate financial or social costs and benefits of more openness to trade or membership in the Eurozone are hard to pinpoint.[3] Therefore, citizens' evaluation of these two country characteristics should be less influenced by their attachment to the national community and the model does not include interaction effects for these characteristics.

3.3 The Impact of EU Enlargement to Central and Eastern Europe 2004/2007 and the Onset of the Financial and Economic Crisis 2008 on Individual Identification with Europe

The explanatory model developed so far has presented a general model of European identification that aims at explaining citizens' identification with Europe across EU member states and over different periods in the EU integration process. The remainder of this chapter takes the general model as a starting point for discussing the implications of two turning points in the integration process for the development of European identification. The aim is to explore whether and how the bases of citizens' identification with Europe change at key moments in the integration process. These turning points are, first, the *accession of Central and Eastern European member states in 2004/2007*, and, second, the *onset of the financial and economic crisis in 2008*. These events are considered turning points in the integration process in that they have caused extensive debates among political elites and in the mass media, resulting in shifts in elite positions on EU integration as well as changes at the level of public opinion.

The accession of Central and Eastern European member states and the financial and economic crisis, followed by sovereign debt crises in a number of EU member states, have affected both the EU and individual member states in significant ways. To give a few examples: In financial terms, eastward enlargement provoked a re-allocation of EU structural and cohesion funds from old to new member states after 2004, whereas the crisis led to the introduction of extensive credit lines for over-indebted Eurozone countries after 2008. Politically, the accession of ten new member states in 2004 required a change in voting weights in the Council and led to

[3]The financial and economic interdependencies between Eurozone countries became clearer after the onset of the crisis. These changes and their implications for the effects or Eurozone membership on European identification are discussed in Sect. 3.3.3.

new majorities within the EU institutions, while, in the wake of the crisis, we observed a shift in decision-making back to member state governments. Finally, both the opening of borders to the East and the crisis stimulated labour migration within the EU, from new to old member states after the 2004/2007 enlargement rounds, and, since 2008, from southern European member states in economic crisis to economically thriving countries in north-western Europe.

Given the impact of enlargement and the crisis on the EU and its member states and the debate these events have raised, we may expect consequences for citizens' feelings of belonging to Europe, too. This is even more so, as enlargement and the crisis have brought about changes with a particular bearing on collective identifications and feelings of belonging together as Europeans. For example, the re-allocation of financial funds to Eastern Europe and southern European member states following enlargement and the crisis invoke principles of solidarity and loyalty that are closely linked to feelings of community and collective identification. Likewise, labour migration leads to social changes in member state societies—both in the host and the sending countries—which have implications for definitions of (national) community and thus may affect collective identifications. Finally, the debates over enlargement and the crisis have been marked by a strong presence of populist right-wing parties that promote the primacy of national interests and the national community, thus also raising questions of solidarity and identity (Bornschier 2011).

The present work argues that the EU's enlargement in 2004/2007 as well as the economic and financial crisis starting in late 2008 have led to an increase in heterogeneity among EU member states and made political, economic, and social differences between EU member states more visible to the general public. Concurrently, we observe an increase in the salience of EU affairs in domestic politics and an increased politicisation and controversy over questions of EU integration (Hutter and Grande 2014; Hutter and Kerscher 2014; Rauh and Zürn 2014). The heightened visibility of member state differences and greater salience of EU affairs in national debates implies that the environment in which citizens receive Europe-related information and make Europe-related experiences have changed with enlargement and the crisis. As the salience of EU affairs increases, citizens have better and easier access to information about the EU and about the implications of EU integration for their home country; at the same time, trends like the influx of workers and students from Eastern Europe and southern member states give citizens a direct experience of the consequences of European integration. All the while, the changes brought about by enlargement and the crisis vary between EU member states. For example, enlargement required adjustments foremost from the newly accessing member states—the adoption of the *acquis communautaire*—while the economic and social consequences of the crisis have been by far more disruptive in countries like Greece or Spain than Germany or Poland. Depending on their country of origin, citizens thus differ in their experience of enlargement and the crisis.

To begin with, the developments in EU integration related to enlargement and the crisis suggest changes in the *level* of citizens' identification with Europe. On the one hand, we may expect citizens' attachment to Europe to increase as measures of

European wide solidarity become more visible. On the other hand, citizens may identify less with Europe if the mutual obligations and interdependencies that come with increased integration at the European level become more perceptible in the domestic context.

What is more, we may also expect changes in the *determinants* of European identification. By raising questions about the future borders of Europe and the EU's capacity to integrate new member states (in the case of enlargement) and testing member states' financial solidarity and willingness to cooperate in severe economic crisis (in the case of the financial and economic crisis), enlargement and the crisis have led to an increased politicisation of European integration (Hutter and Grande 2014; Hutter and Kerscher 2014; Rauh and Zürn 2014; Risse 2015). The economic and financial crisis in particular has brought questions of European integration into national political debates as recent election campaigns and analyses of parliamentary debates in EU member states show (Auel and Höing 2014; Miklin 2014; Puntscher Riekmann and Wydra 2013; Rauh and Zürn 2014; Wendler 2014).

Compared to pre-enlargement and pre-crisis periods, the EU has played a more prominent role in public debate in the member states. This rise in the salience of EU affairs in national debates implies that the environment in which citizens receive Europe-related information and make Europe-related experiences has changed. As a result of these changes in citizens' access to Europe-related information and in the way they experience Europe in their everyday lives, the importance of different determinants for citizens' identification with Europe may also have changed in the course of enlargement and the crisis. In particular, we may expect changes in the effects of *political interest* and *national identification* on European identification due to the greater salience of European affairs in national political debates. Among the country-level predictors, the influence of *macroeconomic indicators* on citizens' propensity to identify with Europe can be expected to have changed as a result of the financial and economic crisis compared to pre-crisis periods.

The following section will briefly outline the consequences of enlargement and the crisis for the EU and its member states and show how both events have increased differences between EU member states and the salience of EU affairs in domestic debates (Sect. 3.3.1). The remainder of the chapter will draw on this discussion to develop hypotheses regarding, first, changes in the effect of macroeconomic indicators on European identification (Sect. 3.3.2) and, second, variation in the effects of political interest and national identification on citizens' propensity to identify with Europe in response to enlargement and the crisis (Sect. 3.3.3).

3.3.1 Consequences of Eastward Enlargement 2004/2007 and the Onset of the Financial and Economic Crisis 2008 for the EU and the Member States

Preparations for *EU enlargement to Central and Eastern Europe* started as early as 1993 when the European Council agreed that 'the associated countries in Central and Eastern Europe that so desire shall become members of the European Union' (European Council 1993, p. 13) and concluded with the accession of Cyprus, the Czech Republic, Estonia, Hungary, Latvia, Lithuania, Malta, Poland, Slovakia, and Slovenia in May 2004 and Bulgaria and Romania in January 2007 (for a detailed account of the 2004/2007 enlargement round, see Nugent 2004a; O'Brennan 2006, esp. Chaps. 2–4).

With 10+2 new member states joining at once, the EU's enlargement to Central and Eastern Europe in 2004/2007 has been the single biggest enlargement round in the history of the EU.[4] It nearly doubled the number of EU member states and increased the EU's population and its territory by about one-third of its previous size. Eastward enlargement thereby led to a noticeable increase in political, economic, and social heterogeneity among member states. Politically, the majority of the 12 new member states had been part of the Eastern bloc until 1989/1990 and consequently had experienced a very different historical trajectory than the 'old' EU15 member states, both before and after the fall of the Iron Curtain.

Economically, enlargement further increased existing disparities within the EU. GDP per capita levels were substantially lower in the new member states than in the EU15, with the average per capita income in the CEE countries reaching no more than 50% of the EU15 average.[5] Likewise, labour market conditions in CEE differed widely from those in the EU15, with markedly lower labour productivity, high structural unemployment and overall higher unemployment, particularly among the young and the long-term unemployed (European Commission 2006).[6] Lower income levels in the CEE member states were accompanied by lower expenditure for social protection (in share of GDP), although the share of population at risk of poverty (measured against the national income distribution) was rather similar in old and new member states (European Commission 2006).[7]

To accommodate the new member states and help them catch up economically, the EU introduced both institutional and policy reforms. At the institutional level, reforms included a re-weighting of votes and reorganisation of decision rules in the Council, a higher number of MEPs and a reallocation of seats between member

[4]Prior to Eastern enlargement, no more than three countries had joined the EU at the same time.

[5]The ten new member states joining the EU in 2004 added only about 5% to the EU's GDP (at current prices). At the time of accession, only Cyprus and Slovenia reached comparable or higher per capita income levels than the least affluent EU15 member states Greece and Portugal. Per capita income in the new member states ranged from about 43% of the EU15 average in Latvia to about 78% in Cyprus. For a detailed account of GDP/capita and comparison of old and new member states, see European Commission (2006).

[6]In 2004, the average labour productivity in the new member states was less than two thirds of the EU15 level. Employment rates stood at 56% in the new member states versus 65% in the EU15, while total unemployment was 13% in CEE and 8% in the EU15. For a detailed account of labour productivity and employment and unemployment rates in old and new member states, see European Commission (2006).

[7]Shares of population at risk of poverty ranged from less than 10% in the Czech Republic, Luxemburg, and Slovenia to more than 20% in Greece, Ireland, and Portugal (European Commission 2006).

states in the Parliament, as well as changes in the size and composition of the Commission (see Nugent 2004b; O'Brennan 2006; Phinnemore 2004 for more information on the unfolding of the 2004/2007 enlargement rounds and the institutional changes at the EU level).

At the policy level, the weaker macroeconomic performance in terms of competiveness, per capita income, and employment led to a reallocation of EU structural and cohesion funds to CEE countries after 2004. With the exception of Cyprus, all CEE member states have been net receivers of EU transfers since 2004/2007. The new member states in Eastern Europe have received a majority of EU structural funds since the EU's budget reform in 2007. In contrast, the share allocated to the 'old' EU15 member states has decreased by about one quarter compared to pre-enlargement levels (European Commission 2009b; Lequesne 2012).[8]

The significance of the 2004/2007 enlargement round resonated in heightened media attention during the accession period. Confirming earlier reports of an increase in EU coverage at key moments of EU integration such as EU summits or treaty negotiations (de Vreese 2001, 2003; de Vreese and Boomgaarden 2006a; Peter and de Vreese 2004), the visibility of the EU in the media intensified during the enlargement period 2004 (Boomgaarden et al. 2010; van Noije 2010; Vliegenthart et al. 2008). Researchers found the press to take a predominantly national perspective and focus on the economic consequences of enlargement, in particular labour migration and the effects of enlargement on national labour markets (Dursun-Ozkanca 2011; Inthorn 2006; Light and Young 2009; van Noije 2010). These findings indicate that the salience of EU affairs indeed increased as a result of enlargement; what is more, the consequences of enlargement for national economies and national labour markets featured prominently in the debate.

The subsequent sections discuss the implications of enlargement and the potential consequences of heightened media attention and new concerns for national economies for the determinants of citizens' identification with Europe. Before that, I briefly recapitulate the financial and economic crisis and its consequences for the EU and its member states.

To summarise broadly, the *financial and economic crisis* set off in 2007 with the collapse of the US subprime mortgage market, which triggered banking crises in both the US and Europe and cumulated in the bankruptcy of the US investment bank Lehman Brothers in September 2008. The financial crisis of 2007/2008 subsequently triggered a global economic crisis, resulting in the 'great recession' of 2009. All EU member states except Poland saw a decline in GDP in 2009; by the following year, the economy had recovered in some member states while others continued to register negative growth rates (European Commission 2011a). In 2010, the economic crisis evolved into sovereign debt crises in a number of EU member states, most notably Greece, Ireland, Italy, Portugal, and Spain. In these

[8]See European Commission (2009b) for a detailed account of types and volume of EU transfers allocated to old and new member states after enlargement.

countries, the economic, social, and political consequences of the crisis have been far more disruptive than in member states like Germany, which emerged quickly from the 2008/2009 recession.

The EU's initial response to the crisis included an agreement to inject up to 2 trillion euros in the European banking sector to end the banking crisis in the short term (October 2008) together with a fiscal stimulus package (December 2008). To contain the sovereign debt crises developing in Southern Europe, member states further agreed on financial support for Greece, Ireland, Portugal, Spain, and other Eurozone countries, most importantly bilateral loans to Greece (May 2010) in exchange for economic austerity policies monitored by the so-called 'troika' of IMF, European Commission, and European Central Bank. Finally, member states agreed on the European Financial Stabilisation Mechanism (EFSM) and the European Financial Stability Facility (EFSF) as temporary rescue mechanisms, followed by the (permanent) European Stability Mechanism (ESM) authorised to lend up to 500 billion euros to Eurozone members in financial difficulties.

In order to refinance their debt on capital markets and/or receive financial assistance from the EU and the IMF, the most highly indebted member states implemented fiscal austerity programmes, agreed to significant reductions of public budget deficits over relatively short time periods, and imposed structural reforms. In most cases, fiscal austerity programmes combined substantial cuts in public expenditure, in particular in social security provisions, pensions, and jobs and wages in the public sector, with a rise in indirect taxes (Armingeon and Baccaro 2012; Theodoropoulou and Watt 2011). Both measures tend to affect disproportionally lower income groups, resulting in an increased risk of poverty and social exclusion. In the context of generally weak economies, the adverse social consequences of cuts in public expenditure were further reinforced by declining incomes and high levels of unemployment, in particular among young people (Bieling 2012; Leschke et al. 2012).

In many of the most affected member states, the economic downturn not only had severe social consequences, but also triggered political and governmental crises. Austerity policies were met with social protests, mass demonstrations, and general strikes, e.g. in Greece and Spain in 2010/2011 and in Portugal in 2012. Analyses of public opinion data show significant declines in trust in national governments and EU institutions in the wake of the crisis (Armingeon and Ceka 2014; Clements et al. 2014; di Mauro 2014; Roth et al. 2013, 2014) as well as a general erosion of citizens' satisfaction with democracy, most notably in the countries hit hardest by the crisis (Armingeon and Guthmann 2014).

At the European level, the EU's reaction to the economic and financial crisis has largely been negotiated and decided by the heads of state and government meeting in the European Council, in smaller configurations, or bilaterally. The crisis has thus led to a reinforcement of the role of national governments in EU integration and, in particular, the European Council, vis-à-vis the Council and other EU institutions (Bickerton et al. 2015; Dinan 2012, 2013a; Hodson and Puetter 2013; Puetter 2012).

Apart from ad-hoc rescue mechanisms, the crisis also led to long-term policy reforms in the field of European fiscal and economic governance. These included the reinforcement of the Stability and Growth Pact and extended fiscal coordination among member states, a reinforcement of the measures of corrective action available to the Commission, minimum requirements for national budgetary frameworks, and a new macroeconomic imbalance procedure.[9]

Similar to enlargement, the economic and financial crisis further led to a rise in the salience of EU integration in the member states (Hutter and Grande 2014; Hutter and Kerscher 2014; Meijers 2013). Media analyses reveal that nationally centred perspectives have dominated the news coverage of the crisis (Gottschalck 2011/2012; Katsourides 2014; Mazzoni and Barbieri 2014).

To summarise, the EU's enlargement to Central and Eastern Europe in 2004/2007 and the onset of the financial and economic crisis in 2008 thus led to three major changes to the environment in which citizens receive Europe-related information and make Europe-related experiences. First, enlargement and the crisis led to an increase in the political, economic, and social heterogeneity among EU member states; second, they initiated extensive institutional and policy reforms at the EU level; third, they triggered a rise in the salience of EU affairs in national debates.

The remainder of this chapter will explore how the consequences of enlargement and the crisis at the EU and national levels affect the sources of citizens' identification with Europe. Since both enlargement and the crisis led to an increase in economic and social differences between EU member states as well as in the salience of EU affairs at the national level, we may initially expect that the two events also lead to similar changes in the determinants of European identification. Accordingly, the discussion starts with the general implications of enlargement and the crisis for the determinants of individual identification with Europe (Sect. 3.3.2). The focus of this section is on changes in the effects of political interest and national identification on individual identification with Europe that should occur equally in response to enlargement and in response to the crisis.

Yet even though we observe similar trends in the consequences of CEE enlargement and the financial and economic crisis, the two events differ in the degree and severity of their effects on member state societies and economies. Compared to enlargement, the crisis had far more disruptive consequences, e.g. in terms of prolonged declines in economic growth, high levels of unemployment, social protests, and governmental crises. Citizens directly witnessed these distortions in their daily lives and their immediate environment. In this way, the crisis also more fundamentally changed the way in which citizens experience the economic dimensions of European integration than the accession of the new CEE member states did. To account for the more disruptive consequences of the crisis compared to

[9]See e.g. Caporaso et al. (2015) and Ioannou et al. (2015) for more detailed summaries of the integrative steps taken in response to the crisis.

enlargement, a second section concentrates on the particular consequences of the economic crisis for sources of European identification (Sect. 3.3.3).

3.3.2 *General Implications of Eastward Enlargement and the Crisis for Individual Identification with Europe*

The EU's enlargement and the economic and financial crisis starting in late 2008 led to an increase in heterogeneity within the Union, making political, economic, and social differences between EU member states more visible to the general public. At the same time, we observe an increase in the salience of EU affairs in domestic politics and greater politicisation and controversy over questions of EU integration (Hutter and Grande 2014; Hutter and Kerscher 2014; Rauh and Zürn 2014). The economic and financial crisis in particular has turned European integration into a salient issue in national election campaigns and parliamentary debates in the member states (Auel and Höing 2014; Miklin 2014; Puntscher Riekmann and Wydra 2013; Rauh and Zürn 2014; Wendler 2014).

This rise in the salience of EU integration at the national level means that the environment in which citizens receive Europe-related information and make Europe-related experiences has changed. As a result, we may expect changes in the importance of different determinants of citizens' identification with Europe, too. In particular, the greater salience of EU integration may affect the importance of *political interest* for European identification, as both the highly politically interested and the less interested have better access to information about Europe. The revived debate over national interests and financial redistribution between member states in connection with enlargement and the crisis, in turn, may affect the relevance of *national identification* for European identification, as citizens reconsider the consequences of European integration for their country and the national community. The following sections discuss these propositions in more detail.

3.3.2.1 Variation in the Effects of Political Interest in Response to Eastward Enlargement and the Crisis

Analyses of national and international news coverage show that both Eastern enlargement and the economic and financial crisis have reverberated in national political debates and the mass media (see, e.g. Boomgaarden et al. 2010; Cross and Ma 2013; Schuck et al. 2011). We observe a rise in the salience of EU integration in the member states in relation to the two events, in particular after the onset of the crisis in 2008 (Hutter and Grande 2014; Hutter and Kerscher 2014; Meijers 2013; Vliegenthart et al. 2008).

The rise in the salience of EU topics in the context of enlargement and the crisis implies that citizens gain better access to Europe-related information during these periods. On the one hand, citizens are likely to receive more information about Europe because, as the mass media devote more time and space to EU integration, they provide a greater amount of information to their audience. On the other hand, more citizens are likely to receive information about Europe because, as media that previously paid little attention to EU integration start covering EU-topics, they provide EU-related information to new audiences. In short, the heightened media attention given to the EU during enlargement and the crisis suggest that more information about Europe is available to citizens during these periods.

The wider availability of Europe-related information also has implications for the importance of political interest as a determinant of European identification. Two contradictory scenarios seem plausible. On the one hand, the greater salience of European affairs at key moments like EU enlargement and the crisis implies that the politically interested have even more chances to inform themselves about Europe in these periods; on the other hand, the less interested, too, are able to access information about Europe relatively easily at such critical moments in the integration process.

In the first case, we should expect the 'knowledge gap' between the politically interested and their less interested peers to *widen* as the salience of EU integration increases during enlargement and the crisis. As a result, political interest should become more important as a determinant of European identification, i.e. the effect of political interest on individual identification with Europe should increase.

In the second case, we should expect the 'knowledge gap' between the politically interested and their less interested peers to *shrink* as the salience of EU integration increases. As a result, political interest should become less influential as a determinant of European identification, i.e. the effect of political interest on individual identification with Europe should decrease.

The (scant) empirical record on changes in the effects of political interest under varying conditions of salience and media coverage is mixed: Zaller finds for the U.S. context that as message intensity grows, attitude change also occurs among respondents at lower levels of political awareness (Zaller 1992, Chap. 8). In contrast, Semetko et al. (2003) find for the European case that under conditions of intense media coverage of EU affairs, for example around EU summits and treaty negotiations, attitude change is more likely among politically more attentive respondents. Finally, de Vreese and Boomgaarden (2006a) find no significant differences in the effect of political sophistication on support for EU enlargement for different levels of news coverage of EU affairs.

From a theoretical point of view, both increases and decreases in the effect of political interest on European identification appear plausible. Given Semetko et al.'s (2003) results regarding effects of EU summits and treaty negotiations, the present analysis proposes that political interest becomes *more* important as a determinant of EU attitudes at key moments of EU integration. That is, the effect of political interest on citizens' identification with Europe should increase during the enlargement period and after the onset of the financial and economic crisis compared to more low-key periods in the integration process. The following hypothesis captures this expectation:

H_{23}: The effect of political interest on individual identification with Europe increases with the accession of the new member states from Central and Eastern Europe in 2004/2007 and the onset of the financial and economic crisis in 2008.

3.3.2.2 Variation in the Effects of National Identification in Response to Eastward Enlargement and the Crisis

The second determinant expected to have stronger effects during the enlargement and crisis periods compared to 'normal' times of EU integration is *national identification*. Enlargement and the crisis increased political, economic, and social differences between EU member states, reviving conflicts over member states' national interests and the overall objectives of European integration. The *accession of new member states from Central and Eastern Europe in 2004/2007* was a first instance that brought to the fore diverging national interests and seemingly jeopardized the integrity of the national community. Commentaries and analyses of enlargement centred primarily on the economic implications of the accession of the new member states. In many (old) member states, the enlargement process triggered debates over issues of immigration, social security benefits for EU migrants, and risks of social dumping and relocation of production lines to CEE countries (see the findings on news coverage of eastward enlargement by e.g. Dursun-Ozkanca 2011; Inthorn 2006; Light and Young 2009; van Noije 2010).

Even if these debates focussed on economic aspects of enlargement, they likely raised concerns for national identity and the well-being of the national community, too. Bornschier (2011), for example, shows that fears of a loss of national identity are associated with economic fears of EU integration, in particular fears of a demise of the national welfare state. At the party level, debates over enlargement were accompanied by the emergence of populist right-wing parties promoting traditionalist-communitarian values and the primacy of the national community while rejecting EU integration and the EU's interference in national politics (Bornschier 2011). Analyses of political conflict show that cultural issues—immigration, cultural diversity, the defence of national traditions and sovereignty, national identity and a national way of life—generally have become more salient in recent years (Bornschier 2010; Hutter and Grande 2014; Kriesi et al. 2006; Stoll 2010).

Like the accession of new member states from CEE, the *financial and economic crisis* and the EU's reaction to it made apparent conflicts between member states' national interests. Across the EU, the crisis and the financial guarantee mechanisms set up to rescue heavily indebted member states[10] sparked vivid debates over questions of national (financial) sovereignty, solidarity between EU member states, and the costs of integration in terms of fiscal and monetary autonomy (Hutter and

[10]Between November 2008 and July 2012, bailout programmes were initiated for Cyprus, Greece, Hungary, Ireland, Latvia, Portugal, Romania, and Spain.

Kerscher 2014; Mazzoni and Barbieri 2014; Schmidt 2014). Media analyses show that, in both debtor and creditor countries, accounts of the crisis predominantly adopted a national perspective, focussing on the (negative) consequences of the crisis for the national economy and setting up an opposition between 'good' and 'bad', fiscally responsible and irresponsible, member states (Mazzoni and Barbieri 2014; Picard 2015). Even those political actors who were supportive of the bailout measures rarely framed their support in terms of solidarity among EU member states, but rather referred to (national) economic interests (Closa and Maatsch 2014; Schmidt 2014).

Like the debate over enlargement, the controversy over the origins of the crisis and appropriate response mechanisms not only raised economic questions, but also pointed to the wider implications of economic and political integration in terms of national sovereignty and the costs of integration for the nation state and its citizens. The expectation is that against this background, national attachments and concerns for the national community have become more important for citizens' feelings of belonging to Europe. Empirically, this assumption is supported by analyses of euroscepticism in the mass public that show a growing influence of national attachments on attitudes towards the EU between 2007 and 2010 (Serricchio et al. 2013).

To summarise, both the accession of new member states from CEE and the onset of the economic and financial crisis have revived controversies over national interests, national sovereignty, and the well-being of the national community in a more integrated EU. As a result, I expect a growing influence of national attachments on citizens' propensity to identify with Europe:

H_{24}: The effect of national identification on individual identification with Europe increases after the accession of the new member states from Central and Eastern Europe in 2004/2007 and the onset of the financial and economic crisis in 2008.

3.3.3 *Financial and Economic Crisis and Individual Identification with Europe*

The overview of the consequences of Eastward enlargement and the financial and economic crisis for the EU and its member states showed that both enlargement and the crisis increased political, economic, and social differences between EU member countries. Compared to enlargement, however, the financial and economic crisis had far more disruptive consequences for member state societies and economies, e.g. in terms of prolonged declines in economic growth, high levels of unemployment, or social protests and governmental crises. In this regard, member state citizens presumably felt the social and economic consequences of the crisis far more directly in their everyday lives than the consequences of enlargement.

Likewise, the role of the EU and the consequences of economic integration were more visibly to citizens in the crisis. The spread of sovereign debt crises made apparent spill-over effects within economic and monetary union; EU summits held to find a coordinated response to the crisis and provide financial rescue measures to indebted member states were highly publicised; and by making financial aid conditional on austerity measures, the EU appeared to intervene directly in member states' fiscal and economic policy.

Against this background, this book argues that the crisis had implications for citizens' identification with Europe that go beyond the general consequences of the increase in political, economic, and social differences between EU member states and the increased politicisation of the EU at the member state level discussed above. Two developments appear to set the financial and economic crisis apart from earlier turning points in the EU integration process: first, the enduring controversy over the EU's response to the crisis that politicised the EU and polarised the debate over EU integration; second, the dominance of economic issues, both in the debate over EU integration and at the national level, which fundamentally changed the way in which citizens experience the economic dimensions of European integration. The implications of these developments for European identification and its determinants are discussed in turn in the following

3.3.3.1 Controversy over EU Integration in the Crisis and Effects of Political Interest on Individual Identification with Europe

The previous section argued that as the salience of EU integration in national political debates and the mass media has risen with Eastern enlargement and the financial and economic crisis, more information about Europe becomes available for citizens and they can more easily access this information. I expected that politically interested citizens disproportionally benefit from the greater amount of and easier access to EU-information. As a result, we should see a widening gap in EU knowledge and familiarity with EU affairs between politically more and less interested citizens as the salience of EU integration increases; in consequence, the effect of political interest on European identification should also increase (cf. H_{23}).

Yet compared to previous periods in the integration process, the financial and economic crisis has not only increased the salience of EU affairs, but also generated substantial and persistent controversy among EU leaders that resonated widely in the media (Dinan 2012, 2013a, b; Puetter 2012). EU integration issues have become increasingly politicised in national election campaigns and party positions over EU integration became more polarised over the course of the crisis (Hutter and Grande 2014; Hutter and Kerscher 2014; Risse 2015). In this regard, the crisis appears to represent a turning point in the degree of polarisation of EU events, changing the context in which citizens receive information about Europe and leading to a higher degree of conflict in Europe-related messages. The higher degree of polarisation, in turn, is expected to mitigate the effects of political interest on citizens' propensity to identify with Europe, with political interest becoming less important for European identification in the course of the crisis.

In fact, Semetko et al. (2003) hypothesise that politically less interested and less attentive citizens respond foremost to media reporting on scandalous or conflict-ridden events. That is, politically less interested citizens are considered to pay attention to increased media coverage mainly if the media cover conflict-ridden events. In this case, they will benefit from the greater availability of political information due to heightened media attention, receive more political communications, and, in this sense, become more alike to their politically more interested peers. As a result, the differences between more and less politically interested citizens with regard to attitude change should diminish.

Semetko et al.'s (2003) considerations regarding the type of event and the degree of polarisation implied by the events covered are instructive for the present analysis. Until recently, key EU events like EU summits and treaty negotiations have indeed been characterised by consensual decision-making and relative broad agreement among European leaders across member states and ideological lines (Bickerton et al. 2015; Hodson and Puetter 2013; Puetter 2012). The ongoing financial and economic crisis, on the contrary, has generated substantial controversy among EU leaders, resonating widely in the media (Dinan 2012, 2013a, b; Puetter 2012). Analyses of electoral campaigns within EU member states, too, show that EU integration issues have become more politicised and party positions over EU integration more polarised over the course of the crisis (Hutter and Grande 2014; Hutter and Kerscher 2014).

In this regard, the crisis appears to represent a turning point in the degree of polarisation of EU events and correspond to the type of conflict-ridden event that Semetko et al. hypothesise to have a greater effect on politically less attentive citizens. That is, before the crisis, high salience of issues of EU integration typically meant intensive coverage of consensus among EU leaders and a focus on the agreements reached among EU member states. After the onset of the crisis, high salience of issues of EU integration typically implies intensive coverage of conflict among EU leaders and controversy over financial assistance for debt-ridden member states and the need for further economic and political integration.

In line with Semetko et al. (2003), we should expect that the ongoing controversy over the causes and responses to the crisis have led also those citizens to consume political information who ordinarily show little interest in political affairs. As a result, differences between politically more and less interested citizens should diminish and the effect of political interest on citizens' identification with Europe should *decrease* rather than increase after the onset of the crisis in 2008. Therefore, an alternative hypothesis to H_{23} formulated above proposes that the effect of political interest on European identification decreases in response to the financial and economic crisis:

H_{25}: The effect of political interest on individual identification with Europe decreases after the onset of the financial and economic crisis in 2008.

3.3.3.2 Effects of Economic Indicators in the Crisis

Having explored the potential consequences of an increased degree of conflict and polarisation over EU integration for European identification, we now turn to the question how the dominance of economic issues over the past years will likely affect the development of individual identification with Europe.

As a basic principle, we can expect economic factors to become more important as determinants of European identification during the crisis. Looking at some of the most important indicators of macroeconomic performance, the crisis was felt across the EU: apart from Poland and Slovakia, all EU member states experienced recessions at some point after the onset of the crisis; likewise, unemployment rates increased in all member states in 2008/2009 (European Commission 2009a, 2012a). Even if citizens were not personally affected by lay-offs or insolvency, they could witness the consequences of the crisis in their everyday lives, be it in terms of rising unemployment, cuts in public spending, higher job insecurity, social protests, falling interest rates on private savings, or credit defaults and unfinished construction projects. In this regard, citizens across the EU experienced the effects of the crisis, not only in the most heavily affected member states like Spain or Greece, but also in those member states that emerged relatively quickly from economic downturn, like Germany or Poland. Election studies indeed confirm that the economic crisis has been among the most important issues for voters in recent years, with economic issues featuring even higher on voters' agenda in the countries hit hardest by the crisis (Singer 2013).

The crisis further had a clearly European dimension. Due to the high market integration within the EU, the mutual importance of EU member states as trading partners and, especially, the interdependencies within the monetary union, economic decline and risks of credit default in one member state could not be contained to national economies, but spread to other member states, too. Concurrently, the EU and its institutions were highly visible actors in the crisis. The European Council, the Eurogroup, the EU Commission, and the ECB in particular played prominent roles, working together, first to end the banking crisis in late 2008, later to establish financial rescue mechanisms for member states experiencing sovereign debt crises and monitor the implementation of austerity policies in the most highly indebted member states. In this way, there was a connection to be made for citizens between the consequences of the crisis they felt at the national level and the causes, actors, and policy responses to the crisis at the EU level.

In short, the crisis fundamentally changed the way in which citizens experience the economic dimension of European integration. It brought to the fore the risks of financial and economic interdependencies in terms of spill-over effects and citizens directly experienced adverse economic effects. What is more, given the length of the crisis and the interdependencies between European economies, these negative experiences accumulated over the years and were not necessarily contained to the actual recession period of the national economy. Germany is a case in point:

although the German economy emerged quickly from the recession and unemployment rates have actually declined since 2010, the crisis has dominated the political debate over the past years.

The expectation is that the sustained experience of the crisis and the association of the crisis with the European level also have consequences for how macroeconomic indicators affect citizens' identification with Europe. The general expectation is that economic considerations have come to play a more important role for citizens when forming attitudes towards Europe. Consequently, we should observe an increase in the effect of economic factors on European identification since the onset of the crisis as the following hypothesis proposes. In particular, one would expect macroeconomic indicators such as unemployment rates, but also redistributive considerations in terms of net contributions to the EU budget to gain importance as economic conditions worsened in the crisis:

H_{26}: The effect of economic factors on individual identification with Europe increases after the onset of the financial and economic crisis.

Although the financial crisis of late 2008 and the ensuing crisis of the real economy hit the entire EU, individual EU member states were affected to different degrees and in different manners. The economic, social, and political consequences of the crisis were particularly severe in member states where the crisis of the real economy triggered sovereign debt crises, notably Greece, Ireland, Portugal, and Spain. In exchange for financial assistance from the EU and the IMF, these countries agreed to austerity programmes, budget cuts, and structural reforms. In the context of generally weak economies, cuts in public expenditure, including social security, pension, jobs, and wages in the public sector, resulted in a growing risk of poverty, declining incomes, and high levels of unemployment (Armingeon and Baccaro 2012; Bieling 2012; Leschke et al. 2012; Theodoropoulou and Watt 2011).

At the public opinion level, we observe a general erosion of trust in national governments and EU institutions in the wake of the crisis (Armingeon and Ceka 2014; Clements et al. 2014; di Mauro 2014; Roth et al. 2013, 2014). This decline was particularly pronounced in the countries hit hardest by the crisis (Armingeon and Guthmann 2014). Presumably, the erosion of trust in the EU in connection with the crisis also has effects for citizens' propensity to identify with Europe, resulting in a decline in European identification as economic conditions worsen in a country:

H_{27}: The worse the economic effects of the financial and economic crisis in a country, the less citizens from this country identify with Europe.

The negative effects of economic decline on European identification will likely be reinforced in member states that received conditional financial aids by the EU and IMF. We can expect a 'blame effect', with citizens attributing economic hardship in their country to the EU and the austerity measures imposed by the EU and IMF in exchange for financial help. Citizens in Greece, Spain, and Portugal very clearly made the connection between the dire social conditions in their countries and the EU's role in imposing national austerity programmes and budget cuts. Mass demonstrations and general strikes not only protested national governments, but also the troika and its influence on national economic and financial policy (*BBC News* 2010). Hence, I expect citizens in countries under IMF/EU conditionality to identify less with Europe than citizens in other EU member states:

H_{28}: Citizens from member states under EU/IMF conditionality identify less with Europe than citizens from other EU member states.

Finally, we may expect differences in the effects of the crisis between member states in and outside the Eurozone. Although both groups of member states experienced economic downturns, Eurozone countries were particularly affected by the risks of sovereign defaults, which put in danger the monetary union as a whole. What is more, the Eurozone member states bore the brunt of bilateral loans and financial guarantees under the framework of the different financial stability mechanisms. While in the debtor countries there was controversy over the conditions for financial assistance in terms of austerity programmes, in the creditor countries, too, the financial guarantees met with criticism, both among political elites and the public.[11] In this regard, the risks of greater market integration became even clearer in the Eurozone than in other EU countries. Against this background, we may expect that the previously hypothesised positive effect of membership in the Eurozone is reversed in the crisis period. Accordingly, the following hypothesis expects a negative effect of Eurozone membership on European identification in the crisis:

H_{29}: After the onset of the financial and economic crisis, individuals from Eurozone member states identify less with Europe than individuals from member states outside the Eurozone.

3.3.3.3 National Identification and the Effects of Economic Indicators in the Crisis

The above discussion showed that, within the EU, we can distinguish two groups of countries that were particularly affected by the financial and economic crisis. On the one hand, the member states at risk of sovereign default, which had to agree to austerity programmes in exchange for financial aid by the EU and IMF; on the other hand, the Eurozone member states, which were particularly affected as the risks of sovereign default spread among Eurozone members and required substantial

[11]By way of example: In Germany, the ESM was challenged in Constitutional Court, most notably by MPs from the government coalition, while public opinion polls showed a clear majority of respondents opposed to bailout payments (see results reported in Bechtel et al. 2014; Forschungsgruppe Wahlen 2010a, b, 2011a, b, c, 2012a, b). In France, too, public opinion polls found a majority to oppose further bailout measures for Greece (*Bloomberg News* 2011). In Slovakia, parliament initially rejected the expansion of EFSF whereas in Finland, parliament only reluctantly agreed to expand the EFSF.

financial guarantees. Accordingly, the previous section hypothesised negative effects of EU/IMF conditionality and Eurozone membership on citizens' identification with Europe in the crisis period.

In addition to these general effects of EU/IMF conditionality and Eurozone membership, we may expect that citizens within these countries differ in their perception and reaction to austerity measures and financial assistance programmes to other member states. We know from analyses of media coverage and political speeches that in both, countries under EU/IMF conditionality and countries providing financial guarantees via the European rescue mechanisms, accounts of the crisis predominantly adopted a national perspective. The debate focussed largely on the (negative) consequences of the crisis for the national economy, juxtaposing 'good' and 'bad', fiscally responsible and irresponsible member states (Mazzoni and Barbieri 2014; Picard 2015). Even those political actors who were supportive of bailout measures tended to frame their support in terms of (national) economic interests (Closa and Maatsch 2014; Schmidt 2014). The expectation is that citizens who feel strongly attached to their national community are particularly concerned by the negative effects of austerity programmes required by the EU/IMF (in countries receiving financial aids) and the amount of financial guarantees given to member states in crisis (in the Eurozone creditor states). As a result, we should see the effect of EU/IMF conditionality and Eurozone membership on European identification vary by citizens' level of national identification as the following hypotheses propose:

H_{30}: In member states receiving conditional financial aid from the EU/IMF, the more individuals identify with the nation, the less they identify with Europe.

H_{31}: In Eurozone member states, the more individuals identify with the nation, the less they identify with Europe.

3.4 Summary of the Explanatory Model of European Identification

The present chapter developed a theoretical model of individual identification with Europe among EU citizens. At its core is the idea that citizens' identification with Europe draws on two general sources—Europe-related information on the one hand and Europe-related personal experiences on the other. Building on this idea, the theoretical model explains citizens' identification with Europe by individual- and country-level factors shaping either citizens' access to Europe-related information or their opportunities for personal experiences with other Europeans and EU politics.

To identify the relevant individual- and country-level attributes and predispositions likely to shape citizens' access to Europe-related information and personal contacts with other Europeans, and thus their propensity to identify with Europe, the theoretical discussion drew on previous research on public opinion and attitudes towards European integration, notably Zaller's work on '*The Nature and Origins of Mass Opinion*' (Zaller 1992) and its adaption to EU public opinion by Fuchs (2011).

The final model combines three sets of individual-level and three sets of country-level determinants in a multilevel framework of European identification. At the individual level, identification with Europe is expected to depend on citizens' political awareness, attitudes towards the European and national community, and personal transnational experiences. At the country level, identification with Europe is expected to depend on national party messages related to the European and national community, member states' economic position and degree of integration in the EU and global markets, and the ethnocultural composition of member state societies. Furthermore, I expect interaction effects between individual- and country-level determinants on citizens' identification with Europe. Table 3.1 summarises the theoretical expectations developed for each set of determinants.

The explanatory model of individual identification with Europe provides an integrated framework for analysis that seeks to explain European identification among EU citizens across all EU member states and periods of European integration without being restricted to a particular political, geographical, or historical context. In a second step, the general model was adapted for two decisive periods in the EU integration process, namely the EU's enlargement to Central and Eastern Europe in 2004/2007 and the onset of the financial and economic crisis in 2008. In this way, the present analysis explores not only general determinants of European identification, but also the implications of key moments in the integration process for the development of European identification in the mass public. Hypotheses with regard to the expected effects of enlargement and the crisis on individual identification with Europe are summarised in the bottom part of Table 3.1.

The following empirical analysis proceeds in three steps. In a first step, it examines the evolution of individual identification with Europe in the EU aggregate and the member states over the period 1992–2013. In a second step, it examines to what extent parties emphasise issues related to the European and national community and their respective collective identities in European election campaigns in the years 1979 to 2009. Finally, the theoretical model of individual identification with Europe developed in the present chapter is tested for the period 2000–2012 to clarify the effects of individual- and country-level determinants on European identification in the mass public.

Table 3.1 Summary of hypotheses of determinants of individual identification with Europe

	Hypotheses
Individual level	
Political awareness	
H_{1a}	The more interested individuals are in politics, the more they identify with Europe.
H_{1b}	The more interested individuals are in politics, the less they identify with Europe.
H_{2a}	The more interested individuals are in EU politics, the more they identify with Europe.
H_{2b}	The more interested individuals are in EU politics, the less they identify with Europe.
H_{3a}	The more knowledgeable individuals are of the EU and EU integration, the more they identify with Europe.
H_{3b}	The more knowledgeable individuals are of the EU and EU integration, the less they identify with Europe.
Attitudes towards European and national community	
H_{4a}	The more individuals associate Europe with a common cultural heritage and/or a common political fate, the more they identify with Europe.
H_{4b}	The more individuals associate Europe with individual benefits, the less they identify with Europe.
H_{5a}	The more individuals identify with the nation, the more they identify with Europe.
H_{5b}	The more individuals identify with the nation, the less they identify with Europe.
H_{6a}	The more individuals associate membership in the national community with common political values, the more they identify with Europe.
H_{6b}	The more individuals identify associate membership in the national community with a common ethnic and religious heritage, the less they identify with Europe.
Personal transnational experiences	
H_7	The more individuals engage in transnational practices involving other Europeans in their daily lives, the more they identify with Europe.
H_8	Individuals with a personal transnational background identify more with Europe than individuals without a transnational background.
H_9	The more transnational human capital individuals possess, the more they identify with Europe.
Country level	
Party messages related to the European and national community	
H_{10}	The more political parties in a country address issues of European community and identity in the national political debate, the more individuals from this country identify with Europe.
H_{11}	The more political parties in a country address issues of national community and identity in the national political debate, the less individuals from this country identify with Europe.
Economic position and degree of integration in the EU and global markets	
H_{12}	Individuals from Eurozone member states identify more with Europe than individuals from member states outside the Eurozone.
H_{13}	Individuals from net contributor countries of EU funds identify less with Europe than individuals from net recipient countries of EU funds.
H_{14}	The more economically integrated a country in the European and global markets, the more individuals from this country identify with Europe.

(continued)

Table 3.1 (continued)

	Hypotheses
Ethnocultural composition of member state societies	
H_{15}	The higher the share of EU nationals in a country, the more individuals from this country identify with Europe.
H_{16a}	The higher the overall share of immigrants in a country, the more individuals from this country identify with Europe.
H_{16b}	The higher the overall share of immigrants in a country, the less individuals from this country identify with Europe.
Interaction effects between individual- and country-level determinants	
Interaction with political interest	
H_{17}	The more interested individuals are in politics, the stronger the relationship between party messages and individual identification with Europe.
H_{17a}	The more interested individuals are in politics, the stronger the positive relationship between party messages on issues of European community and individual identification with Europe.
H_{17b}	The more interested individuals are in politics, the stronger the negative relationship between party messages on issues of national community and identity and individual identification with Europe.
H_{18}	The more interested individuals are in politics, the stronger the effect of member states' status as a net contributor country of EU funds on individual identification with Europe.
H_{19}	The more interested individuals are in politics, the stronger the effect of member states' degree of integration in the European and global markets on individual identification with Europe.
Interaction with national identification	
H_{20}	The more individuals identify with the nation, the stronger the relationship between party messages and individual identification with Europe.
H_{20a}	The more individuals identify with the nation, the stronger the negative relationship between party messages on issues of national community and individual identification with Europe.
H_{21}	The more individuals identify with the nation, the stronger the negative relationship between member states' status as a net contributor country to EU funding and individual identification with Europe.
H_{22}	The more individuals identify with the nation, the greater the negative effect of member states' overall share of immigrants on their propensity to identify with Europe.
Impact of enlargement and the crisis on individual identification with Europe	
General implications of enlargement and the crisis	
H_{23}	The effect of political interest on individual identification with Europe increases after Eastward enlargement and the onset of the financial and economic crisis in 2008.
H_{24}	The effect of national identification on individual identification with Europe increases after Eastward enlargement and the onset of the financial and economic crisis in 2008.
Economic crisis and individual identification with Europe	
H_{25}	The effect of political interest on individual identification with Europe decreases after the onset of the financial and economic crisis in 2008.
H_{26}	The effect of economic factors on individual identification with Europe increases after the onset of the financial and economic crisis.
H_{27}	The worse the economic effects of the financial and economic crisis in a country, the less citizens from this country identify with Europe.

(continued)

Table 3.1 (continued)

	Hypotheses
H_{28}	Individuals from member states under EU/IMF conditionality identify less with Europe than individuals from other EU member states.
H_{29}	After the onset of the financial and economic crisis, individuals from Eurozone member states identify less with Europe than individuals from member states outside the Eurozone.
Interaction with national identification in the crisis	
H_{30}	In member states receiving conditional financial aid from the EU/IMF, the more individuals identify with the nation, the less they identify with Europe.
H_{31}	In Eurozone member states, the more individuals identify with the nation, the less they identify with Europe

References

Anderson, B. (1991). *Imagined communities: Reflections on the origins and spread of nationalism*. London/New York: Verso.

Armingeon, K., & Baccaro, L. (2012). The sorrows of young euro: policy responses to the sovereign debt crisis. In N. Bermeo & J. Pontusson (Eds.), *Coping with crisis: Government reactions to the great recession* (pp. 162–198). New York: Russell Sage Foundation.

Armingeon, K., & Ceka, B. (2014). The loss of trust in the European Union during the great recession since 2007: The role of heuristics from the national political system. *European Union Politics, 15*(1), 82–107.

Armingeon, K., & Guthmann, K. (2014). Democracy in crisis? The declining support for national democracy in European countries, 2007–2011. *European Journal of Political Research, 53*(3), 423–442.

Arnold, C., Sapir, E. V., & de Vries, C. (2012). Parties' positions on European integration: Issue congruence, ideology or context? *West European Politics, 35*(6), 1341–1362.

Auel, K., & Höing, O. (2014). Parliaments in the Euro crisis: Can the losers of integration still fight back? *JCMS: Journal of Common Market Studies, 52*(6), 1184–1193.

Bartle, J. (2000). Political awareness, opinion constraint and the stability of ideological positions. *Political Studies, 48*(3), 467–484.

BBC News. (2010). Greece police tear gas anti-austerity protesters.

Bechtel, M. M., Hainmueller, J., & Margalit, Y. (2014). Preferences for international redistribution: The divide over the Eurozone bailouts. *American Journal of Political Science, 58*(4), 835–856.

Bellucci, P., Sanders, D., & Serricchio, F. (2012). Explaining European identity. In D. Sanders, P. Bellucci, G. Tóka, & M. Torcal (Eds.), *The Europeanization of national polities? Citizenship and support in a post-enlargement union* (pp. 61–90). Oxford: Oxford University Press.

Bickerton, C. J., Hodson, D., & Puetter, U. (2015). The new intergovernmentalism: European integration in the post-maastricht era. *Journal of Common Market Studies, 53*(4), 703–722.

Bieling, H.-J. (2012). EU facing the crisis: Social and employment policies in times of tight budgets. *Transfer: European Review of Labour and Research, 18*(3), 255–271.

Bloomberg News. (2011). French People Oppose Second Greek Bailout, Ifop Poll Shows.

Boomgaarden, H. G., Vliegenthart, R., de Vreese, C. H., & Schuck, A. R. T. (2010). News on the move: Exogenous events and news coverage of the European Union. *Journal of European Public Policy, 17*(4), 506–526.

Bornschier, S. (2010). The new cultural divide and the two-dimensional political space in Western Europe. *West European Politics, 33*(3), 419–444.

Bornschier, S. (2011). National political conflict and identity formation: The diverse nature of the threat from the extreme left and extreme populist right. In D. Fuchs, & H.-D. Klingemann (Eds.), *Cultural diversity, European identity and the legitimacy of the EU* (pp. 171–200, Studies in EU reform and enlargement). Cheltenham: Edward Elgar.

Braun, M., & Müller, W. (2012). National and transnational identities of intra-European migrants. In F. Höllinger & M. Hadler (Eds.), *Crossing borders, shifting boundaries: National and transnational identities in Europe and beyond. Festschrift für Max Haller* (pp. 263–287). Campus Verlag: Frankfurt/New York.

Brewer, M. B. (2001). The many faces of social identity: Implications for political psychology. *Political Psychology, 22*(1), 115–125.

Brubaker, R. (1992). *Citizenship and nationhood in France and Germany*. Cambridge, MA: Harvard University Press.

Bruter, M. (2004). Civic and cultural components of a European identity: A pilot model of measurement of citizens' levels of European identity. In R. K. Herrmann, T. Risse, & M. B. Brewer (Eds.), *Transnational identities. Becoming European in the EU* (pp. 186–213). Lanham: Rowman & Littlefield.

Bruter, M. (2005). *Citizens of Europe? The emergence of a mass European identity*. Basingstoke: Palgrave Macmillan.

Büttner, S., & Mau, S. (2010). Horizontale Europäisierung und Europäische Integration. In M. Eigmüller & S. Mau (Eds.), *Gesellschaftstheorie und Europapolitik. Sozialwissenschaftliche Ansätze zur Europaforschung* (pp. 274–317). VS Verlag für Sozialwissenschaften: Wiesbaden.

Caporaso, J. A., Kim, M.-H., Durrett, W. N., & Wesley, R. B. (2015). Still a regulatory state? The European Union and the financial crisis. *Journal of European Public Policy, 22*(7), 889–907.

Carrubba, C. J. (2001). The electoral connection in European Union politics. *The Journal of Politics, 63*(1), 141–158.

Cerutti, F. (2003). A political identity of the Europeans? *Thesis Eleven, 72*(1), 26–45.

Chong, D., & Druckman, J. N. (2007). Framing theory. *Annual Review of Political Science, 10*(1), 103–126.

Citrin, J., & Sides, J. (2004). More than nationals: How identity choice matters in the New Europe. In R. K. Herrmann, T. Risse, & M. B. Brewer (Eds.), *Transnational identities. Becoming European in the EU* (pp. 161–185). Lanham: Rowman & Littlefield.

Citrin, J., Reingold, B., & Green, D. P. (1990). American identity and the politics of ethnic change. *Journal of Politics, 52*(4), 1124–1154.

Clark, N., & Hellwig, T. (2012). Information effects and mass support for EU policy control. *European Union Politics, 13*(4), 535–557.

Clements, B., Nanou, K., & Verney, S. (2014). 'We no longer love you, but we don't want to leave you': The Eurozone crisis and popular Euroscepticism in Greece. *Journal of European Integration, 36*(3), 247–265.

Closa, C., & Maatsch, A. (2014). In a spirit of solidarity? Justifying the European financial stability facility (EFSF) in national parliamentary debates. *Journal of Common Market Studies, 52*(4), 826–842.

Converse, P. E. (1964). The nature of belief systems in mass publics. In D. E. Apter (Ed.), *Ideology and its discontents*. New York: The Free Press of Glencoe.

Cross, M. K. D., & Ma, X. (2013). EU Crises and the International Media. *ARENA Working Papers*. Oslo: Arena Centre for European Studies, University of Oslo.

Curtis, K. A. (2014). Inclusive versus exclusive: A cross-national comparison of the effects of subnational, national, and supranational identity. *European Union Politics, 15*(4), 521–546.

de Vreese, C. H. (2001). 'Europe' in the news: A cross-national comparative study of the news coverage of key EU events. *European Union Politics, 2*(3), 283–307.

de Vreese, C. H. (2003). *Framing Europe. Television news and European integration* (2nd ed.). Amsterdam: Het Spinhuis Publishers.

de Vreese, C. H. (2007). A spiral of Euroscepticism: The media's fault? *Acta Politica, 42*(2-3), 271–286.

de Vreese, C. H., & Boomgaarden, H. G. (2006a). Media effects on public opinion about the enlargement of the European Union. *JCMS: Journal of Common Market Studies, 44*(2), 419–436.

de Vreese, C. H., & Boomgaarden, H. G. (2006b). Media message flows and interpersonal communication the conditional nature of effects on public opinion. *Communication Research, 33*(1), 19–37.

de Vreese, C. H., & Boomgaarden, H. G. (2006c). News, political knowledge and participation: The differential effects of news media exposure on political knowledge and participation. *Acta Politica, 41*(4), 317–341.

de Vries, C. E., & Arnold, C. (2011). Making the polity: Exploring the linkage between European citizens' and political elites' preference for European Union public policy. In D. Fuchs & H.-D. Klingemann (Eds.), *Cultural diversity, European identity and the legitimacy of the EU* (pp. 201–219). Cheltenham/Northampton, MA: Edward Elgar.

de Vries, C. E., & Edwards, E. E. (2009). Taking Europe to its extremes: Extremist parties and public Euroscepticism. *Party Politics, 15*(1), 5–28.

Delanty, G. (2002). Models of European identity: Reconciling universalism and particularism. *Perspectives on European Politics and Society, 3*(3), 345–359.

Delli Carpini, M. X., & Keeter, S. (1996). *What Americans know about politics and why it matters*. New Haven: Yale University Press.

Deutsch, K. W. (1953a). *Nationalism and social communication: An inquiry into the foundations of nationality*. Cambridge, MA: MIT Press.

Deutsch, K. W. (1953b). *Political community at the international level: Problems of definition and measurement*. Princeton, NJ: Princeton University Press.

Deutsch, K. W., Burrell, S. A., & Kann, R. A. (1957). *Political community and the North Atlantic area: International organization in the light of historical experience*. Princeton, NJ: Princeton University Press.

di Mauro, D. (2014). Is the honeymoon over? Explaining Italy's mass support and opposition towards Europe. *Perspectives on European Politics and Society, 15*(2), 143–164.

Diez Medrano, J. (2003). *Framing Europe: Attitudes to European integration in Germany, Spain, and the United Kingdom*. Princeton, NJ: Princeton University Press.

Diez Medrano, J. (2014). Individual and collective responses to crisis: An analytical framework for the study of social resilience. *Partecipazione e Conflitto. Special issue: New Directions in Political Sociology, 7*(3), 532–550.

Diez Medrano, J., & Gray, E. (2010). Framing the European Union in national public spheres. In R. Koopmans & P. Statham (Eds.), *The making of a European public sphere. Media discourse and political contention* (pp. 195–219). Cambridge: Cambridge University Press.

Diez Medrano, J., & Gutiérrez, P. (2001). Nested identities: National and European identity in Spain. *Ethnic and Racial Studies, 24*(5), 753–778.

Dinan, D. (2012). Governance and institutions: Impact of the escalating crisis. *Journal of Common Market Studies, 50*(s2 – Special Issue: The JCMS Annual Review of the European Union in 2011), 85–98.

Dinan, D. (2013a). EU Governance and institutions: Stresses above and below the waterline. *Journal of Common Market Studies, 51*(S1 – Special Issue: The JCMS Annual Review of the European Union in 2012), 89–102.

Dinan, D. (2013b). The post-Lisbon European council presidency: An interim assessment. *West European Politics, 36*(6), 1256–1273.

Duchesne, S., & Frognier, A.-P. (1995). Is there a European identity? In O. Niedermayer & R. Sinnott (Eds.), *Public opinion and internationalized government. Vol. 2 of Beliefs in government* (pp. 193–226). Oxford: Oxford University Press.

Duchesne, S., & Frognier, A.-P. (2008). National and European identifications: A dual relationship. *Comparative European Politics, 6*(2), 143.

Dursun-Ozkanca, O. (2011). European Union enlargement and British public opinion: The agenda-setting power of the press. *Perspectives on European Politics and Society, 12*(2), 139–160.

Entman, R. M. (1993). Framing: Toward clarification of a fractured paradigm. *Journal of Communication, 43*(4), 51–58.

European Commission. (2006). Enlargement, two years after: An economic evaluation. *European Economy Occasional Papers*. Brussels: European Communities.

European Commission. (2009a). *Economic crisis in Europe: Causes, consequences and responses* (Vol. 7). Luxembourg: Office for Official Publications of the European Communities.

European Commission. (2009b). *Five years of an enlarged EU. Economic achievements and challenges*. European Communities: Brussels.

European Commission. (2011a). *European economic forecast spring 2011*. Brussels: European Union.

European Commission. (2011b). *Media use in the European Union*. Report. Standard Eurobarometer 76, Autumn 2011.

European Commission. (2012a). *Employment and social developments in Europe 2012*. Luxembourg: Publication Office of the European Union.

European Commission. (2012b). *Media use in the European Union*. Report. Standard Eurobarometer 78, Autumn 2012.

European Council. (1993). Conclusions of the presidency. Copenhagen, 21–22 June 1993.

Fligstein, N. (2008). *Euroclash: The EU, European identity, and the future of Europe*. Oxford: Oxford University Press.

Forschungsgruppe Wahlen. (2010a). Politbarometer Dezember II 2010: Mehrheit gegen stärkere Finanzhilfen für verschuldete EU-Staaten. *Politbarometer*.

Forschungsgruppe Wahlen. (2010b). Politbarometer März II 2010: Zwei Drittel der Bürger gegen deutsche Kredite für Griechenland. *Politbarometer*.

Forschungsgruppe Wahlen. (2011a). Politbarometer Juni 2011: Mehrheit gegen weitere Finanzhilfen für Griechenland. *Politbarometer*.

Forschungsgruppe Wahlen. (2011b). Politbarometer Oktober I 2011: Mehrheit gegen Schuldenschnitt für Griechenland. *Politbarometer*.

Forschungsgruppe Wahlen. (2011c). Politbarometer September I 2011: Deutliche Mehrheit gegen Erweiterung des Euro-Rettungsschirms. *Politbarometer*.

Forschungsgruppe Wahlen. (2012a). Politbarometer August 2012: Griechenland: Zwei Drittel gegen mehr Zeit. *Politbarometer*.

Forschungsgruppe Wahlen. (2012b). Politbarometer Januar II 2012: Mehrheit gegen Aufstockung des Euro-Rettungsschirms. *Politbarometer*.

Franklin, M., Marsh, M., & McLaren, L. (1994). Uncorking the bottle – Popular opposition to European unification in the wake of Maastricht. *Journal of Common Market Studies, 32*(4), 455–472.

Fuchs, D. (2011). Cultural diversity, European identity and legitimacy of the EU: A theoretical framework. In D. Fuchs & H.-D. Klingemann (Eds.), *Cultural diversity, European identity and the legitimacy of the EU* (pp. 27–57). Cheltenham: Edward Elgar.

Fuchs, D., & Schneider, C. (2011). Support of the EU and European identity: Some descriptive results. In D. Fuchs & H.-D. Klingemann (Eds.), *Cultural diversity, European identity and the legitimacy of the EU* (pp. 61–85). Cheltenham: Edward Elgar.

Fuchs, D., Guinaudeau, I., & Schubert, S. (2009). National identity, European identity, and Euroscepticism. In D. Fuchs, R. Magni-Berton, & A. Roger (Eds.), *Euroscepticism. Images of Europea among mass publics and political elites* (pp. 91–112). Opladen/Farmington Hills: Barbara Budrich.

Gabel, M. J., & Scheve, K. (2007a). Estimating the effect of elite communications on public opinion using instrumental variables. *American Journal of Political Science, 51*(4), 1013–1028.

Gabel, M. J., & Scheve, K. (2007b). Mixed messages: Party dissent and mass opinion on European integration. *European Union Politics, 8*(1), 37–59.
Garry, J., & Tilley, J. (2009). The macroeconomic factors conditioning the impact of identity on attitudes towards the EU. *European Union Politics, 10*(3), 361–379.
Gottschalck, N. (2011/2012). *The Eurocrisis – a European crisis?* (pp. 1–75). Paris: Centre international de formation européenne – Institut européen – European Institute.
Green, D. M. (2007). *The Europeans: Political identity in an emerging polity*. Boulder, CO: Lynne Rienner.
Guinaudeau, I. (2011). National and European identity: The case of France. In D. Fuchs & H.-D. Klingemann (Eds.), *Cultural diversity, European identity and the legitimacy of the EU* (pp. 123–140). Cheltenham/Northampton, MA: Edward Elgar.
Helbling, M., & Tresch, A. (2011). Measuring party positions and issue salience from media coverage: Discussing and cross-validating new indicators. *Electoral Studies, 30*(1), 174–183.
Hellström, J. (2008). Who leads, who follows? Re-examining the party-electorate linkages on European integration. *Journal of European Public Policy, 15*(8), 1127–1144.
Herrmann, R. K., & Brewer, M. B. (2004). Identities and institutions: Becoming European in the EU. In R. K. Herrmann, T. Risse, & M. B. Brewer (Eds.), *Transnational identities. Becoming European in the EU* (pp. 1–22). Lanham: Rowman & Littlefield.
Hix, S. (1999). Dimensions and alignments in European Union politics: Cognitive constraints and partisan responses. *European Journal of Political Research, 35*(1), 69–106.
Hodson, D., & Puetter, U. (2013). The European Union and the economic crisis. In M. Cini & N. Pérez-Solórzano Borragán (Eds.), *European Union politics* (4th ed., pp. 367–439). Oxford: Oxford University Press.
Hooghe, L., & Marks, G. (2004). Does identity or economic rationality drive public opinion on European integration? *Political Science and Politics, 37*(3), 415–420.
Hooghe, L., & Marks, G. (2005). Calculation, community and cues – Public opinion on European integration. *European Union Politics, 6*(4), 419–443.
Hooghe, L., & Marks, G. (2009). A postfunctionalist theory of European integration: From permissive consensus to constraining dissensus. *British Journal of Political Science, 39*(01), 1–23.
Hooghe, L., Marks, G., & Wilson, C. J. (2002). Does left/right structure party positions on European integration? *Comparative Political Studies, 35*(8), 965–989.
Hooghe, L., Marks, G., & Wilson, C. J. (2004). Does left/right structure party positions on European integration? In G. Marks & M. R. Steenbergen (Eds.), *European integration and political conflict* (pp. 120–140). Cambridge: Cambridge University Press.
Hutter, S., & Grande, E. (2014). Politicizing Europe in the national electoral arena: A comparative analysis of five West European countries, 1970–2010. *Journal of Common Market Studies, 52* (5), 1002–1018.
Hutter, S., & Kerscher, A. (2014). Politicizing Europe in hard times: Conflicts over Europe in France in a long-term perspective, 1974–2012. *Journal of European Integration, 36*(3), 267–282.
Inthorn, S. (2006). What does it mean to be an EU citizen? How news media construct civic and cultural concepts of Europe. *Westminster Papers in Communication and Culture, 3*(3), 71–90.
Ioannou, D., Leblond, P., & Niemann, A. (2015). European integration and the crisis: Practice and theory. *Journal of European Public Policy, 22*(2), 155–176.
Isernia, P., Fiket, I., Serricchio, F., & Westle, B. (2012). But still it does not move: Functional and identity-based determinants of European identity. In D. Sanders, P. C. Magalhaes, & G. Toka (Eds.), *Citizens and the European polity: Mass attitudes towards the European and national polities* (pp. 110–139). Oxford: Oxford University Press.
Kaina, V. (2009). *Wir in Europa: kollektive Identität und Demokratie in der Europäischen Union*. Wiesbaden: VS Verlag für Sozialwissenschaften.
Kam, C. D., & Kinder, D. R. (2007). Terror and ethnocentrism: Foundations of American support for the war on terrorism. *Journal of Politics, 69*(2), 320–338.

Katsourides, Y. (2014). Negative images of Europe in an era of crisis: The media and public opinion in cyprus. *Journal of Contemporary European Studies, 24*(1), 61–85.

Kinder, D. R. (2003). Belief systems after converse. In M. MacKuen & G. Rabinowitz (Eds.), *Electoral democracy*. Ann Arbor, MI: University of Michigan Press.

Kinder, D. R. (2006). Belief systems today. *Critical Review, 18*(1-3), 197–216.

Kinder, D. R., & Kam, C. D. (2010). *Us against them: Ethnocentric foundations of American opinion*. Chicago: University of Chicago Press.

Koopmans, R., & Erbe, J. (2004). Towards a European public sphere? *Innovation: The European Journal of Social Science Research, 17*(2), 97–118.

Koopmans, R., & Pfetsch, B. (2006). Obstacles or motors of Europeanization? German media and the transnationalization of public debate. *Communications, 31*(2), 115–138.

Koopmans, R., Erbe, J., & Meyer, M. F. (2010). The Europeanization of public spheres. Comparisons across issues, time, and countries. In R. Koopmans & P. Statham (Eds.), *The making of a European public sphere. Media discourse and political contention* (pp. 63–96). Cambridge: Cambridge University Press.

Kriesi, H. (2005). *Direct democratic choice: The Swiss experience*. Lanham, MD: Lexington Books.

Kriesi, H. (2007). The role of European integration in national election campaigns. *European Union Politics, 8*(1), 83–108.

Kriesi, H. (2010). Restructuration of partisan politics and the emergence of a new cleavage based on values. *West European Politics, 33*(3), 673–685.

Kriesi, H. (Ed.). (2012). *Political communication in direct democratic campaigns: Enlightening or manipulating?* Basingstoke: Palgrave Macmillan.

Kriesi, H., Grande, E., Lachat, R., Dolezal, M., Bornschier, S., & Frey, T. (2006). Globalization and the transformation of the national political space: Six European countries compared. *European Journal of Political Research, 45*(6), 921–956.

Krosnick, J. A., & Brannon, L. A. (1993). The impact of the Gulf War on the ingredients of presidential evaluations: Multidimensional effects of political involvement. *American Political Science Review, 87*(04), 963–975.

Kuhn, T. (2011). Individual transnationalism, globalisation and euroscepticism: An empirical test of Deutsch's transactionalist theory. *European Journal of Political Research, 50*(6), 811–837.

Kuhn, T. (2012). Why educational exchange programmes miss their mark: Cross-border mobility, education and European identity. *JCMS: Journal of Common Market Studies, 50*(6), 994–1010.

Kuhn, T. (2015). *Experiencing European integration: Individual transnationalism and public orientations towards European integration*. Oxford: Oxford University Press.

Lequesne, C. (2012). Old versus new. In E. Jones, A. Menon, & S. Weatherill (Eds.), *The Oxford handbook of the European Union* (pp. 267–277). Oxford/New York: Oxford University Press.

Leschke, J., Theodoropoulou, S., & Watt, A. (2012). How do economic governance reforms and austerity measures affect inclusive growth as formulated in the Europe 2020 Strategy? In S. Lehndorff (Ed.), *A triumph of failed ideas: European models of capitalism in the crisis*. European Trade Union Institute: Brussels.

Light, D., & Young, C. (2009). European Union enlargement, post-accession migration and imaginative geographies of the 'New Europe': media discourses in Romania and the United Kingdom. *Journal of Cultural Geography, 26*(3), 281–303.

Luskin, R. C. (1987). Measuring political sophistication. *American Journal of Political Science, 31*(4), 856–899.

Luskin, R. C. (1990). Explaining political sophistication. *Political Behavior, 12*(4), 331–361.

Maier, J., & Bathelt, S. (2013). Unbekanntes Europa? Eine vergleichende Analyse zu Verteilung und Determinanten von Kenntnissen über die Europäische Union. In S. I. Keil & S. I. Thaidigsmann (Eds.), *Zivile Bürgergesellschaft und Demokratie* (pp. 413–432). Wiesbaden: Springer Fachmedien.

Maier, M., Adam, S., & Maier, J. (2012). The impact of identity and economic cues on citizens' EU support: An experimental study on the effects of party communication in the run-up to the 2009 European Parliament elections. *European Union Politics, 13*(4), 580–603.

Marks, G., & Wilson, C. J. (2000). The past in the present: A cleavage theory of party response to European integration. *British Journal of Political Science, 30*(03), 433–459.

Marks, G., Wilson, C. J., & Ray, L. (2002). National political parties and European integration. *American Journal of Political Science, 46*(3), 585–594.

Marks, G., Hooghe, L., Nelson, M., & Edwards, E. (2006). Party competition and European integration in the East and West – Different structure, same causality. *Comparative Political Studies, 39*(2), 155–175.

Marks, G., Hooghe, L., Steenbergen, M. R., & Bakker, R. (2007). Crossvalidating data on party positioning on European integration. *Electoral Studies, 26*(1), 23–38.

Mau, S., & Mewes, J. (2012). Horizontal Europeanisation in contextual perspective: What drives cross-border activities within the European Union? *European Societies, 14*(1), 7–34.

Mau, S., & Mewes, J. (2013). Horizontal Europeanization and identification with Europe. In R. McMahon (Ed.), *Post-identity? Culture and European integration* (pp. 176–190). Abingdon: Routledge.

Mau, S., Mewes, J., & Zimmermann, A. (2008). Cosmopolitan attitudes through transnational social practices? *Global Networks, 8*(1), 1–24.

Mazzoni, M., & Barbieri, G. (2014). Grasshoppers against ants or malfunctions of capitalism? The representation of the European economic crisis in the main Italian newspapers. *Perspectives on European Politics and Society*, 1–16.

McGuire, W. J. (1985). Attitudes and attitude change. In G. Lindzey & E. Aronson (Eds.), *Handbook of social psychology: Special fields and applications*. New York: Random House.

McLaren, L. M. (2002). Public support for the European Union: Cost/benefit analysis or perceived cultural threat? *Journal of Politics, 64*(2), 551–566.

Meijers, M. (2013). The Euro-crisis as a catalyst of the Europeanization of public spheres? A crosstemporal study of the Netherlands and Germany. *LSE 'Europe in Question' Discussion Paper Series,* (62).

Miklin, E. (2014). From 'sleeping giant' to left–right politicization? National party competition on the EU and the Euro crisis. *Journal of Common Market Studies, 52*(6), 1199–1206.

Netjes, C. E., & Binnema, H. A. (2007). The salience of the European integration issue: Three data sources compared. *Electoral Studies, 26*(1), 39–49.

Netjes, C. E., & Edwards, E. (2005). *Taking Europe to its extremes. Examining cueing effects of right-wing populist parties on public opinion regarding European integration.* Berlin: Wissenschaftszentrum Berlin für Sozialforschung (WZB).

Nugent, N. (Ed.). (2004a). *European Union enlargement*. Basingstoke: Palgrave McMillan.

Nugent, N. (2004b). The unfolding of the 10+2 enlargement round. In N. Nugent (Ed.), *European Union enlargement* (pp. 34–69). Basingstoke: Palgrave McMillan.

O'Brennan, J. (2006). *The Eastern enlargement of the European Union*. Abingdon: Routledge.

Pennings, P. (2006). An empirical analysis of the Europeanization of national party manifestos, 1960–2003. *European Union Politics, 7*(2), 257–270.

Peter, J., & de Vreese, C. H. (2004). In search of Europe: A cross-national comparative study of the European Union in national television news. *The Harvard International Journal of Press/Politics, 9*(4), 3–24.

Peter, J., Semetko, H. A., & de Vreese, C. H. (2003). EU politics on television news: A cross-national comparative study. *European Union Politics, 4*(3), 305–327.

Phinnemore, D. (2004). Institutions and governance. In N. Nugent (Ed.), *European Union enlargement* (pp. 118–131). Basingstoke: Palgrave McMillan.

Picard, R. G. (Ed.). (2015). *The Euro crisis in the media: Journalistic coverage of economic crisis and European institutions*. London: I.B.Tauris.

Polletta, F., & Ho, K. M. (2006). Frames and their consequences. In R. E. Goodin & C. Tilly (Eds.), *The Oxford handbook of contextual political analysis* (pp. 187–209). Oxford/New York: Oxford University Press.

Puetter, U. (2012). Europe's deliberative intergovernmentalism: The role of the Council and European Council in EU economic governance. *Journal of European Public Policy, 19*(2), 161–178.

Puntscher Riekmann, S., & Wydra, D. (2013). Representation in the European State of emergency: Parliaments against governments? *Journal of European Integration, 35*(5), 565–582.

Rauh, C., & Zürn, M. (2014). Zur Politisierung der EU in der Krise. In M. Heidenreich (Ed.), *Krise der europäischen Vergesellschaftung? Soziologische Perspektiven* (pp. 121–145). Wiesbaden: Springer Fachmedien.

Ray, L. (1999). Measuring party orientations towards European integration: Results from an expert survey. *European Journal of Political Research, 36*, 283–306.

Ray, L. (2003). When parties matter: The conditional influence of party positions on voter opinions about European integration. *Journal of Politics, 65*(4), 978–994.

Ray, L. (2007). Validity of measured party positions on European integration: Assumptions, approaches, and a comparison of alternative measures. *Electoral Studies, 26*(1), 11–22.

Recchi, E. (2008). Cross-state mobility in the EU. *European Societies, 10*(2), 197–225.

Recchi, E. (2012). The Europeanisation of everyday life: Cross-border practices and transnational identifications among EU and third-country citizens. Transnational practices and european identity: From theoretical to policy issues. *EUCROSS Working Paper* (p. 12).

Risse, T. (2001). A European identity? Europeanization and the evolution of the nation-state. In M. G. Cowles, J. A. Caporaso, & T. Risse (Eds.), *Transforming Europe: Europeanization and domestic change* (pp. 198–216). Ithaca: Cornell University Press.

Risse, T. (2010). *A community of Europeans? Transnational identities and public spheres*. Ithaca: Cornell University Press.

Risse, T. (2015). European public spheres, the politicization of EU affairs, and its consequences. In T. Risse (Ed.), *European public spheres: Politics is back* (pp. 141–164). Cambridge: Cambridge University Press.

Risse, T., & Engelmann-Martin, D. (2002). Identity politics and European integration: The case of Germany. In A. Pagden (Ed.), *The idea of Europe. From antiquity to the European Union* (pp. 287–316). Cambridge/New York: Cambridge Unversity Press.

Rohrschneider, R., & Whitefield, S. (2010). Consistent choice sets? The stances of political parties towards European integration in ten Central East European democracies, 2003-2007. *Journal of European Public Policy, 17*(1), 55–75.

Roth, F., Nowak-Lehmann, F., & Otter, T. (2013). Crisis and trust in the national and European governmental institutions. In B. De Witte, A. Heritier, & A. H. Trechsel (Eds.), *The Euro crisis and the state of European democracy: Contributions from the 2012 EUDO dissemination conference* (pp. 392–407). Florence: European University Institute.

Roth, F., Gros, D., & Nowak-Lehmann D, F. (2014). Crisis and citizens' trust in the European Central Bank – Panel data evidence for the Euro Area, 1999–2012. *Journal of European Integration, 36*(3), 303-320.

Rother, N., & Nebe, T. M. (2009). More mobile, more European? Free movement and EU identity. In E. Recchi & A. Favell (Eds.), *Pioneers of European integration: Citizenship and mobility in the EU* (pp. 120–155). Cheltenham: Edward Elgar.

Scharkow, M., & Vogelgesang, J. (2010). Effects of domestic media use on European integration. *Communications, 35*(1), 73.

Schlenker, A. (2013). Cosmopolitan Europeans or partisans of fortress Europe? Supranational identity patterns in the EU. *Global Society, 27*(1), 25–51.

Schlenker-Fischer, A. (2009). *Demokratische Gemeinschaft trotz ethnischer Differenz*. Wiesbaden: VS Verlag für Sozialwissenschaften.

Schlenker-Fischer, A. (2011). Multiple identities and attitudes toward cultural diversity in Europe: A conceptual and empirical analysis. In D. Fuchs & H.-D. Klingemann (Eds.), *Cultural diversity, European identity and the legitimacy of the EU* (pp. 86–122). Cheltenham/Northampton, MA: Edward Elgar.

Schmidt, V. A. (2014). Speaking to the markets or to the people? A discursive institutionalist analysis of the EU's sovereign debt crisis. *The British Journal of Politics and International Relations, 16*(1), 188–209.

Schuck, A. R. T., Xezonakis, G., Elenbaas, M., Banducci, S. A., & de Vreese, C. H. (2011). Party contestation and Europe on the news agenda: The 2009 European Parliamentary Elections. *Electoral Studies, 30*(1), 41–52.

Semetko, H. A., van der Brug, W., & Valkenburg, P. M. (2003). The influence of political events on attitudes towards the European Union. *British Journal of Political Science, 33*(04), 621–634.

Serricchio, F., Tsakatika, M., & Quaglia, L. (2013). Euroscepticism and the global financial crisis. *Journal of Common Market Studies, 51*(1), 51–64.

Sigalas, E. (2010). Cross-border mobility and European identity: The effectiveness of intergroup contact during the ERASMUS year abroad. *European Union Politics, 11*(2), 241–265.

Singer, M. M. (2013). The global economic crisis and domestic political agendas. *Electoral Studies, 32*(3), 404–410.

Slothuus, R., & de Vreese, C. H. (2010). Political parties, motivated reasoning, and issue framing effects. *Journal of Politics, 72*(3), 630–645.

Sniderman, P. M., Brody, R. A., & Tetlock, P. E. (1991). *Reasoning and choice: Explorations in political psychology*. Cambridge: Cambridge University Press.

Spoon, J.-J. (2012). How salient is Europe? An analysis of European election manifestos, 1979–2004. *European Union Politics, 13*(4), 558–579.

Steenbergen, M. R., & Scott, D. J. (2004). Contesting Europe? The salience of European integration as a party issue. In G. Marks & M. R. Steenbergen (Eds.), *European integration and political conflict* (pp. 165–192). Cambridge: Cambridge University Press.

Steenbergen, M. R., Edwards, E. E., & de Vries, C. E. (2007). Who's cueing whom?: Mass-elite linkages and the future of European integration. *European Union Politics, 8*(1), 13–35.

Stoll, H. (2010). Elite-level conflict salience and dimensionality in western Europe: Concepts and empirical findings. *West European Politics, 33*(3), 445–473.

Theodoropoulou, S., & Watt, A. (2011). Withdrawal symptoms: An assessment of the austerity packages in Europe. *ETUI Working Papers,* (WP 2011.02).

Turner, J. C. (1987). A self-categorization theory. In J. C. Turner (Ed.), *Rediscovering the social group. A self-categorization theory* (pp. 42–67). Oxford: Blackwell.

Valentino, N. A., & Nardis, Y. (2013). Political communication: Form and consequence of the information environment. In L. Huddy, D. O. Sears, & J. S. Levy (Eds.), *The Oxford handbook of political psychology* (2nd ed., pp. 557–590). Oxford/New York Oxford University Press.

van Deth, J. (1991). Politicization and political interest. In K. H. Reif & R. Inglehart (Eds.), *Eurobarometer: The dynamics of European public opinion: Essays in honour of Jacques-René Rabier* (pp. 201–213). London: Macmillan.

van Deth, J., & Elff, M. (2004). Politicisation, economic development and political interest in Europe. *European Journal of Political Research, 43*(3), 477–508.

van Noije, L. (2010). The European paradox: A communication deficit as long as European integration steals the headlines. *European Journal of Communication, 25*(3), 259–272.

Vliegenthart, R., Schuck, A. R. T., Boomgaarden, H. G., & de Vreese, C. H. (2008). News coverage and support for European integration, 1990–2006. *International Journal of Public Opinion Research, 20*(4), 415–439.

Wendler, F. (2014). End of consensus? The European leadership discourse of the second merkel government during the Eurozone crisis and its contestation in debates of the Bundestag (2009–13). *German Politics, 23*(4), 446–459.

Westle, B. (2003). Europäische Identifikation im Spannungsfeld regionaler und nationaler Identitäten. Theoretische Überlegungen und empirische Befunde. *Politische Vierteljahresschrift, 44*(4), 453–482.

Westle, B. (2012). European identity as a contrast or an extension of national identity? In S. Salzborn, E. Davidov, & J. Reinecke (Eds.), *Methods, theories, and empirical applications in the social sciences: Festschrift for Peter Schmidt* (pp. 249–254). Wiesbaden: VS Verlag für Sozialwissenschaften.

Westle, B., & Johann, D. (2010). Das Wissen der Europäer/innen über die Europäische Union. In T. Faas, K. Arzheimer, & S. Roßteutscher (Eds.), *Information – Wahrnehmung – Emotion* (pp. 353–374). Wiesbaden: VS Verlag für Sozialwissenschaften.

Whitefield, S., Vachudova, M. A., Steenbergen, M. R., Rohrschneider, R., Marks, G., Loveless, M. P., et al. (2007). Do expert surveys produce consistent estimates of party stances on European integration? Comparing expert surveys in the difficult case of Central and Eastern Europe. *Electoral Studies, 26*(1), 50–61.

Zaller, J. (1990). Political awareness, elite opinion leadership, and the mass survey response. *Social Cognition, 8*(1), 125–153.

Zaller, J. (1992). *The nature and origins of mass opinion*. Cambridge: Cambridge University Press.

Chapter 4
The Development of Citizens' Identification with Europe from Maastricht to the Crisis

The present chapter presents the *descriptive evidence on levels and development of citizens' identification with Europe* as the central phenomenon of interest of this book. Drawing on survey data from the Eurobarometer, it provides information on the prevalence of European identifications in the mass public and draws conclusions about the emergence of a collective European identity among EU citizens. To this end, the following analysis explores the evolution of individual identification with Europe in the EU aggregate and the EU member states over the period 1992–2013. Three questions guide the descriptive analysis of European identification:

- How widespread is European identification among citizens in the EU member states and which trends do we observe in European identification over the 1992–2013 period?
- How widespread are multiple national and European identifications in the EU population and do national and European identifications appear compatible or conflicting in a framework of multiple collective identifications?
- How has citizens' identification with Europe responded to the EU's enlargement to Central and Eastern Europe in 2004/2007 and the onset of the financial and economic crisis in late 2008?

Based on the previous conceptual discussion of individual European identification (cf. Chap. 2), the analysis explores *cognitive*, *evaluative*, and *affective* aspects of identification with Europe. These are operationalised by, first, citizens' *self-categorisation as European* (cognitive identification); second, citizens' *pride in being European* (evaluative identification); and third, citizens' *attachment to Europe/the European Union* (affective identification).

The empirical evidence shows that a collective European identity has developed in the EU public alongside collective national identities, with a majority of citizens seeing themselves (also) as European and expressing attachments to the European community. While European identity cannot match national identities in extent or intensity, multiple collective identities are a reality for EU citizens by now. The

S. Bergbauer, *Explaining European Identity Formation*,
https://doi.org/10.1007/978-3-319-67708-8_4

time series for European identification show a slight increase in citizens' identification with Europe following the accession of new Central and Eastern European member states in 2004; in contrast, attachments to the European Union (moderately) decrease in the aftermath of the financial and economic crisis, especially in the Eurozone and in some of the countries hit hardest by the crisis. Rather than causing a sudden drop in European identification, the negative effects of the crisis appear to accumulate over time, gradually weakening citizens' affective ties to the European community.

The remainder of the chapter proceeds as follows: A first section presents the database for the descriptive analysis and explains the choice of indicators used to operationalise the concept of individual European identification (Sect. 4.1). The subsequent sections present the empirical findings, starting with levels and development of European identification in the EU over the 1992–2013 (Sect. 4.2) and the prevalence of multiple identifications with the European and the national community (Sect. 4.3). The subsequent section concentrates on the consequences of the EU's enlargement to Central and Eastern Europe in 2004/2007 and the onset of the financial and economic crisis in late 2008 for citizens' identification with Europe (Sect. 4.4). A final section draws conclusions with regard to the emergence of a collective European identity among the EU citizens (Sect. 4.5).

4.1 Data and Operationalisation

To assess levels and development of citizens' identification with Europe, the present study relies on survey data from 42 Eurobarometer (EB) waves conducted between March/April 1992 and November 2013[1] (see Table 4.2 in the appendix for a full list of EB waves used in the descriptive analysis). EB surveys are representative samples of the populations of the EU member states aged 15 and over (nationals and non-nationals, but EU citizens), with each survey consisting of approximately 1000 face-to-face interviews per country.[2] The combined dataset for the descriptive analysis comprises around 731,000 individuals, sampled in the then current EU member states at 38 time points, with between 13,000 and 27,000 individuals sampled per time point.

---

[1]Conducted on behalf of the European Commission, the Eurobarometer surveys have been monitoring public opinion in the then current EC/EU member countries since 1973. Standard EB surveys are conducted at least twice a year, including attitudes towards European unification, institutions, and policies; measurements for general socio-political orientations; and respondent and household demographics. For more information on the EB and EB methodology, see www.ec.europa.eu/public_opinion. Primary data and related documentation were obtained from the GESIS Data Archive for the Social Sciences at www.gesis.org

[2]Approximately 1500 interviews in Germany with separate samples for East (500) and West (1000); 1300 in the UK with separate samples for Great Britain (1000) and Northern Ireland (300); and 500 in Cyprus, Luxemburg, and Malta.

Individual identification with Europe has previously been defined as citizens' *self-categorisation* as European together with their *evaluations* of their membership in the European collective and their *affective attachment* to Europe and other Europeans (cf. Chap. 2). The three components of European identification contained in the definition—self-categorisation, evaluation, and attachment—are measured by three different indicators, assessing, respectively, citizens' *self-categorisation as European*, citizens' *pride in being European*, and citizens' *attachment to Europe/the European Union*. All three indicators represent standard measures of European identity in survey-based public opinion research and have been widely used in previous analyses of European identification (see, e.g. Bellucci et al. 2012; Caporaso and Kim 2009; Citrin and Sides 2004; Duchesne and Frognier 2008; Fuchs et al. 2009; Fuchs and Schneider 2011; Isernia et al. 2012; Kaina 2009; Pichler 2008; Risse 2010).

Citizens' *self-categorisation as European* is operationalised by the question: "*In the near future, do you see yourself as …? [Nationality] only; [Nationality] and European; European and [Nationality]; European only*;" This question has been used widely in analyses of citizens' identification with Europe, in particular to operationalise concepts of exclusive and inclusive national identity (see, e.g. de Vries and van Kersbergen 2007; Fuchs et al. 2009; Hooghe and Marks 2005; Risse 2010). The item is recoded into a binary variable distinguishing between respondents who identify only with the nation (seeing themselves as 'nationality only' in the near future) and respondents who show some form of European identification (other response categories). Respondents indicating 'don't know' or 'none' spontaneously and those refusing to answer are omitted from the analysis.

Citizens' *pride in being European* is operationalised by the question "*And would you say you are very proud, fairly proud, not very proud, not at all proud to be European?*" As a measure of citizens' esteem for their status as European, European pride implies a positive evaluation of the group of Europeans and can thus be used to operationalise evaluative aspects of European identification. This operationalisation follows research on national identification that uses measures of pride to assess in-group evaluation and interprets national pride as a generalised positive evaluation of the nation (Blank and Schmidt 2003; Mummendey et al. 2001). The pride item is recoded so that higher values indicate stronger pride in being European. For comparison, levels of European pride are presented alongside levels of national pride.[3] To visualise the development of pride over time, European and national pride are collapsed into binary variables distinguishing between respondents reporting to be not at all/not very proud to be European/[NATIONALITY] and respondents reporting to be fairly/very proud to be European/[NATIONALITY]. Respondents indicating 'don't know' and those refusing to answer are omitted from the analysis. Due to data limitations, we can track levels of European pride only for the years 2000 to 2006.

[3]National pride is assessed by the following item: 'Would you say you are very proud, fairly proud, not very proud, not at all proud to be [NATIONALITY]?'

Citizens' *attachment to Europe*, third, is measured by the question "*People may feel different degrees of attachment to their town or village, to their region, to their country or to Europe. Please tell me how attached you feel to... Europe. Very attached, fairly attached, not very attached, not at all attached.*". Starting with EB 67.2 (April/March 2007), the wording of the item changed and the question thereafter refers to 'the European Union' instead of 'Europe'.[4] Therefore, I analyse citizens' attachment to Europe for the years 1995 to 2007 and citizens' attachment to the European Union for the period 2007 to 2013.

Referring to respondents' *attachment* to Europe/the European Union, this item emphasises affective aspects of European identification. Attachment to Europe is one of the most frequently used indicators of identification with Europe and has been found to be the most appropriate measure of European identification in survey research (Sinnott 2006). Unlike the item assessing respondents' self-description as national and/or European, the attachment item does not force respondents to rank-order national and European identifications, but allows them to express equally strong attachments to multiple levels of community. Hence, we are able to directly compare levels and strength of respondents' attachment to the national and the European level and draw conclusions regarding the relative importance of European identification compared to national attachments.

The attachment item is recoded so that higher values indicate stronger attachment to Europe/the European Union. To compare attachment to Europe/the European Union to attachment to the national level, the following analysis shows levels of attachment to Europe/the European Union alongside levels of attachment to one's own country.[5] To visualise the development of attachment over time, all three items, *attachment to the Europe*, *attachment to the European Union,* and respondents' *attachment to their own country*, are collapsed into binary variables, distinguishing between respondents reporting to be very attached/fairly attached and respondents reporting to be not very attached/not at all attached. Respondents indicating 'don't know' or refusing to answer are omitted from the analysis.

[4]The exact question wording for attachment to the European Union is: People may feel different degrees of attachment to their town or village, to their region, to their country or the European Union. Please tell me how attached you feel to...the European Union. Very attached, fairly attached, not very attached, not at all attached.

[5]Attachment to one's own country is assessed by the same item as attachment to Europe/the European Union. The exact question wording is 'People may feel different degrees of attachment to their town or village, to their region, to their country or to Europe. Please tell me how attached you feel to...[COUNTRY]. Very attached, fairly attached, not very attached, not at all attached.'

4.2 The Development of Citizens' Identification with Europe 1992–2013

The first research question to be explored addresses the level and development of citizens' identification with Europe over time. How widespread are European identifications among EU citizens and which trends do we observe in citizens' identification with Europe over the years 1992–2013? To answer these questions, the following section tracks citizens' identification with Europe in terms of their self-categorisation as European, European pride, and attachment to Europe and the European Union. The aim is to give a general overview of the long-term trends in citizens' identification with Europe in the EU member states. Subsequent sections will discuss in more detail to what extent citizens have developed multiple identifications with both the European and national level and how enlargement and the crisis have affected levels of European identification in the member states. All figures and tables are based on the weighted[6] aggregate of EU member states at the time or on weighted aggregates of selected groups of member countries, e.g. the EU6, CEE member states, or Eurozone countries. Vertical lines in the figures indicate the years 2004 and 2008 to ease interpretation with regard to developments in European identification after EU enlargement to CEE and the onset of the financial and economic crisis.

The Development of Citizens' Self-Categorisation as European 1992–2013 Starting with citizens' self-categorisation as European, a first question to be explored is whether citizens' actively allocate themselves to the European community and thus show a form of cognitive identification with Europe. Figure 4.1 depicts the percentage of respondents describing themselves also as European as opposed to respondents seeing themselves only as members of the national group in the near future.

Over the entire period under analysis, a majority of EU citizens see themselves (also) as Europeans. That is, EU citizens have consistently shown a form of cognitive identification with the group of Europeans over the past two decades. Levels of self-categorisation prove remarkably stable over time, with the percentage of citizens identifying (also) as European vacillating between 52% (autumn 1996/spring 2010) and 66% (autumn 1994). Nonetheless, we also observe a considerable proportion of citizens who continue to describe themselves only by their nationality. For these citizens, European and national identification appear not to go together at all, given that the indicator explicitly offers the choice to identify as both national *and* European.

[6]The descriptive analyses of the EU aggregate as well as sub-groups of EU member states (e.g. EU6, new CEE member states, Eurozone countries) employs population size weighting based on the Eurobarometer's 'European weights', which adjust each national sample in proportion to its share in the total EU population (aged 15 and over) or within different groupings of EU member states. The European population size weights also include post-stratification weighting factors for each sample (minimum sex, age, region, size of locality).

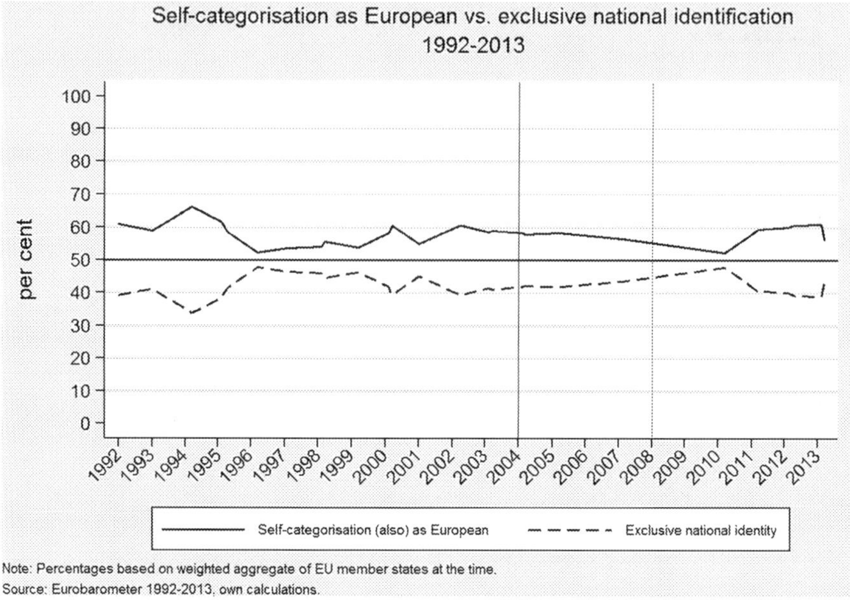

Fig. 4.1 Self-Categorisation as European in the EU Aggregate 1992–2013

The overall trends mask important differences in European identification among EU member states. Figure 4.2 displays levels and development of self-categorisation as European and exclusive national identification by EU member state. In a first group of countries a majority of respondents consistently identifies (also) as European. This is the case notably in France, Luxembourg, Malta, the Netherlands, Poland, Slovakia, and Spain, West Germany since the late 1990s, and Italy except for a brief time span in the early 2000s. In a second group of countries the proportion of respondents identifying (also) as European and the proportion of respondents identifying only by their nationality vacillate around the 50% mark. This group includes notably Austria, Estonia, Finland, Greece, Hungary, Ireland, and Portugal. In these countries, roughly half of respondents identify (also) with Europe while the other half identify only by their nationality. In a third, smaller group of countries a majority of respondents consistently identifies only by their nationality. This is the case notably in Great Britain and, to a lesser extent, in Lithuania.

For the most part, the observed differences in levels of European identification between EU member states appear to reflect long-standing traditions in countries' relations to the EU. Thus, the dominance of exclusive national identifications in Great Britain appears to reflect the view of Europe as 'the other' prevailing in British identity discourses since the 1950s (Risse 2010). On the other hand, we find the greatest proportions of respondents identifying (also) as European in the six founding member states of the EC/EU. In these countries, political elites and mass

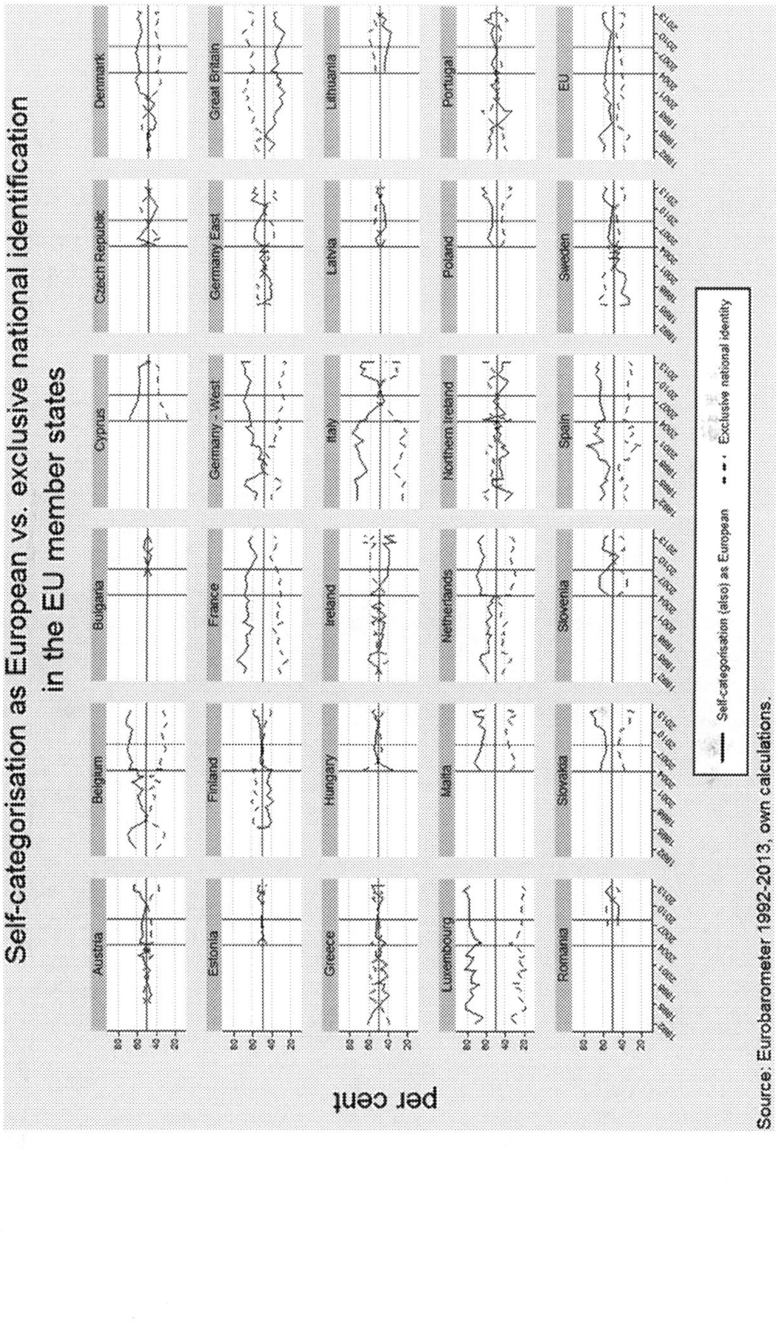

Fig. 4.2 Self-Categorisation as European in the EU Member States 1992–2013

publics have traditionally been supportive of the European project and citizens have the longest experience with EU integration.

The Development of Citizens' Pride in Being European 2000–2006 Levels of European pride confirm the picture of citizens' identification with Europe so far. As Fig. 4.3 shows, citizens' pride in being European remains stable over time, increasing slightly from 68% in early 2000 to 72% in autumn 2004 and 75% in autumn 2006, the last year the pride indicator was included in the Eurobarometer. Levels of European pride remain lower than levels of national pride, with just under 90% of respondents claiming to be proud to be [NATIONALITY] in all years under analysis.

The findings for the EU aggregate are largely replicated at the member state level as the overview of European and national pride in the member states in Fig. 4.4 shows. With the exception of Great Britain, more than 60% of respondents in all EU member states say they are fairly or very proud to be European; in most countries, levels of European pride even exceed the 70%-mark. As in the EU aggregate, levels of European pride remain relatively stable over the years 2000–2006, with levels of national pride being considerably higher than levels of European pride.

The gap in levels of European and national pride differs by member state. At one extreme, we find Greece and Great Britain where high levels of national pride are combined with comparatively low levels of European pride. At the other end, we find Italy and Luxembourg and, to a lesser degree Spain, with comparatively high

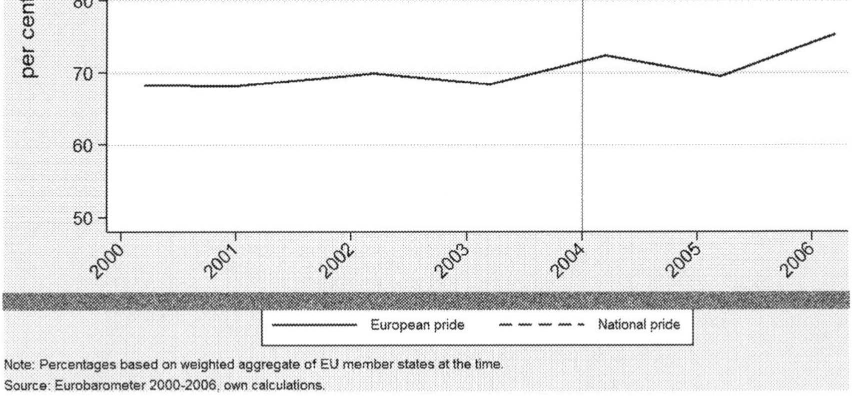

Fig. 4.3 European and National Pride in the EU Aggregate 2000–2006

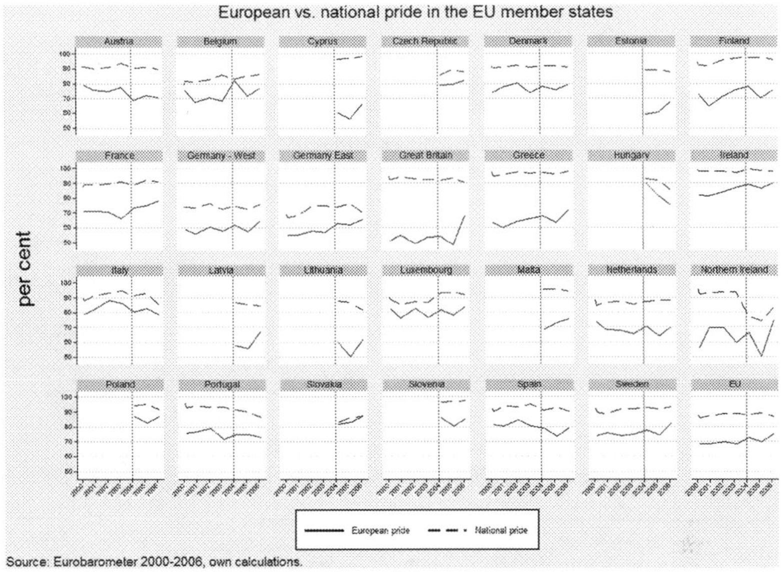

Fig. 4.4 European and National pride in the EU Member States 2000–2006

levels of both national and European pride. Levels of national pride are noticeably lower in Germany, reflecting a long-standing reluctance among Germans to express nationalist sentiments in light of the country's history; the lower level of national pride in Belgium appears to reflect the cleavage between Walloon and Flemish parts of the country and the strong regional identities in the two parts, which may suppress pride in being Belgian.

The Development of Citizens' Attachment to Europe and the EU 1992–2013 Turning to citizens' affective ties to Europe and the community of Europeans and their *attachment to European and the European Union,* we observe similar trends as in the case of citizens' self-categorisation as European and pride in being European.

Figure 4.5 depicts the percentage of respondents indicating to be fairly or very attached to Europe/the European Union alongside the percentage of respondents indicating to be fairly or very attached to their country.

From the late 1990s onwards, a majority of respondents consistently feel fairly or very attached to Europe; by the year 2007, when the question for respondents' *attachment to Europe* was last included in the Eurobarometer survey, the proportion of respondents claiming attachment to Europe had risen to two thirds. Levels of attachment drop considerably if respondents are asked to indicate their attachment to the European Union, although 40–50% of respondents still feel fairly or very attached to the EU over the period under analysis. EU citizens thus appear to have developed stable affective ties to both Europe as the wider region and the European Union as a more narrowly defined political and economic system.

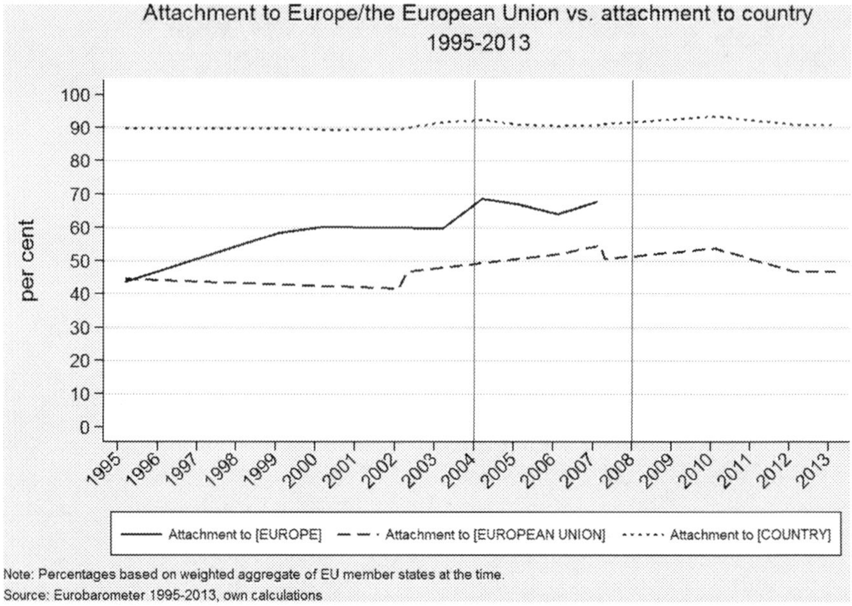

Fig. 4.5 Attachment to Europe/the European Union in the EU Aggregate 1995–2013

Levels of attachment to Europe/the European Union remain far behind respondents' attachment to their own country, however. As the uppermost line in Fig. 4.5 shows, over the entire period under analysis, around 90% of respondents claim to be fairly or very attached to their country. The gap between national and European attachment initially shrank, but widened again in recent years as respondents were asked to indicate their attachment to the European Union. What is more, in nearly all years under analysis, more than half of respondents claim to be 'very attached' to their country, whereas at most a fifth claim to be 'very attached' to Europe and no more than a tenth feel 'very attached' to the European Union.

The overall trends in attachment to Europe/the European Union are widely reflected at the member state level. As Fig. 4.6 shows, national attachments exceed attachment to Europe and the European Union in all member states. Likewise, levels of attachment to Europe generally exceed levels of attachment to the European Union. The upward trend in attachment to Europe which we observed in the EU aggregate from the 1990s onwards is also manifest in most of the member states. Unlike in the case of self-categorisation as European, levels of attachment to Europe are not necessarily higher in the six EC/EU founding states than in countries that joined the EC/EU later in the integration process. Thus, we find about the same or greater proportions of respondents feeling fairly or very attached to Europe in countries like Denmark, Finland, or Sweden as in France, Italy, or the Netherlands.

Some interesting patterns emerge regarding the differences in levels of attachment to Europe and the European Union at the member state level. Although attachment to Europe generally exceeds attachment to the European Union, the

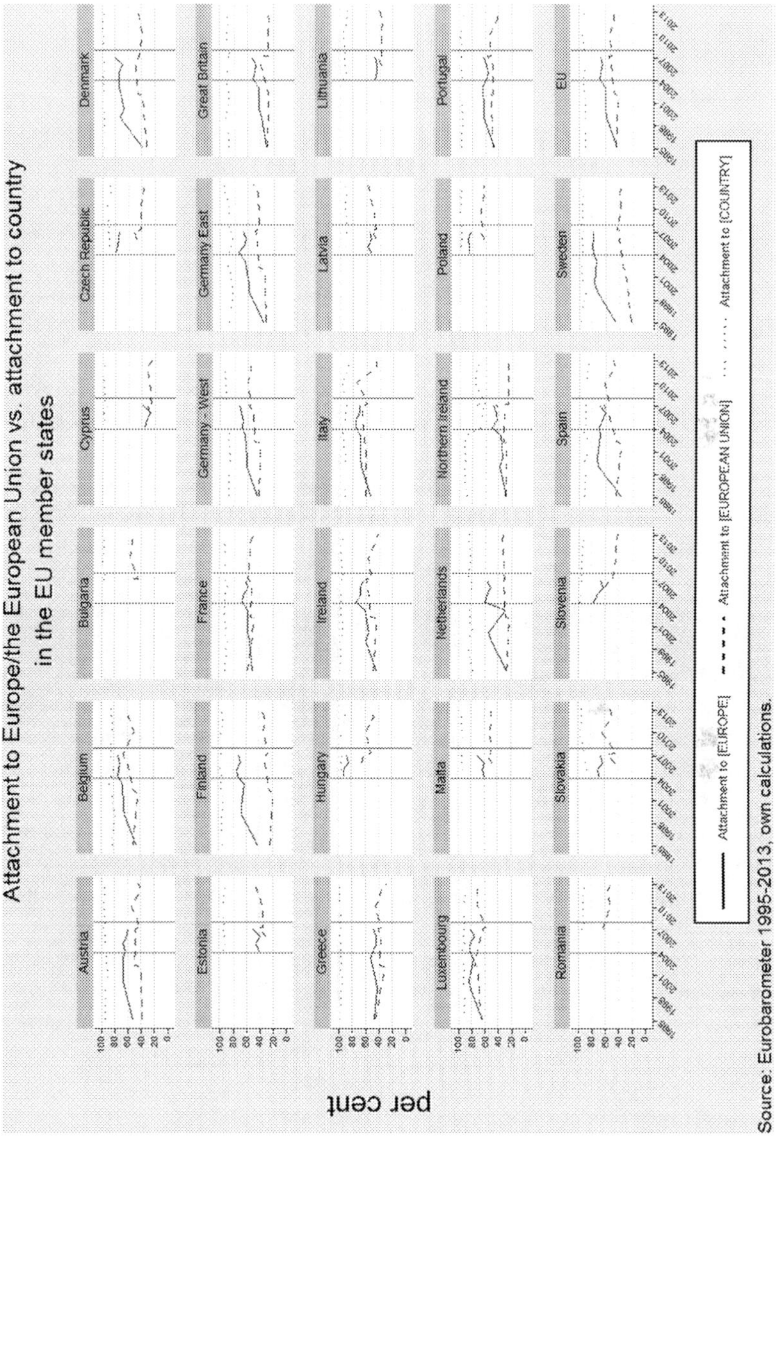

Fig. 4.6 Attachment to Europe/the European Union in the EU Member States 1995–2013

gap between the two differs widely between member states. In a number of countries, such as France, Greece, Ireland, Italy, Portugal, and the Baltic states, attachment to the EU closely traces attachment to Europe. In a second group of countries, notably Denmark, Finland, and Sweden, as well as Spain in the 1990s and early 2000s, we observe a large gap between attachment to Europe and attachment to the European Union. Thus, in spring 2006, the last time attachment to Europe and attachment to the European Union were sampled together in a Eurobarometer survey, the difference in attachment was less than five percentage points in Cyprus, Italy, Spain, and Slovenia, but twenty and more in Denmark, Finland, the Netherlands, Slovakia, and Sweden.[7] These differences do not appear to be related to differences in length of EU membership nor do they divide small and large countries or Western and Eastern European member states. Rather, they suggest that citizens across the EU associate very different meanings with the term 'Europe'.

Thus, the comparatively small gap between attachment to Europe and attachment to the EU in countries like Italy or Slovenia appears to indicate that citizens in these countries largely equate 'Europe' with the 'EU' and/or have developed positive affections to both. As a result, we observe similar levels of attachment regardless of whether respondents are asked to indicate their attachment to Europe or the EU.

In contrast, the large gap in levels of attachment to Europe and the European Union in, e.g. the Nordic countries or the Netherlands, appears to indicate that citizens in these countries differentiate between 'Europe', possibly understood as a cultural sphere or geographical entity, and the EU as a supranational political system and that citizens differ in their affection towards the two objects. Given the comparatively high levels of attachment to *Europe*, citizens in Sweden or Finland do not seem generally averse to developing affective ties to the European level (as seems to be the case for Great Britain, for example, where both levels of attachment to Europe and to the EU are low compared to other EU member states). They appear sceptical towards the European Union, however, as expressed in the lower levels of attachment to the EU. Apparently, the EU has only been partially successful in superimposing itself as the primary meaning of 'Europe' and securing positive affections by its citizens.

Recapitulating our findings so far, we see that a majority of citizens has come to identify with Europe over the past two decades. This is true for all three dimensions of European identification described in the conceptual discussion of individual European identity, i.e. cognitive identification in the form of self-allocation to the European collective, positive evaluations of group membership in the form of European pride, and affective identification in the form of attachment to Europe/the European Union. We can take these results as evidence that EU citizens have indeed started to develop a common European identity.

[7]It should be underlined that EB 65.2 from March/May 2006 employed a split survey design; hence, we cannot compare respondents individually, but only aggregate response behaviour to the two attachment items.

Nonetheless, we find levels of European identification to lag behind levels of national identification over the whole period under analysis. The persistent gap between national and European attachments indicates that for considerable shares of EU citizens, the national community remains an important—and for some the only—object of collective identification. Against this background, the question of multiple collective identifications becomes crucial. Based on the empirical evidence so far, the European Union will not be able to supplant national identification with European identification, at least not in the near future. To guarantee the legitimacy of the EU and EU decision making, it will therefore be necessary that European identification grows alongside national identification. The following section will explore the relationship between national and European identification in more detail. The objective is to determine whether citizens perceive identification with the two levels as compatible or conflicting and how widespread multiple identifications are among the EU population.

4.3 The Prevalence of Multiple European and National Identifications Among EU Citizens

The evidence regarding citizens' identification with Europe presented so far indicates that citizens have developed stable ties to the European community, but the level and intensity of European identifications fall behind those of identification with the national community. This finding raises questions about the relationship between European and national identifications. Are the two forms of collective identification compatible or conflicting? Do citizens discriminate between the two, identifying with *either* the European *or* the national level? Or do citizens combine European and national identifications in the form of multiple collective identifications?

We previously observed that a majority of respondents in the EU describe themselves not only by their nationality, but (also) as European. While we find a less uniform picture at the member state level, in the majority of member states more than half of respondents still see themselves (also) as European. Overall, EU citizens thus appear to combine belongings to the national and the European level relatively easily.

Nonetheless, citizens' self-categorisation as European may be a weak test of the strength of multiple identifications in the EU context. Replies to the question for whether respondents 'see themselves' (also) as Europeans may well be based on a primarily geographic or legal understanding of being European, i.e. based on the location of one's home country on the European continent and its membership in the EU. To fulfil the functions ascribed to a common European identity at the macrosocial level, however, citizens' affective ties to the European level may ultimately be more important than their (cognitive) self-allocation to the European collective. Feelings of attachment are more closely related to the sense of solidarity and obligation to the European community that makes majority decisions and redistributive measures legitimate in the eyes of the citizens. Therefore, the prevalence of multiple *affective* identifications with the national and the

European community in the EU population may be more informative for the role of a common European identity in securing legitimacy and support for the European project than citizens' self-description as European.

To explore multiple affective ties to Europe and the nation among EU citizens, we can cross-tabulate attachment to Europe/the European Union and attachment to country. Following the typology of collective identities proposed by Fuchs and Schneider (2011, p.79).

Table 4.1 provides percentages for four combinations of attachment to the national and European level: respondents who feel attached to both their country and Europe/ the European Union ('multiple identification'); respondents who feel attached only to their country ('national identification only'); respondents who feel attached only to Europe/the European Union ('European identification only'); and respondents who feel attached to neither their country nor Europe/the European Union ('no collective identification'). The upper half of shows cross-tabulations between respondents' attachment to their country and to Europe, the lower half of Table 4.1 shows combinations of respondents' attachment to their country and the European Union.

As we can see from the percentages in the column 'multiple identification', in all years under analysis, a substantial proportion of respondents feel attached to both the national and the European level. In this regard, the comparatively higher levels of national attachment we previously observed do not necessarily imply that citizens find European and national ties incompatible. Rather, multiple collective attachments are the norm for important parts of the EU population.

These rather positive findings need to be qualified, however. First, significant numbers of respondents continue to feel attached only to the national level. What is more, we find important differences in the extent of multiple attachments depending on whether respondents are asked to indicate their attachment to Europe or the European Union. Finally, we observe divergent trends in multiple identifications and exclusive national attachments over time.

Concentrating first on the period 1995 to 2007 and multiple identifications with *Europe* and the home country (upper half of Table 4.1), we see the percentage of respondents with only national attachments decline significantly over time. While in 1995, nearly half of respondents feel attached only to their country, the number has fallen to just over a quarter by 2007. In contrast, the share of respondents feeling attached to both Europe and their country rises from just over 40% in 1995 to nearly 65% in 2007. The increase in multiple identifications between 2003 and 2004 can be partially explained by the greater prevalence of multiple attachments to Europe and the home country in the new CEE member states. Nonetheless, we observe a general upward trend in multiple identifications from the late 1990s to the mid-2000s.

Turning to the lower half of Table 4.1 and multiple identifications with the *European Union* and the home country, we observe significantly lower levels of multiple identifications and higher shares of respondents with only national attachments. What is more, unlike in the case of multiple attachments to Europe and the home country, the share of respondents with multiple identifications increases only intermittently. Multiple attachments to the European Union and the home country peak in spring 2007 and spring 2010, the only times when more than 50% of

Table 4.1 Multiple Identification with Europe/the European Union and [OUR COUNTRY] 1995–2013

Multiple identification with Europe/EU and [COUNTRY] in the EU aggregate (%)						
EB no.	Month	Year	Multiple identification	National identification only	European identification only	No collective identification
Multiple identification with Europe and [OUR COUNTRY]						
EB 43.1bis	May/June	1995	41.0	48.8	2.8	7.5
EB 51	March–May	1999	56.2	33.6	2.4	7.8
EB 54.1	November/December	2000	58.2	31.0	2.2	8.6
EB 60.1	October/November	2003	57.5	34.2	2.4	6.0
EB 62	October/November	2004	66.0	26.2	2.7	5.1
EB 63.4	May/June	2005	64.2	26.7	2.8	6.2
EB 65.2	March/May	2006	61.0	29.3	3.2	6.4
EB 67.1	February/March	2007	64.6	26.1	3.1	6.1
Multiple identification with the EU and [OUR COUNTRY]						
EB 43.1bis	April/May	1995	42.1	47.6	2.4	7.8
EB 56.3	January/February	2002	40.0	49.4	1.7	9.0
EB 58.1	October/November	2002	44.9	45.1	1.7	8.3
EB 65.2	March/May	2006	49.9	40.7	2.0	7.4
EB 67.2	April/March	2007	52.0	39.4	2.7	5.9
EB 68.1	September/November	2007	48.4	42.7	2.3	6.6
EB 73.3	March/April	2010	52.2	41.3	1.6	4.9

(continued)

Table 4.1 (continued)

Multiple identification with Europe/EU and [COUNTRY] in the EU aggregate (%)						
EB no.	Month	Year	Multiple identification	National identification only	European identification only	No collective identification
EB 77.3	May	2012	45.1	45.9	1.8	7.3
EB 80.1	November	2013	44.7	46.2	2.1	7.0

Question wording: People may feel different degrees of attachment to their town or village, to their region, to their country or to Europe. Please tell me how attached you feel to... Europe/The European Union/[OUR COUNTRY]

Note: Typology of identifications based on Fuchs/Schneider (2011), Table 3.7, p.80; Figures are percentages of respondents based on the weighted aggregate of EU member states at the time. Attachment variables are dichotomised by merging the categories 'very attached'/'fairly attached' and 'not very attached'/'not attached at all' and cross-tabulated to construct four types of identifications:

Multiple identification: percentage of respondents feeling fairly or very attached to both country and Europe/the EU;

National identification only: percentage of respondents feeling fairly or very attached to country and not attached to Europe/the EU;

European identification only: percentage of respondents feeling fairly or very attached to Europe/the EU and not attached to country;

No collective identification: percentage of respondents feeling neither attached to Europe/the EU nor to their country;

Source: Eurobarometer, own calculations

respondents feel fairly or very attached to both the national and the European level. We observe the opposite trend in exclusive national attachments: after a temporary drop in early 2007, the share of respondents who feel fairly or very attached only to their home country has risen continually.

The considerable differences in levels of multiple collective identifications depending on whether we examine attachments to Europe or the European Union echo our previous findings with regard to differences in levels of attachment to Europe and the European Union. Citizens in the member states are generally less inclined to develop affective ties to the EU than to Europe, and this tendency is also reflected in the lower prevalence of multiple identifications with the EU and the home country.

The different trends in multiple attachments involving Europe on the one hand and the European Union on the other may (also) be a function of different sampling periods. We observe the highest levels of multiple identifications with Europe and the home country in the mid- to late-2000s, i.e. the post-enlargement period, when public opinion was generally more positively inclined towards European integration (Sanders et al. 2012; Tóka et al. 2012). On the other hand, attachments to the European Union were sampled mainly in the late 2000s and after the onset of the financial and economic crisis when the EU generally faced more criticism. Therefore, the findings from EB 65.2 sampled March/May 2006, which included indicators of both respondents' attachment to Europe and their attachment to the European Union in a split sample design, are particularly informative. In spring 2006, 61% of respondents felt attached to both Europe and their home country, but only about 50% felt attached to the EU and their home country. That is, even in times of relative calm in the EU integration process, considerably fewer respondents held multiple attachments to the EU and the national level than to Europe and the national level. While many citizens appear to see feelings of attachments to *Europe* as compatible with feelings of attachment to their home country, they continue to choose between the *European Union* and their home country.

Presumably, the differences in multiple attachments to country and Europe/the EU are due to differences in how citizens perceive the relationship between 'Europe' and the home country on the one hand and the European Union and the home country on the other. If 'Europe' is understood as referring to the continent or the cultural area, there is little potential for conflicts or rivalry between Europe and the home country as, by definition, all EU member countries are part of the European continent and a European cultural sphere. As a result, respondents probably feel no need to choose between the two, affirming their attachment to both Europe and their home country. The European Union, in contrast, is more likely to be perceived as rival to the nation state as it intervenes directly in national politics and competes for sovereignty with the national political system. Against this background, respondents may feel compelled to choose between the EU and their home country rather than affirm simultaneous attachments to their home country and the EU.

The relative lack of multiple attachments to the EU and the home country seems problematic with regard to the role of affective ties for Europe-wide solidarity and the legitimacy of EU decision-making. As EU integration more and more implies redistributive measures and majority decisions creating (perceived) winners and losers among the EU member states, the EU becomes more dependent on affective sources to legitimise its policies. Yet over the past two decades, multiple attachments to the European Union and the home country have hardly increased and even declined in recent years as interdependencies and mutual obligations between EU member states have become more apparent in the context of the economic crisis. It appears that in situations of conflicts of interest between the national and the European level, citizens still opt for the national level, limiting their affections to their home country and the national community.

4.4 EU Enlargement and the Economic and Financial Crisis and Levels of European Identification

Having explored the general trends in citizens' identification with Europe, the remainder of this chapter will concentrate on the consequences of the EU's enlargement to Central and Eastern Europe in 2004/2007 and the onset of the financial and economic crisis in late 2008 for citizens' identification with Europe.

Levels of European identification are likely to vary between member states due to country-specific experiences with EU integration. Member states joined the EU at different times and against different historical backgrounds. EU enlargement to Central and Eastern Europe and the financial and economic crisis are instances that affected member states in different ways and to different degrees, potentially resulting in different trends in European identification among national publics. To examine these expectations empirically, I distinguish groups of EU member states by length of membership (EU6, EU15, and EU27), countries' pre-accession history (EU15 vs. CEE), and their role in the recent economic crisis (countries at risk of sovereign default; debtor vs. creditor countries; Eurozone vs. non-Eurozone member states). The analysis will be limited to citizens' self-categorisation as European and attachment to Europe and the European Union, as no data on European pride is available for the second half of the 2000s.

4.4.1 EU Enlargement to CEE and Citizens' Identification with Europe

As regards developments in European identification in the context of EU enlargement to Central and Eastern Europe, we observe only minor fluctuations in the EU aggregate in response to the 2004/2007 accession rounds. The share of respondents describing themselves (also) as European (*self-categorisation as European)* decreases slightly: standing at 59% in 2002 (2 years before enlargement), it falls to 55% in 2007 when Bulgaria and Romania accessed the EU (cf. Fig. 4.1). *Attachment to Europe*, on the other hand, temporally peaks in the immediate aftermath of enlargement 2004 (cf. Fig. 4.5). The proportion of respondents feeling fairly or very attached to Europe increases from around 60% in autumn 2003 to about 69% in autumn 2004 and drops back to 64% in spring 2006. The temporal increase suggests a positive effect of enlargement on citizens' attachment to Europe, but also is part of a longer upward trend in European attachment starting in the 1990s. A similar increase is visible in citizens' *attachment to the EU* in the 2000s, starting from a relatively low 42% in early 2002 to 52% in spring 2006 and 55% in spring 2007. *European pride*, finally, does not fluctuate much during the accession period, either (cf. Fig. 4.3). The proportion of respondents' indicating to be fairly or very proud to be European raises temporarily from 68% in autumn 2003 to 72% in autumn 2004, but falls back to 69% in autumn 2005.

Overall, enlargement appears to have caused only minor changes in European identification in the EU population as a whole, but there may be differences between the so-called 'old' member states (EU6, EU15) and the 'new' member states from Central and Eastern Europe. For example, we may expect identification with Europe to be stronger in the old member states because citizens in these countries have had more time to become accustomed to the European Union and experience European integration. Such socialisation effects should lead to higher levels of European identification in the EU15 member states than in the CEE countries (and higher levels of identification in the six EU founding countries than the rest of the EU member states). On the other hand, we may expect 'salience effects' in the CEE countries whereby the prominent role that the EU played in these countries during the accession period leads to higher levels of identification in the aftermath of enlargement.

The trends in European identification by country group only partly confirm these expectations.

Figures 4.7, 4.8, and 4.9 compare levels of self-categorisation as European and attachment to Europe/the EU in the EU6, the EU15, the CEE member states, and the EU aggregate.

Overall, we find similar trends in citizens' self-categorisation as European and European attachment in old and new EU member states, although different country groups start out at different levels of European identification. This is the case for both self-categorisation as European and attachment to Europe/the European Union.

Levels of *self-categorisation with Europe* are initially lower in the CEE member states than in the 'old EU', whereby the gap in identification is larger between the EU6 and the CEE countries than between the EU15 and the CEE member states. After an initial peak in the CEE countries just after accession 2004, we observe similar developments in citizens' self-categorisation as European in the old and the new member states (cf. Fig. 4.7). The shares of respondents seeing themselves (also) as European in the old EU15 and the new CEE member state thus move in

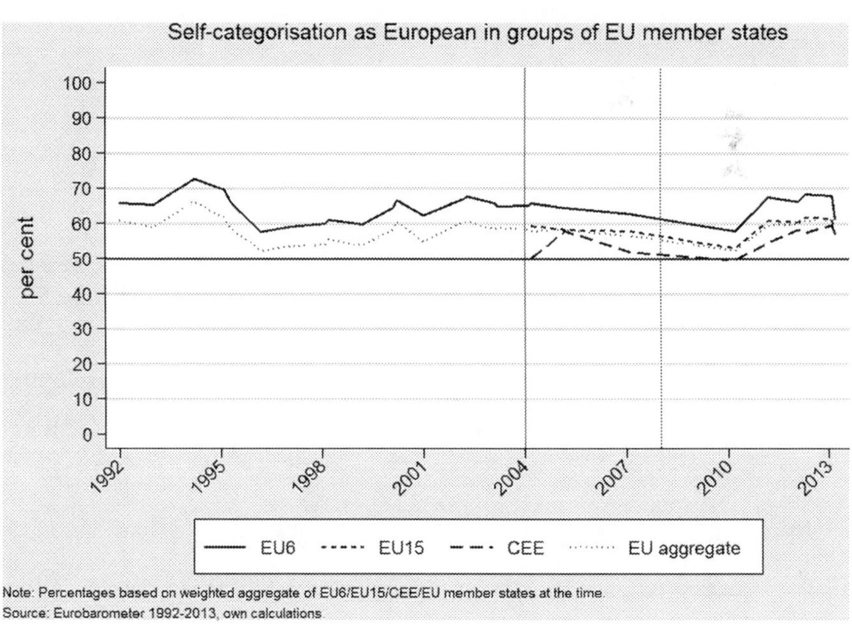

Fig. 4.7 Self-Categorisation as European in Groups of EU Member States 1992–2013

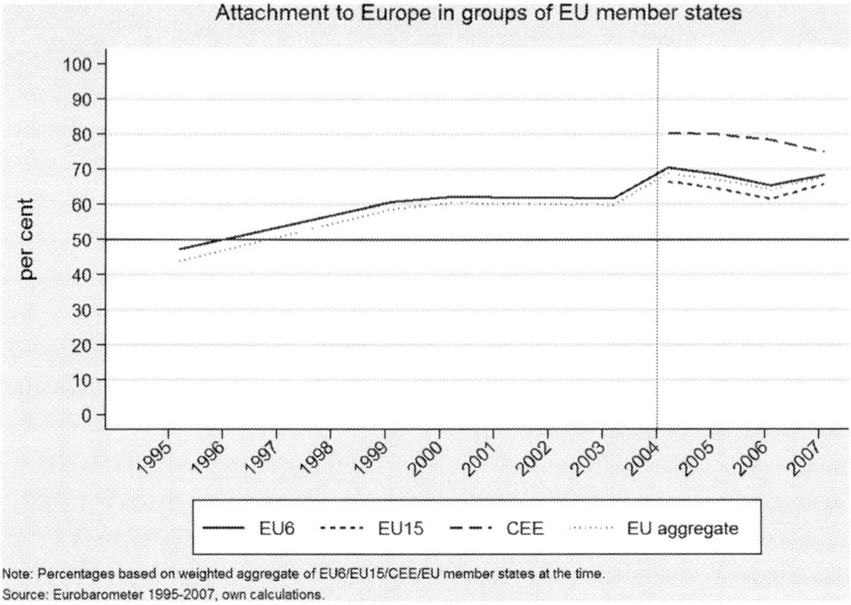

Fig. 4.8 Attachment to Europe in Groups of EU Member States 1995–2007

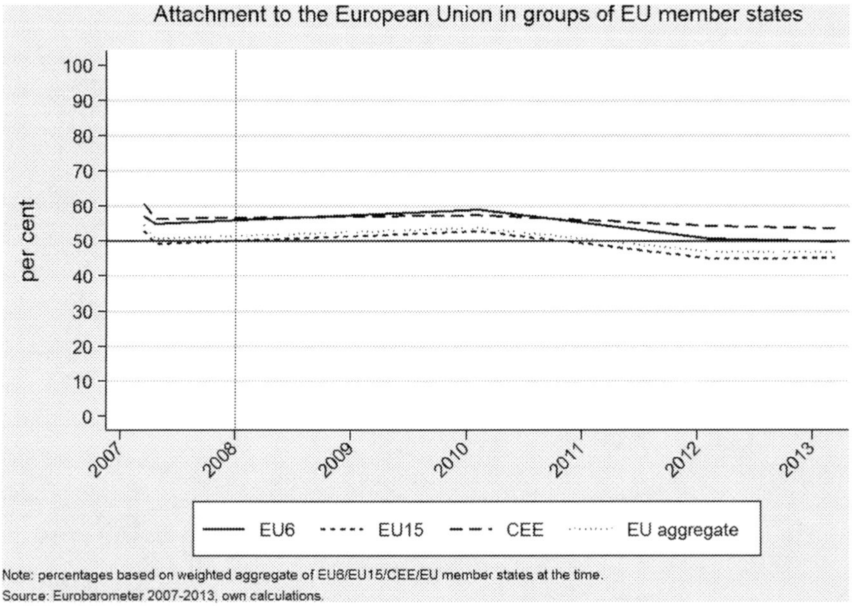

Fig. 4.9 Attachment to the European Union in Groups of EU Member States

parallel in the late 2000s. In 2012/2013, levels of self-categorisation as European in the old and the new member states converge, as European self-categorisation levels off in the old member states.

The picture is reversed in the case of *attachment to Europe*. We observe higher levels of attachment to Europe in the new member states in the immediate aftermath of enlargement; these gradually approach the lower levels of European attachment observed in the old EU15 member states (cf. Fig. 4.8). The differences in attachment between old and new member states persist after 2007, as the indicator changes from attachment to Europe to attachment to the European Union. Levels of *attachment to the European Union*, too, remain slightly higher in the CEE member states than the EU15 in the entire period under analysis (cf. Fig. 4.9).

The findings with regard to the development of European self-categorisation and European attachments in the EU6/EU15 member states and the new member states in Central and Eastern Europe in the aftermath of enlargement allow for different interpretations. On the one hand, the lower levels of self-categorisation as European among citizens in the new CEE member states compared to the EU6/EU15 provide support for hypotheses associating differences in levels of identification with Europe with the length of countries' membership in the EU. In this reading, the higher shares of respondents describing themselves (also) as European in the EU6 compared to the EU15 and in the EU15 compared to the CEE countries are due to socialisation effects. Citizens in the member states that joined the EU earlier in the process have had more time to experience European integration and internalise their status as European. Citizens in the new member states, in contrast, only gradually come to acknowledge their new status as an EU citizen and describe themselves as European.

On the other hand, the persistent gap in self-categorisation as European and European attachment between the EU6 and the EU aggregate as well as the comparatively high levels of European attachment in the CEE member states indicate that socialisation effects alone cannot fully explain differences in European identification. Other than length of EU membership and familiarity with EU politics there appear to be reasons that are specific to certain groups of member states and may explain the observed differences in European identification.

The initially high levels of attachment with Europe in the CEE member states, compared to the EU6 and the EU15, may be an expression of the generally rather pro-European mood in these countries during the accession period (Herzog and Tucker 2010; Wagner 2012). What is more, the history of these countries as former members of the Eastern bloc may add to citizens' attachment to Europe. After the fall of the Iron Curtain and the rapprochement with Western Europe, citizens in the CEE countries may have been all the keener to affirm their belonging to Europe (as opposed to their former membership in the Eastern Bloc and ties to Russia), resulting in the higher levels of attachment to Europe we observe in the CEE member states after 2004.

4.4.2 *The Financial and Economic Crisis and Citizens' Identification with Europe*

Having explored identification with Europe in the aftermath of the EU's enlargement to CEE in 2004/2007, we now turn to the *consequences of the financial and economic crisis for European identification.* The analysis will focus on citizens' self-categorisation as European and their attachment to the European Union as these are the only items available for the post-2008 period.

Starting with developments in the *EU aggregate,* we find only moderate shifts in European identification after the onset of the crisis in late 2008. Levels of citizens' *self-categorisation as European* initially decrease slightly from 55% of respondents seeing themselves (also) as European in early 2007 to 52% in May 2010, but rise again over the following years, reaching 61% in spring 2013 (cf. Fig. 4.1). Aggregate *attachment to the European Union* also remains relatively stable during the crisis. In late 2007, just over 50% of respondents feel fairly or very attached to the European Union. This proportion grows to 54% in spring 2010, and then falls again to just below 47% in November 2013 (cf. Fig. 4.5).

While the crisis thus appears to have had only minor effects on European identification in the EU population as a whole, the aggregate levels may mask differences in identification between member states that were more or less affected by the crisis. Among the EU member states that experienced the most substantial consequences of the crisis are, on the one hand, the member countries of the *Eurozone,*[8] and, on the other, the *countries at risk of sovereign default*[9] in the aftermath of the global recession and, in some cases, receiving conditional financial aid from the EU/IMF.

While the global financial and economic crisis of 2008/2009 initially hit all EU member states, several Eurozone member states experienced sovereign debt crises, putting pressure on the currency area as a whole. Eurozone member states also provided extensive financial guarantees to countries in sovereign debt crises via bilateral loans and the various financial stability mechanisms agreed at EU level. In this regard, economic interdependencies became even more evident within the Eurozone. As a result, we may expect citizens in the Eurozone to become more sceptical and levels of European identification to decrease among Eurozone citizens as the crisis continued.

---

[8]Eurozone member states in the years 2007 to 2013 include Austria, Belgium, Cyprus (from 2008), Estland (from 2011), Finland, France, Germany, Greece, Ireland, Italy, Luxembourg, Malta (from 2008), the Netherlands, Portugal, Slovakia (from 2009), Slovenia, and Spain.

[9]These are Cyprus, Greece, Hungary, Ireland, Italy, Latvia, Portugal, Romania, and Spain. Apart from Italy, all of these countries received funding from one of the European financial assistance programmes and/or bilateral loans from Eurozone partners at some point between 2008 and 2013. Italy is included among the crisis countries as it has commonly been grouped together with Greece, Ireland, Portugal, and Spain—the so-called 'GIIPS' group—based on these countries' economic vulnerability in terms of e.g. debt-to-GDP rations, government bond yields, and current account and trade imbalances.

Likewise, the countries facing sovereign debt crises in the aftermath of the financial and economic crisis experienced more severe economic, social, and political distortions than other EU member states. These countries have seen the strongest decrease in the erosion of trust in national and EU institutions in the wake of the crisis (Armingeon and Guthmann 2014) and we may well expect a decline in levels of European identification, too.

Again, the trends in European identification for different country groups only partly confirm our expectations. Figure 4.10 displays self-categorisation as European in and outside the Eurozone between 2007 and 2013 and Fig. 4.12 shows levels of self-categorisation for the countries risking sovereign defaults after 2008.

Figure 4.11 show levels of attachment to the European Union for the same groups of EU member states.

Starting with the *Eurozone*, we see the trend observed for the EU aggregate repeated in the Eurozone, both with regard to citizens' self-categorisation as European and their attachment to the European Union. Levels of *self-categorisation as European* slightly decrease in the Eurozone in the early crisis years, but increase again after 2010 (cf. the solid line in Fig. 4.10). The trend in self-categorisation as European observed for the Eurozone countries differs little from the trends observed outside the Eurozone; however, the Eurozone-outsiders start out from considerably lower levels of European self-categorisation (62% in the Eurozone vs. 48% outside the Eurozone in 2007).

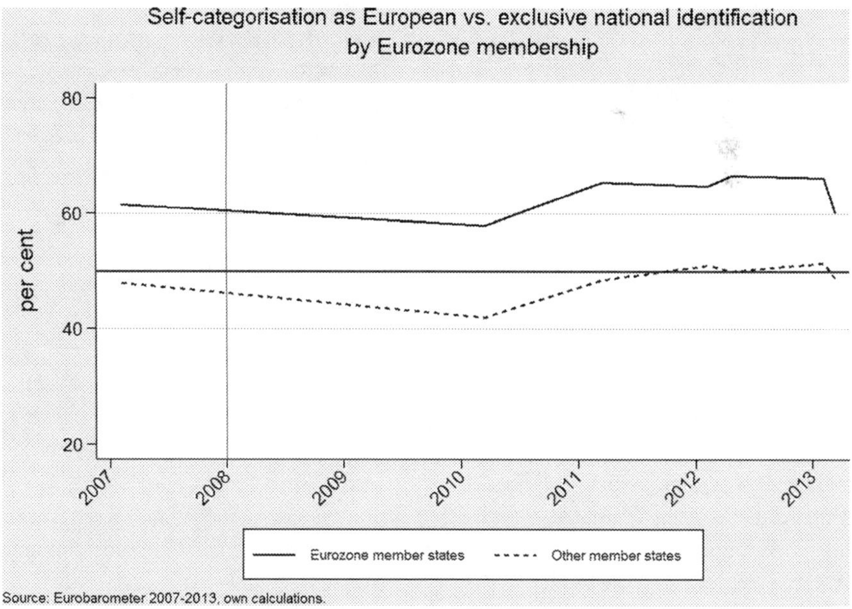

Fig. 4.10 Self-Categorisation as European and Exclusive National Identification in the Eurozone 2007–2013

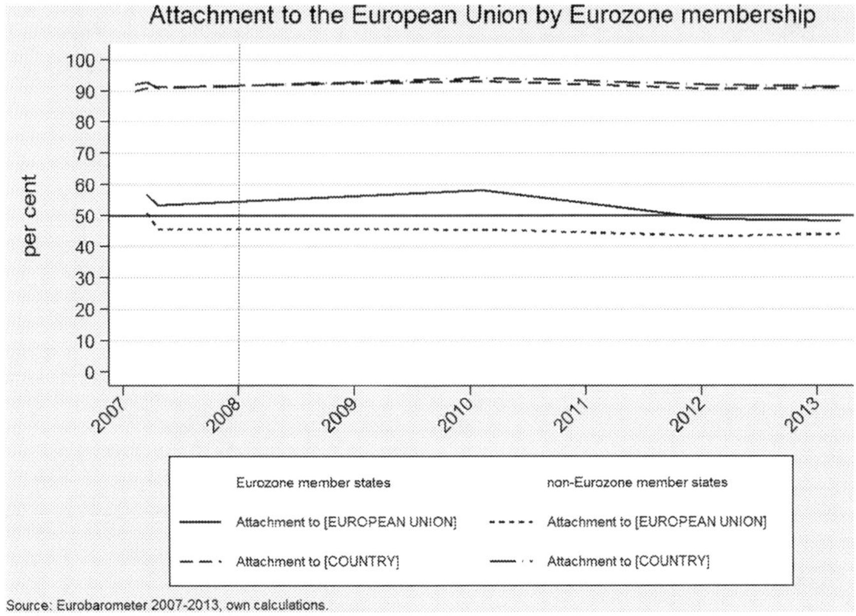

Fig. 4.11 Attachment to the European Union in the Eurozone 2007–2013

The pattern observed in the EU aggregate is repeated for the Eurozone also in the case of citizens' *attachment to the European Union*. Levels of attachment to the European Union rise slightly between 2007 and 2010 and fall again until 2013 (cf. Fig. 4.11). The trend in the Eurozone differs from the trend observed for member states outside the Eurozone. While attachment to the EU in the Eurozone temporally peaks in 2010, it remains stable outside the Eurozone over the crisis period. Levels of attachment to the home country, on the other hand, are virtually the same in and outside the Eurozone, with very little variation over time.

Turning now to levels and development in European identification in the *member states at risk of sovereign default* after 2008, we find more divergence from the general trends observed for the EU aggregate. As regards citizens' *self-categorisation as European* in the member states most affected by the crisis, there are no uniform trends in the shares of respondents identifying (also) as European. As Fig. 4.12 shows, the member states experiencing sovereign debt crises after 2010 started out with very different levels of European identification in 2007. We observe variation in levels of European identification in response to the debt crises in all of these countries, yet to different degrees and in different directions. Thus, in Hungary, Latvia, and Spain, levels of self-categorisation as European remain largely unchanged, with small increases after 2010. In contrast, we observe noticeable increases in the number of respondents identifying (also) as European after 2010 in Greece, Portugal, Romania, and, above all, in Italy, although levels of European identification tend to decrease again in these countries in 2013.

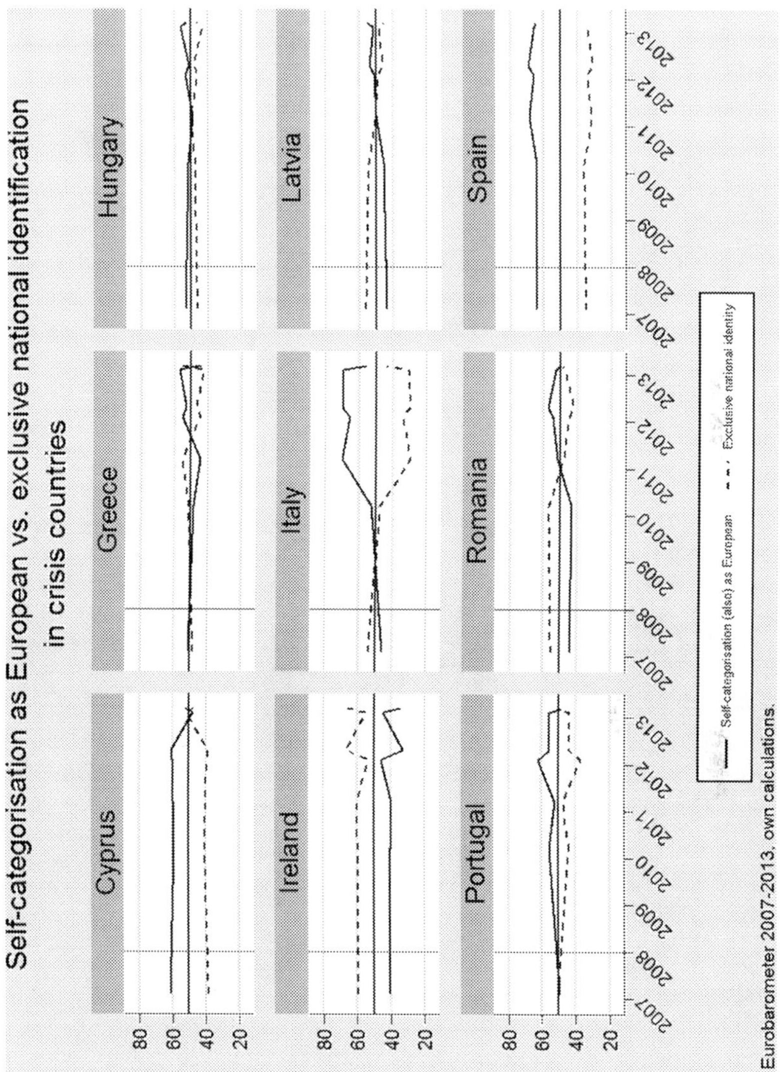

Fig. 4.12 Self-Categorisation as European and Exclusive National identification in the Crisis Countries 2007–2013

In Cyprus and Ireland, finally, we observe a decline in levels of self-categorisation as European from 2012 onwards.

The relative stability in respondents' *attachments to the EU* that we observed in the EU aggregate in the aftermath of the crisis also largely holds for the member states hit hardest by the crisis.

Figure 4.13 shows levels of attachment for the countries that experienced sovereign debt crises after 2010. We observe a notable and comparatively sharp fall in EU attachments after 2010 only in Italy; in the rest of the crisis countries, attachment to the EU remains more or less stable, with a more gradual decrease in Greece after 2010 and a gradual increase in Latvia from 2008 onwards.

To sum up our findings so far, we cannot confirm expectations of a general decrease in European identification in the Eurozone and the crisis countries after 2008. The trends we observe in the level of *European self-categorisation* point upward rather than downward, even as risks of sovereign defaults in a number of Eurozone member states became evident from 2010 onwards. Likewise, we find only scattered evidence for a general decline in levels of *attachment to the European Union* in the wake of the financial and economic crisis. Although fewer respondents express attachment to the EU after 2010, in particular in the Eurozone and some of the countries hit hardest by the crisis, the decrease in EU attachment is moderate in most cases.

A number of reasons may explain this relative resilience of European identifications in the crisis. First, the increase in the level of European self-categorisation between 2010 and 2013 in the EU aggregate and the Eurozone, as well as in some crisis countries, may reflect the high salience of EU affairs at the time. In this regard, the crisis may have alerted citizens to their status as a European and made them more likely to affirm their belonging to the European community. In a similar vein, the social and economic distortions caused by the crisis in member states like Greece, Spain, or Portugal and the media coverage of these events across the EU and in particular in the Eurozone may have led to an increase in feelings of compassion and solidarity among the member state populations that also led to higher levels of self-categorisation as European and/or prevented declines in levels of attachment to the EU. Finally, we might suspect that under the impression of a potential break-up of the Eurozone or even the European Union, citizens respond differently to the stimulus of the self-categorisation item than before and the question whether they see themselves as European 'in the near future'. As an effect of the crisis and the discussions about a break-up of the Union, the self-categorisation item might not only tap into citizens' cognitive identification with Europe, but also their hopes and expectations regarding their country's future within the EU. In this case, the observed increase in the number of Europeans identifying as European after 2010 may reflect not only a heightened sense of European identification, but also citizens' preference for remaining in the EU despite of the crisis.

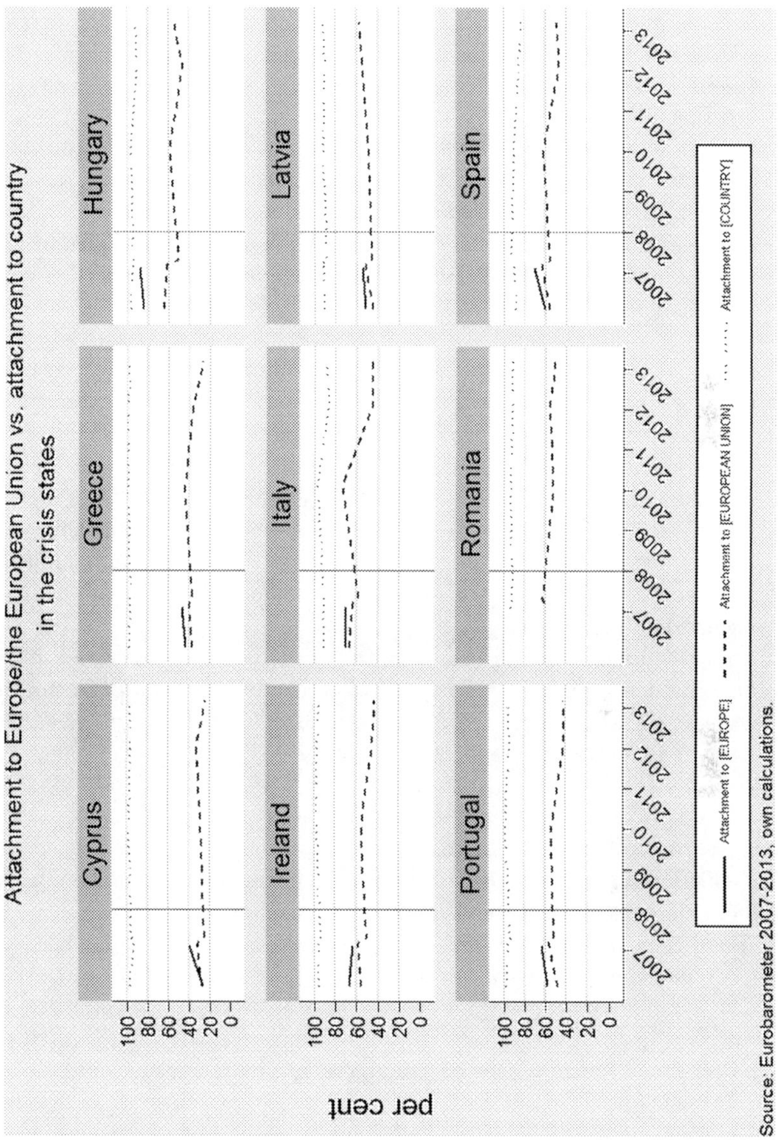

Fig. 4.13 Attachment to the European Union in the Crisis Countries 2007–2013

4.5 The Emergence of a Collective European Identity?

Three questions stood at the beginning of this chapter. We were interested in how widespread European identification is among citizens in the EU member states and which trends we observe in European identification over the 1992–2013 period; whether citizens have developed multiple identifications with both the European and the national collective; and how citizens' identification with Europe responded to Eastward enlargement and the financial and economic crisis. The objective was to explore and describe aggregate levels and development of citizens' identification with Europe that would allow inferences regarding the strength of a collective European identity as a macro-level phenomenon.

As regards general trends in European identification in the EU population, we find a majority of respondents in the EU claiming some form of identification with the European community. Europeans identify cognitively with Europe, describing themselves (also) as European; they show affective identification with Europe, affirming their attachment to Europe/the European Union; and they hold positive evaluations of the European collective, expressing pride in being European. The findings for the EU aggregate also widely hold for individual member states.

We further find substantial proportions of respondents holding multiple collective identifications to the national and the European community. Not only do respondents in their majority describe themselves by both their nationality and being European, but they also feel attached to both the national and the European level. Multiple collective attachments thus appear the norm for important parts of the EU population.

Concerning the impact of the EU's enlargement to Central and Eastern Europe and the financial and economic crisis on citizens' identification with Europe, we find no dramatic shifts in levels of European identification in response to enlargement and the crisis in the EU aggregate. In fact, the proportions of respondents describing themselves (also) as European and those feeling attached to Europe/the European Union increase only slightly after the 2004 accession round. While the EU15 and the new member states from CEE start out from different levels of European identification at the time of accession, the trends we observe in the aftermath of enlargement are largely similar in old and new member states.

Likewise, there is no major decline in European identification after the onset of the financial and economic crisis. We observe an upward rather than downward trend in the number of respondents seeing themselves (also) as European in response to the financial and economic crisis, in particular after the risks of sovereign defaults in the Eurozone became more and more apparent after 2010. Attachments to the European Union decrease over the same period, especially in the Eurozone and some of the countries hit hardest by the crisis; however, the decline is moderate in most cases. Rather than causing a sudden and steep drop in European identification, the negative effects of the crisis appear to accumulate over time, resulting in a gradual weakening of citizens' affective ties to Europe as the crisis wears on.

Which conclusions can we draw from these findings with regard to the emergence of a collective European identity? To recall, the previous conceptual discussion of European identity and individual identification with Europe proposed that a collective European identity will be the stronger, the greater the number of EU citizens identifying with Europe (extensity), and the more intense citizens' identification with Europe (intensity) (cf. Chap. 2).

By these standards, a collective European identity has emerged among EU citizens. More than 50% of respondents see themselves (also) as Europeans and similar proportions feel attached to the European level. This collective European identity has developed alongside rather than in opposition to collective national identities. Although European identity cannot match national identities in extent or intensity, multiple collective identities are a reality in the European Union by now. Collective European identity has also proven remarkably resilient in light of two decisive moments in the EU integration process, the EU's enlargement to Central and Eastern Europe in 2004/2007 and the onset of the financial and economic crisis in late 2008, followed by sovereign debt crises in a number of member states. The stability of European identity in the crisis in particular appears to indicate that the sense of community among Europeans is stronger than expected and may serve as a source for legitimising EU policies and support for European solutions to the crisis.

These rather positive conclusions with regard to the emergence of a collective European identity need to be qualified, however. First, the *extent of collective European identity clearly exceeds its intensity*. While substantial proportions of EU citizens identify with the European collective, their identification is often moderate in degree. Only small proportions describe themselves *only* (or first) as Europeans and few feel *very* attached to the European level. In this regard, European identity falls clearly behind national identities, which can build on intense attachments by large parts of the national public.

What is more, we still observe *distinct national patterns in collective European identity*. European identity is particularly strong in the six EU founding countries. Great Britain, on the other hand, continues to display some of the lowest levels of European identification in the EU. Forty years after EC/EU accession, a collective European identity is still merely nascent in the British public. While the British case may be extreme, it shows that the emergence of a collective European identity is by no means only a matter of time and socialisation into European practices as expected by early theorists of European community building (Deutsch et al. 1957; Haas 1958).

Most importantly, the strength of European identity varies depending on the *collective object of identification*. Collective European identity is strong if '*Europe*' is the reference point. It is noticeable weaker in both extent and intensity if the reference point is the *European Union*. It seems that while Europeans have developed a common we-feeling as inhabitants of the same geographical or cultural sphere, they still lack a common we-feeling as members of the same political community. In this sense, there now is a robust collective *European* identity, whereas a strong collective *European Union* identity is yet to emerge.

Appendix

Table 4.2 Eurobarometer surveys used for descriptive analysis

EB no.	Month of survey	Year of survey	Countries included	Sample size
EB 37	March/April	1992	EU 12	13,082
EB 40	October/November	1993	EU 12	13,073
EB 42	November/December	1994	EU 12	13,063
EB 43.1	April/May	1995	EU 15	16,166
EB 43.1bis	May/June	1995	EU 15	16,300
EB 44.1	November/December	1995	EU 15	16,346
EB 46	October/November	1996	EU 15	16,248
EB 47.1	March/April	1997	EU 15	16,154
EB 49	April/May	1998	EU 15	16,165
EB 50	October/November	1998	EU 15	16,155
EB 51	March/May	1999	EU 15	16,179
EB 52	October/November	1999	EU 15	16,071
EB 53	April/May	2000	EU 15	16,078
EB 54.1	November/December	2000	EU 15	16,067
EB 56.2	October/November	2001	EU 15	15,939
EB 56.3	January/February	2002	EU 15	16,038
EB 57.1	March/May	2002	EU 15	16,012
EB 58.1	October/November	2002	EU 15	16,074
EB 59.1	March/April	2003	EU 15	16,307
EB 60.1	October/November	2003	EU 15	16,082
EB 61	February/March	2004	EU 15	16,216
EB 62	October/November	2004	EU 25	26,807
EB 63.4	May/June	2005	EU 25	26,823
EB 64.2	October/November	2005	EU 25	26,925
EB 65.2	March/May	2006	EU 25	26,665
EB 66.1	September/October	2006	EU 25	26,647
EB 67.1	February/March	2007	EU 27	26,746
EB 67.2	April/March	2007	EU 27	26,717
EB 68.1	September/November	2007	EU 27	26,768
EB 73.3	March/April	2010	EU 27	26,602
EB 73.4	May	2010	EU 27	26,641
EB 76.4	December	2011	EU 27	26,693
EB 77.3	May	2012	EU 27	26,637
EB 78.2	November/December	2012	EU 27	26,739
EB 79.3	May	2013	EU 27	26,605
EB 80.1	November	2013	EU 27	26,829
			Total	730,659

Note: EU 12: Belgium, Denmark, France, Germany, Greece, Ireland, Italy, Luxembourg, Netherlands, Portugal, Spain, United Kingdom; EU 15: EU12 + Austria, Finland, Sweden; EU 25: EU15 + Cyprus, the Czech Republic, Estonia, Hungary, Latvia, Lithuania, Malta, Poland, Slvakia, Slovenia; EU 27: EU25 + Bulgaria, Romania

References

Armingeon, K., & Guthmann, K. (2014). Democracy in crisis? The declining support for national democracy in European countries, 2007–2011. *European Journal of Political Research, 53*(3), 423–442.

Bellucci, P., Sanders, D., & Serricchio, F. (2012). Explaining European identity. In D. Sanders, P. Bellucci, G. Tóka, & M. Torcal (Eds.), *The Europeanization of national polities? Citizenship and support in a post-enlargement union* (pp. 61–90). Oxford: Oxford University Press.

Blank, T., & Schmidt, P. (2003). National identity in a United Germany: Nationalism or patriotism? An empirical test with representative data. *Political Psychology, 24*(2), 289–312.

Caporaso, J. A., & Kim, M.-h. (2009). The dual nature of European identity: Subjective awareness and coherence. *Journal of European Public Policy, 16*(1), 19–42.

Citrin, J., & Sides, J. (2004). More than Nationals: How identity choice matters in the New Europe. In R. K. Herrmann, T. Risse, & M. B. Brewer (Eds.), *Transnational identities. Becoming European in the EU* (pp. 161–185). Lanham: Rowman & Littlefield.

de Vries, C. E., & van Kersbergen, K. (2007). Interests, identity and political allegiance in the European Union. *Acta Politica, 42*(2–3), 307–328.

Deutsch, K. W., Burrell, S. A., & Kann, R. A. (1957). *Political community and the North Atlantic area: International organization in the light of historical experience*. Princeton, NJ: Princeton University Press.

Duchesne, S., & Frognier, A.-P. (2008). National and European identifications: A dual relationship. *Comparative European Politics, 6*(2), 143.

Fuchs, D., Guinaudeau, I., & Schubert, S. (2009). National identity, European identity, and euroscepticism. In D. Fuchs, R. Magni-Berton, & A. Roger (Eds.), *Euroscepticism. Images of Europea among mass publics and political elites* (pp. 91–112). Opladen/Farmington Hills: Barbara Budrich Publishers.

Fuchs, D., & Schneider, C. (2011). Support of the EU and European identity: Some descriptive results. In D. Fuchs & H.-D. Klingemann (Eds.), *Cultural diversity, European identity and the legitimacy of the EU* (pp. 61–85). Cheltenham: Edward Elgar Publishing.

Haas, E. B. (1958). *The Uniting of Europe: Political, social, and economic forces 1950–57*. Stanford, CA: Stanford University Press.

Herzog, A., & Tucker, J. A. (2010). The dynamics of support: The winners-losers gap in attitudes toward EU membership in post-communist countries. *European Political Science Review, 2* (02), 235–267.

Hooghe, L., & Marks, G. (2005). Calculation, community and cues – Public opinion on European integration. *European Union Politics, 6*(4), 419–443.

Isernia, P., Fiket, I., Serricchio, F., & Westle, B. (2012). But still it does not move: Functional and identity-based determinants of European identity. In D. Sanders, P. C. Magalhaes, & G. Toka (Eds.), *Citizens and the European polity: Mass attitudes towards the European and national polities* (pp. 110–139). Oxford: Oxford University Press.

Kaina, V. (2009). *Wir in Europa: Kollektive Identität und Demokratie in der Europäischen Union*. Wiesbaden: VS Verlag für Sozialwissenschaften.

Mummendey, A., Klink, A., & Brown, R. (2001). Nationalism and patriotism: National identification and out-group rejection. *British Journal of Social Psychology, 40*(2), 159–172.

Pichler, F. (2008). Social-structural differences in identification with Europe. *Perspectives on European Politics and Society, 9*(4), 381–396.

Risse, T. (2010). *A community of Europeans? Transnational identities and public spheres*. Ithaca: Cornell University Press.

Sanders, D., Magalhaes, P. C., & Toka, G. (2012). Summary and conclusions: Europe in Equilibrium—Unresponsive Inertia or Vibrant Resilience? In D. Sanders, P. C. Magalhaes, & G. Toka (Eds.), *Citizens and the European polity: Mass attitudes towards the European and national polities* (pp. 245–268). Oxford: Oxford University Press.

Sinnott, R. (2006). An evaluation of the measurement of national, subnational and supranational identity in crossnational surveys. *International Journal of Public Opinion Research, 18*(2), 211–223.

Tóka, G., Henjak, A., & Markowski, R. (2012). Explaining support for European integration. In D. Sanders, P. Bellucci, G. Tóka, & M. Torcal (Eds.), *The Europeanization of national polities? Citizenship and support in a post-enlargement union* (pp. 137–166). Oxford: Oxford University Press.

Wagner, B. (2012). *The formation of support for the European Union in Central and Eastern Europe: The role of national attitudes as cognitive heuristics*. Baden-Baden: Nomos.

Chapter 5
The Salience of European and National Identity for Political Parties in Europe

The theoretical model developed in Chap. 3 introduced party messages related to the European and national community as a country-level determinant of citizens' identification with Europe. Party messages are expected to influence European identification in the mass public to the extent that they provide citizens with arguments and considerations about the European community, a common European identity, and the consequences of European integration for the national community and identity. Depending on whether parties emphasise a common feeling of belonging together as Europeans or a strong sense of national identity, party messages should either reinforce or diminish feelings of European identification among national publics.

This chapter takes a closer look at the messages parties disseminate to the public with regard to a common European identity on the one hand and the national community and national identity on the other. It explores conceptually and empirically how parties emphasise issues related to the European and national community and their respective collective identities. To assess long-term trends in party emphasis on issues of identity, the analysis includes national parties' election manifestos for all seven European parliament elections to date, from the first popular EP elections in 1979 to the latest EP election campaign in 2014. Three questions guide the analysis:

- How salient are issues of European and national community and identity among political parties in the EU member states?
- How has the salience of issues of European and national community and identity developed between the first popular election to the European Parliament in 1979 and the latest EP election campaign 2014?
- Do we see variation in party emphasis on community and identity in response to the EU's eastward enlargement 2004 and/or the onset of the financial and economic crisis in 2008?

Conceptually, the analysis of party manifestos builds on research on party competition over EU integration that explores whether EU integration leads to

S. Bergbauer, *Explaining European Identity Formation*,
https://doi.org/10.1007/978-3-319-67708-8_5

new structural conflicts with potential for political exploitation or links to existing dimensions of political conflict in the domestic context (Hix 1999; Kriesi 2007, 2010; Marks and Steenbergen 2004; Marks and Wilson 2000). These analyses show that European integration not only pits opponents and defenders of economic liberalization against each other, but also creates tensions between cultural liberalists and advocates of national culture and sovereignty (Bornschier 2011; Gabel and Hix 2004; Hooghe et al. 2002, 2004). This line of reasoning ties in with research that sees EU integration as part of a larger process of globalization and denationalisation which leads to intensified economic, political, and cultural competition between and within nation-states (Kriesi *et al.* 2006, 2008). The conflict over Europe thus has an economic *and* a political-cultural dimension. While the former revolves around questions of redistribution and market regulation, the latter is centred on tensions between traditionalist values and cultural and social liberalism, ethnocentrism, and immigration (Bornschier 2011). As EU integration widens and deepens, cultural issues are expected to gain importance for political contestation (Hooghe et al. 2002; Kriesi et al. 2006, 2008).

As regards the contents of party discourse on European integration, previous research has focussed on parties' framing of EU integration (e.g. Helbling et al. 2010), euro-critical party messages (e.g. Statham and Koopmans 2009), and references to specific policy areas and issues of European integration such as the European Constitution, the free movement of people on the common market, or the common agricultural policy (e.g. Arnold and Pennings 2009; Pennings 2006; Whitefield and Rohrschneider 2009; Wüst 2009). By contrast, the specific salience of issues of European and national community in party discourse on European integration has not yet been subject to systematic empirical analysis.[1]

The lack of empirical studies contrasts with the importance attributed to identity issues in the theoretical debate on party contestation over EU integration (see e.g. Hooghe and Marks 2009; Kriesi 2009; Kriesi et al. 2006, 2008). The present work seeks to fill this gap by providing a systematic analysis of the salience that national political parties attach to issues related to European and national community and identity. Previous research has mostly concentrated on how political parties emphasise *national* identity to dispute EU integration and, in particular, on the role of radical right-wing parties in this regard (de Vries and Edwards 2009; Halikiopoulou et al. 2012, 2013; Netjes and Edwards 2005). By contrast, the following analysis will explore party emphasis on both European and national community and identity, for parties across the ideological spectrum.

In so doing, it adds to the literature on party positioning and party competition over European integration in several ways. First, analysing party emphasis on

[1]The exception is the study by Silke Adam and Michaela Maier on 'National parties as politicizers of EU integration? Party campaign communication in the run-up to the 2009 European Parliament elections' (Adam and Maier 2011), which examines the salience of an identity cleavage in party contestation over EU integration in the 2009 European election campaign. However, their analysis is restricted to six countries (Bulgaria, Czech Republic, Germany, the Netherlands, Spain, and the UK) and one election campaign, using parties' televised advertisements as a data source.

European and national community and identity simultaneously allows us to assess the relative importance parties attach to issues of European community and identity compared to the attention given to the national community and national identity. Thus, we are able to explore whether parties actively promote a supranational political community or whether they remain centred on the national level when discussing issues of community and identity.

Concurrently, the focus on issues of European and national community and identity in party discourse allows us to assess claims of an increasing politicisation of identity by national political parties (Hooghe and Marks 2009; Kriesi 2009). By tracking party emphasis on issues related to European and national community over time, we are able to determine whether the salience of identity issues in the political debate over European integration has indeed increased in response to the widening and deepening of European integration.

Furthermore, by exploring party emphasis on European and national community in *domestic* political debates, we are able to assess whether the politicisation of identity issues is more or less pronounced in some member states than in others. While potential country-differences in the salience of issues of community and identity in national party discourses are instructive in their own right, they also allow further inferences with regard to role of political parties in citizens' identification with Europe.

The remainder of this chapter starts by outlining an operational concept of party emphasis on issues of national and European community and identity (Sect. 5.1) and develops a measure for inferring party emphasis on European and national community from parties' election programmes (Sect. 5.2). Subsequently, it presents the empirical evidence on the salience of national and European identity issues in EP election manifestos for the period 1979–2014, starting with a general overview of the salience of European and national identity issues in EP election campaigns between 1979 and 2014 period (Sect. 5.3), followed by an assessment of the consequences of the EU's enlargement to Central and Eastern Europe in 2004/2007 and the onset of the financial and economic crisis in late 2008 for the salience of identity issues in party manifestos (Sect. 5.4). A final section reviews the role of identity as an issue in party contestation over EU integration after the crisis (Sect. 5.5).

5.1 Conceptualising Party Emphasis on European and National Community and Identity

Previous chapters hypothesised that because few citizens interact with other Europeans on a daily basis and have the opportunity to experience communalities among Europeans in direct interactions, citizens need to be reminded of their own status as European through elite messages that emphasise the community of Europeans, its shared norms and values, and the meaning of a common European 'we-feeling' (cf. Chap. 2). The present chapter concentrates on the role of political parties in this regard and the question how and to what degree parties emphasise issues of European and national community and identity in political campaigns and public debates.

The salience of party messages on European and national community and identity refers to the emphasis parties attach to issues of national and European identity relative to other political issues. It can be inferred from the amount of resources (in terms of speech time, manifesto length etc.) parties devote to the distinctive properties and membership criteria of the national or European community compared to the resources devoted to other political issues.

Accordingly, the *salience of European community and identity* in party discourse is the higher, the more parties emphasise the community of Europeans as a group with distinctive shared interests and experiences; the more parties refer to a 'European way of life' and principles common to the European population; and the more they insist on the distinctiveness of the European group and a common 'Europeanness' that demarcates Europeans from non-Europeans.

Vice versa, the salience of national community and identity in party discourse is the higher, the more parties emphasise the distinctive interests and experiences of the national community; the more parties refer to a national way of life and traditions common to the national community; and the more they insist on the uniqueness of the national community, which sets the nation apart as a group and makes national attachments appear incompatible with European identity.

5.2 Data and Operationalisation

Party emphasis on issues of European and national community and identity will be analysed using national party manifestos for European parliament (EP) elections in the EU member states[2] from 1979 to 2014. Data on national party manifestos for EP

[2]To account for the high degree of internal fragmentation and regionalisation of party systems in Belgium and the UK, party manifestos are analysed separately for Flanders and Wallonia and for Great Britain and Northern Ireland, respectively. See de Winter et al. (2006) on the fragmentation of the Belgian party system and Webb (2000) for the distinctiveness of the party system in Northern Ireland compared to the rest of the UK. In both Belgium and the UK, the respective regional party systems have been found to be structured along different dimensions of party competition (left-right in Wallonia vs. ethnocentrism and political alienation in Flanders; left-right in Great Britain vs. Irish nationalism/loyalty to Britain in Northern Ireland). These differences may have consequences for the salience of identity issues in national party manifestos, which might be overlooked if parties were aggregated at the national rather than the regional level. In analysing Flanders and Wallonia and Northern Ireland as separate cases, I follow the EMP's coding scheme for the years 1979 to 2004, which codes Belgium-Flanders/Belgium-Wallonia and Great Britain/Northern Ireland as separate cases at the country level. The EMP country identification variable changes in 2009, now coding Belgium rather than Belgium-Flanders/Belgium-Wallonia and UK rather than Great Britain/Northern Ireland. To ensure comparability over time, I recoded and separated the categories Belgium and UK into Belgium-Flanders and Belgium-Wallonia and Great Britain and Northern Ireland, respectively, based on parties' country codes in previous years.

elections from 1979 to 2009 is provided by the Euromanifestos Project (EMP) at the Mannheim Centre for European Social Research (MZES).[3] The EMP codes manifestos of all parties represented in the European parliament at least once. Overall, the data set used for the present analysis includes information on 730 manifestos issued by 287 national parties in the run-up to seven EP elections from 1979 to 2009.[4] The analysis of the EMP data for the years 1979 to 2009 will be supplemented by excerpts from national party manifestos for the most recent EP election in spring 2014, for which EMP data was not yet available at the time of writing.

Due to different EU accession dates, the number of member states and national parties under analysis varies over the period under analysis. The great majority of countries in the EMP data set has seen at least two elections to the European Parliament, fifteen countries have held at least three EP elections, and eight of the EU27 countries have participated in all EP elections since 1979 (see Table 5.2 in the appendix for a complete list of member states and number of manifestos under analysis in each year).

Manifesto data lends itself in particular to examining party positions on specific issues over time. First, because manifestos are devised in extensive debate and usually ratified by party conventions, these documents are authoritative and representative of party policy at the time of publication (Budge 1987). Second, because parties issue new manifestos ahead of each election, party positions can be compared not only at any one election but also from one election cycle to another. The potential for cross-temporal analyses is one of the major advantages of manifesto data over expert surveys, which typically capture more long-standing ideological positions and appear less suited to observing dynamics in party positioning (McDonald and Mendes 2001). Given the prominent argument in the literature whereby parties' attempts to politicise identity issues in relation with European integration have increased in recent years (Hooghe and Marks 2009), such a diachronic design appears particularly suited for the purpose of the present analysis.

[3]The EMP maintains the approach first developed by the Manifesto Research Group (MRG; Budge 1987; Budge et al. 2001; Klingemann et al. 2006) in coding the number of arguments parties devote to different issues in their electoral programmes. It deviates from the original MRG framework by coding the direction of arguments, i.e. whether parties adopt a pro- or contra-position on the issue in question, and includes additional coding categories for European issues. The EMP coding scheme is 'mirrored' for different levels of government to determine whether a statement has an explicit focus on the party's country (national level), Europe or the EU/EC (supra-national level), or neither as the relevant political arena/actor. Overall, it contains 170 coding categories grouped into seven major policy domains. For more information on the EMP, see the project homepage at http://www.ees-homepage.net (accessed on 01 April 2015). For the 1979–2004 manifesto studies see the documentation by Braun et al. (n.d.), Wüst and Schmitt (2007), and Wüst and Volkens (2003). For the 2009 manifesto study, see the documentation by Braun et al. (2010).

[4]By-elections in new member states, i.e. first elections after a country joined the EU such as in Sweden in 1995, have been omitted from the analysis.

The *salience of party messages on European and national community and identity* has previously been defined as the emphasis parties attach to issues of European and national community and identity *relative* to other political issues. Accordingly, the salience of European and national identity in party discourse will be measured as the share (in percentages) of a party's manifesto dedicated to questions of European and national community and identity. Table 5.1 provides a complete list of coding categories used to operationalise party emphasis on European community and identity (upper half of Table 5.1) and party emphasis on national community and identity (lower half of Table 5.1), respectively. For example, appeals to European solidarity, references to a unique European way of life, and calls for cultural integration within in the European community are treated as indicators of party emphasis on European community and identity. In contrast, appeals to nationalism, demands to retain the national way of life within the EC/EU, and characterisations of the national community as a culturally homogeneous group are treated as indicators of party emphasis on national community and identity.

Three measures of salience are constructed, assessing *overall* party emphasis on issues of community and identity, party emphasis on issues of *European* community and identity, and party emphasis on issues of *national* community and identity respectively. The measure '*total identity salience*' thus refers to the overall proportion of statements devoted to the 17 coding categories listed in Table 5.1 in a party manifesto. Analogously, the salience of European identity ('*European identity salience*') is measured by the proportion of statements devoted to the codes reflecting European identity issues (items listed in the upper half of Table 5.1); finally, the salience of national identity ('*national identity salience*') is measured by the proportion of manifesto statements devoted to codes reflecting national identity issues (items listed in the bottom half of Table 5.1). In addition, a subtractive score ('*net European identity*') is calculated to assess whether statements on European or national identity are dominant in party manifestos. It is defined by the proportion of manifesto statements dedicated to European identity issues minus the proportion of statements dedicated to national identity issues.

5.3 The Salience of European and National Community and Identity in National Party Discourse 1979–2014

The analysis of EP election manifestos covers both the general salience of identity issues in party discourse and the specific salience of issues related to European and national identity. It starts with an overview of the salience of identity issues in the EU aggregate, followed by an analysis of party emphasis on identity issues in the EU member states. A subsequent section discusses potential effects of the EU's enlargement to Central and Eastern Europe in 2004/2007 and the onset of the financial and economic crisis in late 2008 on the salience of identity issues at the party level.

Table 5.1 Constructs and indicators of party positioning on national and European identity

EMP Var #	EMP code	EMP domain	Political level	Direction	Code description
European identity					
p2_601	European way of life	Fabric of society	Europe	Positive	Appeals to European way of life, the Occident, or Western Civilisation
p1_602	National way of life	Fabric of society	National	Negative	Opposition to patriotism/ nationalism
p2_606	Social harmony in EU	Fabric of society	Europe	Positive	Appeals for a common effort and solidarity in Europe, the EC/EU
p2_608	Multiculturalism in EU	Fabric of society	Europe	Negative	Support for enforcement or encouragement of cultural integration in Europe, the EC/EU
p2_302	Decentralization of EU	Political System	Europe	Negative	Support for more unitary, centralized Europe; support for more Europeanization in political and administrative procedures
p2_3021	Transfer of power to EU	Political System	Europe	Positive	Support for transfer of power and competences to the EC/EU
p2_203	Constitutionalism in EU	Freedom and democracy	Europe	Positive	Support for (specified aspects of) the constitution; Emphasis on the need for an European constitution
p2_607	Multiculturalism in EU	Fabric of society	Europe	Positive	Support for cultural diversity, communalism, cultural plurality in Europe, the EC/EU
National identity					
p1_601	National way of life	Fabric of society	National	Positive	Appeals to patriotism/ nationalism; support for established national ideas
p2_602	European way of life	Fabric of society	Europe	Negative	Opposition to a European way of life, the Occident, or Western Civilisation
p2_6021	Retaining national way of life in Europe	Fabric of society	Europe	Positive	Emphasis on need to retain national way of life and national cultures in Europe or the EC/EU
p1_606	Social harmony in country	Fabric of society	National	Positive	Appeals for national effort and solidarity in manifesto country
p1_608	Multiculturalism in country	Fabric of society	National	Negative	Support for enforcement or encouragement of

(continued)

Table 5.1 (continued)

EMP Var #	EMP code	EMP domain	Political level	Direction	Code description
					cultural integration in manifesto country
p2_301	Decentralization of EU	Political System	Europe	Positive	Support for less unitary Europe and more national autonomy; support for keeping up local customs and symbols
p2_3011	Transfer of power to EU	Political System	Europe	Negative	Opposition to transfer of power and competences to the EC/EU; regret for the loss of power and sovereignty of the nation-state
p2_204	Constitutionalism in EU	Freedom and democracy	Europe	Negative	Opposition to (specified aspects of) the constitution; No need for an European constitution
p1_607	Multiculturalism in country	Fabric of society	National	Positive	Support for cultural diversity, communalism, cultural plurality in manifesto country

Note: Notations and descriptions of codes follow the original Euromanifesto coding instructions (Braun et al. 2010, n.d.). *EMP Var #* refers to the variable label of the respective code in the Euromanifesto dataset; *EMP code* refers to the name of the coding category as indicated in the Euromanifesto coding scheme; *EMP Domain* refers to the policy domain in which a coding category falls; *political level* indicates whether the code has an explicit focus on the party's country or Europe/the EC/EU as political protagonist or political arena; *direction* indicates whether the coded statements have a positive or negative connotation with regard to the coding category; *code description* corresponds to the description of coding categories provided in the Euromanifesto coding scheme

Extant research shows an increase in the overall salience of European issues in party discourse over the course of EU integration (Pennings 2006; Ray 1999; Steenbergen and Scott 2004). It shows that parties increasingly address not only EU integration as such, but also the consequences of EU integration for national politics and national customs and traditions (Binder and Wüst 2004; Wüst and Schmitt 2007). These findings give reason to expect that parties will put more emphasis on issues of national community and identity, the more EU integration proceeds and the more EU competencies extend to areas such as monetary policy or immigration and asylum that are closely linked to concepts of national community and identity.

On the other hand, the most visible signs of EU integration such as the common currency and the abolition of border controls also lay bare the growing interdependence among EU member states. By now, the European Community has emerged as a genuine political community with common external borders and common symbols such as the European passport and the European flag. Emphasising common European values and a common European heritage is a way for parties to provide a normative rationale for the European project that goes beyond arguments based on pure cost-benefit calculations. Promoting a collective European identity can provide the necessary underpinning for the form of political integration that the EU has embarked on since Maastricht. In this logic, we should expect an increase in the salience of issues related to *European* community and identity in response to the widening and deepening of EU integration.

In short, the question is whether the growing impact of EU policies at the national level has consequences for how national parties address European integration in their election campaigns. Have parties put more emphasis on issues of *national* community and identity as EU integration proceeds and takes over core competences of the nation state? Or have parties responded to the widening and deepening of EU integration by emphasising the *European* community and a common European heritage so as to provide a normative rationale for the form of political integration that the EU has embarked on since Maastricht?

Figure 5.1 plots aggregate shares of identity issues in party manifestos over time (see Table 5.3 in the appendix for mean shares of identity issues per member state). A first look at the data reveals that identity is not a minor issue in party campaigns. On average, parties in the EU27 dedicate about 9% of their EP election programmes to issues of identity, a higher share than for many other policy domains, including social justice, agricultural policies, and environmental protection (see results in

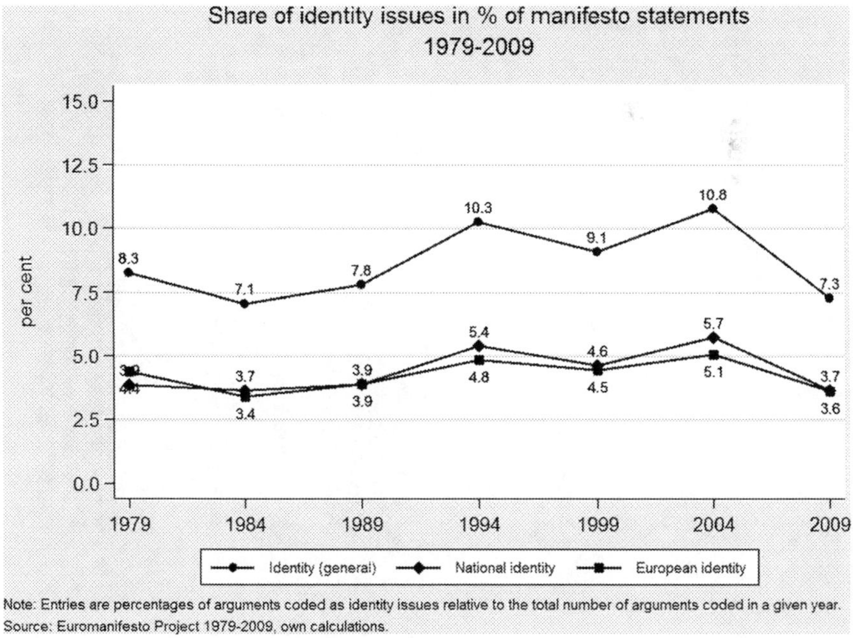

Fig. 5.1 Salience of identity issues in party manifestos 1979–2009

Wüst 2009; Wüst and Schmitt 2007). We also find some evidence for an increase in the salience of identity issues in response to the widening and deepening of European integration. Between 1984 and 1994, i.e. the decade when the Maastricht treaty was negotiated and came into force, the total share of identity issues in party manifestos increased by about three percentage points; identity shares reached a high of 10.8% in 2004 when the EP election campaign coincided with eastward enlargement.

National and European identity are about equally salient in party manifestos; both become more salient from 1989 onwards. The increase in salience is slightly more pronounced for national identity in the 1994 and 2004 campaigns, i.e. just after the entry into force of the Maastricht treaty and the accession of the new member states from Central and Eastern Europe. On the other hand, parties appear quick to shift attention away from questions of identity when other issues become more pressing: identity issues were least salient in 2009 when the economic and financial crisis dominated the agenda.

Turning to the salience of identity issues within EU member states, Figs. 5.2 and 5.3 rank member states by average shares of party manifestos dedicated to issues of European and national identity. Starting with party emphasis on a common European identity and community, we can distinguish three groups of member states (cf. Fig. 5.2). In a first group of member states comprised of Bulgaria, Great Britain, Ireland, Northern Ireland, Latvia, Greece, Estonia, Sweden, and Cyprus, political parties devote little space to European identity, with less than 3% of party

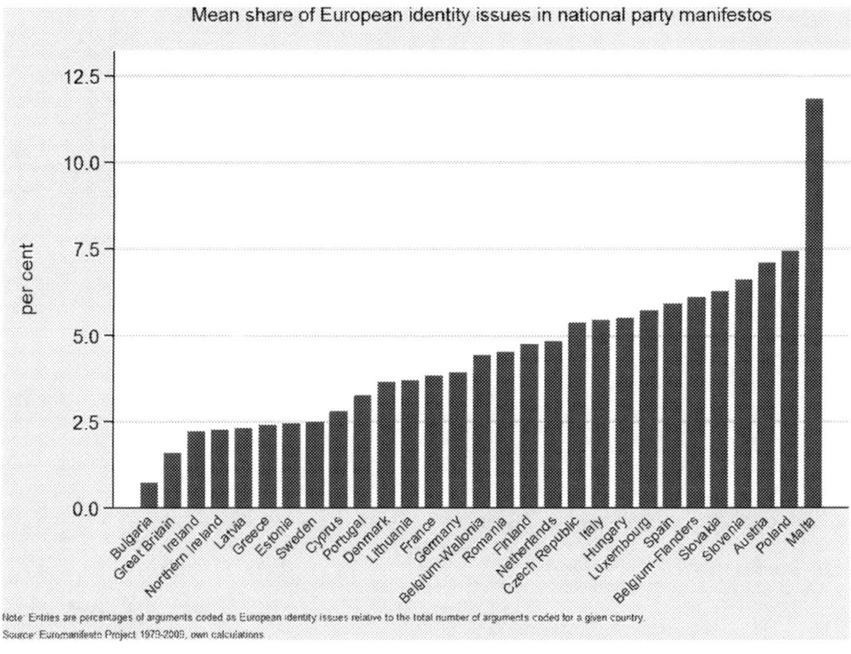

Fig. 5.2 Average salience of European identity issues by member state

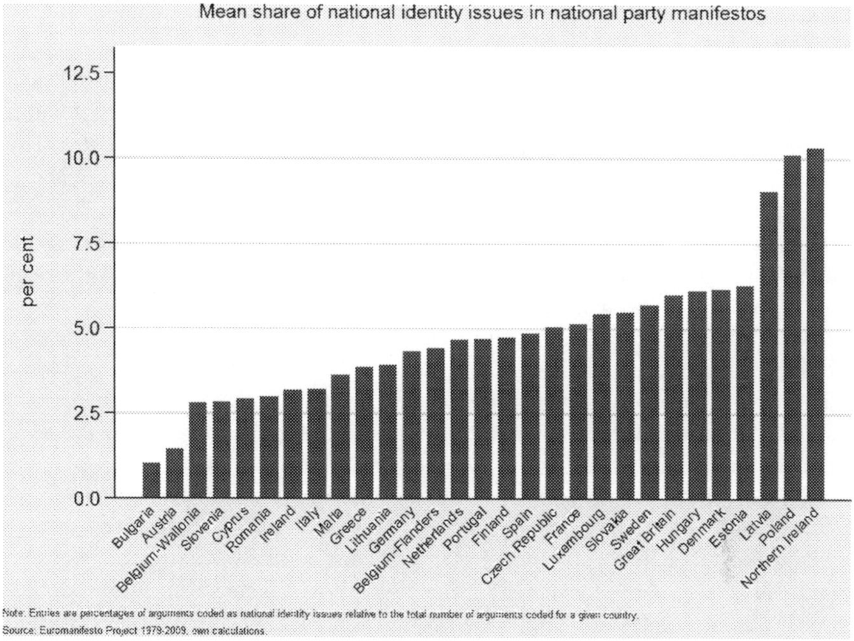

Fig. 5.3 Average salience of national identity issues by member state

manifestos dedicated to issues of European community and identity. In a second group of member states, parties pay moderate attention to questions of European community and identity, with between 3% and 5% of party manifestos addressing these issues (Portugal, Denmark, Lithuania, France, Germany, Belgium-Wallonia, Romania, Finland, and the Netherlands). Finally, in a third group of member states, issues of European identity and community take up more than 5% of party manifestos (Czech Republic, Italy, Hungary, Luxembourg, Spain, Belgium-Flanders, Slovakia, Slovenia, Austria, Poland, and Malta).

Malta, and to a lesser extent Bulgaria, are the clear outliers at the two extremes of the spectrum. In Malta, the high overall share of European identity issues (11.8%) is due mainly to the 2009 EP election campaign, when national parties dedicated nearly 20% of their manifestos to issues of European community and identity. In Bulgaria, on the other hand, parties dedicated less than 1% of their manifestos to issues of European community and identity; however, this share is based on only one EP election campaign (2009), which was generally dominated by the financial and economic crisis.

As regards party emphasis on national community and identity, we can again distinguish three groups of member states (cf. Fig. 5.3). At the low end, we find Bulgaria and Austria, where issues of national community and identity make up less than 2% of national parties' EP election manifestos. In a second group, comprising the majority of EU member states, parties dedicate between 3% and 6% of election manifestos to the national community. At the extreme end, we find Latvia, Poland,

and Northern Ireland, where 9–10% of arguments in EP election manifestos address issues of national community and identity.

With European identity shares ranging between approximately 1% and 12% and national identity shares ranging between approximately 1% and 10%, we find a considerable degree of variation in party emphasis between EU member states. The rank orders of member states in terms of European and national identity salience at the party level further shows that party emphasis on national identity issues does not necessarily come at the expense of issues of European identity, and vice versa. Comparing shares of national and European identity issues for individual member states, we observe significant differences between member states with regard to the relative importance of national and European identity issues in party discourse (see also Table 5.3 in the appendix).

In a first group of countries, most notably Poland, but to a lesser extent also Hungary, Slovakia, Luxembourg, and the Czech Republic, parties dedicate a considerable amount of their manifestos to *both*, European and national identity issues. In contrast, in a second group of countries, *neither* European *nor* national identity issues feature prominently in party discourse. This is the case notably in Bulgaria, but also in Cyprus and Ireland. Between the two extremes, we find countries like Germany, Lithuania, or the Netherlands, where both European and national identity issues are emphasised to moderate extent. Finally, there are the member states in which *either* European *or* national identity issues are dominant in party discourse. Thus, in Malta, Austria, Slovenia, and Italy, parties emphasise issues related to a common *European* identity and community up to three times as much as they emphasise issues related to national identity and community. In contrast, in Northern Ireland, Latvia, and Great Britain, *national* identity issues feature more than three times as often in party discourse than European identity issues. To a lesser extent, issues of national identity and community are also dominant in Estonia, Sweden, and Denmark (see the net European identity shares listed in the rightmost column of Table 5.3 in the appendix).

National patterns of party emphasis on issues of identity and community—and, by implication, member state differences in the relevance of national and European identity issues—remain relatively stable over time. As a result, we find diverging trends in the salience of identity issues at the member state level. Figure 5.4 plots shares of party manifestos dedicated to national and European identity issues as well as the total share of identity issues in party manifestos for the EU member states between 1979 and 2009. While parties in Northern Ireland and Luxembourg have consistently emphasised issues of community and identity, party emphasis on identity issues has been moderate in Germany and the Netherlands. Parties in Ireland as well as in Greece have put only limited emphasis on issues of identity over the last three decades. In a number of member states, notable in the new member states in Central and Eastern Europe, as well as in Austria, Ireland, Portugal, and Spain, party emphasis on questions of identity and community peaks in 2004. Malta is the exception, registering far higher shares of identity issues in 2009 than in 2004. In Denmark, Great Britain, Italy, and, to a lesser extent in France and Germany, we observe a gradual increase in parties' attention to

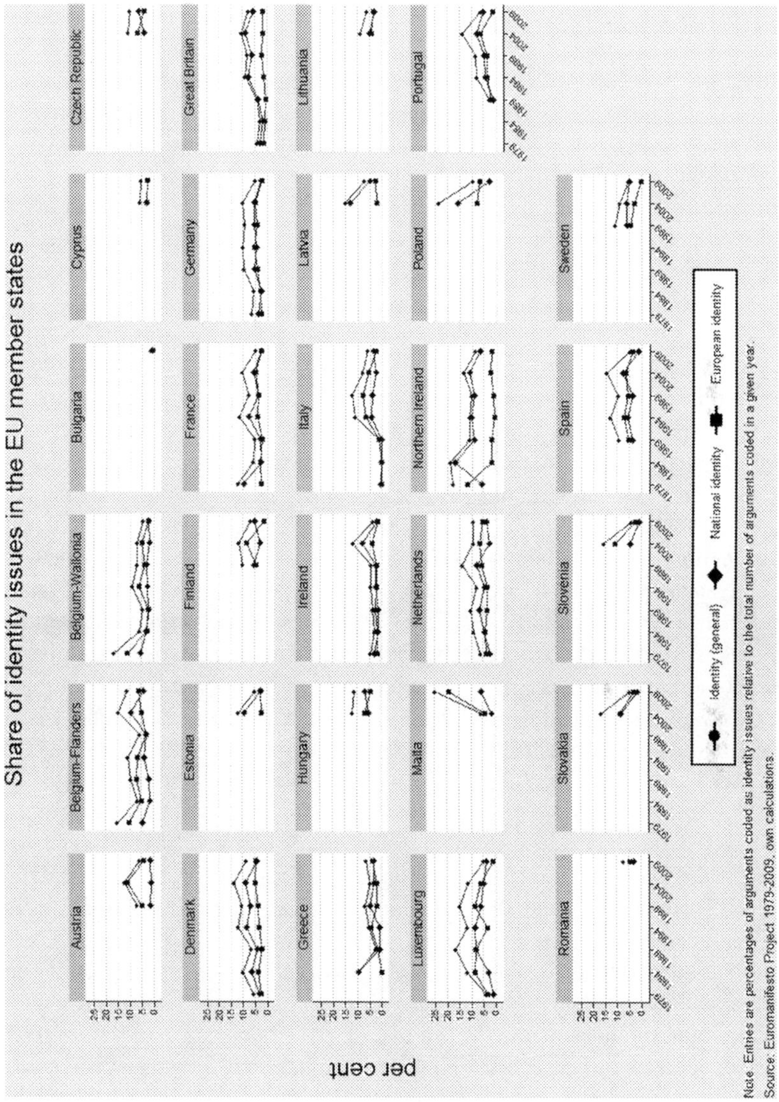

Fig. 5.4 Salience of identity issues in party manifestos by member state, 1979–2009

identity issues. In Luxembourg and in Belgium-Wallonia, in contrast, we observe a gradual decline in party emphasis on identity issues since the late 1990s.

What is more, the relative dominance of either national or European identity issues in party manifestos changes little over time. That is, parties in the member states consistently emphasise *either* national identity issues over European identity issues, *or* European identity issues over national identity issues, *or* emphasise both to the same degree. Figure 5.5 visualises the relative importance of European and national identity issues by plotting net shares of European identity issues in party manifestos by member state over time. Depending on the relative dominance of European and national identity issues in party discourse and the developments in net shares of European identity over time, four distinct patterns emerge.

In a first group of member states, parties consistently put more emphasis on issues of European identity and community than on issues of national identity and community. This is the case in Austria, Belgium, notably in the Flemish part of the country, Malta, and to a lesser extent, in Italy and Slovenia. In a second group of member states, parties dominantly address issues of national identity and community in their manifestos over the entire period under analysis. This is notably the case in Great Britain and Northern Ireland, and, to a lesser extent, in Denmark and Sweden. In a third group of member states, parties consistently dedicate about equal shares of election manifestos to European and national identity and community. This is the case in countries like Bulgaria, Cyprus, Germany, Lithuania, and Slovakia. In a fourth set of member states, the relative importance of national and European identity in party manifestos changes from one election cycle to the next. We observe such dynamics in Greece, Luxembourg, Poland, Finland, and France.

Country differences in party emphasis on issues of European and national identity and community do not correspond to commonly invoked differences between EU member states, e.g. in terms of accession date, size, or location in Eastern or Western Europe. Apart from Italy and Flanders, European identity is not particularly salient for parties from the six EU funding member states; on the other hand, European identity issues are dominant in Austria, which did not join the EU until 1995. Identity issues are relatively salient in the 2004 election campaign in some of the CEE member states; yet with the exception of Poland and Latvia, levels of identity shares in party manifestos observed in Eastern Europe are similar to those observed in some of the Western European countries and fall again in the 2009 election campaign.

To sum up the results of the analysis so far, national and European identity and community have been salient issues in party discourse over the whole period under analysis, accounting for up to 10% of manifesto arguments. Patterns of party emphasis on issues of identity vary between member states, both with regard to the extent to which parties emphasise identity issues and with regard to whether parties put more emphasis on European identity or national identity or emphasise both to the same degree. Finally, national patterns of party emphasis on identity issues change little over time and do not confirm to commonly invoked differences between EU member states in terms of length of membership, size, or geographical location. The following section will discuss to what extent the differences we

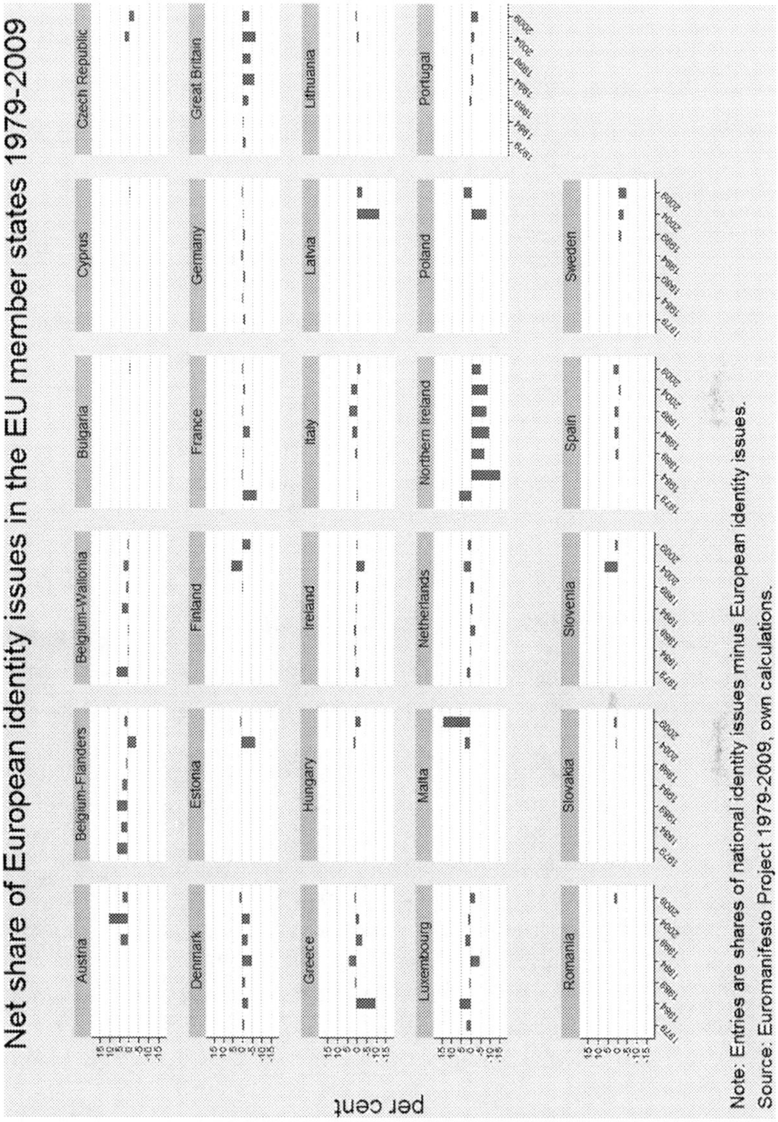

Fig. 5.5 The relative importance of European and national identity issues in national party discourse

observe in the salience of identity issues over time and between member states can be explained by the EU's enlargement to Central and Eastern Europe in 2004/2007 and the onset of the financial and economic crisis in late 2008.

5.4 EU Enlargement and the Economic and Financial Crisis and the Salience of European and National Community and Identity in National Party Discourse

While we find no uniform trend in levels and developments of party emphasis on European and national identity, can some of the differences we observe between member states and/or over time be related to the EU's enlargement to Central and Eastern Europe or the financial and economic crisis?

Starting with the EU enlargement in 2004/2007, we see a peak in the salience of identity issues in party manifestos in a few of the old EU15 member states, notably in Austria, the Flemish part of Belgium, Ireland, Portugal, and Spain (cf. Fig. 5.4). Only in Austria, however, is the spike in identity salience driven by an increase in parties' emphasis on questions of *European* identity and community. In all of the other countries, issues of identity and community become overall more salient because parties put more emphasis on *national* identity and community. Issues of identity are also prominent in the 2004 election manifestos in a number of the new CEE member states, in particular in Estonia, Latvia, Poland, Slovakia, and Slovenia (cf. Fig. 5.4). As in the EU15 member states, the salience of identity issues in these countries is mainly driven by parties' emphasis on national identity and community; Slovenia is the only country among the new members from CEE in which parties put considerably more emphasis on European identity than national identity in the 2004 campaign.

With few exceptions, parties thus did not respond to the accession of ten new member states by putting more emphasis on a common European community, neither in the old nor in the new member states. Increases in the salience of identity issues in the 2004 EP election campaign were mainly due to increased emphasis on national identity and community. One possible explanation of the dominance of the national community we observe in party discourse in both old and new member states may be the framing of domestic debates on enlargement that shaped the political context of the 2004 EP election campaign. We know from media analyses that the coverage of the EU's enlargement to CEE in the member states predominantly focussed on the domestic consequences of enlargement, in particular the effects on national labour markets (Dursun-Ozkanca 2011; Inthorn 2006; Light and Young 2009; van Noije 2010). Although enlargement had already been formally completed by the time of the 2004 EP elections,[5] a closer look at the 2004

[5]The ten new member states from CEE officially joined the EU on 01 May 2004; the 2004 EP elections were held between 10 and 13 June 2004.

manifestos[6] shows that parties still addressed the consequences of enlargement in the election campaign. In Germany, for example, all major parties apart from the PDS opened their election programmes with references to the 2004 enlargement round; all linked the accession of new Central and Eastern European member states to new opportunities for the German export economy (cf. BÜNDNIS 90/DIE GRÜNEN 2004; CDU 2004; FDP 2004; SPD 2004). Likewise, the French UMP not only considered enlargement a victory of the EU and its values, but also pointed to France's large potential on the enlarged Common Market (UMP 2004). In Austria, the ÖVP claimed that 'Austria benefits most of all from enlargement—more than any other EU member country'[7] (ÖVP 2004, p. 6; own translation) while in Ireland, Fianna Fáil declared that 'as a country, we have nothing to fear from the enlargement of the European Union' (Fianna Fàil 2004, p. 6). This cursory overview of the election manifestos indicates that national perspectives on enlargement apparently dominated the 2004 campaign; this may also party explain the higher shares of national identity issues observed in party manifestos.

What is more, in most countries, the rise in the salience of identity issues in party manifestos in the 2004 campaign appears to have been a singular peak rather than a sustained increase. In the majority of countries, identity shares fall again in 2009, in particular in the new CEE member states. It cannot be ascertained, however, whether the decrease in identity salience in 2009 reflects a levelling-off of the effects of enlargement or rather the onset of the financial and economic crisis, which may have redirected parties' attention to issues other than identity and community.

Turning to the 2009 election campaign and changes in party emphasis on identity that can be related to the economic and financial crisis, we thus see a decrease in the salience of identity issues in party manifestos in all EU member states but Malta and Greece (cf. Fig. 5.4). As might have been expected, parties' attention shifted away from questions of identity and community and towards economic issues under the impression of the financial and economic crisis (see also the findings on the dominant issues in the 2009 EP election campaing by Adam and Maier 2011; Bachl and Brettschneider 2011; Brunsbach et al. 2011). What is more, the shift away from issues of identity and community is rather uniform across the EU. We see the salience of identity issues decline in all but two member states and apparently independent of differences between member states, not only in terms of size, location, or length of membership, but also in terms of macroeconomic characteristics such as Eurozone membership and trade dependency. Unlike in the context of enlargement 2004 when parties increasingly addressed concerns for the national community and the consequences of enlargement for national

[6]The election manifestos for the EP elections 2004 and 2009 quoted in the following were retrieved from the Euromanifestos Project website at MZES, accessible via http://www.mzes.uni-mannheim.de/projekte/manifestos/ (accessed on 06 April 2015). Manifestos for the 2014 elections were retrieved from the parties' respective websites.

[7]'Österreich profitiert am meisten von der Erweiterung – mehr als jeder andere Mitgliedsstaat.'(ÖVP 2004, p. 6).

economies and societies, parties apparently did not (yet) link economic issues to identity issues in 2009. The fact that parties focussed on economic issues in 2009, while disregarding the identity- and community-dimension, may well reflect the scope and progression of the crisis at the time. Concurrently, we may expect that parties started to link economic and identity issues more closely as the crisis continued and changed from a financial and economic crisis into a sovereign debt crisis in the Eurozone, requiring extensive financial transfers between member states.

In fact, at the time of the European election campaign in spring 2009,[8] the crisis was still a crisis of the financial sector and the real economy. By mid-2009, all EU member states except Poland and Slovakia were or had been in recession in the previous months; fears of a sovereign debt crisis, on the other hand, did not emerge until the end of 2009/beginning of 2010.[9] As a result, when addressing economic issues and the crisis in the campaign, parties predominantly emphasised the need for investments to stimulate the economy and the need for stricter financial regulation and oversight of the banking system. An overview of the 2009 manifestos shows that parties across the board expressed such demands. To cite a few, on the left, there were calls for a 'strong European stimulus for growth and employment to overcome the crisis and its consequences' (SPÖ 2009); a 'real stimulus package' (PS 2009); more national and European investments in the field of innovation, research, and development, a European pact for labour, and stricter financial regulation at the European and international level (SPD 2009); as well as a 'European investment policy for development', stronger coordination of economic policy and stimulus packages among member states as well as 'new rules for the international financial system' (Partito Democratico 2009). On the right, parties demanded 'clear regulations for secure financial markets' and European funding for small and medium-size enterprises (ÖVP 2009); 'common actions for massive innovation and investment for industries in difficulty' (UMP 2009); a reform of international financial markets, including increased transparency and accountability, better regulation, and the reform of international economic and financial institutions (CDU 2009); and a 'redesign of the international financial system' (PDL 2009). On the other hand, we observe no references to measures of European financial solidarity or aids to individual member states in crisis that might be substantiated by invoking a common European community and identity.

By the time of the next European election campaign in spring 2014, the crisis had evolved into a sovereign debt crisis in several member states; the EU and the Eurogroup had agreed on extensive financial rescue mechanisms, leading to widespread and long-lasting controversy within and between member states; under

[8]The 2009 EP elections were held between 4 and 7 June 2009.

[9]The beginning of the European debt crisis is often dated back to autumn/winter 2009 when Greek Prime Minister George Papandreou had to revise the estimate of the government budget deficit for 2009 from the previous estimate of 6.7% to 12.7% of GDP. This was followed by the downgrade of Greek bond ratings by major rating agencies and a general decline of investor confidence in the Greek economy (Illing 2013; Nelson et al. 2010).

pressure from the EU and the IMF, member states at the risk of sovereign default had implemented austerity programmes and structural reforms in exchange for financial aids; and economic and social disparities between member states had increased as national economies recovered at different speed after the 2008/2009 recession. The crisis and in particular the need for bilateral loans and common financial rescue mechanisms revived debates over member states' mutual obligations, financial solidarity within the EU, and the costs of saving the common currency. In this regard, it not only raised economic questions, but also laid bare the consequences of increased economic and political integration in terms of national (financial) sovereignty and the risk of financial and economic interdependencies for national economies, national finances, and, ultimately, citizens and taxpayers in the member states. In short, as the crisis continued and required financial redistribution between member states, it increasingly raised questions regarding the sovereignty of the national community on the one hand and the strength of solidarity and loyalty within the wider European community on the other. Against this background, we may expect that issues of identity and community again played a greater role in the 2014 EP election campaign than in the 2009 campaign.

While manifesto data for the 2014 campaign was not available at the time of writing, a cursory overview of party manifestos for the 2014 EP elections indicates that parties indeed started to link economic issues to issues of solidarity and community in the 2014 campaign. Unlike in 2009, when parties across the board called for investments and financial regulations, in 2014, parties on the left and the right of the political spectrum appeared more divided with regard to the level of community—national or European—they addressed and appealed to. The left thus emphasised the wider European community and a common European responsibility to overcome the crisis whereas the right was more concerned with the national community and member states' individual responsibility to emerge from the crisis, as the German case exemplifies.

In fact, German Social Democrats highlighted their vision of a 'European Germany, not a German Europe', underlining that the country cannot do well unless its European neighbours do well and rejecting the idea of Germany 'going it alone' (SPD 2014). The Greens pushed this point even further, arguing that 'Europe has become part of our identity just as Germany, their region, city or community for many are [part of their identity]'. Calling for reliable, coordinated, and sustainable politics to avoid fission within the EU, they warned against letting 'break apart what belongs together' (BÜNDNIS 90/DIE GRÜNEN 2014). On the right, in contrast, Christian Democrats advertised 'solidarity in exchange for solidity', stressing their solidarity with the European partners while underlining that 'member states are themselves responsible' for overcoming the crisis (CDU 2014). The CSU put it more bluntly, calling on 'our European neighbours to make an effort and become more competitive' rather than blame Germany for its economic performance, because 'you cannot strengthen the weak by weakening the strong'. Financial aids are only to be granted to member states in crisis in return for structural reforms (CSU 2014). Unsurprisingly, the sentiment that European integration must not come at the expense of the national level was even more commonplace among the eurosceptic AfD who demanded ‘courage for Germany’ and a greater say in the European institutions to avoid further decisions to Germany’s disadvantage (AfD 2014).

While parties did not directly refer to national identity or the national way of life, at least on the right, concerns for the (financial) well-being of the national community appear to have become more prevalent in party discourse, which often also implies pitting national interests against European-wide solidarity. On the left, on the other hand, parties seemed eager to avoid this impression by promoting a sense of ‘being in this together’ as Europeans that transcends national (financial) interests and appeals to European-wide responsibility and solidarity. In this regard, issues of identity and community indeed seem to have become more salient again as the crisis continued and eventually required extensive intra-European transfers.

The above examples from party manifestos are of course restricted to the German case. Given Germany’s position as the main creditor and its role in the negotiations over bailout measures, German parties may be more prone to emphasise the financial responsibilities of the crisis countries and the need for reforms in exchange for financial aids than their counterparts in other member states. Analyses of national media coverage and national parliamentary debates, however, show that juxtapositions between fiscally responsible and irresponsibly member states and references to (national) economic interests rather than appeals to European solidarity were common in other member states, too (Closa and Maatsch 2014; Mazzoni and Barbieri 2014; Picard 2015; Schmidt 2014). The German findings may thus well be representative for parties in other EU member countries, in particular in other creditor countries. Overall, there is reason to assume that in the course of the crisis parties have started to link economic issues to identity issues, making issues of community and identity again more salient in party discourse than in previous years.

We can sum up the findings with regard to the effects of EU enlargement and the financial and economic crisis on the salience of issues of European and national community and identity in party manifestos as follows: Identity issues became more salient in a number of EU member states, both in the old EU15 and in CEE in the 2004 EP election campaign, which took place in the context of the EU’s enlargement to Central and Eastern Europe. This rise in the salience of identity issues in party manifestos was driven mainly by parties’ emphasis on issues of *national* identity and community; a cursory overview of party manifestos further indicates that parties promoted national perspectives on Eastward enlargement in their election programmes. Under the impression of the financial and economic crisis, parties’ attention shifted away from question of identity and community, leading to a decline in the salience of identity issues in almost all member states in 2009. As the crisis continued, turning from a crisis of the financial sector and the real economy into a sovereign debt crisis in the Eurozone, and EU member states agreed to extensive financial guarantees to countries at risk of sovereign default, economic issues appear to have become more closely linked to identity issues again. In effect, excerpts from German party manifestos indicate that parties put more emphasis on (divergent) national interests and national responsibilities on the one hand and European-wide solidarity on the other in 2014 EP election campaign than in previous years. In this regard, the crisis may have led to a renewed increase in the salience of European and national community issues in party discourse.

5.5 Identity as an Issue of Party Contestation Over EU Integration

The present chapter set out to explore the prevalence of issues related to European community and a common European identity on the one hand and the national community and common national identity on the other in party discourse in the member states. The aim was to gain a better understanding of party messages related to the European and national community as one of the main country-level determinants in the explanatory model of individual identification with Europe and contribute to the literature on the contents of party competition over European integration.

The *salience of party messages on European and national community and identity* was conceptualised as the share of issues of national and European identity *relative* to other political issues in parties' election manifestos. The empirical analysis examined the salience of issues related to European and national community and identity in national parties' election manifestos for seven European parliament elections between 1979 and 2014. It confirmed that identity is not a minor issue for political parties, with parties across the board dedicating sizeable shares of their election programmes to identity-related issues. Parties address not only concerns for national community and national identity, but equally emphasise the wider community of Europeans and a collective European identity. Thus, national and European identity and community have been salient issues in party discourse over the whole period under analysis, accounting for up to 10% of manifesto arguments. We find patterns of party emphasis on issues of identity to vary between member states, but remain relatively stable over time. Identity issues became more salient in party manifestos in the context of enlargement in the 2004 EP election campaign, mostly due to a rise in party emphasis on issues related to national identity and community. Under the impression of the financial and economic crisis, parties' attention shifted away from question of identity and community, leading to a decline in the salience of identity issues in almost all member states in 2009. Excerpts from party manifestos for the 2014 EP elections, however, seem to indicate that economic issues have become more closely linked to identity issues again as the crisis continued.

Which conclusions do these findings allow, first with regard to the contents of party contestation over European integration and claims of an increasing politicisation of identity issues in party competition, and, second, with regard to the role of party messages on European and national identity for citizens' identification with Europe?

Starting with claims of an increasing politicisation of identity by national political parties, we find only moderate support for a general rise in party emphasis on identity issues in response to the widening and deepening of EU integration. While we observe increases in parties' emphasis on issues of national community and national identity in individual member states, the European-wide peak in identity salience is limited to the 2004 EP election campaign; in almost all member states, the salience of identity issues dropped considerably in 2009.

Nonetheless, the findings for the three most recent EP elections campaigns (2004, 2009, and 2014) are instructive with regard to party mobilisation on identity issues. First or all, we observe an almost uniform increase in party emphasis on identity issues—and issues of national identity and community in particular—in the context of enlargement 2004, i.e. at a time when the European Union became culturally and economically more heterogeneous and differences between member states became more apparent. In this regard, party manifestos appear to reflect national debates on enlargement, which centred largely on the costs and benefits of enlargement for national societies and economies. After the drop in identity salience in 2009, a first overview of party manifestos for the 2014 EP elections gives reason to assume that issues of identity and community have become more important again in the last EP election campaign, i.e. at a time when the debate over the crisis had moved from stimulus packages and financial regulations to bailouts for highly indebted member states and European financial rescue mechanisms.

The excerpts from the 2014 manifestos show that depending on their position on the political spectrum parties do not only focus on the national level and the costs of intra-European transfers for the national community, but also appeal to feelings of belonging together as Europeans in order to defend bailout measures and European-wide rescue mechanisms. The claim that identity becomes more important as EU integration has more and more redistributive consequences thus also seems to find support at the party level, with parties emphasising both national and European identity in their election programmes.

Apart from inferences about the importance of identity issues in party contestation over European integration, the analysis of party manifestos also allows some conclusions concerning the development of a collective European identity among citizens in the member states. As a preliminary step to testing the effect of party messages on citizens' identification with Europe in statistical analysis in Chap. 6, we can compare the results of the descriptive analyses of individual identification with Europe (cf. Chap. 5) with the above results of the analysis of party manifestos. This gives a first impression of the relationship between identity salience at the party level and collective identifications among citizens in the member states.

Contrasting shares of identity issues in national party manifestos and citizens' identification with Europe by member state, we find parallels between identity shares at the party and the individual level. For example, parties in both parts of the UK predominantly emphasised issues of national identity and community over the whole period under analysis, while paying little attention to issues of European identity and community. This tendency is mirrored at the citizen level where we find some of the highest shares of respondents identifying exclusively with the nation in Great Britain and Northern Ireland. In contrast, in countries like Germany, Italy, France, or Luxembourg where higher shares of respondents identify (also) as Europeans, we also find parties to emphasise European and national identity and community more equally and vice versa. Overall, levels and development of national and European identity at the party and the citizen level thus appear to follow similar rather than divergent trends. Simply comparing levels and development of identity salience at the party level and collective identification at the individual level of course cannot determine whether parties influence individual identification or, on the contrary, parties respond to trends in public opinion by emphasising issues that are salient in public debates in their manifestos. The following explanatory analysis of individual identification with Europe will assess the effect of parties' emphasis on identity issues on European identification at the individual level.

Appendix

Table 5.2 Number of EP election manifestos by year and member state 1979–2009

	No. of party manifestos by year and member state							
	Year of election							
	1979	1984	1989	1994	1999	2004	2009	Total
Austria					5	6	6	17
Belgium-Flanders	4	5	6	6	6	7	8	42
Belgium-Wallonia	2	3	3	3	5	5	5	26
Bulgaria							6	6
Cyprus						5	4	9
Czech Republic						7	6	13
Denmark	8	6	7	9	10	8	8	56
Estonia						6	5	11
Finland					7	7	8	22
France	3	2	4	8	11	20	9	57
Germany	5	5	6	7	7	7	7	44
Great Britain	2	4	5	7	7	8	8	41
Greece		2	1	2	6	6	6	23
Hungary						4	5	9
Ireland	3	1	3	5	5	5	8	30
Italy	1	1	2	8	13	15	10	50
Latvia						7	7	14
Lithuania						10	8	18
Luxembourg	3	3	4	4	4	5	4	27

(continued)

Table 5.2 (continued)

	No. of party manifestos by year and member state							
	Year of election							
	1979	1984	1989	1994	1999	2004	2009	Total
Malta						2	2	4
Netherlands	6	6	8	7	7	9	8	51
Northern Ireland	1	3	3	3	3	4	3	20
Poland						8	6	14
Portugal			3	5	5	4	5	22
Romania							6	6
Slovakia						9	6	15
Slovenia						5	6	11
Spain			8	11	6	13	10	48
Sweden					7	8	9	24
Total	38	41	63	85	114	200	189	730

Table 5.3 Average shares of identity issues in EP election manifestos by member state

	Mean share of identity issues in party manifestos in %			
	Total	National	European	Net European
Austria	8.1	1.7	6.4	4.7
Belgium-Flanders	10.5	4.4	6.1	1.7
Belgium-Wallonia	7.2	2.8	4.4	1.6
Bulgaria	1.8	1.0	0.7	−0.3
Cyprus	5.7	2.9	2.8	−0.1
Czech Republic	10.4	5.0	5.4	0.4
Denmark	9.8	6.2	3.6	−2.6
Estonia	8.7	6.3	2.5	−3.8
Finland	9.4	5.0	4.3	−0.7
France	9.0	5.1	3.8	−1.3
Germany	8.2	4.3	3.9	−0.4
Great Britain	7.6	6.0	1.6	−4.4
Greece	6.3	3.8	2.4	−1.4
Hungary	11.6	6.1	5.5	−0.6
Ireland	5.4	3.2	2.2	−1.0
Italy	8.7	3.2	5.4	2.2
Latvia	11.4	9.0	2.3	−6.7
Lithuania	7.6	3.9	3.7	−0.2
Luxembourg	11.1	5.4	5.7	0.3
Malta	15.5	3.6	11.8	8.2
Netherlands	9.5	4.7	4.8	0.1
Northern Ireland	12.6	10.3	2.3	−8.0
Poland	17.5	10.1	7.4	−2.7

(continued)

Table 5.3 (continued)

	Mean share of identity issues in party manifestos in %			
	Total	National	European	Net European
Portugal	8.1	4.4	3.7	−0.7
Romania	7.5	3.0	4.5	1.5
Slovakia	11.7	5.5	6.3	0.8
Slovenia	9.4	2.8	6.6	3.8
Spain	10.5	4.8	5.7	0.9
Sweden	8.1	5.5	2.6	−2.9
Total	9.1	4.9	4.3	−0.6

Note: Entries are average shares of arguments coded as identity issues (see text and variable list in table) relative to the total number of arguments coded per year and country over the period under analysis. '*total*' refers to the *total* share of identity issues in a campaign; '*national*' refers to *national* identity issues; '*European*' refers to *European* identity issues; *net European* refers to the shares of European identity issues minus shares of national identity issues
Source: Euromanifestos 1979–2009, own calculations

References

Adam, S., & Maier, M. (2011). National parties as politicizers of EU integration? Party campaign communication in the run-up to the 2009 European Parliament election. *European Union Politics, 12*(3), 431–453.

AfD. (2014). Mut zu Deutschland. Für ein Europa der Vielfalt. Programm der Alternative für Deutschland (AfD) für die Wahl zum Europäischen Parlament am 25. Mai 2014 (Beschluss des Bundesparteitags vom 22. März 2014).

Arnold, C., & Pennings, P. (2009). Party positions on the European constitution during the 2004 European Parliament elections. [European Parliament, European constitution, saliency theory, cleavage theory, election campaigns, public opinion]. *Journal of Contemporary European Research, 5*(1), 24–42.

Bachl, M., & Brettschneider, F. (2011). Wahlkämpfe in Krisenzeiten: Ein Vergleich der Medien- und der Bevölkerungsagenda vor den Europa- und Bundestagswahlen 2009. In J. Tenscher (Ed.), *Superwahljahr 2009* (pp. 247–268). Wiesbaden: VS Verlag für Sozialwissenschaften.

Binder, T., & Wüst, A. M. (2004). Inhalte der Europawahlprogramme deutscher Parteien 1979–1999. *Aus Politik und Zeitgeschichte, 17*, 38–45.

Bornschier, S. (2011). National political conflict and identity formation: The diverse nature of the threat from the extreme left and extreme populist right. In D. Fuchs, & H.-D. Klingemann (Eds.), *Cultural diversity, European identity and the legitimacy of the EU* (pp. 171–200, Studies in EU Reform and Enlargement). Cheltenham: Edward Elgar.

Braun, D., Mikhaylov, S. F., & Schmitt, H. (2010). EES (2009) Manifesto study documentation advance release (user beware/pre-release B).

Braun, D., Salzwedel, M., Stumpf, C., & Wüst, A. M. (n.d.). Euromanifesto Documentation.

Brunsbach, S., John, S., Volkens, A., & Werner, A. (2011). Wahlprogramme im Vergleich. In J. Tenscher (Ed.), *Superwahljahr 2009* (pp. 41–64). Wiesbaden: VS Verlag für Sozialwissenschaften.

Budge, I. (1987). The internal analysis of election programmes. In I. Budge, D. Robertson, & D. Hearl (Eds.), *Ideology, strategy and party change: Spatial analyses of post-war election programmes in 19 democracies* (pp. 15–38). Cambridge: Cambridge University Press.

Budge, I., Klingemann, H.-D., Volkens, A., Bara, J., & Tanenbaum, E. (Eds.). (2001). *Mapping policy preferences. Estimates for parties, electors, and governments 1945–1998*. Oxford/New York: Oxford University Press.

BÜNDNIS 90/DIE GRÜNEN. (2004). Europa grün gestalten. Europawahlprogramm 2004 von BÜNDNIS 90/DIE GRÜNEN. Berlin.

BÜNDNIS 90/DIE GRÜNEN. (2014). Europa mitentscheiden—erneuern—zusammenhalten. Europawahlprogramm 2014 von BÜNDNIS 90/DIE GRÜNEN. Berlin.

CDU. (2004). Europa-Manifest der CDU. Beschluss des Bundesvorstands der Christlich Demokratischen Union Deutschlands.

CDU. (2009). Starkes Europa – Sichere Zukunft. Programm der Christlich Demokratischen Union Deutschlands zur Europawahl 2009. Berlin.

CDU. (2014). "Gemeinsam erfolgreich in Europa." Europapolitischer Beschluss des 26. Parteitags der CDU Deutschlands. Berlin.

Closa, C., & Maatsch, A. (2014). In a spirit of solidarity? Justifying the European Financial Stability Facility (EFSF) in National Parliamentary Debates. *Journal of Common Market Studies, 52*(4), 826–842.

CSU. (2014). Europaplan Bayern 2014–2019. Das Programm der CSU zur Europawahl 2014. Beschluss des Kleinen Parteitags vom 10. Mai 2014.

de Vries, C. E., & Edwards, E. E. (2009). Taking Europe to its extremes: Extremist parties and public Euroscepticism. *Party Politics, 15*(1), 5–28.

de Winter, L., Swyngedouw, M., & Dumont, P. (2006). Party system(s) and electoral behaviour in Belgium: From stability to balkanisation. *West European Politics, 29*(5), 933–956.

Dursun-Ozkanca, O. (2011). European Union enlargement and British Public Opinion: The agenda-setting power of the press. *Perspectives on European Politics and Society, 12*(2), 139–160.

FDP. (2004). Wir können Europa besser! – Für eine freies und faires Europa. Programm der FDP zur Europawahl 2004. Beschlossen auf dem Europatag am 17. Januar 2004 in Saarbrücken.

Fianna Fàil. (2004). Untitled.

Gabel, M. J., & Hix, S. (2004). Defining the EU political space: an empirical study of European election manifestos, 1979–1999. In G. Marks & M. R. Steenbergen (Eds.), *European integration and political conflict* (pp. 93–119). Cambridge: Cambridge University Press.

Halikiopoulou, D., Mock, S., & Vasilopoulou, S. (2013). The civic zeitgeist: Nationalism and liberal values in the European radical right. *Nations and Nationalism, 19*(1), 107–127.

Halikiopoulou, D., Nanou, K., & Vasilopoulou, S. (2012). The paradox of nationalism: The common denominator of radical right and radical left euroscepticism. *European Journal of Political Research, 51*(4), 504–539.

Helbling, M., Hoeglinger, D., & Wüest, B. (2010). How political parties frame European integration. *European Journal of Political Research, 49*(4), 496–521.

Hix, S. (1999). Dimensions and alignments in European Union politics: Cognitive constraints and partisan responses. *European Journal of Political Research, 35*(1), 69–106.

Hooghe, L., & Marks, G. (2009). A postfunctionalist theory of European integration: From permissive consensus to constraining dissensus. *British Journal of Political Science, 39*(01), 1–23.

Hooghe, L., Marks, G., & Wilson, C. J. (2002). Does left/right structure party positions on European integration? *Comparative Political Studies, 35*(8), 965–989.

Hooghe, L., Marks, G., & Wilson, C. J. (2004). Does left/right structure party positions on European integration? In G. Marks & M. R. Steenbergen (Eds.), *European integration and political conflict* (pp. 120–140). Cambridge: Cambridge University Press.

Illing, F. (2013). *Deutschland in der Finanzkrise*. Wiesbaden: Springer Fachmedien.

Inthorn, S. (2006). What does it mean to be an EU Citizen? How news media construct civic and cultural concepts of Europe. *Westminster Papers in Communication and Culture, 3*(3), 71–90.

Klingemann, H.-D., Volkens, A., Bara, J., Budge, I., & McDonald, M. D. (Eds.). (2006). *Mapping policy preferences II. Estimates for parties, electors, and Governments in Eastern Europe, European Union and OECD 1990–2003*. Oxford/New York: Oxford University Press.

Kriesi, H. (2007). The role of European integration in national election campaigns. *European Union Politics, 8*(1), 83–108.

Kriesi, H. (2009). Rejoinder to Liesbet Hooghe and Gary Marks, 'A Postfunctional Theory of European Integration: From Permissive Consensus to Constraining Dissensus?'. *British Journal of Political Science, 39*(01), 221–224.

Kriesi, H. (2010). Restructuration of partisan politics and the emergence of a new cleavage based on values. *West European Politics, 33*(3), 673–685.

Kriesi, H., Grande, E., Lachat, R., Dolezal, M., Bornschier, S., & Frey, T. (2006). Globalization and the transformation of the national political space: Six European countries compared. *European Journal of Political Research, 45*(6), 921–956.

Kriesi, H., Grande, E., Lachat, R., Dolezal, M., Bornschier, S., & Frey, T. (2008). *West European politics in the age of globalization*. Cambridge: Cambridge University Press.

Light, D., & Young, C. (2009). European Union enlargement, post-accession migration and imaginative geographies of the 'New Europe': Media discourses in Romania and the United Kingdom. *Journal of Cultural Geography, 26*(3), 281–303.

Marks, G., & Steenbergen, M. R. (Eds.). (2004). *European integration and political conflict* (Themes in European Governance). Cambridge: Cambridge University Press.

Marks, G., & Wilson, C. J. (2000). The past in the present: A cleavage theory of party response to European integration. *British Journal of Political Science, 30*(03), 433–459.

Mazzoni, M., & Barbieri, G. (2014). Grasshoppers against ants or malfunctions of capitalism? The representation of the European economic crisis in the main Italian newspapers. *Perspectives on European Politics and Society*, 1–16.

McDonald, M. D., & Mendes, S. M. (2001). The policy space of party manifestos. In M. Laver (Ed.), *Estimating the policy position of political actors* (pp. 90–114). London/New York: Routledge.

Nelson, R. M., Belkin, P., & Mix, D. E. (2010). Greece's debt crisis: Overview, policy responses, and implications. *CRS Report for Congress*: Congressional Research Service.

Netjes, C. E., & Edwards, E. (2005). Taking Europe to its extremes. Examining Cueing Effects of Right-Wing Populist Parties on Public Opinion Regarding European Integration. Berlin: Wissenschaftszentrum Berlin für Sozialforschung (WZB).

ÖVP. (2004). Europa-Manifest zur Europawahl 2004. Wien.

ÖVP. (2009). Wahlmanifest zur Europawahl 2009. Wien.

Partito Democratico. (2009). L'EUROPA CHE CONVIENE. Le idee e gli impegni del Pd per le elezioni europee.

PDL. (2009). ELEZIONI 2009: Manifesto del Partito Popolare Europeo.

Pennings, P. (2006). An empirical analysis of the Europeanization of National Party Manifestos, 1960–2003. *European Union Politics, 7*(2), 257–270.

Picard, R. G. (Ed.). (2015). *The Euro crisis in the media: Journalistic coverage of economic crisis and European institutions*. London: I.B.Tauris.

PS. (2009). L'Europe face à la crise: la relance des socialistes.

Ray, L. (1999). Measuring party orientations towards European integration: Results from an expert survey. *European Journal of Political Research, 36*, 283–306.

Schmidt, V. A. (2014). Speaking to the markets or to the people? A discursive institutionalist analysis of the EU's sovereign debt crisis. *The British Journal of Politics & International Relations, 16*(1), 188–209.

SPD. (2004). Europamanifest der SPD.

SPD. (2009). Europamanifest der der Sozialdemokratischen Partei Deutschlands für die Wahlen zum Europäischen Parlament 2009. Berlin.

SPD. (2014). Europa eine neue Richtung geben. Wahlprogramm für die Europawahl am 25.Mai 2014.

SPÖ. (2009). Wahlmanifest. Wahl zum Europäischen Parlament 2009. SPÖ-Bundesparteirat. Wien.

Statham, P., & Koopmans, R. (2009). Political party contestation over Europe in the mass media: Who criticizes Europe, how, and why? *European Political Science Review, 1*(03), 435–463.

Steenbergen, M. R., & Scott, D. J. (2004). Contesting Europe? The salience of European integration as a party issue. In G. Marks & M. R. Steenbergen (Eds.), *European integration and political conflict* (pp. 165–192). Cambridge: Cambridge University Press.

UMP. (2004). La France en grand, l'Europe ensemble. Synthèse présentée par la présidence de l'UMP.

UMP. (2009). Le Projet de la Majorité Présidentielle. 30 Propositions pour une Europe qui protége et qui agit. Elections européennes. 7 Juin 2009.

van Noije, L. (2010). The European paradox: A communication deficit as long as European integration steals the headlines. *European Journal of Communication, 25*(3), 259–272.

Webb, P. (2000). *The modern British party system*. London: SAGE Publications.

Whitefield, S., & Rohrschneider, R. (2009). The Europeanization of political parties in Central and Eastern Europe? The impact of EU entry on issue stances, salience and programmatic coherence. *Journal of Communist Studies and Transition Politics, 25*(4), 564–584.

Wüst, A. M. (2009). Parties in European parliament elections: Issues, framing, the EU, and the question of supply and demand. *German Politics, 18*(3), 426–440.

Wüst, A. M., & Schmitt, H. (2007). Comparing the views of parties and voters in the 1999 election to the European Parliament. In W. van der Brug, & C. van der Eijk (Eds.), *European elections & domestic politics. Lessons from the past and scenarios for the future* (pp. 73–93, Contemporary European politics and society). Notre Dame, ID: University of Notre Dame Press.

Wüst, A. M., & Volkens, A. (2003). Euromanifesto coding instructions. *Arbeitspapiere – Mannheimer Zentrum für Europäische Sozialforschung*. Mannheim, Germany: Mannheimer Zentrum für Europäische Sozialforschung (MZES).

Chapter 6
Explaining European Identification: The Impact of Enlargement and the Crisis on Feelings of European Identity Among EU Citizens

The present chapter turns to the *explanation* of individual identification with Europe. It subjects the theoretical model of individual identification with Europe developed in Chap. 3 to empirical testing to provide evidence on the *determinants* of individual identification with Europe. The empirical study employs a cross-sectional design that analyses identification with Europe among citizens in the EU member states at seven occasions between 2000 and 2012. The period under analysis includes two key moments in the recent history of EU integration, namely the EU's enlargement to Central and Eastern Europe in 2004/2007 and the financial and economic crisis starting in late 2008. By spanning a time horizon of over a decade, this research design enables us to examine general trends in the determinants of European identification over the course of EU integration. Furthermore, by estimating separate regression models before and after Eastern enlargement and before and after the onset of crisis, we are able to assess how turning points in the EU integration process affect the sources of European identification at the citizen level.

The statistical analysis shows that individual identification with Europe is influenced mainly by individual-level determinants while country-level characteristics have only limited effects on European identification. The effects of individual-level determinants on European identification remain stable over time. Among the country-level determinants, economic aspects and redistributive considerations become more relevant for European identification in the wake of enlargement and the crisis.

The remainder of this chapter introduces the research design and methods of analysis (Sect. 6.1) as well as the data and indicators used to operationalise the dependent and independent variables (Sect. 6.2). The subsequent sections present the findings of the statistical analysis (Sect. 6.3) and draw conclusions with regard to the sources and mechanisms of citizens' identification with Europe after enlargement and the crisis (Sect. 6.4).

S. Bergbauer, *Explaining European Identity Formation*,
https://doi.org/10.1007/978-3-319-67708-8_6

6.1 Research Design and Methods of Analysis

The present work relies on a cross-sectional design that analyses individual identification with Europe in the EU member states at seven time points between winter 2000 and spring 2012.[1] The comparatively long period under analysis in a first instance allows conclusions about general tendencies in the determinants of European identification and the stability of these determinants over time and as the EU integration process evolves. What is more, the period under analysis includes two turning points in EU integration in recent years, namely the EU's enlargement to CEE in 2004/2007 and the onset of the financial and economic crisis in late 2008. Hence, we are able to assess not only the general trends in the determinants of European identification over time, but also their stability or variation in response to major events in the EU integration process.

To assess potential changes in the determinants of citizens' European identification in response to *EU enlargement*, separate models are estimated for November/December 2000, October/November 2003, October/November 2004, and March/May 2006. These reflect different stages in the accession process, namely a *pre-accession stage* (winter 2000) in which membership negotiations were under way; the actual *accession stage* (autumn 2003 and 2004) stretching from spring 2003 when the accession treaty with the candidate states was signed[2] to their official accession to the EU on 01 May 2004; finally, a *post-accession stage* (spring 2006). Using the year 2000 as a benchmark, this research design allows us to study whether the determinants of citizens' identification with Europe have changed in strength and/or direction in relation to the accession of CEE countries. Furthermore, by including 2006 as an additional point of analysis, we are able to assess whether eastward enlargement is associated with long-term changes in the determinants of European identification or whether changes in the determinants are restricted to the period immediately before and after the accession of the ten new member states in 2004.

To assess potential changes in the determinants of European identification in response to *the onset of the financial and economic crisis,* separate models are estimated for April/May 2007, March/April 2010, and May 2012. Spring 2007 serves as the benchmark year against which we can assess changes in the determinants of European identification over the course of the crisis. Although the US housing and subprime market contracted as early as 2007, and, in Europe, Hungary, Ireland, and Italy had already experienced recessions in 2007,[3] the starting date of

---

[1]Winter 2000, autumn 2003, autumn 2004, spring 2006, spring 2007, spring 2010, and spring 2012.

[2]The Treaty of Accession between the EU and the ten new member states to join the EU in 2004 was signed in Athens, Greece, on April 16th, 2003.

[3]Recession is defined here as a quarter-on-quarter contraction of real GDP for at least two consecutive quarters. By this definition, Hungary was in recession in the first and second quarters of 2007, Ireland in the second and third quarters of 2007, and Italy in the third and fourth quarters

the global financial and economic crisis is typically equated with the default of the US bank Lehmann Brothers in September 2008 and the ensuing breakdown of the inter-bank loan market (European Commission 2009). Therefore, it seems reasonable to assume that the public only became aware of the crisis in late 2008, enabling us to take spring 2007 as the benchmark year representing the pre-crisis period (see Hobolt and Leblonde 2014 for a similar operationalisation of pre-crisis and crisis periods).

March/April 2010, in contrast, coincides with a period of increased tension and acute crisis in the EU. In effect, by spring 2010, the financial crisis of 2007/2008 and the global recession of 2008/2009 had given rise to fears of sovereign debt crises in a number of Eurozone member states. In March 2010, Eurogroup governments had offered financial support mechanisms to Greece, which the Greek government officially requested to activate in April. On 02 May 2010, the Eurozone finance ministers and the IMF agreed on a € 110 billion loan package to Greece, conditional on austerity measures including wage freezes and pension cuts in the public sector, tax rises, and an increase of the retirement age. The negotiations over the Greek bailout were accompanied by intense debates both in the creditor countries and in Greece, where austerity measures drew considerable social protests.[4]

By spring 2012, the economic and financial situation in the EU member countries had greatly diversified: Of the 27 EU member states, seven[5] were still in recession in the second quarter 2012 whereas Germany had seen its economy grow since 2010 and Poland had never gone into recession at all. Likewise, unemployment rates in the second quarter 2012 ranged from 4% in Luxemburg to 24% in Spain; while Germany had seen unemployment fall since late 2009, unemployment rates continued to rise in the EU as a whole throughout 2010/2012, most notably in Greece, Italy, Ireland, Portugal, and Spain (OECD 2014b).

Thus, the three years of analysis represent very different stages in the financial and economic crisis: first, a pre-crisis period in 2007; second, a period of tension and economic and financial turmoil throughout the EU and in particular in the Eurozone in early 2010; third, a period of economic diversification in which some member states were recovering from the crisis and others still experienced economic difficulty. In this way, the research design allows us to examine whether the factors explaining citizens' identification with Europe change in times of severe crisis; in particular, we are able to assess whether macroeconomic indicators

of 2007. For quarterly growth rates of real GDP and changes over previous quarter see the OECD National Accounts Statistics database (OECD 2014a).

[4]After protest marches in Athens and Thessaloniki on 01 May 2010, a nation-wide strike against the proposed austerity measures took place in Greece on 05 May 2010, drawing an estimated 100,000 people in Athens alone. Three people died in violent clashes between protesters and the police on 05 May (BBC News 2010a, b). Mass protests and violent riots erupted again in response to further austerity measures in 2011 and 2012 (BBC News 2011, 2012).

[5]Czech Republic, Greece Hungary, Italy, Portugal, Slovenia, Spain (OECD 2014a).

become more important for citizens' feelings of belonging to Europe as economic conditions worsen.

To test the hypotheses derived from the explanatory model of European identification outlined in Chap. 3, the empirical analysis employs hierarchical linear regression models predicting individual identification with Europe from individual- and country-level predictors.[6] The model specification follows the two-stage model formulation suggested by Raudenbush and Bryk (2002). Thus, models are specified in two separate stages for level 1 and level 2 and distinguishing between level 1 and level 2 covariates, with observations on level 1 (individual level), i.e. EU citizens, nested within level-2 units (country level), i.e. the EU member states.

The general two-level model is defined at level 1 by

$$Y_{ij} = \beta_{0j} + \beta_{1j}X_{1ij} + \beta_{2j}X_{2ij} + \ldots + \beta_{Qj}X_{Qij} + r_{ij} \tag{6.1}$$

where i indexes level-1 units and j indexes level-2 units, β_{0j} is the level-1 intercept, β_{1j} through β_{Qj} denote the effects of level-1 predictors, X_{1ij} through X_{Qij} denote level-1 predictor variables, and r_{ij} denotes the individual-level error, which is assumed to be normally distributed with a mean of zero and a constant level-1 variance, σ^2.The subscript j for the intercept and slopes of the level-1 predictors indicates that each level-2 unit has a unique intercept and unique slopes which can be modelled using predictors at level-2.

At level 2, the general model is defined by

$$\beta_{qj} = \gamma_{q0} + \gamma_{q1}W_{1j} + \gamma_{q2}W_{2j} + \ldots + \gamma_{qSq}W_{Sqj} + u_{qj} \tag{6.2}$$

where γ_{q0} is the level-2 intercept, γ_{q1} through γ_{qSq} denote the effects of the level-2 predictors, W_{1j} through W_{Qj} denote level-2 predictor variables, and u_{qj} denotes the level-2 errors whereby the random components u_{qj}, q $= 0\ldots Q$, are assumed to be multivariate normal, each with a mean of zero and some variance, Var(u_{qj})$= \tau_{qq}$.

Setting the coefficients for the level-1 and level-2 predictors to zero yields a *random intercept only model*. Referred to as the empty model (M_0), this model allows us to assess the relative importance of each level for variation in respondents' identification with Europe. It is defined by

$$M_0 : \textit{EU identification}_{ij} = \gamma_{00} + u_{0j} + r_{ij} \tag{6.3}$$

[6]There is a vast literature on the analysis of hierarchical data in social and political research, refering to multilevel/hierarchical models under a variety of terms, including multilevel linear models, hierarchical linear models, mixed-effects models, random-effects models, or random-coefficient regression models. The present analysis follows the notation and development of the multilevel model in Raudenbush and Bryk (2002) and Steenbergen and Jones (2002). Multilevel and hierarchical models are referred to interchangeably in the following. Technically, multilevel modelling is the more encompassing term in that the general multilevel framework also allows for non-nested models, i.e. data structures where units at level 1 are nested within level-2 units without a clear ordering or hierarchy between the two levels (cf. the discussion in Gelman and Hill 2006, p. 2).

where γ_{00} denotes the grand mean of European identification, u_{0j} captures between-country variation, and r_{ij} captures between-individual variation. The level-2 residual u_{0j} can be viewed as representing country-differences due to member state characteristics not accounted for in the model whereas the level-1 residual r_{ij} represents the random deviation of respondent i's degree of European identification from country j's mean identification with Europe.

The random intercept only model specified above is extended stepwise to include predictor variables at the individual and country level. Adding predictors at the individual level yields a *random intercept model with individual-level covariates* (M_1).

Recall that at the *individual level*, the explanatory model of European identification includes three main sets of explanatory factors, each comprising several predictor variables (abbreviations for the predictors are in parentheses). These are, first, political awareness, including general political interest (*int*), interest in EU politics (*EU int*), knowledge of EU politics (*EU know*); second, attitudes toward the European and national community, including respondents' conception of European community (*EU comm*), national identification (*nat id*), and conception of national community (*nat comm*); and, third, personal transnational experiences, including transnational practices (*transprac*), personal transnational background (*transback*), and transnational human capital (*transcap*). In addition to these, the model includes control variables for gender (*gender*), age (*age*), type of community (*commun*), education (*edu*), occupation (*occ*), and respondents' national and personal economic expectations (*nat_eco*; *pers_eco*). Substituting the individual-level predictors in the level-1 equation and constraining the level-2 predictors again to zero yields the single-equation expression for the random intercept model with individual-level covariates (M_1):

$$\begin{aligned} M_1 : & \; EU\ identification_{ij} \\ & = \gamma_{00} + \gamma_{10} int_{ij} + \gamma_{20} EUint_{ij} + \gamma_{30} EUknow_{ij} + \gamma_{40} EUcomm_{ij} \\ & \quad + \gamma_{50} nat\ id_{ij} + \gamma_{60} nat\ comm_{ij} + \gamma_{70} transprac_{ij} + \gamma_{80} transback_{ij} \\ & \quad + \gamma_{90} transcap_{ij} + \gamma_{100} gender_{ij} + \gamma_{110} age_{ij} + \gamma_{120} commun_{ij} \\ & \quad + \gamma_{130} edu_{ij} + \gamma_{140} occ_{ij} + \gamma_{150} nat\_eco_{ij} + \gamma_{160} pers\_eco_{ij} + r_{ij} + u_{0j} \end{aligned} \tag{6.4}$$

In the next step, the model is extended to include predictor variables at the country level, yielding a *random intercept model with individual- and country-level covariates* (M_2). Recall that at the *country level*, the explanatory model of European identification includes three sets of explanatory factors, again each comprising several predictor variables (abbreviations for the predictors in parentheses). These are, first, party messages related to European and national community, including party messages on European community (*EU party*) and party messages on national community (*nat party*); second, member states' economic position and integration in European and global markets, including euro zone membership (*Euro*), member states' net contribution to EU budget (*budget*), and member states' share in international trade (*trade*); third, member states' ethnocultural composition and international social integration, including the share of EU nationals in the national population (*EU imm*) and the overall share of immigrants in the national population (*imm*). In addition to these, the model includes measures for unemployment (*unemploy*) and EU/IMF conditionality (*IMF*) for the crisis period 2008–2012. The country-level predictors are used to model the level-1 intercept β_{0j}., yielding the following level-2 equation:

$$\beta_{0j} = \gamma_{00} + \gamma_{01} EU\ party_j + \gamma_{02} nat\ party_j + \gamma_{03} Euro_j + \gamma_{04} budget_j + \gamma_{05} trade_j + \gamma_{06} EU\ imm_j + \gamma_{07} imm_j + \gamma_{08} unemploy_j + \gamma_{09} IMF_j + u_{0j} \tag{6.5}$$

In the single-equation expression, the random intercept model with individual- and country-level predictors becomes:

$$\begin{aligned} \mathrm{M}_2 : EU\ identification_{ij} \\ = \gamma_{00} + \gamma_{10} int_{ij} + \gamma_{20} EUint_{ij} + \gamma_{30} EUknow_{ij} + \gamma_{40} EUcomm_{ij} \\ + \gamma_{50} nat\ id_{ij} + \gamma_{60} nat\ comm_{ij} + \gamma_{70} transprac_{ij} + \gamma_{80} transback_{ij} \\ + \gamma_{90} transcap_{ij} + \gamma_{100} gender_{ij} + \gamma_{110} age_{ij} + \gamma_{120} commun_{ij} \\ + \gamma_{130} edu_{ij} + \gamma_{140} occ_{ij} + \gamma_{150} nat\_eco_{ij} + \gamma_{160} pers\_eco_{ij} \\ + \gamma_{01} EU\ party_j + \gamma_{02} nat\ party_j + \gamma_{03} Euro_j + \gamma_{04} budget_j + \gamma_{05} trade_j \\ + \gamma_{06} EU\ imm_j + \gamma_{07} imm_j + \gamma_{08} unemploy_j + \gamma_{09} IMF_j + u_{0j} + r_{ij} \end{aligned} \tag{6.6}$$

The random intercept model with individual- and country-level covariates constitutes the core model for the following analysis. It assumes that intercepts vary across EU member states as a function of country-level characteristics, but holds the slopes of the individual-level predictors fixed across EU member states. In addition to these fixed-effects models, a number of *random coefficient models with cross-level interactions* (M_3) are estimated. In these models, the slopes of (some of) the individual-level predictors are no longer fixed across EU member states, but variability in the level-1 slopes is modelled explicitly as a function of level-2 characteristics. As a result, the combined multilevel model includes cross-level interaction terms between individual- and country-level predictor variables.

The inclusion of random coefficients for some of the individual-level predictors is based on the theoretical expectations developed in the previous chapter. Recall that the explanatory model of European identification included a number of cross-level interactions. Specifically, the theoretical discussion suggested interaction effects between individual political interest and party messages on European and national community, between individual political interest and member states' status as net recipient of EU funding, and between individual political interest and member states' shares in international trade (see hypotheses H_{17} to H_{19} formulated in Chap. 3). Furthermore, I hypothesised interaction effects between individual national identification and party messages on European and national community, between individual national identification and member states' status as net recipient of EU funding, and between individual national identification and member states' share of immigrants (see hypotheses H_{20} to H_{22}). Finally, during the financial and economic crisis, I expected interaction effects between individual national identification and EU/IMF conditionality and Eurozone membership, respectively (see hypotheses H_{30} and H_{31}). Model equations for random coefficient models with cross-level interactions can be found in the appendix.

All models are estimated in Stata 13, using Stata's `mixed` command for multilevel mixed-effects linear regression. Models are fitted using maximum likelihood (ML). Data sets and country samples have been chosen to maximise the number of countries/level-2 units for multilevel modelling while being limited by the number of EU member states at the time. As a result, the number of level-1 (n) and level-2 units (N) varies by period of analysis. The analysis is restricted to the EU15 member states ($N = 15$) for the years 2000 and 2003, and to the EU25 member states ($N = 25$) for the years 2004 and 2006.[7] The number of individual observations under analysis in this period ranges from $n = 12{,}128$ (2006)[8] to $n = 24{,}221$ (2004). For the years 2007 to 2012, the analysis includes the EU27 member states ($N = 27$).[9] The number of individual observations under analysis in this period ranges from 25,964 (2007) to 26,144 (2012). Due to data limitations not all models can be estimated using the full set of predictors at the individual- and/or country-level in all years. Whenever possible, missing indicators are replaced by functional equivalents to ensure the comparability of models over time.

[7]There is an ongoing discussion in the literature regarding the number of level-1 units j and level-2 units J needed to fit a multilevel model (see, e.g. Bryan and Jenkins 2015; Maas and Hox 2005; Paccagnella 2011; Snijders 2005; Stegmueller 2013). Maximum likelihood estimation requires sufficiently large sample sizes at both levels to produce accurate estimates and associated standard errors, raising questions of the acceptable lower limit for the number of level-2 units in particular. Simulation studies show, however, that individual-level estimates remain robust even for small numbers of level-2 units ($N < 15$) and level-2 estimates tend to biased only to a limited degree for level-2 samples of 15 and more (Maas and Hox 2005; Stegmueller 2013). Based on these findings, it seems justified to estimate multilevel models even for the smaller set of the EU15 member states.

[8]The relatively small n for 2006 is due to the split-ballot design of EB 65.2; only half of the sample was given the item used to operationalise the dependent variable European identification.

[9]The changes in country sample included in the analysis in different years raises questions with regard to the assessment of changes in the determinants of European identification in response to enlargement. To exclude that observed changes in the determinants are due to systematic differences in European identification between old and new member states, separate models for the EU15 and the CEE member states were estimated for the years 2004 and 2006 as well as the period 2007 to 2012 in the addition to the pooled models for the EU25/EU27. No significant differences appeared between the EU15 and the CEE group in terms of effect size and direction of effects.

6.2 Data and Operationalisation

The analysis of European identification among the EU member state populations combines individual- and country-level data in a multilevel framework. Individual-level data come from seven EB surveys conducted between 2000 and 2012.[10] All Eurobarometer datasets were retrieved online from the ZACAT provided by GESIS—Leibniz Institute for the Social Sciences. Country-level data mainly come from the Eurostat database, supplemented by data from the EU Commission, the Euromanifestos Project (EMP) at the Mannheim Centre for European Social Research (MZES), the IMF, and the Worldbank. Given the comparatively long time span under analysis, identical indicators are not available for all theoretical concepts for all years under analysis and functionally equivalent indicators are used wherever possible.

Operationalisation of the Dependent Variable The dependent variable *European identification* is operationalised by *citizens' attachment to Europe* for the years 2000 to 2006 and *citizens' attachment to the European Union* for the years 2007 to 2012. Both items have been recoded so that higher values indicate greater attachment to Europe/the European Union. The recoded dependent variable has four categories, ranging from 0 = 'not at all attached' to 3 = 'very attached'. Respondents indicating 'don't know' have been omitted from the analysis (see Table 6.4 in the appendix for descriptive statistics for the dependent variable).

Operationalisation of the Independent Variables Measures and indicators for explanatory variables at individual and country level are discussed in the following. All items have been recoded so that positive regression coefficients indicate a positive effect of the respective explanatory factor on European identification as the dependent variable. Respondents indicating 'don't know' and those refusing to reply have been omitted from the analysis (see Table 6.5 in the appendix for descriptive statistics for the dependent variable).

Operationalisation of Explanatory Variables at the Individual Level Independent variables at the individual level comprise respondents' general political interest (*int*), interest in European politics (*EU int*), and knowledge of European politics (*EU know*); attitudes towards the European and national community, including respondents' conception of European and national community (*EU comm*, *nat comm*) and degree of national identification (*nat id*); and personal transnational experiences, including measures for respondents' transnational practices (*transprac*), transnational background (*transback*), and transnational human capital (*transcap*).

Respondents' *general political interest* (*int*) is operationalised by the frequency of political discussions. *Interest in European politics* (*EU int*) is measured by

[10]EB 54.1 (Nov/Dec 2000), EB 60.1. (Nov/Dec 2003), EB 62.0 (Oct/Nov 2004), EB 65.2 (March/May 2006), EB 67.2 (April/May 2007), EB 73.3 (March/April 2010), EB 77.3 (May 2012).

respondents' self-reported interest in politics and economics in other EU countries (in 2003) and the frequency of discussions on European political matters (2012). Respondents' *knowledge of European politics* (*EU know*) is measured by respondents' factual knowledge of EU politics in 2004, 2006, and 2012, and by respondents' awareness of the main EU institutions in 2000, 2003, and 2007. There are no items available for either respondents' objective knowledge of European politics or their awareness of major EU institutions in EB 77.3 (2010).

Respondents' *conception of the European community* (*EU comm*) is measured based on a question asking respondents to indicate what the EU means to them personally. With the exception of EB 54.1 (2000), the respective item is available for all years under analysis. Respondents could choose multiple answers from a list of EU meanings, including peace, economic prosperity, democracy, social protection, freedom to travel, study and work anywhere in the EU, cultural diversity, stronger say in the world, euro, unemployment, bureaucracy, waste of money, loss of cultural identity, more crime, an not enough control at external borders. The resulting nominal variable *EU comm* has three categories: 'common political project' if respondents chose one or more of the options attributed to an understanding of Europe as a common political project (i.e. peace, democracy, social protection) and none of the other options; 'individual benefits' if respondents chose one or more of the options attributed to an understanding of Europe as individual benefits (i.e. economic prosperity, freedom to travel, study and work anywhere in the EU) and none of the other options; and 'other' if respondents chose any of the other options ('other' as reference category).

National identification (*nat id*) is measured by respondents' attachment to their country. It is available for all years under analysis. The discussion of the relation between respondents' *conception of the national community* and their propensity to identify with Europe in the theoretical section suggested differences between citizens who see their national community primarily based on cultural affinity and a common ethnic and religious heritage and citizens who display a civic understanding of national community built on common political values and acquired traits and behaviours. Only EB 73.3 (2010) includes an item that allows testing this proposition. A binary variable (*nat comm*) indicating a conception of the national community as built on a common cultural heritage is constructed from a question asking respondents to choose the three most important characteristics to be (NATIONALITY) from a list of characteristics, including being Christian, sharing (NATIONALITY) cultural traditions, being born in (COUNTRY), having at least one (NATIONALITY) parents, feeling (NATIONALITY), mastering (COUNTRY LANGUAGE), exercising citizens' rights, for example voting in (OUR COUNTRY), having been brought up in (OUR COUNTRY), and being active in any association or organization in (OUR COUNTRY). Among these options, 'to be a Christian', 'to share (NATIONALITY) cultural traditions', and 'to have at least one (NATIONALITY) parent' best reflect a cultural understanding of national community. Thus, *nat comm* takes the value 1 if respondents chose at least two of the three cultural items as most important characteristic to be (NATIONALITY) and a value of 0 if otherwise. The concept of personal transnational experiences, finally, comprises three predictor variables, namely transnational practices involving other Europeans, personal transnational background, and individual transnational human capital. The frequency of respondents' *transnational practices* (*transprac*) is measured by EB items that assess respondents' opportunities to personally interact with other Europeans in their private or professional lives, for example trough long-term stays abroad for work or study or partners and close friends from other than the home country. Due to data limitations, respondents' transnational practices can only be explored for 2010 and 2012. For both years, additive indices are constructed from questions assessing the frequency of respondents' interactions with other Europeans for private or professional reasons, with higher values indicating more transnational contacts.

Respondents' personal *transnational background* (*transback*) is understood as having a European family background, assuming that respondents have more opportunities to interact with other Europeans—the mechanism presumed to underlie European identification—if they have family in other EU member states (as opposed to coming from an immigrant background outside the EU). *Transnational background* is captured by dummy variable that takes the value 1 if either respondents themselves or at least one parent have been born in another EU member state. Respondents indicating 'don't know' and those refusing to answer have been omitted from the analysis. The indicator for transnational background is available for all years except 2000, 2003, and 2012.

Respondents' *transnational capital* (*capital*) refers to the skills that enable citizens to interact directly with other Europeans. It is operationalised by items assessing respondents' foreign language skills, based on the assumption that meaningful interaction with other Europeans requires a common basis for communication (Gerhards 2010). Transnational capital is measured by an index of respondents' self-reported language skills and readiness to follow news from other countries, with higher values indicating greater (use of) foreign language skills. This index is available for the years 2010 and 2012.

Operationalisation of Explanatory Variables at the Country Level At the country level, the general explanatory model of European identification comprises three sets of explanatory variables: party messages related to the European and national community (*EU party, nat party*); member states' economic position and degree of integration in the EU and global markets in terms of Eurozone membership (*Euro*), net contributions to the EU budget (*budget*), and share of trade in GDP (*trade*); and member states' ethnocultural diversity as assessed by the share of (EU) foreigners in the national population (*EU imm, imm*). The discussion of the impact of the financial and economic crisis on citizens' identification with Europe further expected adverse economic conditions in a country as well as EU/IMF conditionality to affect European identification during the crisis. To assess these hypotheses, the model includes member states' level of unemployment (*unemploy*) as well as a measure for receiving conditional financial aid from the EU/IMF (*IMF*) as additional predictors at the country level. With the exception of the binary variables 'Eurozone membership', 'net contributing country to the EU budget' and 'EU/IMF conditionality' as well as the measures for the salience of identity issues in party manifestos (*EU party*, *nat party*), all country-level predictors are centred around their respective grand means.[11]

The salience of messages related to the European and the national community in national party discourse is operationalised using the measures of party emphasis on issues related to European and national community developed in Chap. 5. These measures are based on the share (in %) of a national party's European election manifesto dedicated to questions of European and national community and identity. The variable *EU party* captures the salience of European identity in party discourse; it corresponds to the proportion of manifesto statements referring to issues of European community and identity. The variable *nat party,* in contrast, captures the salience of national identity in party discourse; it corresponds to the proportion of manifesto statements referring to issues of national community and identity. Both variables range from 0 to 100 with 0 meaning that parties did not refer to issues of European/national community in their manifesto at all and 100 meaning that all manifesto statements were dedicated to issues of European/national community. Data on national party manifestos for EP elections come from the Euromanifestos Project (EMP) at the Mannheim Centre for European Social Research (MZES). They are available for 2004 only as 2004 is the only European election year covered by the analysis.

Eurozone membership (Euro) is a binary variable taking the value 1 if member states have adopted the euro as the common currency and the value 0 if otherwise. The variable *Euro* is first included in the model in 2003, after the introduction of the euro as a physical currency on 01 January 2002. Given that the focus here is on the common currency as a means for citizens' direct experience of European integration, it seems reasonably to take 2002 as the starting date, even though the euro had already been introduced as accounting currency in 1999.

Member states' net contribution to the EU budget is operationalised by the so-called operating budgetary balance, which corresponds to the difference between the expenditures allocated to each member state by the EU and member

[11]Centring the country-level predictors around their respective grand mean eases interpretation of the regression coefficients and helps avoid nonsensical results if a value of 0 is essentially meaningless for the predictor variables. For example, while the variables *trade* and *unemployment* theoretically could take a value of zero, no EU member state has zero imports/exports or zero unemployment (see also the descriptive statistics for the independent variables in Table 6.5 in the appendix). By centring the country-level predictors around their grand means, we can interpret regression coefficients as predicted changes in European identification for one-unit changes in the respective independent variable with e.g. trade shares and unemployment rates held at their *average values* in the data rather than at levels zero, which do not occur empirically. In the case of party messages, in contrast, zero is a meaningful value insofar as we can imagine parties not addressing issues of identity at all in their election manifestos. Centring also eases the interpretation of cross-level interaction terms. Thus, for an interaction term in the form of a product $w_j x_{ij}$, the main effect of X is to be interpreted as the effect of X if $W = 0$ (while the main effect of W is to be interpreted as the effect of W for cases with $X = 0$). See also the discussion of centring choices in Raudenbush and Bryk (2002, pp. 31–35).

states' payments to the EU budget.[12] A dummy variable *budget* is created taking the value 1 if member states are net contributor countries of EU transfers and the value 0 if countries are net recipient of EU transfers. Data on member states' operating budgetary balance come from the European Commission's EU budget 2012 financial report (European Commission 2013) that includes information on net EU transfers for the whole period under analysis.

The explanatory model of European identification further hypothesised individuals from member states that are economically more integrated the European and global markets to identify more with Europe. The variable *trade* measures the sum of exports and imports of goods and services as a share of member states' gross domestic product. Data for trade as a share of GDP come from the Worldbank's World Development Indicators database (Worldbank 2015) and are available for the entire period under analysis.

Besides measures of party discourse and macroeconomic indicators, the *ethnocultural composition of member state societies* is included as a country-level determinant of individual identification with Europe. Member states' *ethnocultural composition* is operationalised using the share of foreigners in the domestic population. Two variables are included: First, the share of EU migrants[13] (in%) living in a member state (*EU imm*), and second, the overall share of immigrants[14] (in%) in member states' populations (*imm*). Both are calculated based on population on 1st January of a given year. Data for both measures come from the Eurostat database (EUROSTAT 2014a). Data for the share of EU migrants are available from 2004 onwards; data on the overall share of immigrant are available for all years under analysis.

To assess the *effects of the financial and economic crisis* on individual identification with Europe, the models include measures for member states' unemployment rates (*unemploy*) and, for the crisis period 2010/2012, a dummy variable (*IMF*) for whether or not member states received financial aids by the IMF/EU conditional on structural and economic reforms. Unemployment is measured by member states' annual average unemployment rate defined as the number of people unemployed as a percentage of the labour force.[15] Data on unemployment rates come from the Eurostat database (EUROSTAT 2014c) and are available for all years under

[12]The operating expenditures received by member states exclude administrative expenditures, e.g. for the maintenance of EU institutions. For more information on member states expenditures and payments and the calculation of member states' operating budgetary balances, see the EU budget 2012 financial report (European Commission 2013, pp. 109–111).

[13]EU migrants refer to the number of foreigners coming from countries that were EU member states at the time, i.e. the EU15 in 2000, EU25 in 2004, EU27 in 2010 etc.

[14]Immigrants are defined as persons holding citizenship other than that of their country of residence.

[15]Eurostat defines the labour force as the total number of people employed and unemployed whereby unemployed refers to all persons aged 15 to 74 (16 to 74 in Spain, Italy, and the UK) who were not employed during the reference week, had actively sought work during the past 4 weeks and were ready to begin working immediately or within two weeks (EUROSTAT 2014b).

analysis.[16] The binary variable *IMF* indicates whether member states have been under EU/IMF conditionality since the onset of the financial and economic crisis. Since the EU and the IMF worked side by side in providing joint loan packages and monitoring the implementation of macroeconomic reforms in creditor countries, EU and IMF influence are captured by the same variable. The operationalisation of EU/IMF conditionality follows (Armingeon and Ceka 2014) who define IMF conditionality 'as having agreed to any active lending arrangement according to IMF records' such as a Stand-By Arrangement (SBA) or Extended Fund Facility (EFF)' (Armingeon and Ceka 2014, p. 91). Under these agreements, countries receive financial aids conditional on the implementation of macroeconomic and structural policies. Since the onset of the financial and economic crisis in late 2008, six EU member states (Greece, Hungary, Ireland, Latvia, Portugal, and Romania) have signed lending agreements with the IMF. The variable *IMF* takes the value 1 for member states under EU/IMF conditionality in the year under analysis and the value 0 otherwise. Data on IMF lending agreements come from the IMF Monitoring of Fund Arrangement (MONA) database (IMF 2015).

Control Variables In addition to the individual- and country-level predictors discussed above, the empirical model includes a number of control variables. At the individual level, these include respondents' socio-demographic characteristics (gender, age, type of community, level of education, occupation) and their expectations with regard to their personal financial situation and the situation of the national economy in the year to come. At the country level, the empirical model includes control variables for member states' level of unemployment to account for the influence of the general economic situation and potential negative effects of worsening economic conditions on attitudes towards Europe and European integration.[17]

6.3 The Determinants of Citizens' Identification with Europe 2000–2012

At the core of this book is the question why people identify with Europe. The remainder of this chapter seeks to reply to this question by presenting the empirical evidence on the sources of citizens' identification with Europe. To this end, the

[16]While national unemployment rates are introduced as an indicator for how hard member states were hit by the economic crisis after 2008, all models include the variable for unemployment in order to control for the influence of the general state of the national economy on citizens' identification with Europe.

[17]Another obvious choice would be to control for member states in Central and Eastern Europe, which joined the EU in 2004/2007. However, CEE membership highly correlates with some of the other country-level predictors, in particular net contributions to the EU budget and Eurozone membership. To avoid multicollinearity among the predictors, no additional control variable is included for CEE member states.

results of the multilevel analysis of individual identification with Europe are presented in three steps.

A first part examines how much of the variation observed in individual identification with Europe lies between individuals and how much lies between EU member states (Sect. 6.3.1). In technical terms, this section presents the results of the empty or random intercept only models for the different years of analysis, which partition the total variance in European identification into between- and within-country variances.

A second section turns to the question which individual and which contextual attributes shape European identification (Sect. 6.3.2). It explores the effects of individual attributes and dispositions on the one hand and member state characteristics on the other on citizens' identification with Europe, presenting estimates for individual- and country-level determinants for different points in time between 2000 and 2012. The aim of this section is to provide *general conclusions with regard to the sources of European identification* at the citizen level and provide insights into long-term trends in the determinants of individual identification with Europe over time.

A third and final section turns to the implications of EU enlargement and the financial and economic crisis for the sources of citizens' identification with Europe (Sect. 6.3.3). Starting with enlargement, it explores changes in the individual- and country-level determinants of European identification that can be traced back to the EU's enlargement to CEE and the onset of the financial and economic crisis. The aim of this section is to draw *conclusions with regard to the stability of European identification and its determinants at key moments in the EU integration process*. The focus is on changes in the importance of different explanations of individual European identification as we observe fundamental changes in EU membership and the salience of EU politics in public debates.

6.3.1 Between and Within Country Variation in Individual European Identification 2000–2012

The random intercept only models provide information on the overall level of identification with Europe in the member states in the years 2000 to 2012 and the degree of variation in European identification between and within EU countries. Table 6.1 presents parameter estimates for each year under analysis, including the intercept, which gives the grand mean of European identification; the variance components τ_{00} and σ^2 , which represent the between-country variability (τ_{00}) and the within-country variability (σ^2) in European identification; and the intraclass correlation coefficient (ICC), which indicates the fraction of the total variability in individual identification with Europe that is due to the member state level. Standard errors are in parentheses. Note that the deviance statistic defined as −2 times the log-likelihood, as well as the Aikake information criterion (AIC) and the Bayesian

Table 6.1 Variance components and intraclass correlation 2000–2012

Year	2000	2003	2004	2006	2007	2010	2012
	Attachment to *Europe*				Attachment to the *European Union*		
Intercept	1.73*** (0.05)	1.70*** (0.06)	1.80*** (0.05)	1.70*** (0.06)	1.50*** (0.01)	1.45*** (0.04)	1.39*** (0.03)
Variance components							
Country level τ_{00}	0.04 (0.02)	0.05 (0.02)	0.07 (0.02)	0.08 (0.02)	0.05 (0.01)	0.05 (0.01)	0.03 (0.01)
Individual level σ^2	0.73 (0.01)	0.67 (0.01)	0.66 (0.01)	0.72 (0.01)	0.74 (0.01)	0.70 (0.01)	0.70 (0.01)
ICC	0.06	0.07	0.09	0.10	0.05	0.07	0.04
Deviance	39,279.46	38,330.15	58,880.592	30,555.72	66,098.248	64,697.886	64,847.44
AIC	39,285.46	38,336.15	58,886.59	30,561.72	66,104.25	64,703.89	64,853.44
BIC	39,308.41	38,359.13	58,910.88	30,583.93	66,128.74	64,728.38	64,877.95
No. of groups (N)	15	15	25	25	27	27	27
No. of individuals (n)	15,515	15,6683	24,221	12,128	25,964	25,990	26,144

Note: Figures are estimates from multilevel regression analyses with random intercept only, standard errors in parentheses. The question wording of the dependent variable 'identification with Europe' changes in 2007 due to changes in the EB survey questionnaire. In the years 2000 to 2006, the item refers to the strength of respondents' attachment to *Europe*, from 2007 onwards the item refers to the strength of respondents' attachment to the *European Union*. The relatively smaller n for 2006 is due to the split-ballot design of EB 65.2.

***$p \leq 0.001$; **$p \leq 0.01$; *$p \leq 0.05$; †$p \leq 0.1$.

Source: Eurobarometer, own calculations.

information criterion (BIC) are given for completeness and further reference only; they cannot be compared across models fitted to different data sets.

Starting with the intercepts, we can assess the mean level of identification with Europe across all member states and individual respondents. The estimates for the intercepts can be interpreted as the expected value of European identification for a random citizen in a randomly drawn EU member state. With values around the midpoint of the European identification scale,[18] the point estimates for the intercepts indicate an overall moderate attachment to Europe among respondents in all years under analysis. As observed in the descriptive part of the analysis, mean levels of identification are slightly higher for respondents' 'attachment to *Europe*' than for 'attachment to the *European Union*'.

Other than the mean level of European identification, we are interested in how much of the variation in individual identification with Europe lies between EU member states and how much lies between individuals. Unsurprisingly with public opinion data, we find that differences in European identification are greater for respondents within the same EU member state than between EU member states. Depending on the year under analysis, the estimates for the variance components τ_{00} and σ^2 yield intraclass correlation coefficients ρ between 0.04 and 0.10. That is, the country level accounts for 4–10% of the variance in respondents' identification with Europe whereas the major part of variation in European identification lies at the individual level.[19] Nonetheless, the ICC ratios reported here provide evidence of nesting within EU member states that warrants further investigation.

6.3.2 *Explaining Individual European Identification 2000–2012*

Which factors explain the variation in European identification that we observe at both the individual and the member state level? The following section presents the empirical evidence on the determinants of European identification among EU citizens based on the results of the multilevel analysis. Tables 6.2 and 6.3 report parameter estimates, standard errors, and variance components for hierarchical linear models with maximum likelihood estimation for the different years under analysis. The result tables further include the deviance as well as the AIC and BIC as measures of fit. R^2 gives the proportional reduction of error for predicting an individual outcome as proposed by Snijders and Boskers (1994, 2011). Results for the years 2000 to 2006 are reported in Table 6.2 and results for the years 2007 to

[18]Recall that identification with Europe is measured on a 4-point scale ranging from 0 (not at all attached to Europe/the European Union) to 3 (very attached to Europe/the European Union).

[19]The ICC ratios reported here are consistent with previous studies of EU public opinion. Few studies report intraclass correlation coefficients. An overview of analyses of EU support shows ICC ratios of between 4% (Braun and Tausendpfund 2013) and 16% (Brinegar and Jolly 2005).

Table 6.2 Individual- and country-level determinants of individual identification with Europe 2000–2006

Multilevel analysis of individual identification with Europe (attachment to Europe)													
	2000		2003			2004					2006		
Year	M_1	M_2	M_{1a}	M_{1b}	M_2	M_1	M_{2a2}	M_{2a2}	M_{2b2}	M_{2b2}	M_1	M_{2a}	M_{2b}
Intercept	0.32*** (0.06)	0.29*** (0.09)	0.31*** (0.07)	0.28*** (0.07)	0.32* (0.16)	0.45*** (0.06)	0.30† (0.17)	0.11 (0.11)	0.19 (0.14)	0.16 (0.12)	0.37*** (0.07)	0.24** (0.08)	0.24*** (0.08)
Individual-level predictors													
Gender (male)	−0.03* (0.01)	−0.03* (0.01)	−0.00 (0.01)	−0.04** (0.01)	−0.00 (0.01)	0.00 (0.01)	0.00 (0.01)	0.00 (0.01)	0.00 (0.01)	0.00 (0.01)	0.00 (0.01)	0.00 (0.01)	0.00 (0.01)
Age	−0.00† (0.00)	−0.00† (0.00)	−0.00† (0.00)	−0.00* (0.00)	−0.00† (0.00)	0.00 (0.00)	0.00 (0.00)	0.00 (0.00)	0.00 (0.00)	0.00 (0.00)	−0.00 (0.00)	−0.00 (0.00)	−0.00 (0.00)
Community (ref.: rural)													
Small town	–	–	0.04** (0.01)	0.04** (0.01)	0.04** (0.01)	0.05*** (0.01)	0.05*** (0.01)	0.05*** (0.01)	0.05*** (0.01)	0.05*** (0.01)	0.02 (0.02)	0.02 (0.02)	0.02 (0.02)
Large town	–	–	0.03 (0.02)	0.01 (0.02)	0.03† (0.02)	0.06*** (0.01)	0.06*** (0.01)	0.06*** (0.01)	0.06*** (0.01)	0.06*** (0.01)	0.06*** (0.02)	0.06*** (0.02)	0.06*** (0.02)
Education	0.07*** (0.01)	0.07*** (0.01)	0.08*** (0.01)	0.05*** (0.01)	0.08*** (0.01)	0.07*** (0.01)	0.07*** (0.01)	0.07*** (0.01)	0.07*** (0.01)	0.07*** (0.01)	0.09*** (0.01)	0.09*** (0.01)	0.09*** (0.01)
Occupation (ref.: other)													
Student	−0.00 (0.03)	−0.00 (0.03)	−0.07** (0.03)	−0.04 (0.03)	−0.07* (0.03)	−0.05* (0.02)	−0.05* (0.02)	−0.05* (0.02)	−0.05* (0.02)	−0.05* (0.02)	−0.05 (0.04)	−0.05 (0.04)	−0.05 (0.04)
Manager	0.04 (0.02)	0.04 (0.02)	0.09*** (0.02)	0.08*** (0.02)	0.09*** (0.02)	0.05** (0.02)	0.05** (0.02)	0.05** (0.02)	0.05** (0.02)	0.05** (0.02)	0.06* (0.03)	0.06* (0.03)	0.06* (0.03)
Nat. economic expect.: worse	−0.14*** (0.02)	−0.14*** (0.02)	−0.09*** (0.01)	−0.08*** (0.01)	−0.09*** (0.01)	−0.13*** (0.01)	−0.13*** (0.01)	−0.13*** (0.01)	−0.13*** (0.01)	−0.13*** (0.01)	−0.16*** (0.02)	−0.16*** (0.02)	−0.16*** (0.02)
Pers. economic expect.: worse	−0.15*** (0.02)	−0.15*** (0.02)	−0.16*** (0.02)	−0.15*** (0.02)	−0.16*** (0.02)	−0.14*** (0.01)	−0.14*** (0.01)	−0.14*** (0.01)	−0.14*** (0.01)	−0.14*** (0.01)	−0.07** (0.02)	−0.07** (0.02)	−0.07** (0.02)
Political interest	0.04*** (0.01)	0.04*** (0.01)	0.11*** (0.01)		0.11*** (0.01)	0.09*** (0.01)	0.09*** (0.01)	0.09*** (0.01)	0.09*** (0.01)	0.09*** (0.01)	0.12*** (0.01)	0.12*** (0.01)	0.12*** (0.01)
European political interest	–	–		0.23*** (0.01)		–	–	–	–	–	–	–	–

(continued)

Table 6.2 (continued)

Multilevel analysis of individual identification with Europe (attachment to Europe)													
	2000		2003			2004					2006		
Year	M_1	M_2	M_{1a}	M_{1b}	M_2	M_1	M_{2a2}	M_{2a2}	M_{2b2}	M_{2b2}	M_1	M_{2a}	M_{2b}
EU knowledge	0.05*** (0.00)	0.05*** (0.00)	0.07*** (0.00)	0.04*** (0.00)	0.07*** (0.00)	0.06*** (0.01)	0.06*** (0.01)	0.06*** (0.01)	0.06*** (0.01)	0.06*** (0.01)	0.10*** (0.01)	0.10*** (0.01)	0.10*** (0.01)
EU Conception (ref.: other)													
Common political project	–	–	−0.07** (0.03)	−0.04 (0.03)	−0.07* (0.03)	0.15*** (0.03)	0.15*** (0.03)	0.15*** (0.03)	0.15*** (0.03)	0.15*** (0.03)	0.22*** (0.04)	0.22*** (0.04)	0.22*** (0.04)
Individual benefits	–	–	0.06 (0.03)	0.06* (0.03)	0.06 (0.03)	0.08*** (0.02)	0.08*** (0.02)	0.08*** (0.02)	0.08*** (0.02)	0.08*** (0.02)	0.12*** (0.03)	0.12*** (0.03)	0.12*** (0.03)
National identification	0.45*** (0.01)	0.45*** (0.01)	0.36*** (0.01)	0.35*** (0.01)	0.36*** (0.01)	0.40*** (0.01)	0.40*** (0.01)	0.40*** (0.01)	0.40*** (0.01)	0.40*** (0.01)	0.36*** (0.01)	0.36*** (0.01)	0.36*** (0.01)
Transnational background						0.20*** (0.02)	0.20*** (0.02)	0.20*** (0.02)	0.20*** (0.02)	0.20*** (0.02)	0.15*** (0.03)	0.15*** (0.03)	0.15*** (0.03)
Country-level predictors													
Party messages													
% national identity		–			–		0.00 (0.02)		0.02 (0.02)			–	–
% European identity		–			–			0.05** (0.03)		0.04* (0.02)		–	–
Eurozone		–			−0.07 (0.14)		0.09 (0.13)	−0.01 (0.11)	0.14 (0.11)	0.04 (0.10)		0.05 (0.11)	0.08 (0.10)
Net paying EU transfers		0.06 (0.12)			0.06 (0.11)		0.17 (0.12)	0.13 (0.11)	0.18† (0.10)	0.16 (0.10)		0.24* (0.11)	0.23* (0.10)
Trade		0.00 (0.00)			0.00* (0.00)		0.00 (0.00)	0.00 (0.00)	0.00** (0.00)	0.00† (0.00)		0.00† (0.00)	0.00** (0.00)
EU immigration		–			–		−0.01 (0.01)	0.00 (0.01)				−0.01 (0.01)	
Total immigration		0.01 (0.01)			−0.00 (0.01)				−0.02** (0.01)	−0.01 (0.01)			−0.01 (0.01)

Unemployment		0.00 (0.02)			0.06* (0.03)		0.01 (0.02)	0.01 (0.01)	0.01 (0.02)	0.01 (0.01)		0.06** (0.02)	0.05** (0.02)
Variance components													
Country level τ_{00}	0.04 (0.02)	0.03 (0.01)	0.04 (0.02)	0.04 (0.02)	0.03 (0.01)	0.07 (0.02)	0.06 (0.02)	0.05 (0.01)	0.05 (0.01)	0.04 (0.01)	0.08 (0.02)	0.05 (0.01)	0.04 (0.01)
Individual level σ^2	0.62 (0.01)	0.62 (0.01)	0.59 (0.01)	0.56 (0.01)	0.59 (0.01)	0.57 (0.01)	0.57 (0.01)	0.57 (0.01)	0.57 (0.01)	0.57 (0.01)	0.62 (0.01)	0.62 (0.01)	0.62 (0.01)
Deviance	36,377.34	36,374.04	35,639.62	34,851.68	35,633.32	54,224.92	54,220.82	54,213.86	54,214.36	54,212.1	28,338.57	28,326.6	28,323.16
AIC	36,403.33	36,408.04	35,637.63	34,885.36	35,677.33	54,260.92	54,268.82	54,261.86	54,262.36	54,260.1	28,374.57	28,372.6	28,369.15
BIC	36,502.66	36,537.93	35,803.58	35,015.28	35,845.5	54,406.27	54,462.62	54,455.66	54,456.16	54,443.9	28,507.54	28,542.5	28,539.05
R^2	0.15	0.16	0.13	0.17	0.15	0.12	0.13	0.15	0.15	0.16	0.12	0.15	0.17
No. of groups (N)	15	15	15	15	15	25	25	25	25	25	25	25	25
No. of individuals (n)	15,377	15,377	15,434	15,398	15,434	23,740	23,740	23,740	23,740	23,740	11,932	11,932	11,932

Note: Figures are estimates from linear hierarchical regression models with random intercept (ML estimation). Standard errors in parentheses. ***$p \leq 0.001$; **$p \leq 0.01$; *$p \leq 0.05$; †$p \leq 0.1$.

Table 6.3 Individual- and country-level determinants of individual identification with Europe 2007–2012

	Multilevel analysis of individual identification with Europe (attachment to the European Union)									
	2007			2010			2012			
Year	M_1	M_{2a}	M_{2b}	M_1	M_{2a}	M_{2b}	M_{1a}	M_{1b}	M_{2a}	M_{2a}
Intercept	0.29*** (0.05)	0.31*** (0.07)	0.29*** (0.06)	0.41*** (0.06)	0.23* (0.10)	0.21* (0.10)	0.18*** (0.05)	0.18*** (0.05)	0.25** (0.08)	0.21** (0.08)
Individual-level predictors										
Gender (male)	0.03** (0.01)	0.03** (0.01)	0.03** (0.01)	0.05*** (0.01)	0.05*** (0.01)	0.05*** (0.01)	0.00 (0.01)	−0.01 (0.01)	0.00 (0.01)	0.00 (0.01)
Age	−0.00*** (0.00)	−0.00*** (0.00)	−0.00*** (0.00)	−0.00*** (0.00)	−0.00*** (0.00)	−0.00*** (0.00)	0.00* (0.00)	0.00 (0.00)	0.00* (0.00)	0.00* (0.00)
Community (ref.: rural)										
Small town	−0.01 (0.01)	−0.01 (0.01)	−0.01 (0.01)	0.02† (0.01)	0.02 (0.01)	0.02 (0.01)	0.01 (0.01)	0.01 (0.01)	0.01 (0.01)	0.01 (0.01)
Large town	0.04** (0.01)	0.04** (0.01)	0.04** (0.01)	0.04** (0.01)	0.04** (0.01)	0.04** (0.01)	0.02 (0.01)	0.02† (0.01)	0.02† (0.01)	0.02† (0.01)
Education	0.11*** (0.01)	0.11*** (0.01)	0.11*** (0.01)	0.10*** (0.01)	0.10*** (0.01)	0.10*** (0.01)	0.09*** (0.01)	0.09*** (0.01)	0.09*** (0.01)	0.09*** (0.01)
Occupation (ref.: other)										
Student	−0.12*** (0.03)	−0.12*** (0.03)	−0.12*** (0.03)	−0.06* (0.03)	−0.06* (0.03)	−0.06* (0.03)	−0.01 (0.01)	0.00 (0.02)	−0.01 (0.02)	−0.01 (0.02)
Manager	0.08*** (0.02)	0.08*** (0.02)	0.08*** (0.02)	0.06** (0.02)	0.06*** (0.02)	0.06*** (0.02)	0.03† (0.02)	0.03† (0.02)	0.03† (0.02)	0.03† (0.02)
National economic expect.: worse	−0.20*** (0.01)	−0.20*** (0.01)	−0.20*** (0.01)				−0.16*** (0.01)	−0.16*** (0.01)	−0.16*** (0.01)	−0.16*** (0.01)
Personal economic expect.: worse	−0.10*** (0.02)	−0.10*** (0.02)	−0.10*** (0.02)	−0.08*** (0.01)	−0.18*** (0.02)	−0.18*** (0.02)	−0.11*** (0.01)	−0.11*** (0.01)	−0.11*** (0.01)	−0.11*** (0.01)
Political interest	0.08*** (0.01)	0.08*** (0.01)	0.08*** (0.01)	–	–	–	0.02*** (0.01)		0.02** (0.01)	0.02** (0.01)

European political interest	–	–	–	–	–	–		0.09*** (0.01)		
EU knowledge	0.12*** (0.01)	0.12*** (0.01)	0.12*** (0.01)	–	–	–	0.10*** (0.01)	0.09*** (0.01)	0.10*** (0.01)	0.10*** (0.01)
EU Conception (ref.: other)										
Common political project	0.26*** (0.03)	0.26*** (0.03)	0.26*** (0.03)	–	–	–	0.22*** (0.03)	0.22*** (0.03)	0.22*** (0.03)	0.22*** (0.03)
Individual benefits	0.05* (0.02)	0.05* (0.02)	0.05* (0.02)	–	–	–	0.09*** (0.02)	0.10*** (0.02)	0.09*** (0.02)	0.09*** (0.02)
National identification	0.26*** (0.01)	0.26*** (0.01)	0.26*** (0.01)	0.29*** (0.01)	0.29*** (0.01)	0.29*** (0.01)	0.26*** (0.01)	0.26*** (0.01)	0.26*** (0.01)	0.26*** (0.01)
Conception of national community				0.01 (0.02)	0.01 (0.02)	0.01 (0.02)				
Transnational practices	–	–	–	0.06*** (0.00)	0.06*** (0.00)	0.06*** (0.00)	0.10*** (0.00)	0.09*** (0.00)	0.10*** (0.00)	0.10*** (0.00)
Transnational capital	–	–	–	0.08*** (0.01)	0.08*** (0.01)	0.08*** (0.01)	0.02*** (0.00)	0.02*** (0.00)	0.02*** (0.00)	0.02*** (0.00)
Transnational background	0.13*** (0.02)	0.13*** (0.02)	0.13*** (0.02)	0.07** (0.02)	0.07** (0.02)	0.07** (0.02)	–	–	–	–
Country-level predictors										
Eurozone		0.05 (0.08)	0.07 (0.08)		0.15 (0.10)	0.18† (0.10)			0.08 (0.08)	0.07 (0.08)
Net paying EU transfers		−0.11 (0.09)	−0.07 (0.08)		−0.07 (0.13)	−0.03 (0.13)			−0.28* (0.20)	−0.18 (0.13)
Trade		0.00 (0.09)	0.00 (0.00)		−0.00 (0.00)	0.00 (0.00)			−0.00 (0.00)	−0.00 (0.00)
EU immigration		0.01 (0.01)			0.00 (0.01)				0.01 (0.01)	
Total immigration			0.00 (0.01)			−0.01 (0.01)				0.00 (0.01)

(continued)

Table 6.3 (continued)

	Multilevel analysis of individual identification with Europe (attachment to the European Union)									
	2007			2010			2012			
Year	M_1	M_{2a}	M_{2b}	M_1	M_{2a}	M_{2b}	M_{1a}	M_{1b}	M_{2a}	M_{2a}
Unemployment		0.05** (0.02)	0.05** (0.02)		0.00 (0.01)	0.01 (0.01)			−0.01 (0.01)	−0.01 (0.01)
IMF conditionality		–	–		0.06 (0.13)	0.07 (0.13)			−0.05 (0.12)	0.00 (0.11)
Variance components										
Country level τ_{00}	0.05 (0.01)	0.03 (0.01)	0.03 (0.01)	0.07 (0.02)	0.06 (0.02)	0.06 (0.02)	0.04 (0.01)	0.04 (0.01)	0.03 (0.01)	0.03 (0.01)
Individual level σ^2	0.66 (0.01)	0.66 (0.01)	0.66 (0.01)	0.64 (0.01)	0.64 (0.01)	0.64 (0.01)	0.60 (0.01)	0.60 (0.01)	0.60 (0.01)	0.60 (0.01)
Deviance	61,296.52	61,285.04	61,286.14	59,048.62	59,027.2	59,026.66	60,005.68	59,997.5	60,000.6	60,002.66
AIC	61,332.51	61,331.04	61,332.13	59,080.62	59,071.21	59,070.67	60,043.68	59,812.04	60,050.59	60,052.66
BIC	61,478.95	61,518.15	61,519.24	59,210.41	59,249.68	59,249.13	60,198.6	59,966.93	60,254.43	60,256.5
R^2	0.08	0.11	0.11	0.06	0.07	0.07	0.12	0.12	0.13	0.13
No. of groups (N)	27	27	27	27	27	27	27	27	27	27
No. of individuals (n)	25,217	25,217	25,217	24,641	24,641	24,641	25,687	25,644	25,687	25,687

Note: Figures are estimates from linear hierarchical regression models with random intercept, standard errors in parentheses. ***$p \leq 0.001$; **$p \leq 0.01$; *$p \leq 0.05$; †$p \leq 0.1$.

2012 are reported in Table 6.3. Building on the empty model reported in Table 6.1, the models are constructed stepwise, adding, first, explanatory variables at the individual level, and, second, explanatory variables at the country level. Finally, cross-level interactions are added.[20] Estimates for random coefficient models with cross-level interactions for the years 2000 to 2012 are reported in the appendix.

To avoid collinearity among predictor variables, separate models have been estimated for predictors that are highly correlated at either the individual or the country level. At the individual level, 'general political interest' and 'interest in European politics' have been included separately in models with individual-level predictors in 2003 and 2012 (the only years for which indicators for both constructs are available). To increase comparability across models, all further analyses are limited to 'general political interest' as this is the more widely available indicator. Likewise, given the overlap in the measurement of 'total share of immigrants' and 'share of EU immigrants', these measures have been entered in separate models. Again, to increase comparability across models, all further analyses include only the total share of immigrants (shares of EU immigrants are only available from 2004). Finally, to avoid collinearity between measures of party messages on national and European identity issues, respectively, these have been entered separately in the models for 2004.[21]

The following discussion of the empirical results seeks to draw general conclusions with regard to the determinants of individual identification with Europe among EU citizens over the past decade. The presentation proceeds in a stepwise way, examining, first, evidence for individual-level influences on European identification, moving on to country-level influences, and, finally, interaction effects between individual- and country-level predictors on respondents' identification with Europe.

---

[20]The model notation in the results tables follows the notation developed previously. That is, column M_1 reports results for random intercept models with individual-level covariates; column M_2 reports results for random intercept models with individual- and country-level covariates, and column M_3 reports results for random coefficient models with cross-level interactions. Additional subscripts $_{a,\ b}$ etc. indicate alternative model specifications to avoid collinearity between predictors. For example, in 2003, column M_{1a} reports results for the random intercept model including *political interest* as an individual-level predictor while column M_{1b} reports results for the random intercept model including *European political interest* as an individual-level predictor.

[21]Issues of multicollinearity in multilevel modelling and the impact of multicollinearity on parameter estimates and standard errors in multilevel regression analyses are rarely discussed in the literature (for exceptions, see Kreft and de Leeuw 1998; Kubitschek and Hallinan 1999; Shieh and Fouladi 2003). Kubitschek and Hallinan (1999) find the standard errors of parameter estimates to increase with multicollinearity between level 1 predictors; Shieh and Fouladi (2003) examine the effects of varying degrees of correlations between level-1 predictors, finding moderate bias in the standard errors of the parameter estimates as well as the variance-covariance components at level 2 for correlations >0.7. Kreft and de Leeuw (1998) illustrate that multicollinearity complicates the interpretation of multilevel model coefficients, in particular the interpretation of cross-level interactions. To minimise the risk of multicollinearity, I examined correlations among level-1 and level-2 predictors for all years under analysis. Correlations among predictors do not exceed 0.5; in the great majority of cases, correlations are smaller than 0.2.

6.3.2.1 Individual-Level Determinants of Citizens' Identification with Europe 2000–2012

The theoretical discussion derived three sets of *explanatory variables at the individual level*: political awareness, attitudes towards the European and the national community, and personal transnational experiences. The statistical analysis provides support for all three sets of hypotheses.

Starting with indicators of *political awareness*, both general political interest and interest in European politics as well as respondents' knowledge of the EU and European politics positively affect European identification in all years under analysis. We find empirical support for hypotheses predicting a positive association between respondents' political awareness and their propensity to identify with Europe ($H_{1a,}$ H_{2a}, and H_{3a}); the alternative hypotheses H_{1b}, H_{2b} and H_{3b} can be rejected.

Attitudes towards the European and the national community also have positive effects on European identification. From 2004 onwards, respondents who conceive of the European community as a common political project are consistently more likely to identify with Europe. Surprisingly, respondents who conceive of the European community primarily as a means for individual benefits, too, tend to identify more with Europe than respondents who hold other conceptions of Europe, although the effect is considerably smaller than the effect of perceiving Europe as a common political project. While we thus find evidence in support of hypothesis H_{4a} expecting positive effects of a conception of Europe as a common political project, we can reject hypothesis H_{4b} predicting a negative effect of conceiving of Europe as a means for individual benefits.

Furthermore, national identification has consistent and substantially important positive effects on European identification in all years under analysis. Respondents who identify more strongly with their national community also feel more attached to Europe. There is strong support for hypothesis $H_{5a,}$ which predicted a positive association between identifications at different levels of community. The alternative hypothesis H_{5b} is rejected. Citizens' conception of the national community, finally, has no significant effect on citizens' propensity to identify with Europe, disconfirming hypotheses H_{6a} and $H_{6b.}$

Personal transnational experiences, finally, also have the theoretically expected positive effect on identification with Europe. Transnational practices, a transnational family background, and higher levels of transnational capital all increase respondents' likelihood to identify with Europe. All three hypotheses referring to individual transnational experiences (H_7, H_8, and H_9) are supported by the empirical evidence.

Among the individual-level controls, only respondents' economic outlooks—and, to a lesser degree, their level of education—consistently affect respondents' identification with Europe in statistically and substantially significant ways. While pessimistic economic outlooks, both with regard to the national economy and the personal financial situation, depress respondents' propensity to identify with Europe, education has the expected positive impact on European identification.

To summarise, at the individual level, identification with Europe draws on cognitive and affective sources as well as on direct experiences of European integration in the form of personal contacts with other Europeans. These results support the concepts of information- and experience-based mechanisms of European identification as proposed in the theoretical section of the analysis.

To the extent that respondents' cognitive involvement with European politics strengthens their affective ties to Europe, an information-based way of European identification is substantiated. Respondents with greater interest in politics and especially those with a greater interest in European affairs and greater knowledge of EU politics feel more attached to Europe and the European Union than their less interested peers. In this way, more and better information about Europe and the EU appear to have the hypothesised beneficial effects for European identification.

Concerning experienced-based ways of European identification, on the other hand, both indirect and direct forms of experience with European integration and other Europeans seem to strengthen respondents' attachment to Europe and the European Union.

In fact, if we consider attitudes towards the European and national community the outcome of socialisation processes, we can think of these attitudes as experience with European integration at one remove; the empirical evidence shows that such attitudes indeed positively affect identification with the European level: Respondents' conception of Europe as a common political project has the expected positive effect on European identification. Even more important are affective ties to the national community: the more respondents feel attached to their country, the more they identify with the European level.

In this manner, European identification appears to be a matter of socialisation within the national community—not only in terms of conveying a certain image of Europe as a democratic political community, but even more so in providing citizens with the experience of belonging to a large-scale political community. National communities constitute 'imagined communities' in the sense of Anderson (Anderson 1991): citizens develop feelings of belonging together as a community and believe in the solidarity and cooperation of the other members of the community even if they personally interact only with a small fraction of their fellow nationals. In this way, the experience with the national political community prepares citizens for cooperation within the community of Europeans, which is a larger version of an 'imagined community'. Presumably, citizens who have positive experiences with belonging together and cooperating with strangers within the national community generalise from this experience and extend it to the European level, resulting in the positive association between national and European attachments.

The idea that respondents extrapolate from experiences in their immediate environment to the wider community of Europeans also finds support when we look at direct experiences with other Europeans. Respondents with a European family background identify significantly more with Europe than their peers. Other forms of transnational practices, including the skills enabling respondents to interact with other Europeans, have positive effects on European identification, too. Transactionalist theories of European identity formation dating back to Deutsch and the very beginnings of the European community (Deutsch 1953a, b; Deutsch et al. 1957) thus are still relevant for the development of European identification today. The more people are personally involved with other Europeans—be it through family and friends at home or through working and/or studying abroad—, the more likely they are to develop attachments to the European level.

We also observe that the effects of the individual predictors change little whether the dependent variable is measured by respondents' 'attachment to *Europe*' (2000 to 2006) or their 'attachment to the *European Union*' (2007 to 2012). Political awareness, national identification, and a European family background are among the most important predictors of European identification, independent of the operationalisation of the dependent variable.

It is interesting to note, however, that national identification has a stronger effect on respondents' attachment to *Europe* than on attachment to the *European Union*. This suggests that the European Union can rely only to a limited extent on affective sources and people's general propensity to identify with large-scale communities. Respondents appear more ready to generalise from positive feelings towards their own country to 'Europe' than to the EU. Presumably, these differences are due to the different prompts given by the two items. While the term 'Europe' leaves open whether it refers to Europe as a geographical or cultural region or the EU institutional system, the stimulus 'EU' is unambiguous; respondents are asked to indicate their attachment to the political system of the EU. Duchesne and Frognier (Duchesne and Frognier 2008) suggest that such differences in the question wording trigger different processes of dual identification with Europe and the nation. For them, identification with large-scale collectives relies on two processes: people's natural tendency to identify with abstract groups and their propensity to identify with the specific group in question that is defined, for example, by a specific territory or a political community. Duchesne and Forgnier hypothesise that national and European identification are cumulative and positively related if questions primarily tap into respondents' general disposition to identify with collectives. In contrast, national and European identification should be in competition and negatively related if questions tap into respondents' disposition to identify with distinct territorial or political communities presented and perceived as rivals. This second, competitive relationship may be manifest in the weaker (albeit still positive) association between national identification and 'attachment to the European Union'. In fact, the stimulus 'European Union' refers to a distinct political regime that is rival to and competes with the nation state for sovereignty. On the other hand, the stimulus 'Europe' remains undefined. In this way, it may appeal primarily to respondents' general tendency to identify with large-scale groups rather than compel them to arbitrate between the national and the European level. The result is the stronger positive association between national identification and 'attachment to Europe'.

6.3.2.2 Country-Level Determinants of Citizens' Identification with Europe 2000–2012

Having explored the individual sources of European identification, we now turn to the influence of the member state level on respondents' propensity to identify with Europe. The theoretical discussion expected three sets of member state characteristics to influence European identification among EU citizens: party messages related to the European and national community; macroeconomic indicators; and the ethnocultural composition of member state societies. The empirical findings support these expectations only to a limited extent.

The degree of *party emphasis on issues of European and national identity* has only small positive effects on respondents' identification with Europe. Party data from EP election manifestos is available only for 2004. In this year, only the regression coefficient for party emphasis on European identity and community reaches statistical significance at conventional levels. This finding supports hypothesis H_{10}, which expected a positive association between party emphasis on European identity and European identification at the individual level, but the effect is small in substantial terms.

It is interesting to note in this regard that the coefficient for party emphasis on national identity issues, too, has a positive sign. Although we should be careful not to overstate the effect given the small effect size and the lack of statistical significance at conventional levels, this finding suggests that, unlike theoretically expected (cf. H_{11}), party emphasis on national identity issues encourages rather than impedes European identification. Apparently, similar mechanisms are at work at the individual and the member state level: just as respondents who identify more with their country tend to identify more with Europe, respondents living in countries where parties put more emphasis on issues of national community and identity are more likely to identify with Europe. One explanation for this counterintuitive finding might be that in contexts where questions of community and identity are generally more salient, citizens are more conscious of their own collective identifications and affiliations with political communities at different levels. As a result, they may also be more aware of their European belongings. Parties may also embed issues of national identity within a generally supportive discourse of EU integration, thus establishing a positive link between national identity and Europe that may be reflected in the positive sign for party emphasis on national identity.

Turning now to member states' *economic position and degree of integration in European and global markets* as the second set of country-level characteristics expected to influence European identification at the individual level, we find little empirical support for the theoretically proposed associations.

The coefficient for *Eurozone membership* has the expected positive sign in most years, but is statistically significant (at the 10%-level) only in 2010. Hypothesis H_{12} expecting respondents from Eurozone countries to identify more with Europe than respondents from outside the Eurozone thus finds limited support.

The findings for member states' status as *net contributors or net recipients of EU funding* are more ambiguous: In the years 2000 to 2006, respondents from net paying countries to the EU budget identified *more* with Europe than respondents from net recipient countries; in the years 2007 to 2012, respondents from net paying countries identified *less* with Europe than respondents from net recipient countries. The strongest positive effect of net contributions to the EU budget on European identification occurs in 2006; the strongest negative effect of member states' status as a net contributor to the EU budget in 2012. Overall, there is only partial support for hypothesis H_{13}, which proposed a negative association between net contributions to the EU budget and European identifications.

We should be careful not to overstate these findings considering that only the coefficients for 2006 and 2012 reach conventional levels of statistical significance. Nonetheless, the change in the direction of the effect of net contributions to the EU budget after 2006 warrants further discussion. A number of explanations seem plausible.

First, we note that the change in the direction of the effect coincides with the change in the operationalisation of the dependent variable from 'attachment to Europe' to 'attachment to the European Union'. Perhaps economic considerations are less important for respondents when prompted to think about their attachment to 'Europe' than when asked to indicate their attachment to the 'European Union'. People may tend to understand 'Europe' as a geographical or cultural sphere, to which one belongs for other reasons (location, cultural affinity in terms of language and religion etc.) than economic benefits. In contrast, the cue 'European Union' may evoke connotations of the Common Market and supranational government, which are more likely to be evaluated based on performance and economic costs/ benefit calculations. In this case, a negative balance of national contributions to the EU budget should depress respondents' identification with Europe as the findings for the years 2007 to 2012 seem to indicate. What is more, in the years 2000 to 2006, the group of net paying member states largely corresponds to the EU founding member states such as Belgium, Germany, Italy, Luxemburg, and the Netherlands, where levels of support for European integration are traditionally high. Hence, the positive effect of net contributions to the EU budget on European identification between 2000 and 2006 may in fact reflect the overall positive outlook on Europe in the net paying countries at the time.

Alternatively, we might interpret the change in the direction of the effect as a long-term consequence of EU enlargement to Central and Eastern Europe. While the new CEE member states lagged behind in economic development and productivity, they also offered cheap labour and opportunities for the relocation of production lines from high-wage member states in Western Europe. The accession of Bulgaria and Romania in 2007 intensified the debate over labour migration from CEE to the 'old' EU15 member states. These implications of enlargement may have taken some time to sink in among the public of the EU15. In this regard, the change in the direction of the effect of the budget variable may reflect a higher awareness of the negative consequences of enlargement in the old member states, which, in the majority, were also net contributors to the EU budget (all new CEE member states except Cyprus have been net receivers of EU funding since EU accession).

Finally, the change in the direction of the effect of net payments to the EU budget, and, in particular, the increase in the effect size for 2012, may be attributed to the onset of the financial and economic crisis in late 2008 and the continuing controversy among member states over the 'right' financial and economic policy responses. By May 2012, the EU had seen over two years of intense discussions over financial assistance to member states in crisis (the Eurozone members first agreed on providing bilateral loans to Greece in April 2010) and the need for structural reforms in economically lagging countries. Questions of financial solidarity, redistribution, debt cuts, potential defaults etc. were highly salient in both debtor and creditor countries at the time (cf. the findings by Kontochristou and Mascha 2014; Mazzoni and Barbieri 2014). The length and intensity of the debate over adequate measures to overcome the crisis likely made citizens aware of the stakes of economic integration and greater interdependencies. This effect may have been compounded by the overlap between the group of member states making net payments to the EU budget and those member states providing the highest credit lines to countries in financial and economic difficulties. Against this background, the negative sign and increased size of the coefficient of the budget variable in 2012 may reflect the heightened awareness of the costs of economic integration among citizens in the contributor countries.

Greater *trade openness* does not appear to influence European identification in any meaningful way given the minuscule effect size and lack of statistical significance. Accordingly, hypothesis H_{14}, which assumed a positive effect of global economic integration on European identification, is rejected.

Similarly, the findings with regard to member states' *ethnocultural composition* provide only limited support for the theoretical expectations. In most of the years under analysis, neither the share of EU immigrants nor the overall share of immigrants in a country affect European identification in substantially and/or statistically significant ways. Furthermore, the effects are not consistent over time. While the coefficients for both total immigration shares and share of EU migrants in a country have negative signs from 2003 to 2006, the direction of the effects changes in the years 2007 to 2012. All in all, the findings with regard to member state societies' ethnocultural composition at best provide scant support for hypothesis H_{16b} predicting a negative association between total immigration shares and European identification (coefficients for total immigration are negative and statistically significant at the 5% level in 2004); none of the other hypotheses (H_{15}, H_{16a}) is supported by the empirical evidence.

As regards country-level controls, *unemployment* does not significantly affect European identification, either, with the partial exception of 2003 and 2006/2007. In these years, we observe small positive effects for unemployment, meaning that respondents from member states with higher levels of unemployment were slightly more likely to identify with Europe.

Taken together, member states' political, economic, and social characteristics influence individual identification with Europe only to a limited degree. While the empirical evidence for the individual-level determinants supported both information- and experience-based ways of identification with Europe, the findings for the country-level determinants are less convincing. Neither party-messages related to the European and national community as a source for Europe-related information nor member states' economic position and degree of integration in the EU and global markets and their ethnocultural composition as sources of Europe-related experiences have a significant influence on respondents' identification with Europe.

Several reasons may explain the limited influence of country-level characteristics on respondents' identification with Europe. As regards the (non)-effect of *party messages*, party-level data was only available for the year 2004. Analyses of media coverage show that the 2004 EP election campaign had only moderate visibility in the news, trailing behind domestic and social policies as well as sports and economic issues (de Vreese et al. 2006). More generally, news coverage of the EU is often dominated by economic topics (Peter et al. 2003; Schuck et al. 2011) and in 2004, the EU's enlargement to CEE played a prominent role in EU coverage. Against this background, we may assume that parties' messages with regard to the European and national community did not reach citizens, because they fell behind other topics in EU news coverage and/or citizens concentrated on more salient topics of EU integration.

With regard to *member states' economic position and degree of integration in the EU and global markets*, it is possible that citizens perceive the euro mainly as an everyday item rather than a symbol of European integration and, therefore, do not relate their experience with the common currency to their membership in the European community. Likewise, trade shares and member state contributions to the EU budget may have too little salience in citizens' everyday lives to matter for attitudes towards EU integration. In this regard, it is interesting to note that member states' net contributions to the EU budget have significant effects on European identification in 2006 and 2012. In these years, questions of financial redistributions and economic differences between EU member states became more salient in the context of EU enlargement and the financial and economic crisis. Public debates in the member states often centred on the national perspective (see the findings by e.g. Dursun-Ozkanca 2011; Gottschalck 2011/2012; Inthorn 2006; Katsourides 2014; Light and Young 2009; Mazzoni and Barbieri 2014; van Noije 2010). It appears that the domestic consequences of European integration do not matter per se, but need to be made salient for citizens to consider them when forming attitudes towards the European community.

This finding also has consequences for how we conceive of the mechanism underlying the relationship between macroeconomic indicators and citizens' identification with Europe. Initially, macroeconomic conditions and member states' economic position within the EU were considered indicators for how citizens experience EU integration in their everyday lives. Yet the finding that member states' contributions to the EU budget significantly affect European identification only at times of high salience of economic issues in the domestic debates indicates that the underlying mechanism may be information- rather than experience-based. That is, citizens' propensity to identify with Europe appears to depend less on living in a net contributor or net recipient member state, but on the amount of information—and probably the degree of controversy—about member states' economic contribution to the EU that citizens encounter in the domestic context.

Finally, the limited effects of (EU) *immigration rates* on respondents' identification with Europe appear to indicate that aggregate shares of foreigners living in a country are only a poor proxy for actual personal interactions between national and foreign citizens. Furthermore, national immigration shares may be too crude a measure for citizens' opportunities to interact with non-nationals in their daily lives as migrant populations typically vary at the regional and local level. That is, opportunities to meet foreigners may be limited to citizens living in certain areas and we would need local rather than national immigration shares to test the effects of immigration levels on European attitudes in a more satisfactory way.

6.3.2.3 Interaction Effects Between Individual- and Country-Level Determinants of Citizens' Identification with Europe 2000–2012

Although few of the country-level determinants proved to have direct effects on European identification, we may still suspect that member state characteristics influence identification with Europe mediated through respondents' individual attributes and predispositions. For example, while party messages may not have a significant impact on European identification in general, they may still prove influential among the most politically interested respondents.

The theoretical discussion suggested two sets of such interaction effects: between individual political interest and member state characteristics on the one hand and between national identification and member state characteristics on the other. The remainder of this section presents the empirical findings on interaction effects between country-level predictors and political interest and national identification, respectively. Parameter estimates, standard errors, and variance components for the models with random coefficients and cross-level interactions can be found in Tables 6.6, 6.7, 6.8, 6.9, 6.10, 6.11, 6.12 in the appendix.

Starting with the empirical findings for political interest, we find no evidence that respondents at different levels of political interest differ with regard to the effects of country characteristics on European identification. The analyses for 2004 show no effect of political interest on the relationship between party messages and European identifications (cf. Table 6.8). That is, neither hypothesis H_{17} nor hypotheses H_{17a} and H_{17b} find empirical support.

Likewise, neither the relationship between member states' net contributions to the EU budget and individual European identification nor the relationship between member states' trade openness and individual European identification depend on respondents' level of political interest. The coefficients for the interaction terms are substantially small and statistically insignificant in all years under analysis (cf. Tables 6.6, 6.7, 6.8, 6.9, 6.10, 6.11, 6.12 in the appendix). We therefore reject both hypotheses H_{18} and H_{19}.

Respondents at different levels of *national identification,* too, appear to differ only to limited extent with regard to the effects of country characteristics on European identification. Starting with the interaction between national identification and party emphasis on identity issues in 2004, we find no substantially or statistically significant effects for the interaction term (cf. Table 6.8 in the appendix). The effect of party messages does not increase among respondents with stronger attachments to the national level; accordingly, hypotheses H_{20} and H_{20a} are rejected.

Turning to the other cross-level interactions involving national identification, we find a substantially and statistically significant interaction effect of national identification and member states' net contributions to the EU budget only in 2004 (cf. Table 6.8 in the appendix). The coefficient for the interaction term has the expected negative sign. However, the effects of the constitutive terms national identification and net contributions to the EU budget remain positive and substantially significant. The differences in the size of the coefficients of the interaction and constitutive terms and the opposite signs of theses coefficients imply that the positive effect of national identification on European identification is smaller in net contributing countries, but remains positive nonetheless. That is, even in net contributing countries to the EU budget, respondents who identify more with the national level also identify more with Europe.

A look at the marginal effects of national identification in net contributing and net recipient countries helps clarify the relationship between national and European identification in the two country groups. The marginal effects of national identification can be thought of as the slope of national identification conditional on whether respondents live in a member state that is a net contributor to the EU budget or a member state that is a net recipient of EU funding.

Figure 6.1 visualises the slopes of national identifications for the two groups of countries, graphing predicted European identification over the range of national identification in net recipient and net contributing member states. Straight lines show predictive margins of national identification in net recipient and net contributing member states to the EU budget. Vertical lines give 95% confidence intervals. Predictive margins are based on Model M_{3b} reported in Table 6.8 in the appendix.

The slopes of national identification are positive in both net recipient and net contributing countries. That is, in both country groups, respondents who identify more with their country also identify more with Europe. Nonetheless, the slope for national identification is steeper in net recipient countries of EU funding than in net contributing countries to the EU budget. That is, an increase in national identification leads to a greater increase in European identification among respondents in net recipient countries than among those in net contributor countries to the EU budget. The confidence intervals around the two slopes indicate that the differences in European identification between respondents in net recipient and net contributing member are statistically significant at all but the highest level of national identification, at which confidence intervals overlap.

Taken together, these results provide partial support for hypothesis H_{21}, which expected a stronger negative relationship between net EU budget contributions and European identification among individuals who identify more with the nation. In

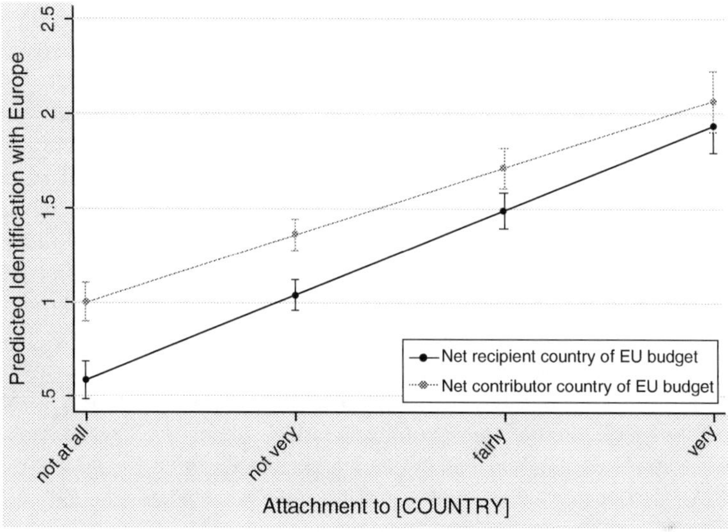

Fig. 6.1 Predicted European identification in net contributing and net recipient countries of EU funding over range of national identification 2004

fact, the effect of living in a net contributing member state on identification with Europe is positive rather than negative and remains positive even for those respondents who identify most with their own country. However, the effect of net EU budget contributions on European identification is weaker among respondents with stronger national attachments (cf. Fig. 6.1). In this sense, we can think of strong national attachment as *dampening* the positive effect of living in a net contributor country to the EU budget, even if they do not reverse the effect.

We should further note that the direction of the effect of the interaction between national identification and net payments to the EU budget changes over the years. While the coefficient for the interaction term has a positive sign until 2003 (cf. Tables 6.6 and 6.7 in the appendix), the sign changes in 2004 and remains negative until 2007 (cf. Tables 6.8, 6.9, 6.10 in the appendix); in 2010 and 2012, it is again positive (cf. Tables 6.11, and 6.12 in the appendix). The timing of these changes suggests a relation to the EU's enlargement to CEE and the onset of the financial and economic crisis, which had significant consequences for the distribution of funds within the EU and raised questions of financial redistribution between EU member states. Section 6.3.3 below will further explore this line of interpretation and discuss the changing effects of the interaction between national identification and net payments to the EU budget in light of the EU's enlargement to CEE and the onset of the economic and financial crisis.

The final hypothesis involving interaction effects between national identification and country-level predictors suggested that member states' overall shares of immigrants have a stronger negative effect on European identification among respondents who identify more with the national level (cf. H_{22}). This hypothesis is rejected given that we observe no substantially or statistically significant interaction effects between national identification and total immigration rates in any of the years under analysis (cf. Tables 6.6, 6.7, 6.8, 6.9, 6.10, 6.11, 6.12 in the appendix).

To sum up the findings with regard to the cross-level interactions, we find only limited empirical evidence that the effects of member state characteristics on identification with Europe depend on respondents' degree of political interest or their attachment to the home country. Several reasons may explain this (non-)result.

The lack of evidence of mediating effects of political interest allows two interpretations. On the one hand, the lack of differences in the effect of member state characteristics between respondents at different levels of political interest may indicate that even the most interested are fairly ignorant of party communications or their home country's economic position within the EU and/or do not draw on this information when forming attachments to the European level. From a more optimistic point of view, we may interpret the lack of differences between respondents at different levels of political interest as a sign that the highly interested do not necessarily have an advantage over their less interested peers when it comes to party messages or the basic facts of the national economy.

The findings for mediating effects of national identification provide some evidence that citizens draw on group sentiments when evaluating the domestic consequences of European integration. As expected, national attachments are particularly important if EU integration has direct financial implications for the national community, as in the case of member states' net contributions to the EU budget. We further observe a time-dependency in the mediating effects of national attachments. National attachments became important for the effect of member state characteristics on European identification at a time when (economic) differences and questions of redistribution between member states became more salient because of the accession of Eastern European countries to the EU.

These findings resonate with previous work that consider economic- and identity-approaches not as competing explanations of EU attitudes, but point to interdependencies between the two (Garry and Tilley 2009). In this view, the effects of national identity on European attitudes are conditional on the national economic context, with national attachments becoming more important for European attitudes as economic competition intensifies. The following section will further pursue this line of analysis. It investigates changes in the determinants of individual identification in response to EU enlargement to CEE and the onset of the financial and economic crisis, i.e. two events that exposed economic differences within the EU and led to financial redistributions between EU member states.

6.3.3 EU Enlargement and the Financial and Economic Crisis and Citizens' Identification with Europe

Having explored European identification in general, we now turn to the implications of EU enlargement and the financial and economic crisis for the development of individual identification with Europe. Do the determinants of citizens' identification with Europe change in response to these key moments in the integration process? Which factors become more or less important for European identification against the background of enlargement and the crisis? Starting with enlargement, the following section discusses shifts in the determinants of European identification that can be traced back to the EU's enlargement to CEE in 2004/2007 and the onset of the financial and economic crisis in late 2008. As before, the discussion will centre first on individual-level determinants of European identification, and, subsequently, turn to country-level determinants and cross-level interactions.

6.3.3.1 The Impact of EU Enlargement on Citizens' Identification with Europe

Chapter 3 outlined the consequences of the 2004/2007 enlargement rounds for the EU and its member states. Most importantly, the EU's eastward enlargement increased economic disparities among EU member states as GDP per capita and income levels were substantially lower in the new member states. Enlargement further led to institutional and policy reforms at the EU level and increased the salience of EU integration issues in national media and public debates, at least for the immediate accession period in spring 2004. In light of the increased attention to EU affairs and the redistributive consequences of enlargement, the theoretical discussion expected changes in the importance of both political interest and national identification for citizens' propensity to identify with Europe (cf. hypotheses H_{23} and H_{24}).

The overview of the regression coefficients for the years 2000 to 2006 listed in Table 6.2 does not reveal dramatic shifts in the individual-level determinants of European identification over the 2000 to 2006 period. We observe moderate increases in the effect sizes of political interest and objective knowledge of EU politics between 2004 and 2006; likewise, there is a small increase in the coefficient for national identification in 2004. Finally, while respondents' conception of Europe as a common political project was negatively related to European identification in 2003, it has a positive effect from 2004 onwards. The change in the direction and size of the effect in 2004 appears to indicate that citizens embraced representations of the EU as a guarantor of freedom and democracy in Europe prominent in the context of the accession of the new democracies in Eastern Europe (Nugent 2004).

The increase in the (positive) effect of political interest and EU knowledge on European identification supports claims whereby the greater salience of the EU due to enlargement has contributed to a widening 'knowledge gap' between politically interested and less interested citizens. The politically interested appear to benefit disproportionally from the heightened media attention to the EU in the context of enlargement. Better information and knowledge of EU affairs, in turn, positively affect people's likelihood to identify with Europe. In this regard, the empirical findings support hypothesis H_{23}, which expected an increase in the importance of political interest as a predictor of European identification in relation to the accession of new member states from Central and Eastern Europe.

As regards the effects of national attachments on European identification, we find only partial evidence of an increasing importance of national identities in the context of enlargement. While national attachments have stronger effects in 2004 compared to 2003 and 2006, these effects do not reach the pre-enlargement level of 2000, and the 2004 increase in the regression coefficient is small in substantial terms.[22] Hence hypothesis H_{24}, which predicted an increase in the effect of national identification in response to enlargement, is only partly supported by the empirical analysis. What is more, national identification has a positive effect on European attachments throughout the accession period. At first sight, eastward enlargement thus does not appear to have stirred widespread concerns for the national community, which would translate into a generally negative association between national and European identifications.

Among the *country-level predictors*, we observe notable changes in effect size during and after the enlargement period only for the coefficient of net contributions to the EU budget. Between 2000 and 2006, living in a net contributing member state is positively related to respondents' identification with Europe; from 2007 onwards, the effect is reversed. While we need to be careful not to overstate these findings given that only the coefficient for 2004 reaches conventional levels of statistical significance, these findings still warrant some discussion.

In a first instance, redistributive concerns do not appear to have become more important for European attachments, even as poorer CEE countries joined the Union. This is evident in the positive effects of net EU budget contributions on European identification throughout the immediate pre- and post-enlargement period (2003–2006). Living in a net paying member state to the EU budget only starts to have negative effects on European identification in 2007, as indicated by the change in the sign of the coefficient in this year.

As has been pointed out before, the change in the sign of the coefficient in 2007 could be due to changes in the operationalisation of the dependent variable from 'attachment to Europe' to 'attachment to the European Union' in 2007. Alternatively, we may see here a long-term effect of the 2004 enlargement round and the impact of the accession of Bulgaria and Romania in 2007. The redistributive consequences of enlargement as well as the consequences for national labour markets (increased competition at home, as Eastern Europeans entered labour markets in the EU15; threats of relocations from the EU15 to low-wage countries in Eastern Europe) may have taken some time for citizens in the EU15 to absorb. The debate over (labour) immigration and wage-dumping by opening the EU15 labour markets to Eastern Europeans was also revived in the context of the

---

[22]Note that only the results for the years 2000 and 2003 on the one hand and for 2004 and 2006 on the other are directly comparable as the analyses for 2000/2003 and 2004/2006 rely on different country samples (EU15 for 2000/2003 and EU25 for 2004/2006). Separate analyses for the EU15 and the new CEE member states for 2004/2006 show largely similar effects as the analyses for the pooled sample of the EU25.

accession of Bulgaria and Romania in early 2007. Hence, the change in the direction of the budget variable after 2007 may be a sign of heightened awareness to redistributive issues in the old member states, which for the most part were also net contributors to the EU budget in this period.

If the change in the direction of the effect of the EU budget variable indeed reflects concerns with regard to enlargement among respondents in the net paying member states, we may expect that these concerns are even more prevalent among respondents with strong attachments to the national level. We can explore this hypothesis by examining the interaction between national identification and net EU budget contributions and its effect on respondents' identification with Europe.

The cross-level interaction between national identification and member states' net budgetary contributions is statistically significant only in 2004 (cf. Table 6.8 in the appendix). Nonetheless, a look at the behaviour of the interaction term and its constituent terms over the years may prove informative and allows some speculation regarding changes in the relationship between national identification, EU transfers, and European identification in response to the EU's enlargement to Central and Eastern Europe. We observe that in the years prior to enlargement, i.e. 2000 and 2003, the coefficient for EU transfers has a negative sign (cf. Tables 6.6 and 6.7 in the appendix), while the coefficients for both national identification and the interaction term have positive signs. After enlargement, i.e. from 2004 to 2007, the sign of the coefficients change: while the coefficients for both constituent terms now have a positive sign, the interaction term takes a negative sign (cf. Tables 6.8 and 6.9 in the appendix). How can we interpret these changes in substantive terms?

We already discussed the interaction effect between national identification and EU budgetary contributions on respondents' identification with Europe for the year 2004 (cf. Sect. 6.3.2.3). We found that national identification increased European identification in both net recipients and net paying member states to the EU budget, but the positive effect of national identification on European identification smaller in net paying member states (cf. Fig. 6.1). In the years 2006 and 2007, the signs for the regression coefficients are the same as in 2004 (positive signs for the constitutive terms of the interaction, negative sign for the interaction term). Hence, similar dynamics seem to be at work in 2004, 2006, and 2007. In the post-enlargement period, national identification has a positive effect on European identification in both net recipient and net contributing member states, but the effect is *smaller* in net *contributing* member states than in the net recipient member states.

Prior to enlargement, in contrast, the relationship between national identification and European identification in net recipient and net contributing member states to the EU budget seems to have been the reverse. In 2000 and 2003, national identification also has a positive effect on European identification in both net recipient and net contributing member states, but in these years, the effect of national identification on European identification is *larger* in net *contributing* member states compared to the net recipient member states.

While we should be careful not to overstate these findings given the lack of statistical significance of the regression coefficients in some years, they still seem to point to changes in the effects of national identification conditional on respondents living in net recipient or net paying member stats of EU transfers that can be traced back to EU enlargement. How can we explain the weakening of national identification as a source of European identification in the net paying member states to the EU budget after enlargement?

The above finding seem to indicate that respondents drew different conclusions from their country's net payments to the EU budget with regard to European identification before and after the accession of the new CEE member states. Presumably, respondents' perception of the costs and benefits of the European project and their consequences for the national level changed with enlargement.

In effect, media reports on enlargement took a predominantly national perspective, focussing in particular on questions of migration and the effects of enlargement on national labour markets (Dursun-Ozkanca 2011; Inthorn 2006; Light and Young 2009; van Noije 2010). Furthermore, the enlargement period coincides with a general trend whereby cultural issues such as immigration, cultural diversity, and the defence of national traditions and sovereignty, national identity, and a national way of life have become more salient in political conflict (Bornschier 2010; Hutter and Grande 2014; Kriesi et al. 2006; Stoll 2010). At the party level, we see the emergence of populist right-wing parties that promote traditionalist-communitarian values and the primacy of the national community and national sovereignty over decision-making at EU level (Bornschier 2011).

We may speculate that respondents in the net paying countries to the EU budget were more responsive to arguments about the cost of enlargement and potential threats to the national community and weighed these more when forming opinions towards Europe than their peers in net recipient countries of EU transfers. As a result, we see the positive effect of national identification diminish in these countries compared to the net recipient countries. This interpretation also ties in with the proposition by Duchesne and Frognier (Duchesne and Frognier 2008) whereby national identification depresses rather than increases identification with Europe if respondents perceive the national and European communities as rivals and arbitrate between the two. Given the relative homogeneity of the old EU15 member states, there was little reason for citizens to perceive the national and the European level as rivals. This changed with the accession of the new CEE member states. For citizens in the EU15 (which corresponds widely to the group of net paying member states after 2004), EU integration and the new, enlarged European community may now have posed threats to the national community in terms of labour competition, immigration and cultural homogeneity etc. Therefore, respondents in the net paying member states who strongly identify with their country may have started to identify less with Europe after enlargement than in the pre-enlargement period. As a result, after enlargement, the relationship between national and European identification becomes weaker in the net contributing member states to the EU budget than in the net recipient countries.

Taken together, the empirical findings with regard to the consequences of EU enlargement for the sources of European identification allow for several conclusions:

As regards the role of individual attributes and predispositions for European identification, enlargement appears to have had only minor consequences. If anything, enlargement appears to have contributed to the 'knowledge gap' between politically interested and less interested citizens as political interest has become a more important predictor of European identification in the aftermath of enlargement.

More importantly, EU enlargement appears to have made redistributive considerations more relevant for respondents' identification with Europe. The (positive) effect of member states' status as a net payer to the EU budget increases over time; it is strongest right after the accession of the ten new CEE member states in 2004 and changes in direction in 2007. In this regard, the present analysis supports claims whereby economic competition and issues of financial redistribution between EU member states have become more relevant for citizens' attitudes towards Europe as EU integration widens and deepens (Eichenberg and Dalton 2007; Garry and Tilley 2015). Unlike what might have been expected, however, net EU transfer payments have a positive effect on European identification throughout the first round of Eastward enlargement (2000–2006). A country's net budget contributions only start to have negative effects on respondents' identification with Europe from 2007 on. This may be interpreted as a long-term effect the 2004 enlargement and/or the effect of the accession of Bulgaria and Romania in January 2007, which revived debates over negative consequences of enlargement on national labour markets and immigration.

Finally, we find enlargement to modify the relationship between national and European identification in net recipient and net contributing countries to the EU budget. National and European identification are positively related in net recipient and net paying member states both before and after enlargement. Yet prior to enlargement, i.e. in 2000 and 2003, the positive influence of national identification on European identification is *larger* in net *contributing* than in net recipient member states while after enlargement, i.e. from 2004 onwards, it is *larger* in net *recipient* than in net contributing member states. In this regard, arguments about the cost of enlargement and the economic and cultural threats it poses to the national community appear to have caught on more in the net paying member states.

These findings are in line with previous work that found the effect of macroeconomic factors on European attitudes to be conditioned by national identity (Garry and Tilley 2009). The present work adds to this research by showing that the relationship between national identity, macroeconomic factors, and attitudes towards the EU are not static, but change over time as EU integration progresses and the composition of EU membership and economic relations between EU member states evolve.

Against this background, a closer investigation of the consequences of the financial and economic crisis for the determinants of European identification is all the more interesting, given that the crisis exposed economic differences between EU member states and led to extensive debates over financial redistributions within the EU. The following section will discuss changes in the determinants of European identification in relation to the financial and economic crisis that started in late

2008, exploring in particular changes in the effects of macroeconomic factors on individual identification with Europe.

6.3.3.2 The Impact of the Financial and Economic Crisis on Citizens' Identification with Europe

The overview of the financial and economic crisis and its consequences for the EU and the member states in Chap. 3 showed that the crisis increased economic disparities within the EU, most notably between member states that experienced sovereign debt crises, e.g. Greece or Portugal, and member states that emerged comparatively quickly from the recession, e.g. Germany. At the same time, debates over member states' mutual obligations and financial interdependence intensified and EU issues became more and more salient in national political debates. In light of these developments, a number of theoretical expectations addressed potential changes in the effects of individual- and country-level determinants of European identification in relation the crisis. A number of hypotheses predicted changes in the importance of political interest ($H_{23,}$ H_{25}), national identification (H_{24}), and macroeconomic factors ($H_{26,}$ H_{27}) as predictors of European identification and a decline in European identification among respondents from member states under EU/IMF conditionality (H_{28}) and Eurozone member states (H_{29}) during the crisis. The negative effects of EU/IMF conditionality and Eurozone membership should be especially pronounced among respondents with strong attachments to the national level ($H_{30,}$ H_{31}).

Taking 2007 as the base year, the remainder of this section will assess to what extent the empirical evidence supports the theoretical expectations regarding the impact of the financial and economic crisis on the determinants of individual identification with Europe. It starts by discussing the individual-level determinants, proceeds to potential changes in the effects of member states' macroeconomic situation on European identification, and finally looks into interaction effects between national identification and macroeconomic conditions on European identification.

The overview of the models for the years 2007 to 2012 summarised in Table 6.3 reveals no major changes in the regression coefficients for the *individual-level determinants* between the pre-crisis year 2007 and the crisis years 2010 and 2012. We observe a minor decrease in the effects of *political interest*, which provides some empirical support for hypothesis H_{25} expecting political interest to have less influence on European identification after the onset of the financial and economic crisis. (Vice versa, this finding disproves hypothesis H_{23}, which expected the effect of political interest on European identification to increase as EU issues gain in salience in the context of the crisis.) Likewise, respondents' *knowledge of EU politics* became slightly less influential between 2007 and 2012. We also find the effect of respondents' *conception of the EU* as a *common political project* to decrease slightly between 2007 and 2012 whereas perceiving the EU mainly as providing *individual benefits* had stronger (positive) effects on respondents' identification with Europe in 2012 than in 2007. *National identification* remained one of the strongest predictors throughout the crisis years; its effect on European identification slightly increased between 2007 and 2010, but goes back to its 2007 level in 2012. Hypothesis H_{24} predicting a growing importance of national attachments for European attachments in the context of the crisis thus cannot be confirmed.

Among the *individual-level control variables*, we note a small decrease in the effects of respondents' level of *education* while differences in European identification between *students, managers,* and respondents in *other professions* become statistically and substantially insignificant in 2012. Finally, the effects of respondents' *evaluations of the national economy* slightly decrease after the onset of the crisis; the effects of respondents' *evaluation of their personal finances* remain virtually unchanged before and after the onset of the crisis.

The smaller effect of political interest together with the reduced effects of educational levels and EU knowledge allow for two interpretations. On the one hand, the smaller effects of political interest and education may indicate that as the EU became more politicised and the debate over EU integration became more polarised, citizens' motivation (political interest) and abilities (education) to inform themselves about the EU became less important for forming an opinion towards the EU. As media coverage of EU issues increased in the crisis, even the politically less aware had easy access to EU-related information and, given the high level of controversy over the EU in the crisis, positions on EU integration were more easily discernible. As a result, we see the differences between more and less politically aware respondents diminish as the crisis continues.

On the other hand, the smaller effects of political interest and education on European identification may indicate that, during the crisis, respondents with more interest in and better knowledge of EU affairs became more aware of the risks of EU integration, and, consequently, less inclined to identify with Europe. In this regard, they may have become more alike to their politically less aware peers, resulting in the observed decrease in the differences in European identification between more and less politically aware respondents.

The findings for respondents' occupation point in the same direction: As issues of EU integration become highly salient and polarised, differences in European identification between students, managers, and other professions disappear. It seems that the greater salience of EU integration at the domestic level helps respondents in other professions to compensate disadvantages vis-à-vis managers and students in terms of education, access to EU-related information, or opportunities to interact with other Europeans abroad and at home.

Turning to *country-level determinants of European identification*, we observe changes for a number of the macroeconomic predictors, notably *Eurozone* membership and *net contributions to the EU budget*. Both become more important as determinants of European identification in the crisis years. In this regard, the models for 2010 and 2012 provide some empirical evidence for the expectation that economic indicators become more important for identification with Europe after the onset of the financial and economic crisis (cf. H_{26}).

Unlike expected, however, economic decline does not negatively affect European identification (cf. H_{27}), at least not if we take national *unemployment* rates as a proxy for the adverse economic effects of the crisis in the member states. In fact, while higher unemployment rates are positively related to European identification in 2007, they no longer have significant effects in 2010 and 2012. The findings for *EU/IMF conditionality* point in the same direction. We do not observe substantially or statistically significant differences in European identification between respondents from member states receiving conditional aid from the EU/IMF and respondents from other EU member states. Hypothesis H_{28} proposing a negative effect of EU/IMF conditionality on European identification is therefore rejected.

These findings seem counterintuitive, especially for the countries under EU/IMF conditionality. The EU played a prominent role in imposing austerity programmes in exchange for financial aids and it should be relatively easy for citizens to make a connection between the negative consequences of austerity measures for their societies, e.g. in terms of social security, public spending, and pension levels, and the EU as (one of) the initiator(s) of these programmes. In the absence of significant negative effects of EU/IMF conditionality on European identification, we may speculate that respondents from member states under EU/IMF conditionality did not so much blame the EU for the economic and social distortions in their country, but understood the need for structural reforms and appreciated the financial aids preventing national bankruptcy. It may also be that the expected 'blame effect' whereby the EU's role in imposing austerity measures weakens European attachments occurred only among certain subsets of the populations in the member states receiving conditional financial aids. This hypothesis is explored below when discussing interactions effects between political interest and national identification and macroeconomic predictors.

The findings for membership in the *Eurozone*, too, run counter to theoretical expectations. We do not see a reversal of the (positive) effects of Eurozone membership on European identification after the onset of the crisis as proposed by hypothesis H_{29}. Throughout 2010 and 2012, Eurozone membership has a positive effect on respondents' identification with Europe (although only the coefficient for 2010 approaches conventional levels of statistical significance). The strongest effect actually occurs in 2010 (significant at the 10% level), i.e. the year the Eurogroup first agreed on bilateral loans and financial stability mechanisms to save member states in sovereign debt crisis.[23] That is, respondents from Eurozone countries became more attached to the EU at a time of high saliency of EU affairs and intense controversy over financial rescue measures at the European level. We

[23]Note that EB 77.3 was in the field in March/April 2010, i.e. during the period when the Eurogroup first negotiated bilateral loans for Greece. Greece officially requested to activate international financial support mechanisms on 23 April 2010; the formal agreement with the IMF was approved on 02 May 2010. The European Council, the Eurogroup, and ECOFIN, together with the IMF, the ECB and the European Commission, had been discussing the Greek financial situation at various meetings in the months leading up to the formal agreement.

may interpret this as a sign that arguments regarding the need for a European solution to the sovereign debt crises in the Eurozone had the intended effects. What is more, respondents in Eurozone countries presumably felt more directly affected by the crisis and the risk of a break-up of the Eurozone than respondents outside the Eurozone. This feeling of being personally affected may have translated into a feeling of 'being in this together', which in turn may have strengthened attachments to the European level.

Finally, we observe that the negative effects of member states' status as *net contributors to the EU budget* become stronger (and statistically significant) as the crisis continues. Over time, calculations in terms of financial costs and benefits appear to become more important for respondents when considering their attachment to Europe. By 2012, the EU had seen more than three years of intense debate over the appropriate response to the economic crisis and, in particular, financial rescue mechanisms to support member states experiencing sovereign debt crises. It also had become clear by then that member states receiving bilateral loans and credits through the various European financial stability measures, Greece in particular, would not be able to repay their debts in the short-run and that some creditors would not be repaid in full.[24] In short, we can assume that, by 2012, respondents in the net contributor countries, which were also the countries providing the largest bilateral loans and financial guarantees, had come to understand the financial risks of bailouts for national budgets and the potential costs incurred by their home country. The greater awareness of financial costs and benefits seems to be reflected in the stronger negative effect of net contributions to the EU budget on respondents' identification with Europe. In this regard, redistributive issues and cost/benefit calculations appear to have gained relevance over the course of the crisis.

Overall, we thus find some evidence that macroeconomic indicators became more important for individual identification with Europe as the crisis continued. Nonetheless, some of the empirical findings appear counterintuitive. In particular, the lack of influence of EU/IMF conditionality on European identification as well as the persistent *positive* effect of the Eurozone dummy in the crisis years is intriguing. Perhaps the overall positive effects of Eurozone membership in the crisis mask differences between subgroups of respondents at different levels of national identification within Eurozone member states (cf. H_{31}). Similarly, we may expect interaction effects between national identification and EU/IMF conditionality on European identification (cf. H_{30}). To assess these hypotheses, the remainder of this section will explore interaction effects between national identification and EU/IMF conditionality and Eurozone membership, respectively.

The results for the models including cross-level interaction terms for the years 2007 to 2012 are listed in Tables 6.10, 6.11, 6.12 in the appendix. Starting with the interaction between national identification and EU/IMF conditionality, we find the expected negative sign for the coefficient of the interaction term in both 2010 and

[24]In October 2011, private creditors holding Greek government bonds agreed to a 50% 'haircut', converting their existing bonds into new loans (Euro Summit 2011; Gow 2011).

2012 (cf. Tables 6.11 and 6.12 in the appendix; no EU member state received financial aids from the EU/IMF in 2007); the effect is statistically significant at the 10% level in 2012. However, the coefficients of the constitutive terms national identification and EU/IMF conditionality remain positive and substantially significant.

Let's explore the results for 2012 in more detail, looking at the slopes of national identification in countries receiving conditional aids from the EU/IMF and those not under EU/IMF conditionality. Figure 6.2 visualises the differences in the effects of national identification in the two groups of member states, graphing predicted European identification over the range of national identification separately for member states under EU/IMF conditionality and other member states. Straight lines show predictive margins of national identification in countries receiving conditional aid from the EU/IMF and countries not under EU/IMF conditionality. Vertical lines give 95% confidence intervals. Predictive margins are based on Model M_{3f} reported in Table 6.12 in the appendix.

We see that while the slope of national identification is positive regardless of EU/IMF conditionality, it is flatter in countries receiving conditional financial aids from the EU/IMF. That is, national identification has a positive effect in both groups of countries, but the effect is *smaller* in countries under EU/IMF conditionality. The confidence intervals around the two slopes indicate that the differences in European identification between respondents in the two country groups are statistically significant at the 95%-level only for respondents who are not at all attached to their home country; confidence intervals overlap at higher levels of national identification. Taken together, these findings only partially support hypothesis H_{30},

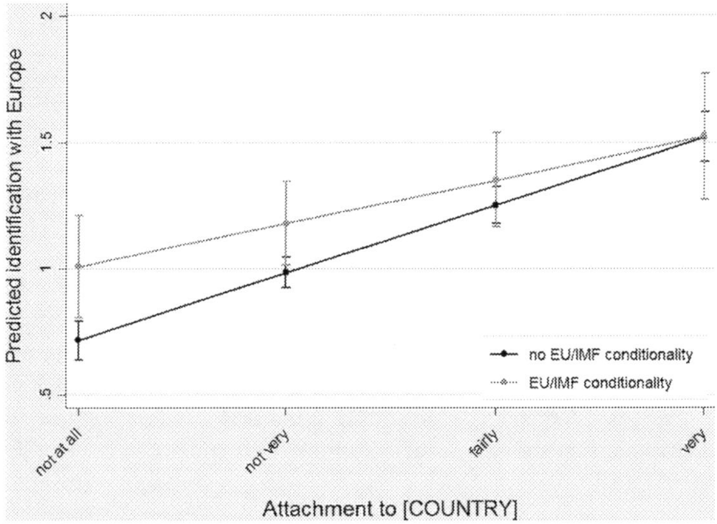

Fig. 6.2 Predicted European identification in countries with and without EU/IMF conditionality over range of national identification 2012

which expected a negative relationship between national identification and European identification in member states under EU/IMF conditionality. Although we do not find a negative relationship between national and European identification in these countries, the relationship is still *weaker* than in countries not under EU/IMF conditionality. That is, the (positive) effect of national identification is reduced among respondents from countries receiving conditional financial aids from the EU/IMF.

Turning to the interaction of *national identification and Eurozone membership* in the period 2007 to 2012, we find similar dynamics at work both before and after the onset of the crisis. The interaction term between national identification and Eurozone membership has a positive sign and is statistically significant in all three years; the coefficient for the constituent term for national identification also remains statistically significant and positive throughout the crisis years while the coefficient for Eurozone membership is negative in all years (albeit it reaches statistical significance only in 2012). Compared to 2007, the size of the coefficient for the interaction term and national identification remain more or less stable whereas the coefficient for Eurozone membership decreases in 2010, but increases again in 2012 (cf. Tables 6.10, 6.11, 6.12 in the appendix). Given that the signs of the coefficients for the interaction and the constituent terms do not change, it appears that the crisis did not alter the fundamentals of the relationship between national identification, Eurozone membership, and European identification.

We can explore this relationship further by examining the results for 2012 in more detail. Figure 6.3 plots predicted European identification over the range of national identification for Eurozone and non-Eurozone member countries. Straight

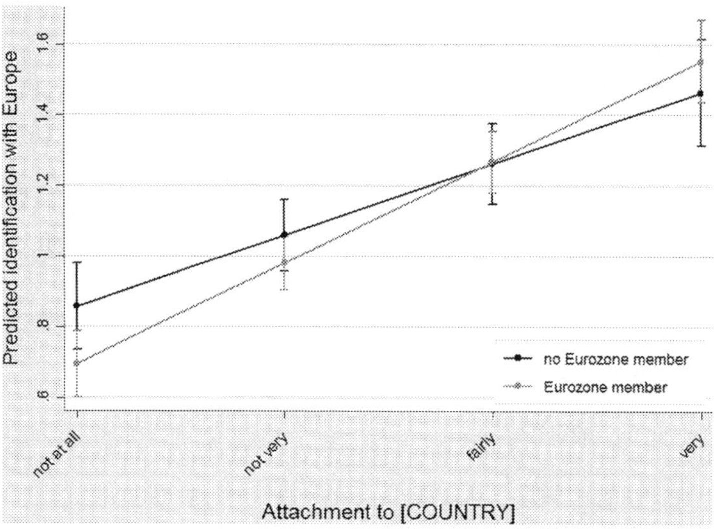

Fig. 6.3 Predicted European identification in and outside the Eurozone over range of national identification 2012

lines show predictive margins of national identification for member states in and outside the Eurozone. Vertical lines give 95% confidence intervals. Predictive margins are based on Model M_{3f} reported in Table 6.12 in the appendix. The ascending slopes for national identification for both Eurozone member states and member states outside the Eurozone indicates that national identification is positively related to European identification in and outside the Eurozone. The slope is steeper for Eurozone countries (grey line), indicating that the effect of national identification is stronger for respondents in the Eurozone than outside (although confidence intervals overlap). This finding clearly rejects hypothesis H_{31}, which expected national identification to be negatively related to European identification in the Eurozone countries after the onset of the crisis.

To sum up, the sources of European identification appear to have changed only to limited degree over the course of the financial and economic crisis. The statistical analysis shows only minor changes in the regression coefficients for the individual-level determinants between 2007 and the crisis years 2010 and 2012. Among the country-level determinants, we observe changes in the effects of macroeconomic predictors. However, these changes often run counter to theoretical expectations. Thus, adverse economic conditions—as expressed by rising unemployment rates and/or the need for financial aid by the EU/IMF—appear to lead respondents to identify *more* rather than less with Europe. Likewise, respondents from Eurozone countries continue to identify *more* with Europe than their peers outside the Eurozone throughout the crisis. Only member states' net budgetary contributions prove to have the expected negative effect on respondents' identification with Europe in the crisis years.

As during the enlargement period, we find national identification to mediate the effect of economic predictors on respondents' identification with Europe. In particular, the relationship between national identification and European identification differs by member states' status as an EU/IMF debtor country and by Eurozone membership. National identification is always positively related to European identification, but the strength of the association differs between the four groups of countries (creditor vs. debtor countries and Eurozone ins and outs). In the case of EU/IMF conditionality, the positive effect of national identification on European identification is stronger in the countries *not* under EU/IMF conditionality. In the case of Eurozone membership, the positive effect of national identification on European identification is stronger in countries *inside* the Eurozone.

If we compare the findings for the interactions between national identification and EU/IMF conditionality and Eurozone membership, respectively, it appears that the relationship between national identification and adverse economic conditions—as represented in the crisis by EU/IMF conditionality and Eurozone membership—does not necessarily run in the same direction. Rather, it seems itself to depend on member state context.

In effect, one could argue that, in the crisis years, both EU/IMF conditionality and Eurozone membership epitomise the risks of greater economic and financial interdependencies. In the case of the countries receiving conditional financial aids by the EU/IMF, the downsides for citizens are clear: the austerity programmes and demands for structural reforms attached to financial support measures led to cuts in pensions and social security systems, rising poverty levels, and generally dire economic and social conditions in the countries under EU/IMF conditionality. In the course of the crisis, Eurozone membership, too, signified risks for member state economies, given the threats of sovereign defaults of some Eurozone member states and the extensive financial guarantees agreed within the Eurozone. Against this background, we would assume that respondents with the strongest attachments to the national community are also the most critical of EU/IMF conditionality and their country's membership in the Eurozone. This should lead respondents with strong national ties in countries under EU/IMF conditionality and the Eurozone to identify less with Europe; we should observe weaker effects of national identification on European identification in these countries compared to countries not under EU/IMF conditionality and/or outside the Eurozone. Empirically, however, this expectation is confirmed only in case of EU/IMF conditionality; we find the (positive) effect of national identification to be smaller in countries receiving financial aids from the EU/IMF compared to those not under EU/IMF conditionality (cf. Fig. 6.2).

In case of Eurozone membership, in contrast, national identification has stronger (positive) effects on European identification inside rather than outside the Eurozone (cf. Fig. 6.3). It seems that the relationship between national identification and European identification under adverse economic conditions depends on context. This could be explained by framing effects and the representations of the economic risks of EU integration in the respective national political contexts.

There is reason to believe that in the countries under EU/IMF conditionality, political elites and media focussed on the negative consequences of austerity measures for the population and the national economy, and the role of external actors, in particular the troika, in imposing austerity programmes on national governments and societies. Analyses of the Greek case, for example, find evidence that political leaders tended to place part of the blame on external actors such as the EU and the IMF (Vasilopoulou et al. 2014) whereas the media concentrated more and more on the suffering of ordinary citizens, 'capitalizing on people's fear, insecurity and despair' (Kouki 2014, p. 19).

In the Eurozone, on the other hand, the dominant discourse may well be summarised by German Chancellor Merkel's dictum that 'if the Euro fails, Europe fails' and that by protecting the common monetary union, national governments first and foremost protected the wealth of the national population.[25] In effect, media analyses in the Eurozone show that bailout measures and financial guarantees to save member states at risk of sovereign default were often framed as being in the national interest and necessary to prevent the breakup of the Eurozone as a whole,

[25]See e.g. Angela Merkel's defense of the first bailout measures for Greece before the Bundestag on 19 May 2010: 'Wir helfen Griechenland, weil wir so der Stabilität unserer gemeinsamen Währung insgesamt helfen. *Wir schützen das Geld der Bürgerinnen und Bürger unseres Landes*—nicht mehr und nicht weniger ist der Auftrag der Bundesregierung genauso wie des Hohen Hauses hier.' (Deutscher Bundestag 2010, p. 4125; emphasis added).

which would have severe consequences for the respective national economy (see, e.g. the findings by Bickes et al. 2014; Drewski 2015; Vaara 2014).

If citizens in the two groups of countries—member states under EU/IMF conditionality on the one hand, Eurozone on the other—subscribed to the respective argumentation, this could explain the differentiated effects of national identification in countries under EU/IMF conditionality and the Eurozone.

In sum, the findings presented here indicate that adverse economic conditions with a clear European dimension do not automatically lead to anti-European reflexes, not even among respondents who identify strongly with the nation. Rather, the tension between the wellbeing of the national community and the role of the EU must be made salient. This appears to have happened in the countries under EU/IMF conditionality, but less so in the Eurozone.

6.4 Sources and Mechanisms of Citizens' Identification with Europe After Enlargement and the Crisis

The present chapter set out to provide empirical evidence on the determinants of individual identification with Europe that help explain European identification in the mass public. To this end, I subjected the previously developed theoretical model of individual identification with Europe to empirical testing. The analysis pursued two objectives. First, we were interested in the individual and country-level characteristics that *generally* shape European identification and the larger trends we observe in these determinants over time. Second, we were interested in the consequences of the EU's enlargement to Central and Eastern Europe and the onset of the financial and economic crisis for the determinants of European identification.

To answer these questions, the empirical analysis employed linear hierarchical regression models combining individual- and country-level data. Separate models were estimated for four occasions before and after the EU's enlargement to Central and Eastern Europe in 2004 and three occasions before and during the economic and financial crisis starting in 2008. With each of these occasions reflecting different stages in the enlargement process and the financial and economic crisis, we were able to assess changes in the determinants of European identification at key moments in the EU integration process.

Starting with the *overall trends in the determinants of European identification*, the empirical results can be summarised as follows: At the *individual level*, identification with Europe is influenced by cognitive factors as well as experiences related to the national and European community. Political interest, interest in European politics, and knowledge about the EU are among the strongest individual-level predictors of European identification. Likewise, national identification and personal transnational experiences have a significant positive influence on European identification. *Country-level characteristics*, on the other hand, influence European identification only to a limited degree. Only member states' net contributions to the EU budget significantly affect identification with Europe in the period under analysis. Finally, the analysis of the *cross-level interactions* finds only weak support for a moderating effect of political interest and national identification. The influence of member states characteristics does not differ by respondents' level of political interest. In contrast, there is some evidence of interaction effects between national attachments and the domestic consequences of European integration. In effect, we find the relationship between national and European identification to depend on member states' status as a net payer to the EU budget, at least in some years under analysis.

Which conclusions can we draw from these findings with regard to the *general mechanisms underlying individual identification with Europe* among citizens in the member states?

To recall, the theoretical discussion suggested two mechanisms by which citizens come to identify with Europe. First, an information-based way of European identification proposing that citizens identify with Europe to the extent that they have access and receive information related to Europe and the European community, thus becoming aware of shared European norms and values underlying a common European 'we-feeling'. Second, an experience-based way of European identification proposing that citizens identify with Europe to the extent that they come in personal contact with other Europeans and thus directly perceive what Europeans have in common in terms of shared experiences, norms, and values.

The empirical evidence provides support for both ways of identifying with Europe. The persistent positive effects of cognitive-based determinants such as political interest and EU knowledge confirm the idea of an information-based mechanism whereby the development of European identification among EU citizens depends on their access to Europe-related information and their capabilities and motivation to process this information. On the other hand, the positive effects of national identification and personal transnational experience support notions of an experience-based mechanism whereby the development of European identification depends on citizens' experience with large-scale political collectives, socialisation processes within the national context, and personal contacts with other Europeans. All in all, the empirical analysis confirmed that European identification draws on different sources, which, to some degree, appear mutually exchangeable. Not every citizen may have the resources and opportunities to come into personal contact with other Europeans; however, high awareness of EU affairs and a positive relationship to the national community can at least partly compensate for the lack of transnational experiences as a source of European identification.

The influence of cognitive mobilisation and national attachments on citizens' identification with Europe underlines the relevance of the second research objective of the present analysis, namely to explore changes in the determinants of individual European identification at key moments in the EU integration process. These were, first, the *accession of Central and Eastern European member states in 2004/2007* and, second, the *onset of the financial and economic crisis in late 2008*. Both EU enlargement to CEE and the financial and economic crisis led to a rise in the salience of EU integration at the domestic level and increased political, social, and, in particular, economic diversity within the EU. Debates over member states' mutual obligations and interdependencies resulting from European integration, already prominent in the context of enlargement, intensified in the course of the financial and economic crisis. The greater salience of EU integration and the revived debate over national interests and financial redistributions between EU member states imply that the environment in which citizens receive Europe-related information and make Europe-related experiences changed with enlargement and the crisis.

The theoretical discussion expected changes in the influence of cognitive factors on European identification as citizen have better access to Europe-related information when issues of EU integration become more salient domestically; it also predicted changes in the importance of national identification and macroeconomic factors for identification with Europe as citizens experience more competition between EU member states and national (economic) interests are pitted against each other in the context of enlargement and the crisis.

Empirically, we observe no major shifts in the individual-level determinants over the accession period and the course of the financial and economic crisis. Neither political interest as an indicator of cognitive mobilisation nor national identification become significantly more or less important for European identification as new member states from CEE enter the EU and EU member states experience economic and financial turmoil in the crisis. As regards country-level predictors, we observe changes in the effects of member states' status as a net contributor to the EU budget, and, for the crisis years, Eurozone membership. In this respect, enlargement and the crisis indeed seem to have increased the relevance of economic aspects and redistributive considerations for citizens' identification with Europe. Finally, we find interaction effects between national identification and macroeconomic factors on European identification. Other than expected, however, strong national ties still are positively related to European identification even under adverse economic conditions.

These findings allow inferences about the broader implications of key developments in the EU integration process for citizens' identification with Europe. First, the empirical results point to a remarkable stability in the determinants of European identification even as the EU and its member states experience significant transformations, be it in terms of EU membership or worsening economic conditions. At the individual level in particular, European identification appears to draw on relatively stable dispositions such as national attachments, which do not vary significantly in the short term. What is more, strong national ties continue to strengthen rather than weaken citizens' attachments to Europe even as member states' political, social, and economic interests and positions become more diverse, and competition for EU funding intensifies. This seems a rather promising result, in particular with regard to a further widening and deepening of European integration.

On the other hand, macroeconomic factors have become more relevant for European attachments over time, in particular those with a clear EU-dimension such as Eurozone membership, EU budgetary contributions, and EU/IMF conditionality of financial aids. Key developments at the EU level, in particular in the context of the crisis, thus seem to reverberate at the citizen level, too.

How macroeconomic conditions affect European identification, however, depends on citizens' relation to their own national community and the domestic context. This is another important finding of the present analysis: the effects of adverse economic conditions, especially among citizens with the strongest national attachments, depend on the domestic context and, presumably, on how developments at the EU level and their impact on the national level are framed domestically.

That is, even if EU integration gains in salience and EU actors and institutions figure as prominently as they did in the crisis, the national context in which citizens experience EU integration remains central. This leaves a crucial role for national political actors and the national media. While key events in EU integration like eastward enlargement and the financial and economic crisis have the potential to change the bases of European identification, it depends on the interpretation of these events in the domestic context whether such key moments in the integration process ultimately lead to a strengthening or weakening of citizens' identification with Europe.

Appendix

Single-Equation Expressions for Random Coefficient Models with Cross-Level Interactions

Interaction of individual political interest and party messages on European community

$$\begin{aligned}
European\ identification_{ij} = {} & \gamma_{00} + \gamma_{10}int_{ij} + \gamma_{20}EUint_{ij} + \gamma_{30}EUknow_{ij} \\
& + \gamma_{40}EUcomm_{ij} + \gamma_{50}nat\ id_{ij} + \gamma_{60}nat\ comm_{ij} \\
& + \gamma_{70}transprac_{ij} + \gamma_{80}transback_{ij} + \gamma_{90}transcap_{ij} \\
& + \gamma_{100}gender_{ij} + \gamma_{110}age_{ij} + \gamma_{120}edu_{ij} + \gamma_{130}commun_{ij} \\
& + \gamma_{140}occ_{ij} + \gamma_{150}nat_eco_{ij} + \gamma_{160}pers_eco_{ij} \\
& + \gamma_{01}EU\ party_j + \gamma_{02}EU\ party_j + \gamma_{03}Euro_j \\
& + \gamma_{04}budget_j + \gamma_{05}trade_j + \gamma_{06}EU\ imm_j + \gamma_{07}imm_j \\
& + \gamma_{08}unemploy_j + \gamma_{09}IMF_j + \gamma_{11}EU\ party_j{}^{*}int_{ij} \\
& + u_{1j}int_{ij} + u_{0j} + r_{ij}
\end{aligned}$$

Interaction of individual political interest and party messages on national community

$$
\begin{aligned}
European\ identification_{ij} = {} & \gamma_{00} + \gamma_{10} int_{ij} + \gamma_{20} EUint_{ij} + \gamma_{30} EUknow_{ij} \\
& + \gamma_{40} EUcomm_{ij} + \gamma_{50} nat\ id_{ij} + \gamma_{60} nat\ comm_{ij} \\
& + \gamma_{70} transprac_{ij} + \gamma_{80} transback_{ij} + \gamma_{90} transcap_{ij} \\
& + \gamma_{100} gender_{ij} + \gamma_{110} age_{ij} + \gamma_{120} edu_{ij} + \gamma_{130} commun_{ij} \\
& + \gamma_{140} occ_{ij} + \gamma_{150} nat\_eco_{ij} + \gamma_{160} pers\_eco_{ij} \\
& + \gamma_{01} EU\ party_j + \gamma_{02} nat\ party_j + \gamma_{03} Euro_j \\
& + \gamma_{04} budget_j + \gamma_{05} trade_j + \gamma_{06} EU\ imm_j + \gamma_{07} imm_j \\
& + \gamma_{08} unemploy_j + \gamma_{09} IMF_j + \gamma_{11} nat\ party_j{}^{*} int_{ij} \\
& + u_{1j} int_{ij} + u_{0j} + r_{ij}
\end{aligned}
$$

Interaction of individual political interest and member states' status as net recipient of EU funding

$$
\begin{aligned}
European\ identification_{ij} = {} & \gamma_{00} + \gamma_{10} int_{ij} + \gamma_{20} EUint_{ij} + \gamma_{30} EUknow_{ij} \\
& + \gamma_{40} EUcomm_{ij} + \gamma_{50} nat\ id_{ij} + \gamma_{60} nat\ comm_{ij} \\
& + \gamma_{70} transprac_{ij} + \gamma_{80} transback_{ij} + \gamma_{90} transcap_{ij} \\
& + \gamma_{100} gender_{ij} + \gamma_{110} age_{ij} + \gamma_{120} edu_{ij} + \gamma_{130} commun_{ij} \\
& + \gamma_{140} occ_{ij} + \gamma_{150} nat\_eco_{ij} + \gamma_{160} pers\_eco_{ij} \\
& + \gamma_{01} EU\ party_j + \gamma_{02} nat\ party_j + \gamma_{03} Euro_j \\
& + \gamma_{04} budget_j + \gamma_{05} trade_j + \gamma_{06} EU\ imm_j + \gamma_{07} imm_j \\
& + \gamma_{08} unemploy_j + \gamma_{09} IMF_j + \gamma_{13} budget_j{}^{*} int_{ij} \\
& + u_{1j} int_{ij} + u_{0j} + r_{ij}
\end{aligned}
$$

Interaction of individual political interest and member states' share in international trade

$$
\begin{aligned}
European\ identification_{ij} = {} & \gamma_{00} + \gamma_{10} int_{ij} + \gamma_{20} EUint_{ij} + \gamma_{30} EUknow_{ij} \\
& + \gamma_{40} EUcomm_{ij} + \gamma_{50} nat\ id_{ij} + \gamma_{60} nat\ comm_{ij} \\
& + \gamma_{70} transprac_{ij} + \gamma_{80} transback_{ij} + \gamma_{90} transcap_{ij} \\
& + \gamma_{100} gender_{ij} + \gamma_{110} age_{ij} + \gamma_{120} edu_{ij} + \gamma_{130} commun_{ij} \\
& + \gamma_{140} occ_{ij} + \gamma_{150} nat\_eco_{ij} + \gamma_{160} pers\_eco_{ij} \\
& + \gamma_{01} EU\ party_j + \gamma_{02} nat\ party_j + \gamma_{03} Euro_j \\
& + \gamma_{04} budget_j + \gamma_{05} trade_j + \gamma_{06} EU\ imm_j + \gamma_{07} imm_j \\
& + \gamma_{08} unemploy_j + \gamma_{09} IMF_j + \gamma_{15} trade_j{}^{*} int_{ij} + u_{1j} int_{ij} \\
& + u_{0j} + r_{ij}
\end{aligned}
$$

Interaction of individual national identification and of party messages on European community

$$\begin{aligned} \textit{European identification}_{ij} = {} & \gamma_{00} + \gamma_{10} int_{ij} + \gamma_{20} EUint_{ij} + \gamma_{30} EUknow_{ij} \\ & + \gamma_{40} EUcomm_{ij} + \gamma_{50} nat\ id_{ij} + \gamma_{60} nat\ comm_{ij} \\ & + \gamma_{70} transprac_{ij} + \gamma_{80} transback_{ij} + \gamma_{90} transcap_{ij} \\ & + \gamma_{100} gender_{ij} + \gamma_{110} age_{ij} + \gamma_{120} edu_{ij} + \gamma_{130} commun_{ij} \\ & + \gamma_{140} occ_{ij} + \gamma_{150} nat\_eco_{ij} + \gamma_{160} pers\_eco_{ij} \\ & + \gamma_{01} EU\ party_j + \gamma_{02} nat\ party_j + \gamma_{03} Euro_j \\ & + \gamma_{04} budget_j + \gamma_{05} trade_j + \gamma_{06} EU\ imm_j + \gamma_{07} imm_j \\ & + \gamma_{08} unemploy_j + \gamma_{09} IMF_j + \gamma_{51} EU\ party_j{}^{*}\ nat\ id_{ij} \\ & + u_{1j} nat\ id_{ij} + u_{0j} + r_{ij} \end{aligned}$$

Interaction of individual national identification and salience of party messages on national community

$$\begin{aligned} \textit{European identification}_{ij} = {} & \gamma_{00} + \gamma_{10} int_{ij} + \gamma_{20} EUint_{ij} + \gamma_{30} EUknow_{ij} \\ & + \gamma_{40} EUcomm_{ij} + \gamma_{50} nat\ id_{ij} + \gamma_{60} nat\ comm_{ij} \\ & + \gamma_{70} transprac_{ij} + \gamma_{80} transback_{ij} + \gamma_{90} transcap_{ij} \\ & + \gamma_{100} gender_{ij} + \gamma_{110} age_{ij} + \gamma_{120} edu_{ij} + \gamma_{130} commun_{ij} \\ & + \gamma_{140} occ_{ij} + \gamma_{150} nat\_eco_{ij} + \gamma_{160} pers\_eco_{ij} \\ & + \gamma_{01} EU\ party_j + \gamma_{02} nat\ party_j + \gamma_{03} Euro_j \\ & + \gamma_{04} budget_j + \gamma_{05} trade_j + \gamma_{06} EU\ imm_j + \gamma_{07} imm_j \\ & + \gamma_{08} unemploy_j + \gamma_{09} IMF_j + \gamma_{52} nat\ party_j{}^{*}\ nat\ id_{ij} \\ & + u_{1j} nat\ id_{ij} + u_{0j} + r_{ij} \end{aligned}$$

Interaction of individual national identification and status as net recipient of EU funding

$$\begin{aligned} \textit{European identification}_{ij} = {} & \gamma_{00} + \gamma_{10} int_{ij} + \gamma_{20} EUint_{ij} + \gamma_{30} EUknow_{ij} \\ & + \gamma_{40} EUcomm_{ij} + \gamma_{50} nat\ id_{ij} + \gamma_{60} nat\ comm_{ij} \\ & + \gamma_{70} transprac_{ij} + \gamma_{80} transback_{ij} + \gamma_{90} transcap_{ij} \\ & + \gamma_{100} gender_{ij} + \gamma_{110} age_{ij} + \gamma_{120} edu_{ij} + \gamma_{130} commun_{ij} \\ & + \gamma_{140} occ_{ij} + \gamma_{150} nat\_eco_{ij} + \gamma_{160} pers\_eco_{ij} \\ & + \gamma_{01} EU\ party_j + \gamma_{02} nat\ party_j + \gamma_{03} Euro_j \\ & + \gamma_{04} budget_j + \gamma_{05} trade_j + \gamma_{06} EU\ imm_j + \gamma_{07} imm_j \\ & + \gamma_{08} unemploy_j + \gamma_{09} IMF_j + \gamma_{53} budget_j{}^{*}\ nat\ id_{ij} \\ & + u_{1j} nat\ id_{ij} + u_{0j} + r_{ij} \end{aligned}$$

Interaction of individual national identification and share of immigrants

$$
\begin{aligned}
\textit{European identification}_{ij} = {} & \gamma_{00} + \gamma_{10}\textit{int}_{ij} + \gamma_{20}\textit{EUint}_{ij} + \gamma_{30}\textit{EUknow}_{ij} \\
& + \gamma_{40}\textit{EUcomm}_{ij} + \gamma_{50}\textit{nat id}_{ij} + \gamma_{60}\textit{nat comm}_{ij} \\
& + \gamma_{70}\textit{transprac}_{ij} + \gamma_{80}\textit{transback}_{ij} + \gamma_{90}\textit{transcap}_{ij} \\
& + \gamma_{100}\textit{gender}_{ij} + \gamma_{110}\textit{age}_{ij} + \gamma_{120}\textit{edu}_{ij} + \gamma_{130}\textit{commun}_{ij} \\
& + \gamma_{140}\textit{occ}_{ij} + \gamma_{150}\textit{nat\_eco}_{ij} + \gamma_{160}\textit{pers\_eco}_{ij} \\
& + \gamma_{01}\textit{EU party}_{j} + \gamma_{02}\textit{nat party}_{j} + \gamma_{03}\textit{Euro}_{j} \\
& + \gamma_{04}\textit{budget}_{j} + \gamma_{05}\textit{trade}_{j} + \gamma_{06}\textit{EU imm}_{j} + \gamma_{07}\textit{imm}_{j} \\
& + \gamma_{08}\textit{unemploy}_{j} + \gamma_{09}\textit{IMF}_{j} + \gamma_{57}\textit{imm}_{j}{}^{*}\textit{nat id}_{ij} \\
& + u_{1j}\textit{nat id}_{ij} + u_{0j} + r_{ij}
\end{aligned}
$$

Interaction of individual national identification and EU/IMF conditionality

$$
\begin{aligned}
\textit{European identification}_{ij} = {} & \gamma_{00} + \gamma_{10}\textit{int}_{ij} + \gamma_{20}\textit{EUint}_{ij} + \gamma_{30}\textit{EUknow}_{ij} \\
& + \gamma_{40}\textit{EUcomm}_{ij} + \gamma_{50}\textit{nat id}_{ij} + \gamma_{60}\textit{nat comm}_{ij} \\
& + \gamma_{70}\textit{transprac}_{ij} + \gamma_{80}\textit{transback}_{ij} + \gamma_{90}\textit{transcap}_{ij} \\
& + \gamma_{100}\textit{gender}_{ij} + \gamma_{110}\textit{age}_{ij} + \gamma_{120}\textit{edu}_{ij} + \gamma_{130}\textit{commun}_{ij} \\
& + \gamma_{140}\textit{occ}_{ij} + \gamma_{150}\textit{nat\_eco}_{ij} + \gamma_{160}\textit{pers\_eco}_{ij} \\
& + \gamma_{01}\textit{EU party}_{j} + \gamma_{02}\textit{nat party}_{j} + \gamma_{03}\textit{Euro}_{j} \\
& + \gamma_{04}\textit{budget}_{j} + \gamma_{05}\textit{trade}_{j} + \gamma_{06}\textit{EU imm}_{j} + \gamma_{07}\textit{imm}_{j} \\
& + \gamma_{08}\textit{unemploy}_{j} + \gamma_{09}\textit{IMF}_{j} + \gamma_{59}\textit{IMF}_{j}{}^{*}\textit{nat id}_{ij} \\
& + u_{1j}\textit{nat id}_{ij} + u_{0j} + r_{ij}
\end{aligned}
$$

Interaction of individual national identification and euro zone membership

$$
\begin{aligned}
\textit{European identification}_{ij} = {} & \gamma_{00} + \gamma_{10}\textit{int}_{ij} + \gamma_{20}\textit{EUint}_{ij} + \gamma_{30}\textit{EUknow}_{ij} \\
& + \gamma_{40}\textit{EUcomm}_{ij} + \gamma_{50}\textit{nat id}_{ij} + \gamma_{60}\textit{nat comm}_{ij} \\
& + \gamma_{70}\textit{transprac}_{ij} + \gamma_{80}\textit{transback}_{ij} + \gamma_{90}\textit{transcap}_{ij} \\
& + \gamma_{100}\textit{gender}_{ij} + \gamma_{110}\textit{age}_{ij} + \gamma_{120}\textit{edu}_{ij} + \gamma_{130}\textit{commun}_{ij} \\
& + \gamma_{140}\textit{occ}_{ij} + \gamma_{150}\textit{nat\_eco}_{ij} + \gamma_{160}\textit{pers\_eco}_{ij} \\
& + \gamma_{01}\textit{EU party}_{j} + \gamma_{02}\textit{nat party}_{j} + \gamma_{03}\textit{Euro}_{j} \\
& + \gamma_{04}\textit{budget}_{j} + \gamma_{05}\textit{trade}_{j} + \gamma_{06}\textit{EU imm}_{j} + \gamma_{07}\textit{imm}_{j} \\
& + \gamma_{08}\textit{unemploy}_{j} + \gamma_{09}\textit{IMF}_{j} + \gamma_{53}\textit{Euro}_{j}{}^{*}\textit{nat id}_{ij} \\
& + u_{1j}\textit{nat id}_{ij} + u_{0j} + r_{ij}
\end{aligned}
$$

Table 6.4 Descriptive statistics for individual identification with Europe by year

	Attachment to Europe/the European Union					
Year	Range	Min	Max	Mean	s.d.	no. of 'don't knows'
2000	0–3	0	3	1.71	0.88	552
2003	0–3	0	3	1.69	0.85	399
2004	0–3	0	3	1.81	0.85	570
2006	0–3	0	3	1.71	0.92	280
2007	0–3	0	3	1.49	0.88	753
2010	0–3	0	3	1.44	0.87	612
2012	0–3	0	3	1.38	0.85	493

Question wording 2000–2006: 'People may feel different degrees of attachment to their town or village, to their region, to their country or to Europe. Please tell me how attached you feel to. . .Europe. Very attached, fairly attached, not very attached, not at all attached.'
Question wording 2007–2012: 'People may feel different degrees of attachment to their town or village, to their region, to their country or the Europe Union. Please tell me how attached you feel to. . .the *European Union*. Very attached, fairly attached, not very attached, not at all attached.'
Note: Higher values indicate more intense attachment to Europe/the European Union. 'No. of 'don't knows' refers to the number of respondents having answered 'don't know' spontaneously to the above questions

Table 6.5 Descriptive statistics for independent variables

Descriptive statistics for the independent variables by year of analysis													
		2000			2003			2004			2006		
	Range	Min/Max	Mean	s.d.	Min/Max	Mean	s.d.	Min/ Max	Mean	s.d.	Min/Max	Mean	s.d.
Individual level predictors													
Political interest	0–2	0/2	0.83	0.64	0/2	0.85	0.64	0/2	0.89	0.64	0/2	0.88	0.64
European political interest	0–3				0/3	1.39	0.86						
EU knowledge	0–3/0-5[a]	0/5	3.92	1.44	0/5	3.99	1.40	0/3	1.62	1.02	0/3	1.43	0.94
Conception of Europe													
Other	0–1				0/1	0.90	0.30	0/1	0.93	0.26	0/1	0.92	0.28
Common political project	0–1				0/1	0.07	0.25	0/1	0.03	0.17	0/1	0.03	0.18
Individual benefits	0–1				0/1	0.04	0.19	0/1	0.04	0.21	0/1	0.05	0.22
National identification	0–3	0/3	2.41	0.70	0/3	2.48	0.66	0/3	2.54	0.65	0/3	2.49	0.67
European background	0–1							0/1	0.06	0.24	0/1	0.06	0.24
Individual level controls													
Gender (male)	0–1	0/1	0.48	0.50	0/1	0.48	0.50	0/1	0.44	0.50	0/1	0.43	0.50
Age	15–99	15/99	44.63	17.92	15/95	45.13	18.27	15/97	47.22	18.20	15/95	47.73	18.29
Type of community (ref.: rural/village)													
Rural	0–1				0/1	0.33	0.47	0/1	0.36	0.48	0/1	0.37	0.48
Small town	0–1				0/1	0.39	0.49	0/1	0.37	0.48	0/1	0.37	0.48
Large town	0–1				0/1	0.28	0.45	0/1	0.27	0.44	0/1	0.26	0.44
Education	0–3	1/3	2.01	0.75	1/3	2.03	0.75	3	2.07	0.74	0/3	2.04	0.75
Occupation													
Other	0–1	0/1	0.81	0.39	0/1	0.82	0.39	0/1	0.81	0.39	0/1	0.81	0.39
Student	0–1	0/1	0.10	0.30	0/1	0.10	0.30	0/1	0.08	0.28	0/1	0.09	0.28

Manager	0–1	0/1	0.09	0.29	0/1	0.09	0.28	0/1	0.11	0.31	0/1	0.10	0.30
National eco. Expect.: worse	0–1	0/1	0.24	0.42	0/1	0.43	0.50	0/1	0.39	0.49	0/1	0.32	0.47
Personal eco. Expect.: worse	0–1	0/1	0.12	0.32	0/1	0.18	0.39	0/1	0.21	0.41	0/1	0.18	0.38
Country level predictors													
Party messages													
Over all identity shares	0–100							4.99/ 23.71	11.96	3.70			
EU identity shares	0–100							1.87/ 11.23	5.60	2.56			
National identity shares	0–100							1.20/ 15.71	6.37	3.39			
Eurozone	0–1				0/1	0.79	0.50	0/1	0.49	0.50	0/1	0.49	0.50
Net paying EU transfers	0–1	0/1	0.56	0.50	0/1	0.75	0.50	0/1	0.46	0.50	0/1	0.46	0.50
Trade	Open-ended	52.60/ 279.00	93.84	51.95	48.30/ 250.20	85.67	44.75	49.7/ 280.50	101.60	43.84	55.10/ 309.00	111.02	46.69
EU Immigration rate	0–100							0/33.00	2.25	4.81	0/33.00	2.20	4.69
Total immigration	0–100	1.70/ 35.80	6.30	6.40	2.00/ 38.10	9.61	9.99	0.10/ 39.00	6.66	6.94	0.10/ 40.80	6.48	6.95
Unemployment rate	0–100	2.20/ 11.70	6.80	2.84	3.80/ 11.40	7.29	2.32	4.50/ 19.10	8.81	3.85	3.90/ 13.90	7.46	2.48

(continued)

Table 6.5 (continued)

		2007			2010			2012		
	Range	Min/Max	Mean	s.d.	Min/Max	Mean	s.d.	Min/Max	Mean	s.d.
Individual level predictors										
Political interest	0–2	0/2	0.88	0.64				0/2	1.00	0.67
European political interest	0–2							0/2	0.81	0.66
EU knowledge	0–3	0/3	2.33	1.01				0/3	2.00	0.95
Conception of Europe										
Other	0–1	0/1	0.91	0.29				0/1	0.91	0.29
Common political project	0–1	0/1	0.04	0.19				0/1	0.03	0.18
Individual benefits	0–1	0/1	0.06	0.23				0/1	0.06	0.24
National identification	0–3	0/3	2.54	0.65	0/3	2.55	0.63	0/3	2.48	0.68
Conception of national community	0–1				0/1	0.09	0.28			
Transnational practices	0–8/0-6[b]				0/8	1.38	1.62	0/6	1.61	1.61
European background	0–1	0/1	0.06	0.24	0/1	0.07	0.25			
Transnational capital	0–2/0-4[c]				0/2	0.85	0.79	0/4	1.43	1.55
Individual level controls										
Gender (male)	0–1	0/1	0.43	0.50	0/1	0.46	0.50	0/1	0.46	0.50
Age	15–99	15/98	47.69	18.23	15/97	47.97	18.20	15/98	48.66	18.15
Type of community										
Rural/village	0–1	0/1	0.37	0.48	0/1	0.36	0.48	0/1	0.35	0.48
Small town	0–1	0/1	0.36	0.48	0/1	0.35	0.48	0/1	0.38	0.48
Large town	0–1	0/1	0.27	0.44	0/1	0.28	0.45	0/1	0.27	0.45
Education	0–3	0/3	2.07	0.73	0/3	2.10	0.72	0/3	2.13	0.72
Occupation										
Other	0–1	0/1	0.81	0.40	0/1	0.82	0.38	0/1	0.82	0.38
Student	0–1	0/1	0.09	0.28	0/1	0.08	0.27	0/1	0.08	0.27
Manager	0–1	0/1	0.11	0.31	0/1	0.09	0.29	0/1	0.10	0.30

National economic expect.: worse	0–1	0/1	0.28	0.45				0/1	0.36	0.48
Personal economic expect.: worse	0–1	0/1	0.17	0.37	0/1	0.09	0.29	0/1	0.22	0.41
Country level predictors										
Eurozone	0–1	0/1	0.49	0.50	0/1	0.57	0.50	0/1	0.61	0.50
Net paying EU transfers	0–1	0/1	0.45	0.50	0/1	0.43	0.50	0/1	0.45	0.50
Trade	Open-ended	55.50/319.50	112.09	47.64	53.30/10.80	111.11	48.58	57.10/325.50	120.78	52.96
EU Immigration rate	0–100	0/35.90	2.59	5.14	0/37.10	2.94	5.37	0/37.90	3.13	5.45
Total immigration	0–100	0.10/41.60	6.71	6.96	0/43.00	7.19	6.91	0.10/43.80	7.43	7.00
Unemployment rate	0–100	3.60/11.20	6.50	1.96	4.40/20.10	10.24	4.31	4.30/25.00	10.62	5.09
IMF conditionality	0–1				0/1	0.19	0.39	0/1	0.15	0.36

Note:
[a]The range for EU knowledge is 0–5 in 2000 and 2003, and 0–3 in the other years under analysis
[b]The range for transnational practices is 0–8 in 2010 and 0–6 in 2012
[c]The range for transnational capital is 0–2 in 2010 and 0–4 in 2012

Table 6.6 Cross-level interaction effects for individual identification with Europe (2000)

Cross-level interaction effects for individual identification with Europe 2000				
	M_{3a}	M_{3b}	M_{3c}	M_{3d}
Intercept	0.28** (0.05)	0.30*** (0.09)	0.36*** (0.07)	0.34*** (0.07)
Individual level predictors				
Gender (male)	−0.03* (0.01)	−0.03* (0.01)	−0.03* (0.01)	−0.03* (0.01)
Age	−0.00† (0.00)	−0.00 (0.00)	−0.00† (0.00)	−0.00† (0.00)
Education	0.07*** (0.01)	0.07*** (0.01)	0.07*** (0.01)	0.07*** (0.01)
Occupation (ref.: other)				
Student	−0.00 (0.03)	−0.00 (0.03)	0.00 (0.03)	0.00 (0.03)
Manager	0.04 (0.02)	0.04 (0.02)	0.03 (0.02)	0.03 (0.02)
National economic expect.: worse	−0.14*** (0.02)	−0.14*** (0.02)	−0.14*** (0.02)	−0.14*** (0.02)
Personal economic expect.: worse	−0.15*** (0.02)	−0.15*** (0.02)	−0.15*** (0.02)	−0.15*** (0.02)
Political interest	0.05*** (0.02)	0.04*** (0.01)	0.04*** (0.01)	0.04*** (0.01)
EU knowledge	0.05*** (0.00)	0.05*** (0.00)	0.05*** (0.00)	0.05*** (0.00)
National identification	0.45*** (0.01)	0.45*** (0.01)	0.42*** (0.03)	0.44*** (0.02)
Country level predictors				
Net paying EU transfers	0.08 (0.12)	0.04 (0.12)	−0.04 (0.10)	0.01 (0.09)
Trade	−0.00 (0.00)	0.00 (0.00)	0.00 (0.00)	0.00 (0.00)
Total immigration	0.01 (0.01)	0.01 (0.01)	0.01 (0.01)	0.01 (0.01)
Unemployment rate	0.00 (0.02)	0.00 (0.02)	0.01 (0.02)	0.01 (0.02)
Cross-level interactions				
Pol interest × Net paying EU transfer	−0.04 (0.03)			
Pol interest × Trade		−0.00 (0.00)		
Nat ident × Net paying EU transfers			0.05 (0.04)	
Nat ident × total immigration				0.00 (0.00)

(continued)

Table 6.6 (continued)

Cross-level interaction effects for individual identification with Europe 2000				
	M_{3a}	M_{3b}	M_{3c}	M_{3d}
Variance components				
Country level τ_{00}	0.04 (0.02)	0.04 (0.02)	0.02 (0.01)	0.02 (0.01)
Individual level σ^2	0.62 (0.01)	0.62 (0.01)	0.62 (0.01)	0.62 (0.01)
Var (pol interest/nat ident)	0.00 (0.00)	0.00 (0.00)	0.01 (0.00)	0.01 (0.00)
Cov(pol interest/nat ident, constant)	−0.00 (0.00)	−0.00 (0.00)	−0.00 (0.00)	−0.00 (0.00)
−2 × Log Likelihood	36,367.92	36,366.88	36,311.94	36,312.48
AIC	36,407.91	36,406.87	36,351.94	36,352.48
BIC	36,560.72	36,559.69	36,504.75	36,505.3
R^2	0.15	0.15	0.15	0.15
No. of groups (N)	15	15	15	15
No. of individuals (n)	15,377	15,377	15,377	15,377

Note: Figures are estimates from linear hierarchical regression models with random coefficients and cross level interactions. Standard errors in parentheses. ***p ≤ 0.001; **p ≤ 0.01; *p ≤ 0.05; †p ≤ 0.1

Table 6.7 Cross-level interaction effects for individual identification with Europe (2003)

Cross-level interaction effects for individual identification with Europe 2003					
	M_{3a}	M_{3b}	M_{3c}	M_{3d}	M_{3e}
Intercept	0.39* (0.19)	0.37* (0.15)	0.45*** (0.14)	0.40*** (0.13)	0.44** (0.14)
Individual level predictors					
Gender (male)	−0.00 (0.01)	−0.00 (0.01)	−0.00 (0.01)	−0.00 (0.01)	−0.00 (0.01)
Age	−0.00† (0.00)	−0.00† (0.00)	−0.00† (0.00)	−0.00† (0.00)	−0.00† (0.00)
Type of community (ref.: rural/village)					
Small town	0.04** (0.01)	0.04** (0.01)	0.04** (0.01)	0.04** (0.01)	0.04** (0.01)
Large town	0.03† (0.02)	0.03 (0.02)	0.03† (0.02)	0.03† (0.02)	0.03† (0.02)
Education	0.08*** (0.01)	0.08*** (0.01)	0.08*** (0.01)	0.08*** (0.01)	0.08*** (0.01)
Occupation (ref.: other)					
Student	−0.07* (0.03)	−0.07* (0.03)	−0.07* (0.03)	−0.07* (0.03)	−0.07* (0.03)
Manager	0.09*** (0.02)	0.09*** (0.02)	0.10*** (0.02)	0.10*** (0.02)	0.10*** (0.02)

(continued)

Table 6.7 (continued)

Cross-level interaction effects for individual identification with Europe 2003					
	M_{3a}	M_{3b}	M_{3c}	M_{3d}	M_{3e}
National economic expect.: worse	−0.09*** (0.01)	−0.09*** (0.01)	−0.09*** (0.01)	−0.09*** (0.01)	−0.09*** (0.01)
Personal economic expect.: worse	−0.16*** (0.02)	−0.16*** (0.02)	−0.16*** (0.02)	−0.16*** (0.02)	−0.16*** (0.02)
Political interest	0.11*** (0.02)	0.11*** (0.01)	0.10*** (0.01)	0.10*** (0.01)	0.10*** (0.01)
EU knowledge	0.07*** (0.00)	0.07*** (0.00)	0.07*** (0.00)	0.07*** (0.00)	0.07*** (0.00)
Conception of Europe (ref.: other)					
Common political project	−0.07* (0.03)	−0.07* (0.03)	−0.07* (0.03)	−0.07** (0.03)	−0.07** (0.03)
Individual benefits	0.06 (0.03)	0.06 (0.03)	0.05 (0.03)	0.05 (0.03)	0.05 (0.03)
National identification	0.36*** (0.01)	0.36*** (0.01)	0.32*** (0.05)	0.37*** (0.02)	0.33*** (0.05)
Country level predictors					
Eurozone	−0.13 (0.17)	−0.12 (0.13)	−0.08 (0.11)	−0.08 (0.11)	−0.13 (0.13)
Net paying EU transfers	0.03 (0.13)	0.04 (0.10)	−0.11 (0.10)	−0.05 (0.08)	−0.05 (0.08)
Trade	0.00* (0.00)	0.00** (0.00)	0.00 (0.00)	0.00 (0.00)	0.00 (0.00)
Total immigration	−0.00 (0.01)	−0.00 (0.00)	0.00 (0.00)	0.00 (0.00)	0.00 (0.00)
Unemployment rate	0.05 (0.03)	0.05* (0.03)	0.05** (0.03)	0.05** (0.03)	0.05** (0.03)
Cross-level interactions					
Pol interest × Net paying EU transfer	−0.00 (0.02)				
Pol interest × Trade		−0.00 (0.00)			
Nat ident × Net paying EU transfers			0.06 (0.05)		
Nat ident × total immigration				−0.00 (0.00)	
Nat ident × Eurozone					0.05 (0.06)

(continued)

Table 6.7 (continued)

Cross-level interaction effects for individual identification with Europe 2003					
	M_{3a}	M_{3b}	M_{3c}	M_{3d}	M_{3e}
Variance components					
Country level τ_{00}	0.04 (0.02)	0.02 (0.01)	0.02 (0.01)	0.02 (0.01)	0.02 (0.01)
Individual level σ^2	0.59 (0.01)	0.59 (0.01)	0.58 (0.01)	0.58 (0.01)	0.58 (0.01)
Var (pol interest/nat ident)	0.00 (0.00)	0.00 (0.00)	0.01 (0.00)	0.01 (0.00)	0.01 (0.00)
Cov(pol interest/nat ident, constant)	0.00 (0.00)	0.00 (0.00)	−0.01 (0.01)	−0.01 (0.01)	−0.01 (0.01)
−2 × Log Likelihood	35,772.26	35,630.6	35,556.58	35,557.5	35,557.14
AIC	35,822.26	35,672.61	35,606.57	35,607.51	35,607.13
BIC	36,013.37	35,833.14	35,797.68	35,798.61	35,798.24
R^2	0.13	0.12	0.13	0.12	0.12
No. of groups (N)	15	15	15	15	15
No. of individuals (n)	15,434	15,434	15,434	15,434	15,434

Note: Figures are estimates from linear hierarchical regression models with random coefficients and cross level interactions. Standard errors in parentheses. ***$p \leq 0.001$; **$p \leq 0.01$; *$p \leq 0.05$; †$p \leq 0.1$

Table 6.8 Cross-level interaction effects for individual identification with Europe (2004)

Cross-level interaction effects for individual identification with Europe 2004										
	M_{3a}	M_{3b}	M_{3c}	M_{3d}	M_{3e}	M_{3f}	M_{3g}	M_{3h}	M_{3i}	M_{3j}
Intercept	−0.03 (0.18)	0.19 (0.15)	0.14 (0.13)	0.02 (0.16)	0.04 (0.16)	0.15 (0.14)	0.13 (0.11)	0.02 (0.12)	0.07 (0.12)	0.06 (0.12)
Individual level predictors										
Gender (male)	0.00 (0.01)	0.01 (0.01)	0.00 (0.01)	0.00 (0.01)	0.00 (0.01)	0.00 (0.01)	0.01 (0.01)	0.00 (0.01)	0.00 (0.01)	0.00 (0.01)
Age	0.00 (0.00)	0.00 (0.00)	0.00 (0.00)	0.00 (0.00)	0.00 (0.00)	0.00 (0.00)	0.00 (0.00)	0.00 (0.00)	0.00 (0.00)	0.00 (0.00)
Community (ref.: rural)										
Small town	0.05*** (0.01)	0.05*** (0.01)	0.05*** (0.01)	0.05*** (0.01)	0.05*** (0.01)	0.04*** (0.01)	0.04*** (0.01)	0.04*** (0.01)	0.04*** (0.01)	0.04*** (0.01)
Large town	0.06*** (0.01)	0.06*** (0.01)	0.06*** (0.01)	0.06*** (0.01)	0.06*** (0.01)	0.06*** (0.01)	0.06*** (0.01)	0.06*** (0.01)	0.06*** (0.01)	0.06*** (0.01)
Education	0.07*** (0.01)	0.07*** (0.01)	0.07*** (0.01)	0.07*** (0.01)	0.07*** (0.01)	0.07*** (0.01)	0.07*** (0.01)	0.07*** (0.01)	0.07*** (0.01)	0.07*** (0.01)
Occupation (ref.: other)										
Student	−0.05* (0.02)	−0.05* (0.02)	−0.05* (0.02)	−0.05* (0.02)	−0.05* (0.02)	−0.05* (0.02)	−0.05* (0.02)	−0.05* (0.02)	−0.05* (0.02)	−0.05* (0.02)
Manager	0.04** (0.02)	0.04** (0.02)	0.04** (0.02)	0.04** (0.02)	0.04** (0.02)	0.04** (0.02)	0.04** (0.02)	0.04** (0.02)	0.04** (0.02)	0.04** (0.02)
National econ expect.: worse	−0.13*** (0.01)	−0.13*** (0.01)	−0.13*** (0.01)	−0.13*** (0.01)	−0.13*** (0.01)	−0.13*** (0.01)	−0.13*** (0.01)	−0.13*** (0.01)	−0.13*** (0.01)	−0.13*** (0.01)
Personal econ expect.: worse	−0.14*** (0.01)	−0.14*** (0.01)	−0.14*** (0.01)	−0.14*** (0.01)	−0.14*** (0.01)	−0.14*** (0.01)	−0.13*** (0.01)	−0.13*** (0.01)	−0.13*** (0.01)	−0.13*** (0.01)
Political interest	0.13*** (0.04)	0.11*** (0.03)	0.11*** (0.03)	0.10*** (0.02)	0.10*** (0.01)	0.10*** (0.01)	0.10*** (0.01)	0.09*** (0.01)	0.10*** (0.01)	0.10*** (0.01)

EU knowledge	0.06*** (0.01)	0.06*** (0.01)	0.06*** (0.01)	0.06*** (0.01)	0.06*** (0.01)	0.06*** (0.01)	0.06*** (0.01)	0.06*** (0.01)	0.06*** (0.01)	0.06*** (0.01)
Concept of EU (ref.: other)										
Common political project	0.14*** (0.03)	0.14*** (0.03)	0.14*** (0.03)	0.14*** (0.03)	0.14*** (0.03)	0.14*** (0.03)	0.14*** (0.03)	0.14*** (0.03)	0.14*** (0.03)	0.14*** (0.03)
Individual benefits	0.08*** (0.02)	0.08*** (0.02)	0.08*** (0.02)	0.08*** (0.02)	0.08*** (0.02)	0.08*** (0.02)	0.08*** (0.02)	0.08*** (0.02)	0.08*** (0.02)	0.08*** (0.02)
National identification	0.40*** (0.01)	0.40*** (0.01)	0.40*** (0.01)	0.40*** (0.01)	0.40*** (0.01)	0.33*** (0.08)	0.42*** (0.05)	0.45*** (0.03)	0.40*** (0.02)	0.41*** (0.03)
Transnational background	0.20*** (0.02)	0.20*** (0.02)	0.20*** (0.02)	0.20*** (0.02)	0.20*** (0.02)	0.20*** (0.02)	0.20*** (0.02)	0.20*** (0.02)	0.20*** (0.02)	0.20*** (0.02)
Country level predictors										
Party messages										
% overall identity	0.03* (0.01)			0.02* (0.01)	0.02* (0.01)	0.01 (0.01)		0.02* (0.01)	0.02* (0.01)	0.02* (0.01)
% national identity		0.02 (0.02)					0.02 (0.01)			
% European identity			0.04† (0.02)							
Eurozone	0.18* (0.09)	0.20* (0.10)	0.11 (0.09)	0.18* (0.09)	0.18* (0.09)	0.02 (0.06)	0.05 (0.07)	0.02 (0.06)	0.02 (0.06)	0.03 (0.08)
Net paying EU transfers	0.12 (0.09)	0.13 (0.10)	0.11 (0.09)	0.16 (0.11)	0.12 (0.09)	0.23*** (0.06)	0.34*** (0.07)	0.41*** (0.08)	0.32*** (0.06)	0.32*** (0.06)
Trade	0.00** (0.00)	0.00** (0.00)	0.00* (0.00)	0.00** (0.00)	0.00** (0.00)	0.00† (0.00)	0.00* (0.00)	0.00† (0.00)	0.00† (0.00)	0.00† (0.00)
Total immigration	−0.02** (0.01)	−0.02* (0.01)	−0.01 (0.01)	−0.02** (0.01)	−0.02** (0.01)	−0.01* (0.00)	−0.01** (0.00)	−0.01* (0.00)	−0.01* (0.01)	−0.01* (0.01)
Unemployment rate	0.01 (0.01)	0.01 (0.01)	0.02 (0.01)	0.01 (0.01)	0.00 (0.01)	0.00 (0.01)	0.01 (0.01)	0.00 (0.01)	0.00 (0.01)	0.00 (0.01)

(continued)

Table 6.8 (continued)

Cross-level interaction effects for individual identification with Europe 2004										
	M_{3a}	M_{3b}	M_{3c}	M_{3d}	M_{3e}	M_{3f}	M_{3g}	M_{3h}	M_{3i}	M_{3j}
Cross-level interactions										
Pol interest × party messages (total id %)	−0.00 (0.00)									
Pol interest × party messages (nat id %)		−0.00 (0.00)								
Pol interest × party messages (EU id %)			−0.00 (0.00)							
Pol interest × Net paying EU transfer				−0.02 (0.02)						
Pol interest × Trade					−0.00 (0.00)					
Nat ident × party messages (total id %)						0.01 (0.01)				
Nat ident × party messages (nat id %)							−0.00 (0.01)			
Nat ident × Net paying EU transfers								−0.09* (0.04)		
Nat ident × total immigration									−0.00 (0.00)	
Nat ident × Eurozone										−0.01 (0.05)
Variance components										
Country level τ_{00}	0.05 (0.02)	0.06 (0.02)	0.06 (0.02)	0.05 (0.02)	0.05 (0.02)	0.02 (0.01)	0.02 (0.01)	0.02 (0.01)	0.02 (0.01)	0.02 (0.01)
Individual level σ^2	0.57 (0.01)	0.57 (0.01)	0.57 (0.01)	0.57 (0.01)	0.57 (0.01)	0.57 (0.01)	0.57 (0.01)	0.57 (0.01)	0.57 (0.01)	0.57 (0.01)

Var (pol interest/nat ident)	0.00 (0.00)	0.00 (0.00)	0.00 (0.00)	0.00 (0.00)	0.00 (0.00)	0.01 (0.00)	0.01 (0.00)	0.01 (0.00)	0.01 (0.00)	0.01 (0.00)
Cov(pol interest/nat ident, cons)	−0.01 (0.00)	−0.01 (0.00)	−0.01 (0.00)	−0.01 (0.00)	−0.01 (0.00)	−0.01 (0.01)	−0.01 (0.01)	−0.01 (0.01)	−0.01 (0.01)	−0.01 (0.01)
−2 × Log Likelihood	54,191.58	54,194.88	54,192.6	54,191.84	54,192.26	54,014.82	54,016.54	54,011.82	54,015.74	54,015.72
AIC	54,245.57	54,248.89	54,246.59	54,245.84	54,246.26	54,068.81	54,070.55	54,065.82	54,069.74	54,069.71
BIC	54,463.59	54,466.91	54,464.62	54,463.86	54,464.28	54,286.83	54,288.57	54,283.84	54,287.76	54,287.74
R^2	0.13	0.13	0.13	0.13	0.13	0.14	0.13	0.13	0.13	0.13
No. of groups (N)	25	25	25	25	25	25	25	25	25	25
No. of individuals (n)	23,740	23,740	23,740	23,740	23,740	23,740	23,740	23,740	23,740	23,740

Note: Figures are estimates from linear hierarchical regression models with random coefficients and cross level interactions. Standard errors in parentheses. ***$p \leq 0.001$; **$p \leq 0.01$; *$p \leq 0.05$; †$p \leq 0.1$

Table 6.9 Cross-level interaction effects for individual identification with Europe (2006)

Cross-level interaction effects for individual identification with Europe 2006					
	M_{3a}	M_{3b}	M_{3c}	M_{3d}	M_{3e}
Intercept	0.24*** (0.08)	0.24*** (0.08)	0.26*** (0.08)	0.26*** (0.08)	0.27*** (0.08)
Individual level predictors					
Gender (male)	0.00 (0.01)	0.00 (0.01)	0.00 (0.01)	0.00 (0.01)	0.00 (0.01)
Age	−0.00 (0.00)	−0.00 (0.00)	−0.00 (0.00)	−0.00 (0.00)	−0.00 (0.00)
Type of community (ref.: rural/village)					
Small town	0.02 (0.02)	0.02 (0.02)	0.01 (0.02)	0.01 (0.02)	0.01 (0.02)
Large town	0.06*** (0.02)	0.06*** (0.02)	0.06** (0.02)	0.06** (0.02)	0.06** (0.02)
Education	0.09*** (0.01)	0.09*** (0.01)	0.09*** (0.01)	0.09*** (0.01)	0.09*** (0.01)
Occupation (ref.: other)					
Student	−0.05 (0.04)	−0.06 (0.04)	−0.05 (0.04)	−0.05 (0.04)	−0.05 (0.04)
Manager	0.06* (0.03)	0.06* (0.03)	0.06* (0.03)	0.06* (0.03)	0.06* (0.03)
National economic expect.: worse	−0.16*** (0.02)	−0.16*** (0.02)	−0.16*** (0.02)	−0.16*** (0.02)	−0.16*** (0.02)
Personal economic expect.: worse	−0.07** (0.02)	−0.07** (0.02)	−0.07*** (0.02)	−0.07*** (0.02)	−0.07*** (0.02)
Political interest	0.13*** (0.02)	0.12*** (0.02)	0.12*** (0.01)	0.12*** (0.01)	0.12*** (0.01)
EU knowledge	0.10*** (0.01)	0.10*** (0.01)	0.10*** (0.01)	0.10*** (0.01)	0.10*** (0.01)
Conception of Europe (ref.: other)					
Common political project	0.22*** (0.04)	0.22*** (0.04)	0.22*** (0.04)	0.22*** (0.04)	0.22*** (0.04)
Individual benefits	0.12*** (0.03)	0.12*** (0.03)	0.13*** (0.03)	0.13*** (0.03)	0.13*** (0.03)
National identification	0.36*** (0.01)	0.36*** (0.01)	0.37*** (0.04)	0.37*** (0.03)	0.36*** (0.03)
Transnational background	0.15*** (0.03)	0.15*** (0.03)	0.14*** (0.03)	0.14*** (0.03)	0.14*** (0.03)
Country level predictors					
Eurozone	0.07 (0.10)	0.07 (0.10)	0.06 (0.07)	0.06 (0.07)	0.05 (0.11)
Net paying EU transfers	0.25* (0.10)	0.23* (0.10)	0.19† (0.11)	0.18* (0.07)	0.18* (0.07)
Trade	0.00*** (0.00)	0.00*** (0.00)	0.00 (0.00)	0.00** (0.00)	0.00** (0.00)

(continued)

Table 6.9 (continued)

Cross-level interaction effects for individual identification with Europe 2006					
	M_{3a}	M_{3b}	M_{3c}	M_{3d}	M_{3e}
Total immigration	−0.01* (0.01)	−0.01* (0.01)	−0.01 (0.00)	−0.00 (0.01)	−0.01 (0.01)
Unemployment rate	0.05** (0.02)	0.05** (0.02)	0.02† (0.01)	0.02† (0.01)	0.02† (0.01)
Cross- level interactions					
Pol interest × Net paying EU transfer	−0.02 (0.03)				
Pol interest × Trade		−0.00* (0.00)			
Nat ident × Net paying EU transfers			−0.01 (0.06)		
Nat ident × total immigration				−0.00 (0.00)	
Nat ident × Eurozone					0.00 (0.06)
Variance components					
Country level τ_{00}	0.04 (0.01)	0.04 (0.01)	0.04 (0.02)	0.04 (0.02)	0.04 (0.02)
Individual level σ^2	0.62 (0.01)	0.62 (0.01)	0.62 (0.01)	0.62 (0.01)	0.62 (0.01)
Var (pol interest/nat ident)	0.00 (0.00)	0.00 (0.00)	0.02 (0.01)	0.02 (0.01)	0.02 (0.01)
Cov(pol interest/nat ident, constant)	0.00 (0.00)	0.00 (0.00)	−0.02 (0.01)	−0.02 (0.01)	−0.02 (0.01)
−2 × Log Likelihood	28,316.58	28,313.38	28,198.2	28,198	28,198.26
AIC	28,368.57	28,365.37	28,250.23	28,249.99	28,250.26
BIC	28,560.63	28,557.44	28,442.3	28,442.05	28,442.33
R^2	0.13	0.13	0.13	0.13	0.13
No. of groups (N)	25	25	25	25	25
No. of individuals (n)	11,932	11,932	11,932	11,932	11,932

Note: Figures are estimates from linear hierarchical regression models with random coefficients and cross level interactions. Standard errors in parentheses. ***$p \leq 0.001$; **$p \leq 0.01$; *$p \leq 0.05$; †$p \leq 0.1$

Table 6.10 Cross-level interaction effects for individual identification with Europe (2007)

Cross-level interaction effects for individual identification with Europe 2007					
	M_{3a}	M_{3b}	M_{3c}	M_{3d}	M_{3e}
Intercept	0.28*** (0.07)	0.28*** (0.07)	0.29*** (0.07)	0.33*** (0.07)	0.39*** (0.08)
Individual level predictors					
Gender (male)	0.03** (0.01)	0.03** (0.01)	0.03** (0.01)	0.03** (0.01)	0.03** (0.01)
Age	−0.00*** (0.00)	−0.00*** (0.00)	−0.00*** (0.00)	−0.00*** (0.00)	−0.00*** (0.00)
Type of community (ref.: rural/village)					
Small town	−0.01 (0.01)	−0.01 (0.01)	−0.01 (0.01)	−0.01 (0.01)	−0.01 (0.01)
Large town	0.04** (0.01)	0.04** (0.01)	0.04** (0.01)	0.04** (0.01)	0.04** (0.01)
Education	0.11*** (0.01)	0.11*** (0.01)	0.11*** (0.01)	0.11*** (0.01)	0.11*** (0.01)
Occupation (ref.: other)					
Student	−0.12*** (0.03)	−0.12*** (0.03)	−0.12*** (0.03)	−0.12*** (0.03)	−0.12*** (0.03)
Manager	0.08*** (0.02)	0.08*** (0.02)	0.08*** (0.02)	0.08*** (0.02)	0.08*** (0.02)
National economic expect.: worse	−0.20*** (0.01)	−0.20*** (0.01)	−0.20*** (0.01)	−0.20*** (0.01)	−0.20*** (0.01)
Personal economic expect.: worse	−0.10*** (0.02)	−0.10*** (0.02)	−0.10*** (0.02)	−0.10*** (0.02)	−0.10*** (0.02)
Political interest	0.07*** (0.02)	0.08*** (0.01)	0.07*** (0.01)	0.07*** (0.01)	0.07*** (0.01)
EU knowledge	0.12*** (0.01)	0.12*** (0.01)	0.12*** (0.01)	0.12*** (0.01)	0.12*** (0.01)
Conception of Europe (ref.: other)					
Common political project	0.26*** (0.03)	0.26*** (0.03)	0.26*** (0.03)	0.26*** (0.03)	0.26*** (0.03)
Individual benefits	0.05* (0.02)	0.05* (0.02)	0.05* (0.02)	0.05* (0.02)	0.05* (0.02)
National identification	0.26*** (0.01)	0.26*** (0.01)	0.28*** (0.03)	0.25*** (0.02)	0.21*** (0.03)
European background	0.13*** (0.02)	0.13*** (0.02)	0.13*** (0.02)	0.13*** (0.02)	0.13*** (0.02)
Country level predictors					
Eurozone	0.10 (0.08)	0.10 (0.08)	−0.02 (0.07)	−0.02 (0.07)	−0.14 (0.10)
Net paying EU transfers	−0.08 (0.09)	−0.07 (0.08)	0.09 (0.10)	−0.01 (0.07)	−0.01 (0.07)
Trade	0.00 (0.00)	0.00 (0.00)	0.00 (0.00)	0.00 (0.00)	0.00 (0.00)
Total immigration	0.00 (0.01)	−0.00 (0.01)	0.00 (0.00)	0.00 (0.01)	0.00 (0.01)

(continued)

Table 6.10 (continued)

Cross-level interaction effects for individual identification with Europe 2007					
	M_{3a}	M_{3b}	M_{3c}	M_{3d}	M_{3e}
Unemployment rate	0.06** (0.02)	0.06** (0.02)	0.04* (0.02)	0.04* (0.02)	0.04* (0.02)
Cross-level interactions					
Pol interest × Net paying EU transfer	0.00 (0.02)				
Pol interest × Trade		−0.00 (0.00)			
Nat ident × Net paying EU transfers			−0.06 (0.04)		
Nat ident × total immigration				0.00 (0.00)	
Nat ident × Eurozone					0.07† (0.04)
Variance components					
Country level τ_{00}	0.04 (0.01)	0.04 (0.01)	0.05 (0.02)	0.05 (0.02)	0.05 (0.02)
Individual level σ^2	0.66 (0.01)	0.66 (0.01)	0.66 (0.01)	0.66 (0.01)	0.66 (0.01)
Var (pol interest/nat ident)	0.00 (0.00)	0.00 (0.00)	0.01 (0.00)	0.01 (0.00)	0.01 (0.00)
Cov(pol interest/nat ident, constant)	−0.00 (0.00)	−0.00 (0.00)	−0.02 (0.01)	−0.02 (0.01)	−0.02 (0.01)
−2 × Log Likelihood	61,275.42	61,274.88	61,172.56	61,174.28	61,174.28
AIC	61,327.42	61,326.88	61,224.56	61,226.29	61,226.29
BIC	61,538.93	61,538.4	61,436.08	61,437.81	61,437.81
R^2	0.10	0.10	0.10	0.10	0.10
No. of groups (N)	27	27	27	27	27
No. of individuals (n)	25,217	25,217	25,217	25,217	25,217

Note: Figures are estimates from linear hierarchical regression models with random coefficients and cross level interactions. Standard errors in parentheses. ***$p \leq 0.001$; **$p \leq 0.01$; *$p \leq 0.05$; †$p \leq 0.1$.

Table 6.11 Cross-level interaction effects for individual identification with Europe (2010)

Cross-level interaction effects for individual identification with Europe 2010							
	M_{3a}	M_{3b}	M_{3c}	M_{3d}	M_{3e}	M_{3f}	M_{3g}
Intercept	0.17 (0.11)	0.23* (0.11)	0.24* (0.11)	0.29** (0.09)	0.28** (0.09)	0.27** (0.09)	0.33*** (0.09)
Individual level predictors							
Gender (male)	0.05*** (0.01)	0.05*** (0.01)	0.05*** (0.01)	0.05*** (0.01)	0.05*** (0.01)	0.05*** (0.01)	0.05*** (0.01)
Age	−0.00*** (0.00)	−0.00*** (0.00)	−0.00*** (0.00)	−0.00*** (0.00)	−0.00*** (0.00)	−0.00*** (0.00)	−0.00*** (0.00)
Type of community (ref.: rural/village)							
Small town	0.02 (0.01)	0.02 (0.01)	0.02 (0.01)	0.02 (0.01)	0.02* (0.01)	0.02* (0.01)	0.02* (0.01)
Large town	0.04** (0.01)	0.04** (0.01)	0.04** (0.01)	0.04** (0.01)	0.04** (0.01)	0.04** (0.01)	0.04** (0.01)
Education	0.12*** (0.02)	0.10*** (0.01)	0.10*** (0.02)	0.10*** (0.01)	0.10*** (0.01)	0.10*** (0.01)	0.10*** (0.01)
Occupation (ref.: other)							
Student	−0.07* (0.03)	−0.06* (0.03)	−0.06* (0.03)	−0.06* (0.03)	−0.06* (0.03)	−0.06* (0.03)	−0.06* (0.03)
Manager	0.06*** (0.02)	0.06*** (0.02)	0.06*** (0.02)	0.06*** (0.02)	0.06*** (0.02)	0.06*** (0.02)	0.06*** (0.02)
Personal economic expect.: worse	−0.18*** (0.02)	−0.18*** (0.02)	−0.18*** (0.02)	−0.18*** (0.02)	−0.18*** (0.02)	−0.18*** (0.02)	−0.18*** (0.02)
National identification	0.29*** (0.01)	0.29*** (0.01)	0.29*** (0.01)	0.28*** (0.02)	0.28*** (0.01)	0.29*** (0.02)	0.24*** (0.03)
Conception of national community	0.01 (0.02)	0.01 (0.02)	0.01 (0.02)	0.01 (0.02)	0.01 (0.02)	0.01 (0.02)	0.01 (0.02)
Transnational practices	0.05*** (0.00)	0.05*** (0.00)	0.05*** (0.00)	0.06*** (0.00)	0.06*** (0.00)	0.06*** (0.00)	0.06*** (0.00)
Transnational capital	0.08*** (0.01)	0.08*** (0.01)	0.08*** (0.01)	0.08*** (0.01)	0.08*** (0.01)	0.08*** (0.01)	0.08*** (0.01)
Transnational background	0.06** (0.02)	0.06** (0.02)	0.07** (0.02)	0.06** (0.02)	0.06** (0.02)	0.06** (0.02)	0.06** (0.02)
Eurozone	0.16† (0.10)	0.16† (0.10)	0.16† (0.10)	0.06 (0.09)	0.06 (0.09)	0.06 (0.09)	−0.03 (0.09)
Net paying EU transfers	0.08 (0.14)	−0.05 (0.12)	−0.05 (0.12)	−0.05 (0.12)	−0.05 (0.11)	−0.04 (0.11)	−0.03 (0.11)
Trade	0.00 (0.00)	0.00 (0.00)	0.00 (0.00)	−0.00 (0.00)	−0.00 (0.00)	−0.00 (0.00)	−0.00 (0.00)
Total immigration	−0.00 (0.01)	−0.00 (0.01)	−0.00 (0.01)	0.00 (0.01)	0.00 (0.01)	0.00 (0.01)	0.00 (0.01)
Unemployment rate	0.01 (0.01)	0.01 (0.01)	0.01 (0.01)	0.00 (0.01)	0.00 (0.01)	0.00 (0.01)	0.00 (0.01)
IMF conditionality	0.06 (0.13)	0.06 (0.13)	0.00 (0.16)	0.13 (0.11)	0.11 (0.11)	0.19 (0.13)	0.13 (0.12)
Cross-level interactions							
Education × Net paying EU transfer	−0.04 (0.02)						

(continued)

Table 6.11 (continued)

Cross-level interaction effects for individual identification with Europe 2010							
	M_{3a}	M_{3b}	M_{3c}	M_{3d}	M_{3e}	M_{3f}	M_{3g}
Education × Trade		−0.00 (0.00)					
Education × IMF			0.02 (0.03)				
Nat ident × Net paying EU transfers				0.01 (0.04)			
Nat ident × total immigration					−0.00 (0.00)		
Nat ident × IMF						−0.05 (0.05)	
Nat ident × Eurozone							0.08* (0.03)
Variance components							
Country level τ_{00}	0.08 (0.02)	0.09 (0.03)	0.09 (0.03)	0.04 (0.02)	0.04 (0.02)	0.04 (0.02)	0.04 (0.01)
Individual level σ^2	0.64 (0.01)	0.64 (0.01)	0.64 (0.01)	0.64 (0.01)	0.64 (0.01)	0.64 (0.01)	0.64 (0.01)
Var (education/ nat ident)	0.00 (0.00)	0.00 (0.00)	0.00 (0.00)	0.01 (0.00)	0.01 (0.00)	0.01 (0.00)	0.00 (0.00)
Cov(education/ nat ident, constant)	−0.01 (0.00)	−0.01 (0.00)	−0.01 (0.00)	−0.00 (0.00)	−0.00 (0.00)	−0.00 (0.00)	−0.00 (0.00)
−2 × Log Likelihood	58,973.18	58,975.66	58,975.44	58,952.58	58,951.88	58,951.34	58,948
AIC	59,023.18	59,025.67	59,025.44	59,002.57	59,001.87	59,001.34	58,998.01
BIC	59,225.99	59,228.47	59,228.25	59,205.38	59,204.68	59,204.14	59,200.81
R^2	0.09	0.08	0.08	0.08	0.08	0.08	0.08
No. of groups (N)	27	27	27	27	27	27	27
No. of individuals (n)	24,641	24,641	24,641	24,641	24,641	24,641	24,641

Note: Figures are estimates from linear hierarchical regression models with random coefficients and cross level interactions. Standard errors in parentheses. ***$p \leq 0.001$; **$p \leq 0.01$; *$p \leq 0.05$; †$p \leq 0.1$

Table 6.12 Cross-level interaction effects for individual identification with Europe (2012)

Cross-level interaction effects for individual identification with Europe 2012							
	M_{3a}	M_{3b}	M_{3c}	M_{3d}	M_{3e}	M_{3f}	M_{3g}
Intercept	0.23** (0.08)	0.23** (0.08)	0.23** (0.08)	0.23*** (0.07)	0.22*** (0.07)	0.20** (0.07)	0.27*** (0.07)
Individual level predictors							
Gender (male)	0.00 (0.01)	0.00 (0.01)	0.00 (0.01)	0.00 (0.01)	0.00 (0.01)	0.00 (0.01)	0.00 (0.01)
Age	0.00* (0.00)	0.00* (0.00)	0.00* (0.00)	0.00** (0.00)	0.00** (0.00)	0.00** (0.00)	0.00** (0.00)
Community (ref.: rural)							
Small town	0.01 (0.01)	0.01 (0.01)	0.01 (0.01)	0.01 (0.01)	0.01 (0.01)	0.01 (0.01)	0.01 (0.01)
Large town	0.02† (0.01)	0.02† (0.01)	0.02† (0.01)	0.02† (0.01)	0.02† (0.01)	0.02† (0.01)	0.02† (0.01)
Education	0.09*** (0.01)	0.09*** (0.01)	0.09*** (0.01)	0.09*** (0.01)	0.09*** (0.01)	0.09*** (0.01)	0.09*** (0.01)
Occupation (ref.: other)							
Student	−0.01 (0.01)	−0.01 (0.01)	−0.01 (0.02)	−0.01 (0.01)	−0.01 (0.01)	−0.01 (0.01)	−0.01 (0.01)
Manager	0.03* (0.02)	0.03* (0.02)	0.03* (0.02)	0.03* (0.02)	0.03* (0.02)	0.03* (0.02)	0.03* (0.02)
National economic expect.: worse	−0.16*** (0.01)	−0.16*** (0.01)	−0.16*** (0.01)	−0.16*** (0.01)	−0.16*** (0.01)	−0.16*** (0.01)	−0.16*** (0.01)
Personal economic expect.: worse	−0.11*** (0.01)	−0.11*** (0.01)	−0.11*** (0.01)	−0.11*** (0.01)	−0.11*** (0.01)	−0.11*** (0.01)	−0.11*** (0.01)
Political interest	0.02* (0.01)	0.02** (0.01)	0.02** (0.01)	0.03*** (0.01)	0.03** (0.01)	0.03*** (0.01)	0.03*** (0.01)
EU knowledge	0.10*** (0.01)	0.10*** (0.01)	0.10*** (0.01)	0.10*** (0.01)	0.10*** (0.01)	0.10*** (0.01)	0.10*** (0.01)
EU Conception (ref.: other)							
Common political project	0.22*** (0.03)	0.22*** (0.03)	0.22*** (0.03)	0.22*** (0.03)	0.22*** (0.03)	0.22*** (0.03)	0.22*** (0.03)
Individual benefits	0.09*** (0.02)	0.09*** (0.02)	0.09*** (0.02)	0.09*** (0.02)	0.09*** (0.02)	0.09*** (0.02)	0.09*** (0.02)
National identification	0.26*** (0.01)	0.26*** (0.01)	0.26*** (0.01)	0.24*** (0.03)	0.25*** (0.02)	0.27*** (0.02)	0.20*** (0.02)
Transnational contacts	0.10*** (0.00)	0.10*** (0.00)	0.10*** (0.00)	0.09*** (0.00)	0.09*** (0.00)	0.09*** (0.00)	0.09*** (0.00)
Transnational capital	0.02*** (0.00)	0.02*** (0.00)	0.02*** (0.00)	0.02*** (0.00)	0.02*** (0.00)	0.02*** (0.00)	0.02*** (0.00)
Country level predictors							
Eurozone	0.06 (0.08)	0.06 (0.08)	0.06 (0.08)	−0.07 (0.07)	−0.07 (0.07)	−0.07 (0.07)	−0.16* (0.08)
Net paying EU transfers	−0.19 (0.12)	−0.19 (0.12)	−0.19 (0.12)	−0.04 (0.11)	−0.01 (0.10)	−0.00 (0.10)	−0.00 (0.11)
Trade	−0.00 (0.00)	−0.00 (0.00)	−0.00 (0.00)	0.00 (0.00)	0.00 (0.00)	0.00 (0.00)	0.00 (0.00)
Total immigration rate	0.00 (0.01)	0.00 (0.01)	0.00 (0.01)	−0.00 (0.01)	−0.01 (0.01)	−0.00 (0.01)	−0.00 (0.01)

(continued)

Table 6.12 (continued)

Cross-level interaction effects for individual identification with Europe 2012							
	M_{3a}	M_{3b}	M_{3c}	M_{3d}	M_{3e}	M_{3f}	M_{3g}
Unemployment rate	−0.01 (0.01)	−0.01 (0.01)	−0.01 (0.01)	0.01 (0.01)	0.01 (0.01)	0.01 (0.01)	0.01 (0.01)
IMF conditionality	−0.02 (0.11)	−0.02 (0.11)	−0.01 (0.11)	0.18† (0.09)	0.18† (0.09)	0.29** (0.11)	0.18† (0.09)
Cross-level interactions							
Pol interest × Net paying EU transfer	0.02 (0.02)						
Pol interest × Trade		−0.00 (0.00)					
Pol interest × IMF			0.02 (0.03)				
Nat ident × Net paying EU transfers				0.03 (0.04)			
Nat ident × total immigration					0.00 (0.00)		
Nat ident × IMF						−0.10† (0.06)	
Nat ident × Eurozone							0.08* (0.04)
Variance components							
Country level τ_{00}	0.03 (0.01)	0.03 (0.01)	0.03 (0.01)	0.02 (0.01)	0.02 (0.01)	0.02 (0.01)	0.02 (0.01)
Individual level σ^2	0.60 (0.01)	0.60 (0.01)	0.60 (0.01)	0.60 (0.01)	0.60 (0.01)	0.60 (0.01)	0.60 (0.01)
Var (pol interest/nat ident)	0.00 (0.00)	0.00 (0.00)	0.00 (0.00)	0.01 (0.00)	0.01 (0.00)	0.01 (0.00)	0.01 (0.00)
Cov(pol interest/ nat ident, constant)	0.00 (0.00)	0.00 (0.00)	0.00 (0.00)	−0.01 (0.01)	−0.01 (0.00)	−0.01 (0.00)	−0.01 (0.00)
−2 × Log Likelihood	59,994.84	59,994.88	59,994.86	59,851.56	59,848.64	59,849.26	59,847.92
AIC	60,050.48	60, 050.88	60, 050.85	59,907.56	59,904.63	59,905.26	59,903.92
BIC	60,278.78	60,279.19	60,279.16	60,135.87	60,132.94	60,133.56	60,132.23
R^2	0.13	0.13	0.13	0.13	0.13	0.13	0.13
No. of groups (N)	27	27	27	27	27	27	27
No. of individuals (n)	25,687	25,687	25,687	25,687	25,687	25,687	25,687

Note: Figures are estimates from linear hierarchical regression models with random coefficients and cross level interactions. Standard errors in parentheses. ***$p \leq 0.001$; **$p \leq 0.01$; *$p \leq 0.05$; †$p \leq 0.1$

References

Anderson, B. (1991). *Imagined communities: Reflections on the origins and spread of nationalism*. London/New York: Verso.

Armingeon, K., & Ceka, B. (2014). The loss of trust in the European Union during the great recession since 2007: The role of heuristics from the national political system. *European Union Politics, 15*(1), 82–107.

BBC News. (2010a). Greece police tear gas anti-austerity protesters.

BBC News. (2010b). Three dead as Greece protest turns violent.

BBC News. (2011). Greece crisis: MPs vote on austerity package.

BBC News. (2012). Buildings ablaze as Greek MPs vote on austerity plan.

Bickes, H., Otten, T., & Weymann, L. C. (2014). The financial crisis in the German and English press: Metaphorical structures in the media coverage on Greece, Spain and Italy. *Discourse & Society, 25*(4), 424–445.

Bornschier, S. (2010). The new cultural divide and the two-dimensional political space in Western Europe. *West European Politics, 33*(3), 419–444.

Bornschier, S. (2011). National political conflict and identity formation: The diverse nature of the threat from the extreme left and extreme populist right. In D. Fuchs, & H.-D. Klingemann (Eds.), Cultural diversity, European identity and the legitimacy of the EU (pp. 171–200, Studies in EU reform and enlargement). Cheltenham: Edward Elgar.

Braun, D., & Tausendpfund, M. (2013). Immigration als Erklärung für die Zustimmung zur weiteren Europäischen Integration. Eine europaweite empirische Analyse. *Zeitschrift für Vergleichende Politikwissenschaft, 7*(3), 205–226.

Brinegar, A. P., & Jolly, S. K. (2005). Location, location, location: National contextual factors and public support for European integration. *European Union Politics, 6*(2), 155–180.

Bryan, M. L., & Jenkins, S. P. (2015). Multilevel modelling of country effects: A cautionary tale. *European Sociological Review, 32*, 3–22.

de Vreese, C. H., Banducci, S. A., Semetko, H. A., & Boomgaarden, H. G. (2006). The news coverage of the 2004 European parliamentary election campaign in 25 countries. *European Union Politics, 7*(4), 477–504.

Deutsch, K. W. (1953a). *Nationalism and social communication: An inquiry into the foundations of nationality*. Cambridge, MA: MIT Press.

Deutsch, K. W. (1953b). *Political community at the international level: Problems of definition and measurement*. Princeton, NJ: Princeton University Press.

Deutsch, K. W., Burrell, S. A., & Kann, R. A. (1957). *Political community and the North Atlantic area: International organization in the light of historical experience*. Princeton, NJ: Princeton University Press.

Deutscher Bundestag. (2010). Plenarprotokoll 17/42: Stenografischer Bericht, 42. Sitzung. Berlin, Mittwoch, den 19. Mai 2010. Berlin.

Drewski, D. (2015). Has there been a European public discourse on the Euro crisis? A systematic content analysis of newspaper editorials on the Euro crisis in Germany in Spain. Berliner Studien zur Soziologie Europas – BSSE-Arbeitspapier (33).

Duchesne, S., & Frognier, A.-P. (2008). National and European identifications: A dual relationship. *Comparative European Politics, 6*(2), 143.

Dursun-Ozkanca, O. (2011). European Union enlargement and British public opinion: The agenda-setting power of the press. *Perspectives on European Politics and Society, 12*(2), 139–160.

Eichenberg, R. C., & Dalton, R. J. (2007). Post-maastricht blues: The transformation of citizen support for European integration, 1973–2004. *Acta Politica, 42*(2–3), 128–152.

EUROSTAT. (2014a). Unemployment—LFS adjusted series (une)—Reference Metadata in Euro SDMX Metadata Structure (ESMS). *Eurostat database*. Accessed January 05, 2015, from http://ec.europa.eu/eurostat/cache/metadata/en/une_esms.htm

EUROSTAT. (2014b). Population on 1 January by five year age group, sex group and citizenship [migr_pop1ctz]. *Eurostat database*. Accessed January 05, 2015, from http://appsso.eurostat.ec.europa.eu/nui/show.do?dataset=migr_pop1ctz&lang=en

EUROSTAT. (2014c). Unemployment rate by sex and age groups—annual average, % [une_rt_a]. *Eurostat database*. Accessed January 05, 2015, from http://appsso.eurostat.ec.europa.eu/nui/show.do?dataset=une_rt_a&lang=en

Euro Summit. (2011). Euro summit statement. Brussels.

European Commission. (2009). *Economic crisis in Europe: Causes, consequences and responses* (Vol. 7). Luxembourg: Office for Official Publications of the European Communities.

European Commission. (2013). *EU budget 2012 financial report*. Luxembourg: Publications Office of the European Union.

Garry, J., & Tilley, J. (2009). The macroeconomic factors conditioning the impact of identity on attitudes towards the EU. *European Union Politics, 10*(3), 361–379.

Garry, J., & Tilley, J. (2015). Inequality, state ownership and the European Union: How economic context and economic ideology shape support for the European Union. *European Union Politics, 16*(1), 139–154.

Gelman, A., & Hill, J. (2006). *Data analysis using regression and multilevel/hierarchical models*. Cambridge/New York: Cambridge University Press.

Gerhards, J. (2010). Transnationales linguistisches Kapital der Bürger und der Prozess der Europäischen Integration. In M. Eigmüller, & S. Mau (Eds.), Gesellschaftstheorie und Europapolitik. Sozialwissenschaftliche Ansätze zur Europaforschung (pp. 213–243, Neue Bibliothek der Sozialwissenschaften). Wiesbaden: VS Verlag für Sozialwissenschaften.

Gottschalck, N. (2011/2012). *The Eurocrisis – A European crisis?* (pp. 1–75). Paris: Centre international de formation européenne – Institut européen – European Institute.

Gow, D. (2011). Eurozone crisis: Banks agree 50% reduction on Greece's debt. *The Guardian*.

Hobolt, S. B., & Leblonde, P. (2014). Economic insecurity and public support for the Euro: Before and during the financial crisis. In N. Bermeo & L. M. Bartels (Eds.), *Mass politics in tough times: Opinions, votes and protest in the great recession* (pp. 128–147). Oxford/New York: Oxford University Press.

Hutter, S., & Grande, E. (2014). Politicizing Europe in the national electoral arena: A comparative analysis of five West European countries, 1970–2010. *Journal of Common Market Studies, 52* (5), 1002–1018.

IMF. (2015). Monitoring of fund arrangements database Accessed January 05, 2015, from http://www.imf.org/external/np/pdr/mona/index.aspx

Inthorn, S. (2006). What does it mean to be an EU Citizen? How news media construct civic and cultural concepts of Europe. *Westminster Papers in Communication and Culture, 3*(3), 71–90.

Katsourides, Y. (2014). Negative images of Europe in an era of crisis: The media and public opinion in Cyprus. *Journal of Contemporary European Studies, 24*(1), 61–85.

Kontochristou, M., & Mascha, E. (2014). The Euro crisis and the question of solidarity in the European Union: Disclosures and manifestations in the European press. *Review of European Studies, 6*(2), 50–62.

Kouki, H. (2014). European crisis discourses: The case of Greece. In T. Murray-Leach (Ed.), *Background paper: Crisis discourses in Europe. Media EU-phemisms and alternative narratives* (pp. 16–20). London: Civil Society and Human Security Research Unit, London School of Economics and Political Science.

Kreft, I. G. G., & de Leeuw, J. (1998). *Introducing multilevel modeling*. London: Sage Publications.

Kriesi, H., Grande, E., Lachat, R., Dolezal, M., Bornschier, S., & Frey, T. (2006). Globalization and the transformation of the national political space: Six European countries compared. *European Journal of Political Research, 45*(6), 921–956.

Kubitschek, W. N., & Hallinan, M. T. (1999). Collinearity, bias, and effect size: Modeling "the" effect of track on achievement. *Social Science Research, 28*(4), 380–402.

Light, D., & Young, C. (2009). European Union enlargement, post-accession migration and imaginative geographies of the 'New Europe': Media discourses in Romania and the United Kingdom. *Journal of Cultural Geography, 26*(3), 281–303.

Maas, C. J. M., & Hox, J. J. (2005). Sufficient sample sizes for multilevel modeling. *Methodology: European Journal of Research Methods for the Behavioral and Social Sciences, 1*(3), 86–92.
Mazzoni, M., & Barbieri, G. (2014). Grasshoppers against ants or malfunctions of capitalism? The representation of the European economic crisis in the main Italian newspapers. *Perspectives on European Politics and Society*, 1–16.
Nugent, N. (2004). The unfolding of the 10+2 enlargement round. In N. Nugent (Ed.), *European union enlargement* (pp. 34–69). Basingstoke: Palgrave McMillan.
OECD. (2014a). Quarterly National Accounts: Quarterly Growth Rates of real GDP, change over previous quarter. *OECD National Accounts Statistics (database)*. Accessed December 15, 2014, from http://stats.oecd.org/Index.aspx?QueryName=350&QueryType=View&Lang=en#
OECD. (2014b). Revisions Analysis Dataset. Infra-annual Indicators: Harmonised Unemployment Rates. *OECD Revisions Analysis Dataset*. Accessed December 15, 2014, from http://stats.oecd.org/Index.aspx?querytype=view&queryname=211#
Paccagnella, O. (2011). Sample size and accuracy of estimates in multilevel models: New simulation results. *Methodology: European Journal of Research Methods for the Behavioral and Social Sciences, 7*(3), 111–120.
Peter, J., Semetko, H. A., & de Vreese, C. H. (2003). EU politics on television news: A cross-national comparative study. *European Union Politics, 4*(3), 305–327.
Population on 1 January by five year age group, sex group and citizenship [migr_pop1ctz] (2014). Accessed January 05, 2015, from http://appsso.eurostat.ec.europa.eu/nui/show.do?dataset=migr_pop1ctz&lang=en
Raudenbush, S. W., & Bryk, A. S. (2002). *Hierarchical linear models: Applications and data analysis methods* (Second ed.). Thousand Oaks, CA: SAGE.
Schuck, A. R. T., Xezonakis, G., Elenbaas, M., Banducci, S. A., & de Vreese, C. H. (2011). Party contestation and Europe on the news agenda: The 2009 European parliamentary elections. *Electoral Studies, 30*(1), 41–52.
Shieh, Y.-Y., & Fouladi, R. T. (2003). The effect of multicollinearity on multilevel modeling parameter estimates and standard errors. *Educational and Psychological Measurement, 63*(6), 951–985.
Snijders, T. A. B. (2005). Power and sample size in multilevel linear models. In B. S. Everitt & D. C. Howell (Eds.), *Encyclopedia of statistics in behavioral science* (Vol. 3, pp. 1570–1573). Chicester: Wiley.
Snijders, T. A. B., & Bosker, R. J. (1994). Modeled variance in two-level models. *Sociological Methods & Research, 22*(3), 342–363.
Snijders, T. A. B., & Bosker, R. J. (2011). *Multilevel analysis: An introduction to basic and advanced multilevel modeling* (2nd ed.). London: SAGE.
Steenbergen, M. R., & Jones, B. S. (2002). Modeling multilevel data structures. *American Journal of Political Science, 46*(1), 218–237.
Stegmueller, D. (2013). How many countries for multilevel modeling? A comparison of frequentist and Bayesian approaches. *American Journal of Political Science, 57*, 748–761.
Stoll, H. (2010). Elite-level conflict salience and dimensionality in Western Europe: Concepts and empirical findings. *West European Politics, 33*(3), 445–473.
Vaara, E. (2014). Struggles over legitimacy in the Eurozone crisis: Discursive legitimation strategies and their ideological underpinnings. *Discourse & Society, 25*(4), 500–518.
van Noije, L. (2010). The European paradox: A communication deficit as long as European integration steals the headlines. *European Journal of Communication, 25*(3), 259–272.
Vasilopoulou, S., Halikiopoulou, D., & Exadaktylos, T. (2014). Greece in crisis: Austerity, populism and the politics of blame. *JCMS: Journal of Common Market Studies, 52*(2), 388–402.

Chapter 7
The State of European Identity After the Crisis: Implications for Research and Policymaking

A common identity of Europeans has long been a concern for scholars of European integration and European policymakers alike. Despite the importance attributed to the emergence of European identity among EU citizens for the legitimacy and long-term survival of the EU, the individuals seeing themselves as 'Europeans' and the processes leading them to identify with Europe have received less attention. Empirically, European identification is widespread among the EU population today. If asked about their European allegiances, a majority of EU citizens express some form of identification with the European level. Yet although important steps towards an 'ever closer union' among Europeans have been completed at the institutional level—Europeans can now move freely between member states, rarely need to show their passport at national borders, and pay with the same currency in large parts of the EU—, the share of citizens identifying with Europe has hardly changed over the past decades. Based on this observation, the present study set out from the basic question: Why do people identify with Europe?

7.1 Taking Stock of Citizens' Identification with Europe from the Maastricht Treaty to Eastward Enlargement and the Crisis

Empirically, this book took stock of levels and development of citizens' identification with Europe and its determinants from the adoption of the Maastricht Treaty 1992 to the EU's enlargement to Central and Eastern Europe in 2004/2007 and the financial and economic crisis that has been affecting the EU and its member states since late 2008.

It started by describing *levels and development of European identification among EU citizens* from 1992, the year the Maastricht Treaty was signed, until 2013, when the financial and economic crisis of 2008/2009 had turned into a

S. Bergbauer, *Explaining European Identity Formation*,
https://doi.org/10.1007/978-3-319-67708-8_7

sovereign debt crisis in the Eurozone. Exploring changes in European identification over the past two decades, it provided an update on the strength and development of European identification among EU citizens in recent years and in particular since the EU's enlargement to Central and Eastern Europe in 2004/2007 and the onset of the financial and economic crisis in late 2008. The empirical evidence showed that identification with Europe is a widespread phenomenon among EU citizens by now. The majority of EU citizens see themselves as Europeans, express attachment to Europe and the European Union, and are proud to be European. Neither the EU's enlargement to Central and Eastern Europe nor the financial and economic crisis led to dramatic shifts in citizens' identification with Europe. Levels of European identification increased slightly after the 2004 accession round and although the new CEE member states started out from lower levels of European identification than the EU15 in 2004, they have since shown largely similar trends in identification. After the onset of the financial and economic crisis in late 2008, more rather than less respondents saw themselves (also) as Europeans. In contrast, affective attachments to the European Union decreased over the same period, especially in the Eurozone and in some of the member states hit hardest by the crisis. Rather than causing a sudden drop, the crisis thus appears to have resulted in a gradual weakening of citizens' affective ties to Europe.

Large parts of the EU population hold multiple identifications, identifying with the national and the European community at the same time. They describe themselves as nationals *and* Europeans and feel attached to both the national and the European level. The number of citizens with multiple identifications has remained fairly stable over the two decades under analysis. Neither the EU's enlargement to CEE nor the onset of the crisis led to a rise in national identifications to the detriment of European identifications; rather, citizens continued to identify as both nationals and Europeans even as the EU became more heterogeneous and economic conditions worsened. This seems remarkable especially in the case of the economic and financial crisis, which sparked vivid debates over mutual obligations within the EU and made apparent conflicts of (financial) interest between member states. Media accounts of the EU's response to the crisis often took the form of 'good' vs. 'bad' member states and reported widely on controversies among national governments over financial rescue measures (Dinan 2012, 2013a, b; Mazzoni and Barbieri 2014; Puetter 2012). The tendency of posing national against European interests did not catch on at the citizen level. Unlike what might have been expected, there was no generalised upsurge of exclusive national identifications during the crisis years.

In a second step, the empirical analysis turned to the party level and examined the *salience of European identity issues among national political parties* from 1979 to 2014. It tackled the question whether parties' emphasis on European identity issues changed over the course of EU integration and in response to the EU's eastward enlargement 2004/2007 and the onset of the financial and economic crisis in 2008. In this way, it provided information on a theoretically important influence on European attitudes—namely messages and communications by political elites—that had not been examined with a view to European identification so far. The analysis of party manifestos showed that European identity is not a minor issue for national political parties, either. Across the EU, parties dedicate sizeable shares of their election programmes to identity-related issues, which account for up to 10% of manifesto arguments. In the 2004 EP election campaign that took place in the context of CEE enlargement, identity issues became more salient in manifestos as parties put more emphasis on issues of national identity and community. In contrast, the salience of identity issues decreased in almost all member states in the 2009 campaign as parties' attention shifted to economic issues in the wake of the financial and economic crisis of 2008/2009. Manifesto excerpts from the most recent EP election campaign in 2014 indicate a renewed emphasis on identity. It seems that parties started to link economic issues more closely to identity issues in their campaign as the crisis turned from a crisis of the financial system and the real economy into a sovereign debt crisis in the Eurozone that required extensive financial rescue measures and increased controversies over member states' obligations for mutual support and (financial) solidarity.

Comparing the salience of European identity at the citizen and the party level, we observed similar trends. European identity is widespread at the citizen level in member states like Germany, Italy, France, or Luxembourg and political parties in these countries, too, tend to emphasise a common European identity and community alongside issues of national identity and community. In contrast, in the UK, European identity is comparatively weak at the citizen level and political parties devote little attention to issues of European identity. The member-state specific patterns remain relatively stable over time. At least to some extent, the measures of European identity at the citizen and the party level thus seem to reproduce the general relevance of questions of identity and community in member state societies rather than short-time concerns in public opinion and party strategies in a given campaign. In a way, there appears to be a third variable at work that influences the relevance of European and national identity at both the citizen and the party level. We may think of this 'third variable' as the national 'European' political culture or national 'collective memory' of European integration that comprises country-specific narratives of European integration, member states' historical approaches to European integration, and their relationship to the European Union. This 'collective memory' with regard to Europe and the EU is transmitted to citizens in socialisation processes, but also structures political debates and the discourse of political elites and could thus explain the parallels in the importance of European and national identities among national populations and political parties.

The third part of the empirical analysis turned to *explanation of citizens' identification with Europe*. It provided evidence on the factors influencing individual identification with Europe and changes in the determinants of European identification in the period 2000 to 2012. It was particularly interested in changes in the sources of European identification over time and in response to the EU's enlargement to CEE 2004/2007 and the onset of the financial and economic crisis in late 2008. The statistical analysis found individual identification with Europe to depend on individual-level attributes rather than country-level characteristics in all years under analysis.

At the individual level, political interest, interest in European politics, and knowledge about the EU were among the strongest predictors of European identification; likewise, national identification and personal transnational experiences had strong positive effects on European identification. EU citizens identify with Europe because they are interested in and familiar with (European) politics, because they identify strongly with their home country, and because they have family and friends abroad or otherwise engage in trans-border activities. The more citizens are cognitively and practically engaged with Europe—by discussing European politics with friends and relatives and following the European and international news, by socialising with people from other EU member states, e.g. because they attend school abroad, study at a foreign university, or work outside their home country—the more see themselves as Europeans and develop affective ties to Europe.

At the country level, only member states' net contributions to the EU budget had significant effects on European identification in the period under analysis. Until the late 2000s, citizens from countries that paid more into the EU budget than they got out, i.e. the net payers of EU transfers, identified more with Europe; since the onset of the financial and economic crisis in 2008, this effect has been reversed. As the crisis evolved into a sovereign debt crisis in the Eurozone, citizens in the net payer states—which also gave the largest financial guarantees—appear to have become more critical. Now, they identify less with Europe than their peers in the net recipient countries of EU funding.

The analysis also tested whether the effects of country-level determinants depend on respondents' degree of political interest or the strength of their national attachments. The influence of member state characteristics did not differ by respondents' level of political interest. For example, party messages on issues of European and national community and identity had similar effects among citizens claiming to be highly interested in political affairs and those with little interest in politics. Neither did citizens in the net paying member states identify more or less with Europe if they were more interested in politics. This non-finding may be interpreted as the result of a generalised obliviousness to party communications and the national costs of EU integration; in a more optimistic view, it may also indicate that the 'knowledge gap' between the highly interested and those with little interest in politics is less significant than expected.

National attachments, on the other hand, appeared to have different effects on European identification in different domestic contexts and under different economic conditions. In particular, we found interaction effects between citizens' national identification and economic indicators such as member states' contributions to the EU budget, Eurozone membership, and whether or not member states received conditional financial aids from the EU/IMF. In most cases, however, the results ran counter to theoretical expectations. First of all, national identification positively affected European identification in all groups of member states, whether or not they were net contributors to the EU budget, members of the Eurozone, or under EU/IMF conditionality. Intuitively, we might have expected citizens' with strong national attachments to be more critical of their country's contributions to the EU budget, the loss of monetary sovereignty in the Eurozone, or interventions by EU and IMF, resulting in negative or at least weaker effects of national identification on European identification in these country groups. Empirically, this is not always the case. Until 2003, national identification had stronger (positive) effects on European identification in net contributing rather than in net recipient countries of EU transfers; only from 2004 onwards have citizens with strong national attachments in net paying member states identified less with Europe than their peers in net recipient member states. Living inside or outside the Eurozone only starts to matter for the relationship between national and European identification in the late 2000s; yet even in the crisis, we find that national identifications have stronger positive effects on European identification within the Eurozone than outside. In countries under EU/IMF conditionality, finally, we find the expected relationship between national identification, adverse economic conditions, and European identification. National identification has smaller effects on European identification in countries under EU/IMF conditionality than in other member states. That is, respondents who feel strongly attached to the nation and who experienced austerity programmes as conditions of financial aids by the EU and IMF identify less with Europe than their peers with equally strong national attachments, but living in countries not under EU/IMF conditionality. Still, even in countries under EU/IMF conditionality, national identification remains positively related to identification with Europe.

As regards changes in the sources of European identification related to the EU's enlargement to CEE in 2004/2007 and the onset of the financial and economic crisis in late 2008, no major shifts in the individual-level determinants took place over the accession period or in the course of crisis. Neither political interest nor national identification had significantly more or less influence on citizens' propensity to identify with Europe as new member states from CEE entered the EU and EU member states experienced economic and financial turmoil in the crisis. At the country level, we found changes in the effects of member states' status as a net contributor to the EU budget in the wake of enlargement and the crisis; likewise, the effect of Eurozone membership increased during the crisis years. Until 2006, citizens in net paying member states identified more with Europe; after 2007, citizens in net paying member states identified less with Europe than their peers from net recipient member states. This effect intensified as the crisis continued. Citizens in the Eurozone always tended to identify more with Europe than citizens form countries outside the monetary union, yet in the crisis years, and in particular in 2010 at the height of the discussion over a Greek bail-out, the difference between those living within the Eurozone and those living outside the Eurozone became even more pronounced. In this respect, enlargement and the crisis indeed seem to have increased the relevance of economic aspects and redistributive considerations for citizens' identification with the European level.

Finally, we find interaction effects between national identification and EU/IMF conditionality and Eurozone membership. National identification remains positively related to European identification both in countries receiving and not receiving conditional financial aids from the EU/IMF and as well as inside and outside the

Eurozone. Still, the positive influence of national identification is reduced in countries under EU/IMF conditionality. In contrast, it is stronger within the Eurozone than outside the monetary union. That is, although in the crisis, both EU/IMF conditionality and Eurozone membership seem to represent the risks of economic and financial interdependencies, strong national attachments have different consequences for European identification in the two country groups. Hence, the relationship between national identification and European identification under adverse economic conditions seems to depend on context and the way the crisis was represented domestically. In countries receiving conditional financial aids from the EU/IMF, Greece in particular, the domestic debate focussed on the negative consequences of austerity measures for the population and the national economy, and the role of external actors, in particular the troika, in imposing austerity programmes on national governments and societies (Kouki 2014, p. 19; Vasilopoulou et al. 2014). In the Eurozone, on the other hand, the focus was on the need to save the common currency in the interest of the national economy (see e.g. findings by Bickes et al. 2014; Drewski 2015; Vaara 2014). Citizens seem to have adopted these argumentations at least so some extent, leading to the observed differences in the effects of national identification on European identification in countries under EU/IMF conditionality and the Eurozone. Overall, the findings presented here indicate that even if adverse economic conditions have a clear European dimension, they do not automatically lead to anti-European reflexes, not even among respondents who identify strongly with the national level. Rather, the tension between the wellbeing of the national community and the role of the EU must be made salient.

7.2 European Identity and EU Legitimacy After Maastricht

The evidence on European identification presented in this book also has implications for the debate on the legitimacy of the EU and a future widening and deepening of EU integration. From a functional perspective, the emergence of a collective European identity among citizens in the member states is a crucial precondition for citizens to accept majority decisions and redistributive policies at the EU level (Beetham and Lord 1998; Fuchs 2011; Herrmann and Brewer 2004; Offe 1998; Zürn 2000). At first sight, the empirical findings allow a rather positive outlook on the development of a European identity among the member state populations. More than half of those surveyed saw themselves (also) as European and similar proportions felt attached to the European level between 1992 and 2013. Large parts of the EU population hold multiple identifications, expressing attachments to both the national and the European level. These are signs of an emergent collective identity among Europeans.

European identity has also proven remarkably stable in critical periods of EU integration such as the accession of twelve new member states from Central and Eastern Europe in 2004/2007 and the onset of the financial and economic crisis in late 2008. The resilience of European identity in the crisis in particular seems encouraging. In this perspective, the sense of community among Europeans appears already stronger than expected and may thus provide legitimacy to EU policies and European solutions to the crisis.

This rather positive outlook on the state of European identity requires some qualifications, however. First, the *extent of collective European identity exceeds its intensity*. While European identification is widespread among EU citizens, it often remains moderate in degree. Few citizens see themselves *only* as Europeans or feel *very* attached to the European level. In this regard, European identity falls clearly behind national identities, which build on intense attachments by large parts of the national public. Second, *European identity follows distinct national patterns*. We find consistently high levels of European identity in countries like Germany and Italy while European identification remains a minority phenomenon in Britain. Third, *the strength of European identity varies depending on the collective object of identification*. Collective European identity is strong if '*Europe*' is the reference point, but noticeable weaker in extent and intensity if the reference point is the *European Union*. Apparently, Europeans have developed a common we-feeling as inhabitants of the same geographical or cultural sphere, yet still lack a common we-feeling as members of the same political community. A robust collective *European* identity thus faces a comparatively weaker collective *European Union* identity.

This last finding in particular seems crucial for the question of EU legitimacy. The requirements put on a collective European identity are high. A common European identity is seen as a means for legitimising the European polity that can remedy deficits in EU democracy, and strengthen solidarity and loyalty among EU member states and their populations. It becomes all the more important as output-oriented forms of EU legitimacy, e.g. based on the effectiveness and generalised welfare gains of the common market, become less persuasive (Cerutti 2008; Cerutti and Lucarelli 2008; Scharpf 2015). The financial and economic crisis and the measures taken by the EU to avoid sovereign defaults in the Eurozone have raised the stakes further. The extent of fiscal transfers between member states requires unprecedented levels of solidarity and mutual obligation within the EU and among citizens in the member states. The crisis thus calls for a common we-feeling as *EU citizens*, i.e. as members of an overarching political system that is threatened by the crisis (rather than a we-feeling as Europeans in the sense of inhabitants of the same continent or cultural sphere, which will persist regardless of the outcome of the crisis). In Easton's terms, citizens in the member states need to develop a feeling of belonging together as members of a political community, as 'a group which, because it shares a political structure, also shares a political fate' (Easton 1965, p. 185). It is unclear, however, whether the observed levels of *identification with the EU* fulfil these requirements and provide the necessary degree of political cohesion and solidarity to legitimate (further) intra-European redistribution and financial transfers.

National political actors are likely to play a crucial role in this regard. As the financial and economic crisis continued, EU affairs became more salient and more politicised in domestic political debates and national elections campaigns (Auel and Höing 2014; Hutter and Grande 2014; Hutter and Kerscher 2014; Miklin 2014; Puntscher Riekmann and Wydra 2013; Rauh and Zürn 2014; Risse 2015; Wendler 2014). Across the EU, the crisis and in particular the financial guaranteed to member states at risk of sovereign default sparked vivid debates over questions of national (financial) sovereignty, solidarity between EU member states, and the costs of integration in terms of fiscal and monetary autonomy (Hutter and Kerscher 2014; Mazzoni and Barbieri 2014; Schmidt 2014). In debtor and creditor countries alike, however, accounts of the crisis adopted a national perspective, focussing on the (negative) consequences of the crisis for the national economy and setting up an opposition between 'good' and 'bad', fiscally responsible and irresponsible, member states (Mazzoni and Barbieri 2014). Even political actors supporting the bailout measures rarely framed their support in terms of intra-European solidarity, but referred to (national) economic interests that were best served by giving financial guarantees to member states in financial difficulty (Closa and Maatsch 2014; Schmidt 2014). The evidence presented in this book with regard to the recent EP election campaigns echoes these findings. As the crisis turned from a crisis of the real economy into a sovereign debt crisis requiring financial rescue measures and intra-European transfers, parties appeared to link economic issues more closely to issues of solidarity and community. Especially on the right, we found parties pitting national interests against European-wide solidarity. Rather than appealing to a feeling of 'being in this together' as Europeans, political actors appear to have responded to the crisis by emphasising national (economic) interests over intra-European solidarity. This tendency is likely to continue given the ongoing controversy over financial aids for Greece or the debate over proper measures to boost the economy in the Eurozone, which equally reveals diverging interests between member states. At the citizen level, these debates are likely to reinforce concerns for the national (economic) well-being and the cost of EU integration for the national community. Such concerns risk to weaken ties to the European level and thus run counter to the development of a strong collective identity as *EU citizens* that would be needed to legitimise a further widening and deepening of EU integration.

7.3 The State of European Identity After the Crisis and Implications for Policymaking

Which are the implications of the present findings for policymakers and practitioners? The EU has long tried to encourage the formation of a common European identity among EU citizens through active identity politics (Stråth 2002). Among its most prominent programmes is the Erasmus exchange programme in higher education, which has recently been transformed into the Erasmus+ programme for education, training, youth and sport covering exchange programmes for students in secondary and higher education as well as vocational training.

The findings presented by this book suggest that such efforts to bring Europeans together are steps in the right direction. The positive effects of personal transnational experiences on citizens' identification with Europe we observed in all years under analysis support notions of an experience-based formation of European identification whereby personal contacts with other Europeans foster citizens' identification with the European community.

We further found that a high awareness of EU affairs can at least partly compensate for a lack of personal transnational contacts as a source of European identification as not all EU citizens may have the resources and opportunities necessary for transnational activities and personal interactions with other Europeans. With European identification thus drawing on different—and to some degree complementary—sources, policy programmes aimed at strengthening a common identity among Europeans could pursue different strategies: On the one hand, policymakers could create further opportunities for direct exchanges between Europeans. Given that transnational experiences are highly stratified by socio-economic status, with the highly educated and those in managerial positions being significantly more likely to engage in transnational exchanges (Fligstein 2008; Kuhn 2015), exchange programmes should target in particular citizens in non-academic professions and those at lower levels of education. These could take the form of work exchanges for apprentices and students in vocational training or non-professional exchange programmes, for example in the form of twinning towns across Europe, which allow transnational contacts outside the workplace and educational systems as well as for older age groups.

Still, even if intra-European exchange programmes are substantially extended and succeed in creating contacts between previously not transnationally active citizens, they will never reach entire member state populations. Complementary to exchanges programmes, a second line of action could stimulate citizens' interest in and improve their knowledge of European politics, e.g. through teaching and information campaigns about European politics and the EU institutions. In this way, policymakers could work towards strengthening European identity along an information-based way of identification. Concrete measures in this regard could be to work closely with member state authorities to implement EU topics in national curricula in primary and secondary education or invest in the EU's local information and documentation centres in the member states. By actively providing EU-related information and hosting EU-focused events, the latter could thus take on a role in educating the public about EU affairs similar to that of the German federal and regional agencies for civic education in providing political information at the national level. From this vantage point, we may also welcome the recent efforts by the candidates for the Commission presidency to conduct a truly pan-European EP election campaign, which sought to draw public attention to the European level and the EU institutions.

7.4 Suggestions for Further Research on Individual Identification with Europe

Drawing on the findings of this book, further research on individual identification with Europe could go in three main directions. First, it could carry forward the *conceptual discussion* of individual identification with Europe and its *operationalisation*, exploring in more depth citizens' understanding of the terms 'Europe' or 'the European Union' in survey items to improve the measurement of European identification in the mass public. Second, future contributions could add to the *explanation* of European identification in the mass public by examining theoretically and empirically the role of the mass media for citizens' identification with Europe. Third, research on European identification should continue to analyse *levels and determinants of European identification in times of economic crisis* beyond the timeframe of this book.

How could researchers carry forward the conceptualisation and operationalisation of European identification in future analyses of European identity? The present work conceptualised European identification as citizens' self-categorisation as European together with their evaluations of their membership in the European collective and affective attachments to Europe and other Europeans. Ideally, researchers could rely on indicators referring to 'the Europeans' as collective object of identification to operationalise European identification in empirical analyses. However, most available public opinion surveys, the Eurobarometer in particular, do not include items referring to 'the Europeans'; rather, survey items refer to 'Europe', the 'European Union', or 'EU citizenship'. This was also the case for the present analysis. In the absence of indicators of respondents' relationship to 'the Europeans', it relied on respondents' 'attachments to Europe' to operationalise affective identification with the European level; due to changes in the Eurobarometer questionnaires, the operationalisation changed from 'feelings of attachment to Europe' to 'feelings of attachment to the European Union' during the period of analysis. Yet there remains some ambiguity as to what people feel attached to when affirming their attachment to Europe/the European Union. Do respondents associate different meanings with 'Europe' on the one hand and 'the European Union' on the other? Or has the EU succeeded in superimposing itself as the primary understanding of 'Europe'? Do respondents equate the terms Europe/the European Union with the collective of Europeans and/or EU citizens? Does the reference to the European Union really tap respondents' attachment to the European community or rather their evaluation of the EU, its institutions, and policies? And do respondents' understandings of Europe/the European Union differ by member state?

Answers to these questions would allow a validation of how the concept of European identification has been measured so far and inform the interpretation of empirical results. For example, a better understanding of the meanings citizens associate with 'Europe' on the one hand and 'the European Union' on the other could help explain the differences we observe in levels of attachments to Europe and the European Union and, in particular, the observed country differences in the gap between attachment to Europe and attachment to the European Union. Large-n survey instruments and quantitative research can only provide limited information on respondents' understanding of 'Europe' or the 'European Union'. Qualitative research could provide further insights by using in-depth interviews to get a better grasp on response behaviour in the context of EU integration research. Such analyses could tie in with previous qualitative work pointing to the heterogeneity of citizens' understanding of 'Europe', 'European identity', or 'being European' (Diez Medrano 2003, 2010; Duchesne 2010). At the theoretical level, the inquiry into citizens' understanding of 'Europe' ought to be accompanied by a discussion of the implications of the different objects of identification—Europe on the one hand, the European Union on the other—for conceptualisations of European identification rooted in social psychology. Social psychological approaches to identity are primarily concerned with identification with 'social groups' or 'social categories' such as gender, nation, or race. Conceptually, future research ought to discuss more thoroughly, why 'Europe'/the 'European Union', too, represent social categories of this type. An in-depth analysis of citizens' understanding of different stimuli—Europe, the European Union, the Europeans etc.—could inform this discussion by clarifying whether, empirically, citizens perceive Europe indeed as a social group or rather as a geographic region, cultural sphere, or something else entirely.

A second question for further research could be the role of the mass media in citizens' identification with Europe. The present analysis only implicitly took into account media effects on European identification, assuming for example that party manifesto contents are disseminated via the mass media or that the increased media attention to EU affairs in the course of the crisis gave citizens easier access to EU-related information. Experimental research by Michael Bruter and Sarah Harrison suggests that EU-related news and the tone of EU coverage indeed affect citizens' identification with Europe (Bruter 2009; Harrison and Bruter 2015). Media effects are a well-known phenomenon in public opinion research (McGuire 1985; Zaller 1992). In the context of EU integration studies, media coverage of EU affairs has been shown to affect attitudes towards EU integration in general (de Vreese 2007; Scharkow and Vogelgesang 2010; Semetko et al. 2003; Vliegenthart et al. 2008), support for EU enlargement (Azrout et al. 2012; de Vreese and Boomgaarden 2006), and voting decisions in EU referenda (Hobolt 2009; Schuck and de Vreese 2011). So far, however, no large-n comparative study has systematically assessed the role of the media in citizens' *identification* with Europe.[1]

Conceptually, research on media effects on European identification could tie in with the idea of information-based identification introduced by this book. Citizens regularly cite the mass media as their primary source for news on European political matters and information about the EU, its institutions, and policies (European

[1]The analyses by Bruter (2009) and Harrison and Bruter (2015) are based on data from the period 1999–2003 and include only six member states (Belgium, France, Germany, Portugal, Sweden, and the UK).

Commission 2013). The mass media are thus an important factor on the supply side of EU-related information, regulating citizens' access to information about EU affairs and the type of information they receive about EU affairs. Researchers could introduce the amount and tone of media coverage of EU integration as an additional country-level determinant in an explanatory model of individual identification with Europe.

Third, future research should assess what is next for European identity. This book presented evidence on levels and development of European identification until November 2013. It last assessed the determinants of individual identification with Europe in spring 2012. Future work ought to explore the development of European identification among EU citizens beyond the period of analysis of the present work and examine the long-term effects of economic decline on citizens' identification with Europe. There is reason to assume that negative effects of the crisis on citizens' attitudes towards EU integration accumulate over time, leading to a gradual weakening of citizens' ties to the European level. By extending the time series presented in this book, future research could draw more solid conclusions with regard to the long-term consequences of economic crisis and heightened controversy over EU integration for citizens' identification with Europe. This should include time series for both the EU aggregate and individual member states to assess whether the ongoing crisis has resulted in diverging trends in European identification among EU member states.

Beyond describing the evolution of European identity over the course of the crisis, future research should also reassess the determinants of European identification among EU citizens. The present work found macroeconomic indicators to become more relevant for citizens' identification with Europe as the crisis continued; it also showed that the effects of national identification on European identification depend on (economic) context. Since 2012, economic disparities in the EU have further increased while controversies over the best way to consolidate national finances and stimulate economic growth have intensified, especially in the Eurozone. Are these developments reflected in changes in the determinants of European identification? Have macroeconomic predictors become yet more important? Does national identification still have a positive influence on European identification, despite growing conflicts over member states' national interests? More explanatory analyses of European identification could help answer these questions and thus allow conclusions about the sources of European identification and their stability in times of crisis.

Besides the evolution of collective European identity among EU citizens in the crisis, political parties and their role in making identity issues salient in national political debates also warrant further analysis. In particular, future contributions could reassess the role of political parties in the formation of individual identification with Europe. A more thorough analysis of the 2014 EP election manifestos could help establish to what extent parties have started to link identity issues more closely to economic issues as the crisis brought to the fore diverging (economic) interests between member states. The present analysis only found weak effects of party messages on citizens' identification with Europe when assessing the influence of the *overall* salience of identity issues in national party systems. Future research could match parties with their respective supporters, using party-specific rather than national salience scores as an explanatory variable of European identification. This would allow an assessment of whether parties succeed in influencing their own supporters when emphasising issues of European and national identity in their campaigns.

References

Auel, K., & Höing, O. (2014). Parliaments in the Euro Crisis: Can the losers of integration still fight back? *JCMS: Journal of Common Market Studies, 52*(6), 1184–1193.

Azrout, R., van Spanje, J., & de Vreese, C. (2012). When news matters: Media effects on public support for European Union enlargement in 21 countries. *Journal of Common Market Studies, 50*(5), 691–708.

Beetham, D., & Lord, C. (1998). *Legitimacy and the EU (Political dynamics of the EU)*. London/New York: Longman.

Bickes, H., Otten, T., & Weymann, L. C. (2014). The financial crisis in the German and English press: Metaphorical structures in the media coverage on Greece, Spain and Italy. *Discourse and Society, 25*(4), 424–445.

Bruter, M. (2009). Time bomb? The dynamic effect of news and symbols on the political identity of European citizens. *Comparative Political Studies, 42*(12), 1498–1536.

Cerutti, F. (2008). Why political identity and legitimacy matter in the European Union. In F. Cerutti, & S. Lucarelli (Eds.), *The search for a European idenity. Values, policies and legitimacy of the European Union* (pp. 3–22, Routledge/GARNET series: Europe in the World). Abingdon/New York: Routledge.

Cerutti, F., & Lucarelli, S. (2008). *The search for a European identity: Values, policies and legitimacy of the European Union*. London: Routledge.

Closa, C., & Maatsch, A. (2014). In a spirit of solidarity? Justifying the European financial stability facility (EFSF) in national parliamentary debates. *Journal of Common Market Studies, 52*(4), 826–842.

de Vreese, C. H. (2007). A spiral of Euroscepticism: The media's fault? *Acta Politica, 42*(2–3), 271–286.

de Vreese, C. H., & Boomgaarden, H. G. (2006). Media effects on public opinion about the enlargement of the European Union. *JCMS: Journal of Common Market Studies, 44*(2), 419–436.

Diez Medrano, J. (2003). *Framing Europe: Attitudes to European Integration in Germany, Spain, and the United Kingdom*. Princeton, NJ: Princeton University Press.

Diez Medrano, J. (2010). Unpacking European identity. *Politique Européenne, 30*, 45–66.

Dinan, D. (2012). Governance and institutions: Impact of the escalating crisis. *Journal of Common Market Studies, 50*(s2 – Special Issue: The JCMS Annual Review of the European Union in 2011), 85–98.

Dinan, D. (2013a). EU governance and institutions: Stresses above and below the waterline. *Journal of Common Market Studies, 51*(S1 – Special Issue: The JCMS Annual Review of the European Union in 2012), 89–102.

Dinan, D. (2013b). The post-Lisbon European Council Presidency: An interim assessment. *West European Politics, 36*(6), 1256–1273.

Drewski, D. (2015). Has there been a European public discourse on the Euro crisis? A systematic content analysis of newspaper editorials on the Euro crisis in Germany in Spain. *Berliner Studien zur Soziologie Europas – BSSE-Arbeitspapier*, (33).

Duchesne, S. (2010). L'identité européenne, entre science politique et science fiction. *Politique Européenne, 30*(1), 7–16.

Easton, D. (1965). *A systems analysis of political life*. New York: Wiley.

European Commission. (2013). *Standard Eurobarometer 80. Autumn 2013*. Media use in the European Union. Report (Vol. 80). Brussels.

Fligstein, N. (2008). *Euroclash: The EU, European identity, and the future of Europe*. Oxford: Oxford University Press.

Fuchs, D. (2011). Cultural diversity, European identity and legitimacy of the EU: A theoretical framework. In D. Fuchs & H.-D. Klingemann (Eds.), *Cultural diversity, European identity and the legitimacy of the EU* (pp. 27–57). Cheltenham: Edward Elgar.

Harrison, S., & Bruter, M. (2015). Media and identity: The paradox of legitimacy and the making of European citizens. In T. Risse (Ed.), *European public spheres: Politics is back* (pp. 165–189). Cambridge: Cambridge University Press.

Herrmann, R. K., & Brewer, M. B. (2004). Identities and institutions: Becoming European in the EU. In R. K. Herrmann, T. Risse, & M. B. Brewer (Eds.), *Transnational identities. Becoming European in the EU* (pp. 1–22). Lanham: Rowman & Littlefield.

Hobolt, S. B. (2009). *Europe in question: Referendums on European integration*. Oxford: Oxford University Press.

Hutter, S., & Grande, E. (2014). Politicizing Europe in the national electoral arena: A comparative analysis of five West European countries, 1970–2010. *Journal of Common Market Studies, 52* (5), 1002–1018.

Hutter, S., & Kerscher, A. (2014). Politicizing Europe in hard times: Conflicts over Europe in France in a long-term perspective, 1974–2012. *Journal of European Integration, 36*(3), 267–282.

Kouki, H. (2014). European crisis discourses: The case of Greece. In T. Murray-Leach (Ed.), *Background paper: Crisis discourses in Europe. Media EU-phemisms and alternative narratives* (pp. 16–20). London: Civil Society and Human Security Research Unit, London School of Economics and Political Science.

Kuhn, T. (2015). *Experiencing European integration: Individual transnationalism and public orientations towards European integration*. Oxford: Oxford University Press.

Mazzoni, M., & Barbieri, G. (2014). Grasshoppers against ants or malfunctions of capitalism? The representation of the European economic crisis in the main Italian newspapers. *Perspectives on European Politics and Society*, 1–16.

McGuire, W. J. (1985). Attitudes and attitude change. In G. Lindzey & E. Aronson (Eds.), *Handbook of social psychology: Special fields and applications*. New York: Random House.

Miklin, E. (2014). From 'sleeping giant' to left–right politicization? National party competition on the EU and the Euro crisis. *Journal of Common Market Studies, 52*(6), 1199–1206.

Offe, C. (1998). Demokratie und Wohlfahrtsstaat: Eine europäische Regimeform unter dem Stress der europäischen Integration. *Swiss Political Science Review, 4*(4), 35–56.

Puetter, U. (2012). Europe's deliberative intergovernmentalism: The role of the Council and European Council in EU economic governance. *Journal of European Public Policy, 19*(2), 161–178.

Puntscher Riekmann, S., & Wydra, D. (2013). Representation in the European state of emergency: Parliaments against governments? *Journal of European Integration, 35*(5), 565–582.

Rauh, C., & Zürn, M. (2014). Zur Politisierung der EU in der Krise. In M. Heidenreich (Ed.), *Krise der europäischen Vergesellschaftung? Soziologische Perspektiven* (pp. 121–145). Wiesbaden: Springer Fachmedien.

Risse, T. (2015). European public spheres, the politicization of EU affairs, and its consequences. In T. Risse (Ed.), *European public spheres: Politics is back* (pp. 141–164). Cambridge: Cambridge University Press.

Scharkow, M., & Vogelgesang, J. (2010). Effects of domestic media use on European integration. *Communications, 35*(1), 73.

Scharpf, F. W. (2015). Political legitimacy in a non-optimal currency area. In O. Cramme & S. B. Hobolt (Eds.), *Democratic politics in a European Union under stress* (pp. 19–47). Oxford: Oxford University Press.

Schmidt, V. A. (2014). Speaking to the markets or to the people? A discursive institutionalist analysis of the EU's sovereign debt crisis. *The British Journal of Politics and International Relations, 16*(1), 188–209.

Schuck, A. R. T., & de Vreese, C. H. (2011). Public support for referendums: The role of the media. *West European Politics, 34*(2), 181–207.

Semetko, H. A., van der Brug, W., & Valkenburg, P. M. (2003). The influence of political events on attitudes towards the European Union. *British Journal of Political Science, 33*(04), 621–634.

Stråth, B. (2002). A European identity. To the historical limits of a concept. *European Journal of Social Theory, 5*(4), 387–401.

Vaara, E. (2014). Struggles over legitimacy in the Eurozone crisis: Discursive legitimation strategies and their ideological underpinnings. *Discourse and Society, 25*(4), 500–518.

Vasilopoulou, S., Halikiopoulou, D., & Exadaktylos, T. (2014). Greece in crisis: Austerity, populism and the politics of blame. *JCMS: Journal of Common Market Studies, 52*(2), 388–402.

Vliegenthart, R., Schuck, A. R. T., Boomgaarden, H. G., & de Vreese, C. H. (2008). News coverage and support for European integration, 1990–2006. *International Journal of Public Opinion Research, 20*(4), 415–439.

Wendler, F. (2014). End of consensus? The European leadership discourse of the second merkel government during the Eurozone crisis and its contestation in debates of the Bundestag (2009–13). *German Politics, 23*(4), 446–459.

Zaller, J. (1992). *The nature and origins of mass opinion*. Cambridge: Cambridge University Press.

Zürn, M. (2000). Democratic governance beyond the nation-state: The EU and other international institutions. *European Journal of International Relations, 6*(2), 183–221.